'96 Terry Bradshaw Fantasy Football Journal

The Bible for Playing Fantasy Football—

- The ABC's of setting up your league
- Drafting strategies
- Team-by-team reviews
- Last year's top players
- Three-year NFL and FFL player stats
- Official FFL rules and scoring
- Quick start guides for DOS & Windows

Eighth Edition

A Fantasy Sports Properties, Inc. Trade Paperback

by Terry Bradshaw with Dick Giebel

A Fantasy Sports Properties Paperback—

Published by:
Fantasy Sports Properties, Inc.
P.O. Box 2698
Reston, Virginia 22091

If you purchased this book without a cover, you should be aware that this book is stolen property. It was reported as "*unsold and destroyed*" to the publisher, and neither the author nor the publisher has received any payment for this "*stripped book.*"

No part of this publication may be reproduced or transmitted in any form or by any means, electronic or mechanical, including photocopying, recording, or by any information and retrieval system (except excerpts which may be used for reviews) without the express written consent of the publisher, except where permitted by law.

FSPI, FBL, Franchise Baseball League, FFL, Franchise Football League, FBBL, Franchise Basketball League, Fantasy Basketball, FHL, Franchise Hockey League, and Fantasy Hockey are all registered trademarks of Fantasy Sports Properties, Inc. Patent No. 4,918,603. Additional Patents Pending.

© Copyright 1996 Fantasy Sports Properties, Inc. All Rights Reserved. Printed in the U.S.A.

Terry Bradshaw Fantasy Football is also patent and copyright protected by FSPI, and may not be duplicated for distribution in any way. Only printed output from the league reports section of the software program may be reproduced and distributed.

ISBN 0-9636895-5-X

Printed in the United States of America
Cover and Book Design by:
Eddie Byrd, Byrd Graphic Design, Inc., Arlington, Virginia.
(703) 524-5020, (703) 243-7061 FAX, BGDI@MSN.COM

June 1996   10 9 8 7 6 5 4 3 2 1

Contents

	v	Foreword
	vii	Introduction
	viii	Abbreviations
Chapter 1—		**What is Terry Bradshaw Fantasy Football?**
	1.2	*Wow, do I really need to know all these stats for these players?*
	1.3	*Putting it all in context*
	1.4	*I missed the opening kickoff. Can I still play?*
Chapter 2—		**Starting a Terry Bradshaw Fantasy Football League**
	2.1	*Getting the Right People*
	2.1	*Select a Commissioner*
	2.2	*Franchise Requirements*
	2.2	*Draft Sequence*
	2.3	*Running a Smooth Draft*
	2.3	*Weekly Starting Lineups*
	2.4	*Supplemental Draft*
	2.4	*Trades and Waivers*
	2.4	*League Newsletters*
	2.5	*Team-vs-Team Setup*
	2.5	*FFL Scoring System*
	2.5	*Summary*
	2.6	*Official Terry Bradshaw Fantasy Football Scoring System*
Chapter 3—		**Free Agency and the NFL Draft**
	3.2	*Players on the Move*
	3.5	*Team-by-Team Free Agent Reviews*
Chapter 4—		**Team-by-Team Reviews**
	4.1	*Drafting Head Coaches*
	4.6	*Arizona Cardinals*
	4.8	*Atlanta Falcons*
	4.10	*Baltimore Ravens*
	4.12	*Buffalo Bills*
	4.14	*Carolina Panthers*
	4.16	*Chicago Bears*
	4.18	*Cincinnati Bengals*
	4.20	*Dallas Cowboys*
	4.22	*Denver Broncos*
	4.24	*Detroit Lions*
	4.26	*Green Bay Packers*
	4.28	*Houston Oilers*

	4.30	*Indianapolis Colts*
	4.32	*Jacksonville Jaguars*
	4.34	*Kansas City Chiefs*
	4.36	*Miami Dolphins*
	4.38	*Minnesota Vikings*
	4.40	*New England Patriots*
	4.42	*New Orleans Saints*
	4.44	*New York Giants*
	4.46	*New York Jets*
	4.48	*Oakland Raiders*
	4.50	*Philadelphia Eagles*
	4.52	*Pittsburgh Steelers*
	4.54	*St. Louis Rams*
	4.56	*San Diego Chargers*
	4.58	*San Francisco 49ers*
	4.60	*Seattle Seahawks*
	4.62	*Tampa Bay Buccaneers*
	4.64	*Washington Redskins*

5 QB Chapter 5— **Quarterbacks**
  5.1 *Drafting Quarterbacks*
  5.1 *Drafting Backup Quarterbacks*
  5.3 *Free Agent Quarterbacks*
  5.4 *Quarterback Question Marks*
  5.5 *'95 Official Bombers (Two or More TDS Over 40 Yards)*
  5.5 *Fast Feet Feats ('95 Quarterback Rushing Stats)*
  5.6 *'96 Quarterback Review*
  5.16 *Best of the Rest*
  5.17 *'96 Pre-Season Quarterback Ranking*

6 RB Chapter 6— **Running Backs**
  6.1 *Drafting Running Backs*
  6.1 *The Running Back Draft Plan*
  6.2 *Bonus Scoring*
  6.3 *Free Agent Running Backs*
  6.3 *Who are these guys? The True Sleepers*
  6.4 *Question Marks at Running Back*
  6.6 *'95 Top Receiving Running Backs*
  6.8 *'96 Running Back Review*
  6.28 *Best of the Rest*
  6.30 *'96 Pre-Season Running Back Ranking*

This year's Journal is dedicated with love to Kim Lohmann and Mark Giebel. May your wedding day, September 7, 1996 be the first day of a beautiful life together!

— Dick Giebel

Acknowledgements

Special thanks go out to all those contributed their time and efforts to make this eighth edition of our Journal a success. Thanks have to first go out, for all their love and support, to my children Matt, Tim, and Caitlin.

Thanks, of course, to Larry Weisman, Dave Douglas, John Weiss, and Kevin Lynch for the exceptional work on the *Team-by-Team Reviews*—well done as usual, gang! A special thanks go out the usual fantasy football gurus at FSPI. For Pat and Cheryl Hughes, the signing of Terry Bradshaw is finally the payoff for years of hard work keeping this show on the road. And speaking of Terry, what a class guy to get endorsing our game! *(Hey, Terry, feel free to give us a plug on any Sunday!!!)*

FSPI's Bill Kelly and Sean Moran get a tip of the ol' helmet for their undying editorial support of this book during the crunch time. Brett Coffman is the man responsible for the majority of the stats found in this book, so you can thank, blame, or curse him as well! And a big heartfelt thanks go out once again to the "*Editor Extraordinaire*" Dave Warner, who is responsible for putting it all together and turning my random musings into comprehensible paragraphs. Thanks also go out to the original "*Design Man*" himself, Eddie Byrd, for his unflagging contributions to the design, layout, and production of all the marketing materials for FSPI this year, including the ads, the game box, and especially this Journal—great job!

I gotta give a plug to the the always entertaining and top-notch sports radio team of Dan Miller and Rick "*Doc*" Walker, heard in the nation's capital on WTEM. I sincerely hope they will get a shot at a national gig! And there is always the hope that WTEM's own brilliantly underrated Tony Kornheiser—a creative and talented writer for *The Washington Post*—will be a national network discovery—soon! FSPI would also like to thank WTEM's Bruce Murray, Billy Karlin, and Gary Edell at "*Roto-Talk*" for their support and assistance as well.

A personal thanks to Sarah Vogel for encouragement, advice and technical assistance; to Mike Goodman, marketing and media wiz and Marty McGrath, publishing guru—thanks, guys. To my brother and fantasy football partner, Greg, thanks for the teamwork and for reminding me constantly how terrible our team was last season. Congratulations have to go out to the SHH franchise (Mike Holp, Scott Smeds, and Mike Healey) for completely dominating the HFL fantasy football league in '95. Ahh, the HFL—thanks to Steve Jacobs and everyone in our rapidly growing league for making each season nothing less than an event—it's still a blast! So on that note, let's get down to some serious fun! *Pass that bowl of chips, will ya?* ★

Chapter 7—		**Wide Receivers**	7
	7.1	*Drafting Wide Receivers*	WR
	7.2	*Who are these guys? The True Sleepers*	
	7.2	*What about Deion Sanders?*	
	7.3	*Question Marks at Wide Receiver*	
	7.5	*Quarterback/Wide Receiver Listing*	
	7.6	*'96 Wide Receiver Review*	
	7.22	*Best of the Rest*	
	7.29	*'96 Pre-Season Wide Receiver Ranking*	

Chapter 8—		**Tight Ends**	8
	8.1	*Drafting Tight Ends*	TE
	8.1	*Who are these guys? The True Sleepers*	
	8.2	*Question Marks at Tight End*	
	8.4	*'96 Pre-Season Tight End Review*	
	8.12	*Best of the Rest*	
	8.14	*'96 Pre-Season Tight End Ranking*	

Chapter 9—		**Kickers and Punters**	9
	9.2	*Question Marks at Kicker*	K
	9.4	*'96 Pre-Season Kicker Review*	
	9.14	*'96 Pre-Season Kicker Ranking*	
	9.15	*'95 Punter Review*	

Chapter 10—		**Defenses and Special Teams**	10
	10.2	*'95 Interception Leader Review*	DT
	10.3	*'95 Sack Leader Review*	
	10.4	*'95 Defense Average Total Yards Allowed per Game*	
	10.5	*'96 Pre-Season Defensive Team Ranking*	
	10.6	*'96 Pre-Season Defense/Special Team Review*	
	10.16	*Drafting Special Team Returners*	
	10.16	*Special Team Drafting Tips*	
	10.17	*What about Deion, Rod, and Tim?*	
	10.18	*'95 Punt Returner Review*	
	10.19	*'95 Kick Returner Review*	
	10.20	*'96 Pre-Season Special Team Returner Ranking*	

Chapter 11—		**Offensive Teams**	11
	11.2	*3-Year Offensive Line Review*	OT
	11.7	*Quarterback Team Review*	

Chapter 12—		**Rookies and Free Agents**	12
	12.1	*Drafting Rookies*	RK
	12.2	*The Best of the New: The '96 Rookies*	

Chapter 13—		**Dick's Picks**	13
	13.1	*Top 200 Scoring and Performance Picks*	DP

Appendix A
A.1 NFL Schedule

Appendix B
B.1 All-Fantasy '93-95 Dream Teams

Appendix C
C.1 Three-Year Fantasy Rankings

Appendix D
D.1 Final '95 Fantasy Rankings

Appendix E
E.1 FFL Merchandise

Appendix F
F.1 Quick Start, '96 Terry Bradshaw Fantasy Football for DOS

Appendix G
G.1 Quick Start, '96 Terry Bradshaw Fantasy Football for Windows

Foreword

After eight years of long hours, annual development cycles updating our software, manuals and Journals, not to mention the enormous financial struggle, we finally got our big breakthrough last year when FOX Sports tapped our company to assist them in developing FOX Fantasy Football, an Internet-based fantasy football contest. While enjoying our invitation to visit FOX's studios in Los Angeles and watch a live telecast of "FOX NFL Sunday", we met FOX Studio co-host Terry Bradshaw, the NFL Hall of Fame and four-time Super Bowl champion quarterback. We took advantage of this meeting to eventually sign Terry to what hopefully will become a long-term relationship, in which his likeness will be the focus of our patented fantasy football league administration software, this Journal, and other corresponding promotions.

The primary reason that we started Fantasy Sports Properties was to develop products capable of assisting league commissioners and team owners in administering their leagues. We wanted them to have the best insight for playing, while making it fun and less time consuming. We saw the potential for millions of football fans to become *interactive* football fans, and as I am sure you will agree, to discover the fun, camaraderie, and good spirit that the games bring as well as the new perspective that it generates while following the NFL. *The Wall Street Journal* recently published an article that confirms our original goals. It said major corporations are finally discovering that as many as two to six million fans worldwide already participate. We think that with the endorsement by Terry, millions more sports fans will uncover what you and I already know: the incredible fun and excitement of playing in a fantasy football league.

In addition to Terry's presence, we continue to bring you new products and services, and this year are proud to announce that Terry Bradshaw Fantasy Football is now available for both DOS and Windows. In addition, America's most popular online service, America Online, now has a special section devoted just to our company. And speaking of things online, check out our new updated web site at HTTP://WWW.FSPI.COM. In addition to the software and stat services that have made our company the industry leader, you will find roster transactions, up-to-date NFL rosters, Dick Giebel's inside predictions, and much more.

In summary, we believe that this is finally the year when
fantasy football will be recognized as the market force that it is, and
given the long overdue credit by the press and the TV networks.
Terry Bradshaw's presence brings a newfound credibility and spotlight
to a three-decade-old game, and the best that could come about
is increased media focus, which means more stats and
information for you, the players. So sit back, and enjoy what we truly
believe will be the best season yet for fantasy football.

And as always, I hope to hear from you about your league,
your "*war stories*", sleeper picks, and draft nightmares. I wish you, your
franchise and your league the best this season, and hope that
my fantasy team finishes about eight places higher than last year! ★

Patrick J. Hughes, President
Fantasy Sports Properties, Inc.
P.O. Box 2698
Reston, Virginia 22091
703-391-0533 FAX
FSPI@FSPI.COM

Introduction

I am pleased to lend a hand to the splendid folks at Fantasy Sports Properties in order to bring fantasy football fans worldwide the best resources available to play the hottest interactive game in sports today. I am of course speaking of the incomparable Terry Bradshaw Fantasy Football software program, and this Journal.

My fantasy football pals Dick Giebel, Dave Douglas and John Weiss at NFL Films, Kevin Lynch at Pro Sports Xchange, and the always humorous Larry Weisman at USA *Today* are the finest group of football experts assembled this side of Hollywood, (which is where the *greatest* group of experts are—*me, Howie and J.B.!*) Their insights, rankings and lists in the following chapters will hopefully help you draft and coach your team to victory. However, in the event that they give any bad advice, don't blame me, for I don't even know these guys!

As Pat Hughes points out in his foreword, I hope that my association with fantasy football will help bring this incredibly fun and compelling game to millions of fans worldwide. FSPI has proven themselves to be the far and away leaders in fantasy football, and I am proud to be a part of the excitement.

Last year, with the right roster moves and a lot of luck, I won my fantasy league at FOX, and I know you can too. Best of luck to you and your league this year, and I'll be seeing you every Sunday all the way through the *Super Bowl* on FOX! ★

Abbreviations

The following abbreviations are used extensively throughout the 1996 Terry Bradshaw Fantasy Football Journal. For your convenience, other legends are provided at the beginning of chapters which present tabular information containing additional abbreviations. ★

AZ	Arizona Cardinals	NFL	National Football League
ATL	Atlanta Falcons	FFL	Franchise Football League
BAL	Baltimore Ravens	NFC	National Football Conference
BUF	Buffalo Bills	AFC	American Football Conference
CAR	Carolina Panthers	FG	Field Goal
CHI	Chicago Bears	PAT	Point after Touchdown
CIN	Cincinnati Bengals	YDS	Yards
CLE	Cleveland Browns	DT	Defensive Team
DAL	Dallas Cowboys	TD	Touchdown
DEN	Denver Broncos	PTS	Points
DET	Detroit Lions	AVG	Average
GB	Green Bay Packers	REC	Receptions
HOU	Houston Oilers	FUM	Fumble
IND	Indianapolis Colts	INT	Interception
JAX	Jacksonville Jaguars	QB	Quarterback
KC	Kansas City Chiefs	RB	Running Back
RAI	Oakland Raiders	HB	Halfback
MIA	Miami Dolphins	FB	Fullback
MIN	Minnesota Vikings	WR	Wide Receiver
NE	New England Patriots	TE	Tight End
NO	New Orleans Saints	PR	Pass Receiver
NYG	New York Giants	K	Kicker
NYJ	New York Jets	P	Punter
PHI	Philadelphia Eagles	S	Safety
PIT	Pittsburgh Steelers	C	Center
SD	San Diego Chargers	G	Guard
SF	San Francisco 49ers	T	Tackle
SEA	Seattle Seahawks	FS	Free Safety
RAM	St. Louis Rams	SS	Strong Safety
TB	Tampa Bay Buccaneers	DB	Defensive Back
WAS	Washington Redskins	CB	Cornerback
		LB	Linebacker
		OLB	Outside Linebacker
		MLB	Middle Linebacker
		ILB	Inside Linebacker
		RS	Return Specialist

1 What is Terry Bradshaw Fantasy Football?

Terry Bradshaw Fantasy Football is a game that allows you the opportunity to be the owner, general manager and head coach of your own NFL team. You can't tell me that you have never watched a game and said to your chip'n'dip pals, "These coaches are nuts! I could coach better than them with my eyes closed!". Well, here's your chance. No longer is that just a fantasy. Now you can have fantasy football—the Terry Bradshaw way! You draft players, build your own team, and compete against other teams in your fantasy league.

Imagine the feeling of matching wits against your family, buddies, or co-workers.

- *Will your draft strategy work?*
- *Who will be the hot scorers, the big surprises, the sleeper picks and the flat-out busts in 1996?*
- *Which rookies will jump into the limelight?*
- *Which quarterback will have the hot hand this year— Marino, Elway, Young, Favre, Mitchell, or a young guy like Jeff Blake?*

No one says that these decisions will be easy. Occasionally you bench a guy that scores like mad, or you keep a guy in your lineup on his bye week—*ouch*! But it's the weekly competition, the chance to interact with other football fans and take charge of your team's destiny, hey, that's the fun of playing fantasy football—making these key personnel decisions each week as you take charge and draft a fantasy football team. Why miss all that fun? Get a group of football maniacs like yourself, arm yourself with good literature and our *Terry Bradshaw Fantasy Football* league management software program, and get rolling!

So the choice is yours, my friend: sit back and spend another boring season watching your favorite team make some bonehead moves with your favorite players, or call your own shots and see how you rate as a franchise owner in your own fantasy football league! So if you are up to the challenge, read on. I promise you that you will never watch football the same way again.
Enjoy!

| 1 | Wow, do I really need to know all these stats for these players? This looks complicated! |

Well, this is no *Fantasy Football for Dummies* book, but what we have done here is put together "*The Bible*" that you can use no matter what your fantasy football experience or football knowledge level. Although this Journal contains a lot of information, we have tried to present it in such a way that the hard-core football stat heads of the world get what they need, but then the average football fan trying this for the first time gets a taste of the fun of playing fantasy football.

We analyze all the draft picks, free agent moves, NFL teams, last year's stats, and current rosters in an effort to predict for you, as best we can, what we think will happen this year in fantasy football. This is somewhat akin to predicting the stock market, or calling *Dionne's Psychic Love Connection*—you just never know what you are gonna get. For example, who could have predicted that Denver RB Terrell Davis or St. Louis WR Isaac Bruce would explode like they did last year? Similarly, not many had an inkling that QB Drew Bledsoe, after two successful seasons, was doomed from the start last year. However, our recommendations are well-researched and thought-out, although they do place some of the responsibility on you, the reader.

Since we go to press in June, lots of things can happen in the NFL between June 1 and September 3, so you do have to pay attention to what has happened in the pros over the summer. People are hurt in training camp, GMs make last-minute changes to their rosters, or the hot rookie is shown up by the experienced veteran. Whatever the case, use the picks and tips as a guide to make your selections. By and large, we're not too far off the mark.

But my point is that you don't have to study *all* the stats for *all* the players in order to get a feel for who's hot in the NFL anyway. Chances are you know the *"hot"* players in the NFL already. But in this era of free agency, it's knowing the full rosters, and the context of the players and the teams that makes you a successful fantasy football player. So we urge you to keep this Journal handy, and make it one of a few weapons in your drafting arsenal. In fantasy football, the franchise owner that prepares the most usually wins or comes really close.

Putting it all in context—

In the real estate market, the key to success is, *"location, location, location"*. Well, in fantasy football, the key to your success is *"context, context, context"*. For example, the points in this book, where available, are based on the FFL scoring system. Now this is fine if you use the FFL system, but in my 14 years of playing this game, I have never seen two established leagues use the exact same scoring system. So what you must do is take our stats, and our recommendations, and put them in the context of your own scoring system.

For example, in this book we rate Barry Sanders very high, because most leagues use a scoring system that awards points for yardage. Now in my league, which does not use yardage at all, he would actually rate a bit lower. Not too much lower, but he is not going to be as big a scorer as, say, an Emmitt Smith or a Marshall Faulk. But in another league that gives points for yardage, Sanders might actually be more valuable than either Smith or Faulk. Also, if a league gives extra points to running backs that receive the ball out of the backfield, a Brian Mitchell or Dorsey Levens suddenly merits attention. Therefore, it is critical that you make your draft determinations based on your own scoring systems.

This Journal was on sale in October, and I missed the opening kickoff. Can I still play?

Part of the intrigue of drafting a fantasy football team is the great unknown. Drafting a fantasy team several days before the NFL season kicks off is exciting because there are still many decisions to be made by NFL coaches—decisions such as who's gonna start, who might be their key running back, last-minute trades or injuries, etc.

Obviously we suggest forming a league prior to the start of the NFL season. However, if by chance you have already missed the start of the season but still want to play, by all means join in. It's simple to just hold your draft and play an abbreviated schedule. On the plus side, you and your cronies will know firsthand who's starting full-time, who's hot, and who's not. Also, you will know who's injured—so why worry? Start today, no matter what week of the season it is.

Okay, I'm hooked. How do I do this?

I knew you would come around. Well, read on, and let's take a look at the Terry Bradshaw way of doing things, and see why we are considered by many the leader of this phenomena called fantasy football. ★

2 Starting a Terry Bradshaw Fantasy Football League

By now you have learned why you need to play fantasy football, and why this Journal makes that simple by giving you all the stat analysis you need. But, you might ask, how do I get going? What do I do now? Where do I begin?

Getting the Right People—

The first thing you need, of course, is a desire to play and some friends, family or co-workers. The *Terry Bradshaw Fantasy Football* software can administer from 2 to 30 leagues, although for practicality's sake we recommend that you keep the size of your league between 6 and 16 franchises. If you have 2 or 4 franchises, all the teams are stocked with superstars, and there is much less of a challenge. If you have more than 16 teams, not everyone will have 2 QBs on their team that start each week, since there are only 30 starting QBs each week. So we recommend that, if you have a lot of people interested in playing in a league, you try to get them to double up owners in a smaller league. For example, in my league I have over 50 owners, but only 12 franchises. We have done this on purpose, just to keep the league size and schedule manageable.

The other key here is to find players that will not lose interest five minutes into the draft, and that can pay attention to their rosters for the whole season. There is nothing worse than having half of the owners in a league really into it and paying attention, and the other owners not making roster moves and putting in *"lame duck"* franchises. This drags down the entire league, and can sometimes make the rest of the league actually less interested—a no-win situation for sure. So make it clear to the league members in advance— don't play if they think they might lose interest.

Select a Commissioner—

Once you have found the players for your league, one of them should be designated (or voted, or commanded) to be Commissioner. The Commissioner's responsibilities begin before *Draft Day*, and extend past the end of the season. He or she is in charge of setting up and running the league, organizing the logistics of *Draft Day*, and coordinating the weekly lineups. Typically this person should have access to a computer and a fax machine to make the processing and distribution of the weekly rosters and lineups easier. The tip here is to pick someone who is both a good organizer (*there is nothing worse than getting your weekly reports four days late each week*) and a good mediator. Often times a scoring play, a league rule, or some other matter will have to be dealt with, and having a *wimp* that caves in to pressure is bad, but having a *bully strongman* will ruin your league!

Franchise Requirements— By giving plenty of notice for the fantasy draft you will ensure that every franchise is represented. A missing franchise puts a damper on the draft, and having another franchise draft for the phantom team is both a drag and an inconvenience. It is difficult enough keeping track of who's drafting whom and deciding just what your own next move will be; adding the responsibility of drafting for another team is a complete bummer! Therefore, make it clear that all franchises are to be represented.

Draft Sequence— As a rule of thumb, an existing league generally will operate the draft just like the NFL—based on the final standings from the previous season. The last-place team receives the first pick, next-to-last gets the second pick, etc. Obviously, this sequence will give last season's champ the final pick in *Round One* and the first pick in *Round Two*.

Example Draft Sequence for a Ten-Team League:

Round One:		Round Two:	
Team #10	Pick #1	Team #1	Pick #1
Team #9	Pick #2	Team #2	Pick #2
Team #8	Pick #3	Team #3	Pick #3
Team #7	Pick #4	Team #4	Pick #4
Team #6	Pick #5	Team #5	Pick #5
Team #5	Pick #6	Team #6	Pick #6
Team #4	Pick #7	Team #7	Pick #7
Team #3	Pick #8	Team #8	Pick #8
Team #2	Pick #9	Team #9	Pick #9
Team #1	Pick #10	Team #10	Pick #10

Round Three would lead off with Team #8 picking first as the order reverses every round. If you are a new league, just pick numbers from a hat to determine the *Round One* draft order.

Team #1 through Team #10 (*Round One*)
Team #10 through Team #1 (*Round Two*)
Team #1 through Team #10 (*Round Three*)
Team #10 through Team #1 (*Round Four*)

Remember to reverse the order every round. The *Terry Bradshaw Fantasy Football* software now lets you modify the draft order each round, or to change the draft order once and for all. For more information, see Appendices F and G.

Running a Smooth Draft—

Set the Draft Date:

Just before the start of the NFL regular season the league Commissioner sets a date for the FFL *Fantasy Draft*. The Commissioner must be prepared to list the players chosen round-by-round. An easel and a marker will help the Commissioner or an assistant to record each round and will allow league members to review their choices.

Don't Let the Draft Drag:

To move the draft along, set a time limit per selection— for example, many leagues suggest one minute between picks. If you don't set a time limit initially, your draft will drag and tempers will flare. Trust me, without a time limit per selection, your draft will become a nightmare! Have fun, but move the selection process along to ensure a successful draft.

Suggested Number of Players:

The numbers of players the FFL suggests to draft per team are listed below. This is not a hard-and-fast rule, but with these amounts you will have enough players at each position to cover situations such as the always-wonderful bye week, injuries, etc. Many existing leagues change these numbers slightly, so use them as general guidelines. Clearly, if you have more than 15 teams in your league, you may only draft one defensive team.

4 Quarterbacks (QB)
6 Running Backs (RB)
6 Wide Receivers (WR)
2 Tight Ends (TE)
2 Kickers (K)
2 Defenses/Special Teams (DT/ST)

Weekly Starting Lineups—

Right after *Draft Night*, each franchise must submit a weekly lineup for the first week of play. After the first week, typically the Commissioner takes lineup changes right up until the beginning of the one o'clock game on Sunday. Other leagues make the Thursday or Friday before the week's games the cut-off time. This is up to your league. Whatever the case, we do recommend that the Commissioner get an answering machine or voice mail to record the weekly lineups. There is no better tool to resolve disputes than a tape recording, plus this is the most reliable method for recording the entire league's selections. Other leagues might use a central fax machine, or even E-MAIL. The *Terry Bradshaw Fantasy Football* software program allows you to print out *Starting Lineup Worksheets*, and these are often used by Commissioners for distribution to the league members.

Typically, we recommend that you limit your starting lineup to nine players—eight position players and one defensive/special team. You may customize these numbers as much as needed. Many leagues do not have any benched players—everyone starts. Others individual defensive and special teams players rather than whole defenses; this is entirely up to your league's rules and scoring system.

Supplemental Draft—

Do you remember just how smart you felt immediately after the draft? Now, several weeks later, you may begin to notice your team fraying around the edges. That starting QB may have gone down in the first game. That hot rookie may have been not-so-hot. Well, if you need to give yourself a quick fixer-upper, then you need a quick trip to the *Supplemental Draft*. Many leagues hold a *Supplemental Draft* to fix draft night mistakes. Not only will the *Supplemental Draft* correct flaws, but it is also helpful in cases where your key players are benched or, worse, injured! I recommend that you hold a *Supplemental Draft* after Week 5 or 6 in order to supplement rosters with NFL players not chosen at the outset. I also recommend that you set a draft limit of six players to be selected for each team.

Trades and Waivers—

One other reason to hold the *Supplemental Draft* is that it is a great opportunity to get the whole gang back together. This is also a good chance to make trades, in case your franchise is suffering.

As with real NFL teams, franchise owners can trade or transfer one or more NFL players from one franchise to another. However, all trades must be approved by the Commissioner, and in order to play a traded player on Sunday, the trade usually must be finalized prior to the time set aside for turning in your weekly lineups. In the FFL, no trades are allowed during the final four weeks of the season, in order to prevent loser franchises from selling their talent to the good teams. In most leagues, a franchise owner may also waive a player on his/her current roster and add a non-roster player up to a maximum of eight times during the season.

League Newsletters—

Beyond just the starting lineups, weekly communication with league owners is critical to prevent a loss of interest from your franchise owners. We find that the best way is through a weekly newsletter. One league may simply use the one built into the *Terry Bradshaw Fantasy Football* software; it allows you to type out text and attach it to your weekly reports. Others go to the opposite extreme, scanning in photos and weekly reports into a professional-looking weekly document. Often times these are extremely funny and inventive, and really display the passion these players have for fantasy football, on top of being extremely informative. Usually the Commissioner does this, and it typically includes the following information:

1. *Weekly winners*
2. *Past week's scoring results, team-by-team*
3. *YTD league standings*
4. *Rules interpretations*
5. *Head-to-Head schedules*
6. *League business, and any other league news*

Team-vs-Team Setup—	Leagues typically handle their weekly scoring in one of two ways. Either they will have one weekly winner, based on the total number of points scored in a week, or they will set up a weekly schedule and base their league on the total number of wins and losses, like the NFL. This also provides a playoff structure similar to the NFL's. For ease and convenience, we have created schedules that are included in the *Terry Bradshaw Fantasy Football* software program.
FFL Scoring System—	Years ago, when we first developed the software and Journal, we created our own scoring system which was based solely on scoring plays. Over time, we discovered that including scoring for performance plays, such as rushing and passing yards, interceptions, sacks, and tackles, made drafting your players a lot more challenging and a whole lot more fun. Our scoring system has therefore evolved to the one found on the following page. Most leagues take our scoring system and customize it based on their own experience, and you and your league should feel free to do the same. Most leagues will begin with ours, then vote on changes and improvements in successive years. As I have said, though, you must always take the scoring system that your league uses into account when you are drafting your players.
Summary—	Well, you've seen how to set up and run a league, how to coordinate your draft night, and how to run the league from week to week. Now the only question is, *"Who should I pick?"*, and that's where it gets really fun. In order to provide you with the best information possible, we have now included three-year stats for the most popular players, as well as my rankings at the end of each chapter. We also have a *Free Agent Review*, so that you can keep up with the myriad of free agent moves that occurred this offseason. There are *Team-by-Team Reviews*, a *Rookie Highlights* section, and of course the *"Dick's Picks"* section, where I list the top 200 players in the NFL. I hope you enjoy the insight that I and my writers provide you, and wish you the best of luck in your season. *Happy drafting!* ★

Official *Terry Bradshaw Fantasy Football* Scoring System—

Regular Scoring Plays—

	0-9 YDS:	10-39 YDS:	40+ YDS:
QB Pass for TD:	6 PTS	9 PTS	12 PTS
RB Run for TD:	6 PTS	9 PTS	12 PTS
WR/TE Catch for TD:	6 PTS	9 PTS	12 PTS
DT/ST* or LB, DB, and DL Return for TD:	6 PTS	9 PTS	12 PTS

*If your league uses the defensive/special teams unit method—in which franchise owners pick an entire defensive and special teams unit rather than individual players—and any player from that unit scores a TD, the points, as specified above, are awarded to that franchise.

	1-39 YDS:	40-49 YDS:	50+ YDS:
Field Goal:	3 PTS	5 PTS	10 PTS

Two-Point Conversion—

QB Pass, RB Run, WR/TE Catch:	2 PTS
QB Run/Catch:	4 PTS
RB Pass/Catch:	4 PTS
WR/TE Run/Pass:	4 PTS
K Pass/Run/Catch:	4 PTS

Bonus Scoring Plays—

	0-9 YDS:	10-39 YDS:	40+ YDS:
QB Run/Catch for TD:	12 PTS	18 PTS	24 PTS
RB Pass/Catch for TD:	12 PTS	18 PTS	24 PTS
WR/TE Run/Pass for TD:	12 PTS	18 PTS	24 PTS
K Pass/Run/Catch for TD:	12 PTS	18 PTS	24 PTS

Optional Performance Scoring—

		EACH ADDT'L. 10 YDS:
QB Passing Yards:	10 PTS @ 250 YDS	1 PT
QB Rushing/Receiving Yards:	5 PTS @ 50 YDS	1 PT
RB Rushing Yards:	10 PTS @ 100 YDS	1 PT
RB Passing/Receiving Yards:	5 PTS @ 50 YDS	1 PT
WR/TE Receiving Yards:	10 PTS @ 100 YDS	1 PT
WR/TE Passing/Rushing Yards:	5 PTS @ 50 YDS	1 PT

Safety Scored by DT/ST, DB, LB, or DL:	4 PTS
INT Thrown/Sack Received by QB:	4 PTS
Point After Touchdown (PAT):	1 PT

Abbreviations:

	QB	Quarterback	DL	Defensive Lineman
	RB	Running Back	TD	Touchdown
	WR	Wide Receiver	YDS	Yards
	TE	Tight End	PTS	Points
	K	Kicker	DT/ST	Defensive Team/Special Team
	LB	Linebacker	INT	Interception
	DB	Defensive Back		

3 Free Agency and the NFL Draft

When the NFL and the NFL Players came to their milestone player agreement a few years ago, in which all players were given free agency in exchange for a team salary cap, it was a blessing for the players and a curse for fantasy footballers everywhere. Gone are the days of knowing, from year to year, who was a member of your favorite NFL team. These days, every team is shifting a myriad of players each year, in an effort to get the best possible team under the salary cap. While this may be the status quo in the NFL how do you deal with all the roster moves in the NFL, and come to grips with players jumping teams like there's no tomorrow?

We at the FFL have tracked all the roster moves in the offseason, and have provided the most updated list available. In this chapter we have included both a quick look at the major free agent changes, as well as a comprehensive review of each NFL team's free agent gains, free agent losses, and top draft picks. This information can be found elsewhere in the book, in the position and NFL team-by-team review chapters, but we feel that this gives you a one-stop look at all the major offseason action in the NFL. ★

Players on the Move—

Position:	Player:	Old Team:	1996 Team:
Quarterback	Jeff George	Atlanta Falcons	Free Agent
	Neil O'Donnell	Pittsburgh Steelers	New York Jets
	Boomer Esiason	New York Jets	Arizona Cardinals
	Steve Walsh	Chicago Bears	St. Louis Rams
	Randall Cunningham	Philadelphia Eagles	Free Agent
	Ty Detmer	Green Bay Packers	Philadelphia Eagles
	Frank Reich	Carolina Panthers	New York Jets
	David Krieg	Arizona Cardinals	Chicago Bears
	David Klingler	Cincinnati Bengals	Free Agent
	Steve Beuerlein	Jacksonville Jaguars	Carolina Panthers
	Sean Salisbury	Free Agent	San Diego Chargers
	Kent Graham	Detroit Lions	Arizona Cardinals
	Erik Wilhelm	New York Jets	Cincinnati Bengals
	Bucky Richardson	Free Agent	Kansas City Chiefs
	Kelly Stouffer	Free Agent	Carolina Panthers
	Jack Trudeau	Carolina Panthers	Free Agent
	Brad Goebel	Free Agent	Washington Redskins
	Will Furrer	Houston Oilers	Free Agent
Running Back	Natrone Means	San Diego Chargers	Jacksonville Jaguars
	Tommy Vardell	Cleveland Browns	San Francisco 49ers
	Johnny Johnson	Free Agent	San Francisco 49ers
	Jerome Bettis	St. Louis Rams	Pittsburgh Steelers
	Lorenzo White	Cleveland Browns	New Orleans
	Todd McNair	Houston Oilers	Free Agent
	Lewis Tillman	Chicago Bears	Free Agent
	Anthony McDowell	Free Agent	Washington Redskins
	Leroy Thompson	Kansas City Chiefs	Free Agent
	John L. Williams	Pittsburgh Steelers	Free Agent
	Tracy Johnson	Seattle Seahawks	Free Agent
Wide Receiver	Fred Barnett	Philadelphia Eagles	Miami Dolphins
	Quinn Early	New Orleans Saints	Buffalo Bills
	Willie Davis	Kansas City Chiefs	Houston Oilers
	Jeff Graham	Chicago Bears	New York Jets
	Irving Fryar	Miami Dolphins	Philadelphia Eagles
	Shawn Jefferson	San Diego Chargers	New England Patriots
	Keenan McCardell	Cleveland Browns	Jacksonville Jaguars
	Charles Jordan	Green Bay Packers	Miami Dolphins
	Haywood Jeffires	Houston Oilers	Free Agent
	Gary Clark	Miami Dolphins	Free Agent

Position:	Player:	Old Team:	1996 Team:
Wide Receiver	Don Beebe	Carolina Panthers	Free Agent
(Continued)	Webster Slaughter	Kansas City Chiefs	Free Agent
	Michael Bates	Cleveland Browns	Carolina Panthers
	Ray Crittenden	New England Patriots	Carolina Panthers
	Rico Smith	Cleveland Browns	New York Jets
	Bryan Reeves	Arizona Cardinals	Washington Redskins
	Greg McMurtry	Free Agent	Washington Redskins
	Jeff Query	Free Agent	Green Bay Packers
	Bill Brooks	Buffalo Bills	Washington Redskins
Tight End	Johnny Mitchell	New York Jets	Free Agent
	Wesley Walls	New Orleans Saints	Carolina Panthers
	Pete Metzelaars	Carolina Panthers	Detroit Lions
	Walter Reeves	Arizona Cardinals	San Diego Chargers
	Rodney Holman	Detroit Lions	Free Agent
Kicker	Chip Lohmiller	Free Agent	St. Louis Rams
	Bjorn Nittmo	Free Agent	Kansas City Chiefs
	Lin Elliott	Kansas City Chiefs	Free Agent
	Roman Anderson	Free Agent	Kansas City Chiefs
	Scott Szeredy	Free Agent	Kansas City Chiefs
Defensive Back	Ronnie Lott	Kansas City Chiefs	Retired
	Troy Vincent	Miami Dolphins	Philadelphia Eagles
	Ashley Ambrose	Indianapolis Colts	Cincinnati Bengals
	Larry Brown	Dallas Cowboys	Oakland Raiders
	Kevin Ross	Atlanta Falcons	San Diego Chargers
	Lorenzo Lynch	Arizona Cardinals	Oakland Raiders
	Dana Hall	Cleveland Browns	Jacksonville Jaguars
	Darryl Williams	Cincinnati Bengals	Seattle Seahawks
	Mark McMillian	Philadelphia Eagles	New Orleans Saints
	Eric Davis	San Francisco 49ers	Carolina Panthers
	Jimmy Spencer	New Orleans Saints	Cincinnati Bengals
	Willie Clay	Detroit Lions	New England Patriots
	Patrick Bates	Oakland Raiders	Atlanta Falcons
	Bo Orlando	San Diego Chargers	Cincinnati Bengals
	Curtis Buckley	Tampa Bay Buccaneers	San Francisco 49ers
	Marcus Turner	New York Jets	Green Bay Packers
	Frankie Smith	Miami Dolphins	Free Agent
	Robert Bailey	Dallas Cowboys	Miami Dolphins
	Anthony Prior	New York Jets	Free Agent
	Eric Thomas	Denver Broncos	Free Agent
Linebacker	Cornelius Bennett	Buffalo Bills	Atlanta Falcons
	Kevin Greene	Pittsburgh Steelers	Carolina Panthers
	Chris Spielman	Detroit Lions	Buffalo Bills
	Bryan Cox	Miami Dolphins	Chicago Bears

Position:	Player:	Old Team:	1996 Team:
Linebacker (Continued)	Robert Jones	Dallas Cowboys	St. Louis Rams
	Dixon Edwards	Dallas Cowboys	Miami Dolphins
	Fred Strickland	Green Bay Packers	Dallas Cowboys
	Gerald Dixon	Cleveland Browns	Cincinnati Bengals
	Bill Romanowski	Philadelphia Eagles	Denver Broncos
	Michael Brooks	New York Giants	Detroit Lions
	Eddie Robinson	Houston Oilers	Jacksonville Jaguars
	Kurt Gouveia	Philadelphia Eagles	San Diego Chargers
	Darryl Talley	Atlanta Falcons	Free Agent
	Broderick Thomas	Minnesota Vikings	Dallas Cowboys
	Jack Del Rio	Minnesota Vikings	Miami Dolphins
	Joe Kelly	Green Bay Packers	Free Agent
	Tracy Haworth	Detroit Lions	Atlanta Falcons
	Jaime Fields	Kansas City Chiefs	Free Agent
Defensive Line	Leslie O'Neal	San Diego Chargers	St. Louis Rams
	Russell Maryland	Dallas Cowboys	Oakland Raiders
	Sean Gilbert	St. Louis Rams	Washington Redskins
	Marco Coleman	Miami Dolphins	San Diego Chargers
	Santana Dotson	Tampa Bay Buccaneers	Green Bay Packers
	Chris Doleman	Atlanta Falcons	San Francisco 49ers
	Darren Mickell	Kansas City Chiefs	New Orleans Saints
	Kenny Davidson	Houston Oilers	Free Agent
	Pio Sagapolutele	Cleveland Browns	New England Patriots
	Simon Fletcher	Denver Broncos	Retired
	Fred Stokes	St. Louis Rams	New Orleans Saints
	Alfred Williams	San Francisco 49ers	Denver Broncos
	Mark Wheeler	Tampa Bay Buccaneers	New England Patriots
	Ray Childress	Houston Oilers	Free Agent
	Jumpy Geathers	Atlanta Falcons	Free Agent
	Karl Wilson	Buffalo Bills	Free Agent
	James Harris	Minnesota Vikings	Free Agent
	Craig Veasey	Houston Oilers	Free Agent

Team-by-Team Free Agent Review—

Team:	Gains:	Top Drafts:	Losses:
Arizona Cardinals	QB Boomer Esiason OT Lomas Brown OG Mike Devlin QB Kent Graham	DE Simeon Rice RB Leland McElroy TE Johnny McWilliams	QB David Krieg C Ed Cunningham SS Lorenzo Lynch
Atlanta Falcons	LB Cornelius Bennett	DT Shannon Brown RB Richard Huntley	DE Chris Doleman LB Darryl Talley DT Jumpy Geathers S Kevin Rosso L Gene Williams
Baltimore Ravens	OL Jeff Blackshear	OT Jonathan Ogden LB Ray Lewis	LB Carl Banks RB Lorenzo White FB Tommy Vardell WR Keenan McCardell WR Rico Smith WR Michael Bates P/QB Tom Tupa OG Bob Dahl LB Gerald Dixon S Dana Hall DT Pio Sagapolutele
Buffalo Bills	WR Quinn Early LB Chris Spielman	WR Eric Moulds DE Gabe Northern	LB Cornelius Bennett FB Carwell Gardner S Matt Darby S Chris Green DE Karl Wilson OL Mike Devlin WR Bill Brooks
Carolina Panthers	TE Wesley Walls WR Michael Bates WR Ray Crittenden OT Greg Skrepenak QB Kelly Stouffer CB Eric Davis LB Kevin Greene	RB Tim Biakabutuka WR Mushin Muhammad	WR Don Beebe TE Pete Metzelaars OT Derrick Graham
Chicago Bears	LB Bryan Cox C Ed Cunningham QB Dave Krieg	CB Walt Harris WR Bobby Engram	WR Jeff Graham RB Lewis Tillman C Jay Leeuwenberg OT Troy Auzenne

Team:	Gains:	Top Drafts:	Losses:
Cincinnati Bengals	CB Ashley Ambrose S Bo Orlando LB Gerald Dixon CB Jimmy Spencer QB Erik Wilhelm	OT Willie Anderson TE Marco Battaglia	S Darryl Wiliams
Dallas Cowboys	LB Fred Strickland	DE Kavika Pittman LB Randall Godfrey WR Stepfret Williams	DT Russell Maryland LB Dixon Edwards LB Robert Jones CB Larry Brown CB Clayton Holmes CB Robert Bailey C Derek Kennard OT Ron Stone
Denver Broncos	LB Bill Romanowski DE Alfred Williams WR Mike Sherrard	LB John Mobley CB Tory James	RB/WR Glyn Milburn DE Simon Fletcher CB Eric Thomas QB Hugh Millen
Detroit Lions	WR Glyn Milburn LB Michael Brooks OT Ray Roberts TE Pete Metzelaars	LB Reggie Brown OG Jeff Hartings	OT Lomas Brown LB Chris Spielman S Willie Clay OT David Lutz OG Doug Widell TE Rodney Holman QB Kent Graham LB Tracy Hayworth
Green Bay Packers	DT/DE Santana Dotson CB/S Marcus Turner WR Jeff Query	OT John Michels WR Derrick Mayes RB Chris Darkins	DT John Jurkovic QB Ty Detmer WR Charles Jordan LB Fred Strickland LB Joe Kelly
Houston Oilers	WR Willie Davis RB Ronnie Harmon	RB Eddie George DE Bryant Mix	WR Haywood Jeffires DE Ray Childress DE Kenny Davidson LB Eddie Robinson DL Doug Veasey RB Todd McNair QB Will Furrer

Team:	Gains:	Top Drafts:	Losses:
Indianapolis Colts	OT Troy Auzenne OT Tony Mandarich OG Jay Leeuwenburg OG Doug Widell LB Quentin Coryatt	WR Marvin Harrison DB Dedric Mathis	CB Ashley Ambrose OT Will Wolford
Jacksonville Jaguars	RB Natrone Means OT Leon Searcy WR Keenan McCardell DT John Jurkovic S Dana Hall LB Eddie Robinson	LB Kevin Hardy DE Tony Brackens	OG Eugene Chung
Kansas City Chiefs	QB Bucky Richardson K Bjorn Nittmo K Roman Anderson K Scott Szeredy	S Jerome Woods S Reggie Tongue	WR Willie Davis WR Webster Slaughter DE Darren Mickell K Lin Elliott S Ronnie Lott (Retired) RB Leroy Thompson OL Joe Valerio LB Jaime Fields
Miami Dolphins	WR Fred Barnett WR Charles Jordan OT James Brown LB Jack Del Rio QB Mike Buck	DT Daryl Gardener CB Dorian Brew RB Karim Abdul-Jabbar	WR Irving Fryar WR Gary Clark LB Bryan Cox DE Marco Coleman CB Troy Vincent CB Frankie Smith OG Tom McHale OG Bert Weidner
Minnesota Vikings	LB Dixon Edwards	DE Duane Clemons DT James Manley RB Moe Williams	LB Broderick Thomas DE Roy Barker DE James Harris LB Jack Del Rio S Charles Mincy OG Chris Hinton

Team:	Gains:	Top Drafts:	Losses:
New England Patriots	WR Shawn Jefferson S Willie Clay P/QB Tom Tupa DT Mark Wheeler DT Pio Sagapolutele CB Frankie Smith	WR Terry Glenn S Lawyer Milloy	DE Aaron Jones
New Orleans Saints	DE Darren Mickell DE Fred Stokes CB Mark McMillian OT Clarence Jones	CB Alex Molden S Je'Rod Cherry	WR Quinn Early TE Wesley Walls CB Jimmy Spencer OT Richard Cooper OG Chris Port
New York Giants	OT Ron Stone	DE Cedric Jones WR Amani Toomer QB Danny Kanell	LB Michael Brooks OT Jumbo Elliott
New York Jets	QB Neil O'Donnell WR Jeff Graham OT Jumbo Elliott OT David Williams WR Rico Smith C John Hudson QB Frank Reich	WR Keyshawn Johnson WR Alex Van Dyke	QB Boomer Esiason TE Johnny Mitchell QB Bubby Brister QB Erik Wilhelm DT Tony Casillas CB/S Marcus Turner S Anthony Prior OT James Brown
Oakland Raiders	DT Russell Maryland CB Larry Brown S Lorenzo Lynch OT Charles McRae	TE Rickey Dudley LB Lance Johnstone	Don Mosebar (Retired) OT Greg Skrepenek
Philadelphia Eagles	CB Troy Vincent QB Ty Detmer OT Richard Cooper WR Mark Seay WR Irving Fryar	OT Jermaine Mayberry TE Jason Dunn QB Bobby Hoying	WR Fred Barnett LB Bill Romanowski LB Kurt Gouveia CB Mark McMillian C John Hudson

3.8

Team:	Gains:	Top Drafts:	Losses:
Pittsburgh Steelers	RB Jerome Bettis OT Will Wolford	OT Jamain Stephens LB Steven Conley FB Jon Witman	QB Neil O'Donnell OT Leon Searcy FB John L. Williams
St. Louis Rams	QB Steve Walsh DE Leslie O'Neal LB Robert Jones CB Maurice Hurst K Chip Lohmiller	RB Lawrence Phillips WR Eddie Kennison QB Tony Banks TE Ernie Conwell FB Jerald Moore	DT Sean Gilbert RB Jerome Bettis QB Chris Miller DE Fred Stokes OT Clarence Jones
San Diego Chargers	DE Marco Coleman LB Kurt Gouveia S Kevin Ross TE Walter Reeves QB Sean Salisbury	WR Bryan Still LB Patrick Sapp TE Brian Roche WR Charlie Jones	RB Natrone Means WR Shawn Jefferson LB Leslie O'Neal S Bo Orlando TE Duane Young OT Stan Brock
San Francisco 49ers	RB Johnny Johnson FB Tommy Vardell DE Chris Doleman DE Roy Barker S Curtis Buckley OG Ray Brown OG Eugene Chung	DE Isarael Ifeanyi WR Terrell Owens	WR John Taylor CB Eric Davis DE Alfred Williams OT Steve Wallace
Seattle Seahawks	S Darryl Williams OG Derrick Graham	OT Pete Kendall CB Fred Thomas RB Reggie Brown	OT Ray Roberts OT/OG Jeff Blackshear FB Tracy Johnson

Team:	Gains:	Top Drafts:	Losses:
Tampa Bay Buccaneers	DE Lamar Mills	DE Regan Upshaw DT Marcus Jones FB Mike Alstott	DT/DE Santana Dotson DT Mark Wheeler OT Charles McRae S Curtis Buckley
Washington Redskins	DT Sean Gilbert DT Leonard Renfro OG Bob Dahl FB Anthony McDowell WR Greg McMurtry WR Bryan Reeves WR Bill Brooks	OT Andre Johnson RB Stephen Davis	OG Ray Brown

4 Team-by-Team Reviews

Drafting Head Coaches—

One fun part added to the Journal two years ago was an idea presented by you, the reader. People had written in to suggest including head coaches as part of their leagues. This little addition added even more fun and helped tweak the game. Obviously, you don't want to draft a head coach who appears headed for the gallows—this year, that would be Oakland's leader—so even if this pick won't turn your season around, it could help out and allow you to squeak out a weekly victory in a close head-to head game.

Now buck up here if you don't draft head coaches, because you should be aware of any player that you want to draft that could be on a real stink-a-roo of a team. For example, last season the New York Jets fell completely apart. When a team begins to smell foul, the whole team eventually begins to perform like boneheads.

So a tip here is to study the head coaches and regardless if you agree with my assessment, think about drafting players that will see action, can score, and can gobble yardage on a team that isn't losing 20-0 two minutes after the opening kickoff! ★

Coach:	Team:	Projected '96 Wins:	The Inside Skinny:
George Seifert	SF	13-3	Everything here depends on Steve Young. If Young suffers a crucial injury again, the 'Niners will be cooked. Grbac is adequate and learning, but he is no Steve Young (*who is, huh?*). Will Johnny Johnson check his attitude at the door and play with mental and physical toughness? Maybe he can look over at Jerry Rice and catch onto his professional attitude. Expect William Floyd to give 'Niners a second half lift.
Marv Levy	BUF	13-3	Guess what? *They're baaack!* The Bills are rejuvenated and look solid and healthy. This team has perhaps the best positive outlook of any NFL team. This team rallies around Marv and each other. Jim Kelly is healthier than he has been in years and Quinn Early and Eric Moulds will help the Bills offensively. *I smell Super Bowl!*

Coach:	Team:	Projected '96 Wins:	The Inside Skinny:
Mike Holmgren	GB	12-4	It is hard not to like what Holmgren has done to the Pack—Brett Favre is playing hell-bent on the Super Bowl. The defense has tightened up a bit with Santana Dotson, but they will miss John Jurkovic. The big key here is keeping Favre healthy.
Barry Switzer	DAL	12-4	*Super Barry* needs to first solve the "*Michael*" situation. Second, he needs to add Deion Sanders to the offensive mix as a receiver. Can't miss with Emmitt Smith! Despite the Cowpokes' stand—they have been hit hard with two seasons of heavy free agent losses.
Wayne Fontes	DET	11-5	Wayne needs to make that charge *now!* What an awesome offense with an improved Scott Mitchell hitting Moore, Perriman, Morton, and Milburn, and handing off to Barry Sanders. Still, the Lions will find ways to blow some and to win some they shouldn't. It's always interesting with *Wayne's World*.
June Jones	ATL	10-6	Jeff George can be a rockhead, but he can also flat-out rocket the ball. Will Ironhead keep the edge or lose his spot to the achieving Jamal Anderson? Metcalf by himself is worth at least 2-3 wins with his game-breaking abilities. Speaking of winning games by himself, Morten Andersen is worth several wins as well!
Jimmy Johnson	MIA	10-6	I don't care what team J.J. inherits, he will make them improve and win. Having Dan Marino doesn't hurt either. The question will be that glut at running back and how to cover *all* those defensive holes. Jimmy will figure a way to win 10!
Rich Kotite	NYJ	10-6	Don't be shocked if the Jets win 11! No team made so many positive changes in the off-season as the Jets. Sure, the jury is still out on Neil O'Donnell, but he will deliver much more than folks believe. Solid defense and if the offense clicks with Neil, Adrian Murrell, and rookies Keyshawn Johnson and Alex Van Dyke—watch out!

Coach:	Team:	Projected '96 Wins:	The Inside Skinny:
Dennis Green	MIN	10-6	What a season Warren Moon had last year—can he duplicate it? Will Robert Smith play injury-free? The *Vikes* need a full-time runner whether it be Smith or James Stewart. The receivers are pure class—Cris Carter, Jake Reed, Qadry Ismail, and flashy David Palmer. Major loss may be Tony Dungy going to Tampa.
Dave Wannstedt	CHI	10-6	Erik Kramer and Curtis Conway sort of hit the skids by the close of '95. Salaam is a stud, but he is already showing signs of a runner that gets bruised and banged up fairly easily. Wannstedt will have to be concerned about offensive injuries and the loss of Jeff Graham.
David Shula	CIN	10-6	Yes that's right, I think that the Bengals will greatly improve and whip the opposition. First of all, the offense is a lethal weapon and they can score anywhere. Secondly, the defense is mean and fast. Look out, Steelers!
Marty Schottenheimer	KC	9-7	Good defense, but can Steve Bono really dig in and deliver for a full season? How long can this team rely on Marcus Allen? Time for young guys like Greg Hill, Tamarick Vanover, and Lake Dawson to take over.
Dom Capers	CAR	9-7	I really like what Capers is doing with the Panthers—they are legit. Tim Biakabutuka is a huge threat and Kerry Collins demonstrated last season that he is a complete QB and very advanced for such a young player. The guy is a natural winner.
Lindy Infante	IND	9-7	Great fairy tale last season but the Colts will have to scramble this season, since they won't sneak up on anyone this time. I question whether Jim Harbaugh can have similar success (as last year). Craig Erickson is *still* a better passer.

Coach:	Team:	Projected '96 Wins:	The Inside Skinny:
Norv Turner	WAS	9-7	First things first—*Nervous Norv* needs to select a starting QB and live with him. Improved offense and a much tighter defense with offseason acquisitions. Big key for Norv within conference is that he has Dallas' number. With a healthy season and Terry Allen the *'Skins* could win 10!
Ray Rhodes	PHI	9-7	That quarterback situation is still very dicey and losing Fred Barnett is going to hurt. Ricky Watters and Charlie Garner will need to help pump the "*Jersey*" offense.
Mike Shanahan	DEN	9-7	Once again, Elway is the key to a good Bronco season. This could be their "return to glory" year, or another also-ran season. Watch Terrell Davis—he's hot!
Teddy Marchibroda	BAL	8-8	Okay, will Vinny Testaverde finally open up and play? Coach Teddy is a great quarterback coach and will soothe and stroke Vinny. Will Andre Rison more than just show up? Will Leroy Hoard get to carry the ball? A lot of questions.
Bill Cowher	PIT	8-8	Too many player losses and adding Jerome Bettis doesn't alleviate the loss of Bam Morris. Losing Neil O'Donnell is crucial— Jim Miller and Mike Tomczak won't carry you to the super bowl. Kordell Stewart is a year away from becoming an actual starting quarterback.
Jeff Fisher	HOU	8-8	Steadily improving and off-season acquisitions will enable the Oilers to at least hit 8-8. If Eddie George is as good as advertised, the Oilers will be very effective.
Mike White	RAI	8-8	This could be it for Mike White (Joe Bugel is in the wings). Jeff Hostetler needs to stay healthy and the offense needs to decide if they are going to "go long" or "go short".
Rich Brooks	RAM	8-8	Steve Walsh isn't going to shake anyone up. Lawrence Phillips should be an immediate rushing and scoring star and Isaac Bruce is on his way to becoming another Jerry Rice. But I don't see domination here. The defense *is* dominating and will keep the Rams in plenty of games.

Coach:	Team:	Projected '96 Wins:	The Inside Skinny:
Tony Dungy	TB	8-8	The 'Bucs will be an improved team under Tony Dungy, but I really wonder about Trent Dilfer. He needs to move the ball in the air this season and there is no excuse now since the 'Bucs have solid receivers. I question the handling of Errict Rhett's contract. Will he show this summer? What will his attitude be? Stay tuned.
Dennis Erickson	SEA	8-8	Rick Mirer really needs to deliver here. Chris Warren and Joey Galloway are exceptional.
Bill Parcells	NE	7-9	Drew Bledsoe will be back to '94 form and Curtis Martin will gain a ton of yards, but this team is dysfunctional. Parcells has made it clear that he will be out in '97. Not a good sign for his faith in the owner and the team.
Vince Tobin	AZ	7-9	Hey, this is still the Cardinals and it will take some time for Tobin to soothe all those banged-up egos. Can Boomer really zip passes to the streaky Rob Moore and hot second year receiver Frank Sanders? Will Garrison Hearst deliver or be a problem? A ton of questions on this squad!
Bobby Ross	SD	7-9	Scratch that entire backfield and two receivers from last season's roster. I think you can also scratch the season for the Chargers. Too many questions, although I expect Stan Humphries to overcome the bad odds. Plus I like Aaron Hayden.
Tom Coughlin	JAX	7-9	Great season last year, but Tom will have trouble duplicating '95. Improving but they will be short of the mark.
Jim Mora	NO	6-10	Losing pros like Quinn Early and Wesley Walls will hamper Jim Everett. Mario Bates is talented but he hasn't shown signs of really taking over and demanding the ball like Emmitt, Barry, etc. Still a lot of questions with the Saints.
Dan Reeves	NYG	5-11	Sorry, but this will be it for the classy Dan Reeves—there is just not enough fire power outside of Rodney Hampton and Tyrone Wheatley. Amani Toomer is a solid rookie, but this is an old, boring team and they will show the effects this year.

By Larry Weisman
Sports Columnist
USA Today

Arizona Cardinals

Projected Starters:

QB Boomer Esiason
RB Larry Centers
RB Garrison Hearst
WR Rob Moore
WR Frank Sanders
WR Anthony Edwards
K Greg Davis

We can only imagine Vince Tobin wanted to be a head coach in the worst way. And that's the way he became one. Tobin inherits a terrible mess made by Buddy Ryan and this year the Cardinals seem ready to embark on another of their rebuilding programs. Two years ago the Cardinals handed Ryan a team built by Joe Bugel that was ready to win and Ryan turned it into a handpicked collection of cronies and underachievers. The "quarterback of the year" program instituted by the Cardinals brings Boomer Esiason to town to follow in Dave Krieg's legendary footsteps. Krieg, of course, stepped in for Steve Beuerlein, who stepped in for…you get the picture! The Cardinals do have some players who will be worth watching in fantasy leagues and their defense might also be worth a look. Taken as a whole, this team has much work ahead of it before 4-12 seasons become distant memories.

Quarterback—

Not many teams would consider Esiason an upgrade. His arm looks lifeless and three seasons with the New York Jets qualify him to judge mercilesss beatings as an expert. Esiason ranked 15th in the AFC in passer ratings last year but he had no receivers, no line and no running game. Here he'll have former teammate Rob Moore, second-year standout Frank Sanders and fullback Larry Centers. Forget about the first two ever catching anything deep. Esiason must dump the ball short or work the middle zones off play action. The betting here is he'll pile up some cheap yards, hit very few deep touchdowns for big fantasy-league points and, considering the Arizona line, will probably be hurt at some point. The backup is Stoney Case, who's untested and unproven. This is not a great situation for fantasy league general managers to dabble in.

Running Back—

We told you last year this was Garrison Hearst's big chance to break out. We were half-right. He did rush for 1,070 yards and at times looked like the player the Cardinals hoped he could be. But he only scored one rushing touchdown and that just won't do. Of course, Arizona scored only three rushing touchdowns (only the Esiason-equipped Jets rushed for fewer, two). A restricted free agent, Hearst was unsigned at press time and the sujbect of trade rumors at the NFL draft. And though the Cards couldn't move him, they did select Texas A&M's Leland McElroy. That should end the Hearst era before it ever really began. McElroy is productive but not overly big or durable. He's not worth risking an early pick on in so iffy a scheme as Arizona's. Centers is a different story. He set a record for running backs last year with 101 receptions (two for touchdowns) and scored twice on rushes in earning his first Pro Bowl bid. He'll pile up yards, for those in leagues that count yardage bonuses. Will he score touchdowns? We see him getting the call more in short-yardage and goal-line situations, making him a decent late-round selection.

Wide Receiver—

The Cardinals have some fair talent here in Moore and Sanders. Neither is a streak. Both are bigger, possession-type receivers though Moore can make the acrobatic catch downfield. The question is: Can anyone get them the ball downfield? It looks like the answer is no, given the quarterback.

This duo ought to be be fairly productive but isn't going to provide the long-distance lightning strikes that create big points. The Cardinals don't have a lot of depth here. Holdover Anthony Edwards looks like the #3 guy. How exciting for all of us.

Defense/Special Teams—

Let's dispense with the "special" teams first. They ain't. They don't break big returns, they don't score touchdowns and they don't belong on your roster. They were one of three teams last year to allow two kickoff returns for scores. Perhaps McElroy will put a little life in the return game.

The defense could be interesting. True, the Cardinals ranked 30th (last) against the run and 26th overall. But here's what they did well: They led the NFL in takeaways with 42, had 31 sacks and scored on four interception returns. That's not too shabby. Simeon Rice ought to help them step up the pressure.

Tobin's not quite as extreme in attack mentality as Ryan but he likes an aggressive front seven. The Cardinals can get bombed for points but can also score some on defense. It's a gamble but might be a good one.

Kicker—

If Greg Davis didn't have to try six field goals of 50 yards or longer, which everyone but the coaches seemed to know was outside his range, he'd have been unbelievable last year. Throw out the 50-plus tries and he was 29 of 33. Now look at that 1 of 6 stat from 50-plus. The one he made was 55 yards.

Expect Tobin to make better use of Davis and not to ask the ridiculous. Davis can make field goals. He just won't get the opportunity to kick a lot of extra points. ★

By Kevin Lynch
Pro Sports Xchange

Atlanta Falcons

Projected Starters:

QB Jeff George
RB Craig Heyward
WR Eric Metcalf
WR Terance Mathis
WR Bert Emanuel
WR J.J. Birden
K Morten Andersen

The *Run-and-Shoot* is alive, barely! If the Falcons hadn't upset the 49ers on the last game of the season and eked into the playoffs, HC June Jones probably would have been fired, and his beloved 4 WR, pass-crazy offense would have gone with him. The *Run-and-Shoot* was introduced by the Lions in the late 80's and subsequently adopted by the Oilers and Falcons. The Lions and Oilers have since dropped it for traditional schemes. Jones refuses to change and says that he will go down with his *Run-and-Shoot* ship, which has certainly sprung a few leaks. In all fairness to the pass-happy offense, the Falcons DT has been so bad the last few seasons, the offense hasn't had a chance to flourish. Jones also experimented with new-fangled defenses such as a 5 DB/2 LB alignment called the *Big Nickel* which ended up as the *Big Flop*. Returning to a standard 4-3 scheme in '95, the Falcons finished 29th in overall defense. They are quickly learning that without good players, nothing works.

Quarterback—

Two seasons ago, fantasy owners were tantalized by the prospect of QB Jeff George getting out of the offensive desert in Indianapolis and heading up the Falcons' *Run-and-Shoot* offense. His dormant talents would surely flourish in Atlanta. In reality, George was downright disappointing (23 TDS/18 INTS in '94, 24 TDS/11 INTS in '95). Not bad, but certainly not what most people expected. At age 29 and in his third *Run-and-Shoot* year, don't expect his numbers to go up significantly. Also, he has been mired in a contract standoff with the Falcons throughout the off-season. He figures to sign, but for probably less than he wants, which could impact his play on the field. A good late-round pick could be Bobby Hebert. Some defensive players around the league think he's the better QB. Hebert, a great short range passer, was 28 of 45 passing for 313 yards (2 TDS/1 INT) in limited play during '95. He also beat the 49ers after George was knocked out of the game in the second quarter.

Running Back—

No team ran the ball less than the Falcons last year. That said, Craig "Ironhead" Heyward was the NFC's seventh leading runner with 1,083 yards on 236 carries and six TDS (*his career best*). Another bane of the *Run-and-Shoot* is that RBS not only don't get the ball much, they don't score much either. Without a consistent FB or TE those tough yards inside the red zone are hard to get. Yet, Heyward could be an excellent fantasy player. Heyward also catches the ball—37 receptions for 350 yards and a TD last season. His production last season and the league-wide trend away from the *Run-and-Shoot* might dictate that he get the ball more. Jamal Anderson spelled Heyward well, racing for 161 yards in 39 attempts and scoring a TD. Eric Metcalf was also productive in his occasional carry, which will be explored in the receivers section. It's unclear how fourth round rookie Richard Huntley will fit in.

Wide Receiver—

Here's where a fantasy owner can really cash in with the Falcons. Three of their four WRs crested the 1,000 receiving barrier! Eric Metcalf was a smash hit in his first season as a full-time WR (104 receptions for 1,189 yards) along with 28 carries for a 4.8 average and a TD. Metcalf also returns kicks and punts, giving him more opportunities to score. Coming off a stellar season and with a year in the system behind him, Metcalf only figures to get better. Terance Mathis has certainly benefited from the *Run-and-Shoot*. He came to the Falcons in '94 from the Jets (where his previous season high in catches was 24) and he exploded for 111 receptions for 1,342 yards and 11 TDs. He numbers dipped slightly last season (78 for 1,039) partially because of a knee injury, but he led the team with nine receiving TDs. The Falcons and Mathis were haggling over contract numbers late into the off-season but he is expected to re-sign. Bert Emanuel was the third wide receiver who toppled the 1,000 mark and is expected back, despite rumors he was offered in draft day trades. Fourth wideout J.J. Birden was a slight disappointment. Hamstring and back injuries limited him to ten games, where he caught 31 passes for 303 yards and a TD.

4 TM

Defensive/Special Teams—

What's eye-catching about the Falcons DT is their plus-nine turnover ratio. But, actually, it was the offense that should get most of the credit for that, having the fewest turnovers in the league (21). As usual the DT was notoriously bad, ranking 29th in the league.

Over the off-season, the Falcons did little to improve themselves. They did add former Bills Pro Bowl LB Cornelius Bennett, but then lost DE Chris Doleman. They also traded away safety Roger Harper, but got Raider FS Patrick Bates in return. Bates, a former top-round draft choice quit the Raiders in training camp last year, saying he was retiring from football. He then announced his intention to comeback and was traded around draft time to the Falcons. Upon his arrival he said it was the Raiders he didn't like, not necessarily football. If Bates can reach his first-round potential it will be a significant addition to the usually porous Falcons secondary.

The free agent flight of Doleman, likely retirement of Pierce Holt, and aging of Clay Matthews leaves holes in Atlanta's front seven that they've had to spackle with free agency. Former Bronco Shane Dronett will replace Doleman, and Dan Owens will likely step in for Holt. Neither is as talented as the players they're replacing, but they're younger. Rookie Shannon Brown also figures to see playing time. The Falcons will need for young DE Chuck Smith to stay healthy and get after the QB after rewarding him with a $10 million four year deal in the off-season. Their LB corps is aging but excellent. Jesse Tuggle is a tackle-mad MLB in his 10th season. Darryl Talley returns for his 14th season and will once again be paired with old Bills teammate Bennett. The Falcons weren't bad in the turnover department, as they picked off 18 passes and returned two of them for scores. Metcalf is the main threat on kick and punt returns. He'll probably get a helping hand from rookie running back Richard Huntley.

Kicker—

None better than Morten Andersen, who's one of the best free agent pickups to date. When the Saints wanted to reduce his million-dollar salary, Andersen jumped to the division rival Falcons and turned in the best season of his incredible career. He made 31 of 37 kicks, including five of over 50 yards. He'd be an excellent player to have on anyone's fantasy team despite the fact he'll be 36 when the season begins. ★

By Dave Douglas
NFL Films

Baltimore Ravens

Projected Starters:

QB Vinny Testaverde
RB Leroy Hoard
RB Earnest Byner
WR Andre Rison
WR Michael Jackson
WR Derrick Alexander
K Matt Stover

In Cleveland, Art Modell ranks right down there with the Unabomber. Browns fans still haven't recovered from last October's bombshell of an announcement. But in Baltimore, the Ravens have exploded on to the scene and fans there couldn't be happier. While Cleveland mourns and the crab cakers rejoice, the reaction among fantasy drafters is, *"Who cares? Let's see what they have in the way of fantasy guys."* The truth is there are a few Ravens worth raving about. What makes the situation so difficult to judge is the uncertainty concerning the effort players put forth when the team became a lame duck franchise.

Quarterback—

Number one draft pick Jon Ogden (T) will help protect the blind side of somebody—but who? It's Vinny Testaverde vs. Eric Zeier and it's a shame the Ravens can't morph the ability of the Vin-man with the calm decision-making demeanor of Zeier because then they'd really have something special. The job is up for grabs. Last season, Testaverde (241 of 392, 2,883 yards, 17 TDS) picked right up where he left off in '94, then seemed to unravel. Rookie Eric Zeier stepped in and started strong then faded as well. Zeier (82 of 161, 864 yards, 4 TDS) is probably their quarterback of the future but neither are first-tier fantasy guys. See who wins the job and perhaps select one as your backup.

Running Back—

Last season, the Browns used a three-back rotation which is lethal in the fantasy world. You want a ball carrier who does just that, not one who splits time and shares the load. Leroy Hoard (547 yards and 0 TDS), Earnest Byner (432 yards and 4 TDS) and Lorenzo White (163 yards and 1 TD) were the trio used and not one of the three is a top-flight draft pick. If Hoard returns to previous form he could be your third back.

Wide Receiver—

Andre Rison was last year's first round fantasy draft bust. What happened? Some blame the Browns' quarterbacks. Some blame Rison's tempe-rmental nature. Still others say he's purely a run and shoot receiver. The third observation is probably the closest to the truth. Rison (47 catches, 701 yards, 3 TDs) has something to prove and that is when he's at his best. He's still a top 15 receiver and his preseason performance will be the true indicator of exactly where his mind and game is. Michael Jackson (44 catches, 714 yards, 9 TDs) put up excellent fantasy numbers. Keenan McCardell (56 catches, 709 yards, 4 TDs) was lost to free agency. What happened to Derrick Alexander? He could be a force too. Do your homework in August to see who will start on opening day.

Defense/Special Teams—

I believe the Ravens defense will be one of the league's best. I think the unit will take root in Baltimore and be *Cal Ripken-like*—steady, durable, and no nonsense. Stevon Moore is a big hitter and his 5 picks led the team. Draft pick Ray Lewis (LB-Miami) could step in and start. Up front, the Ravens will unleash Anthony Pleasant (8 sacks), Rob Burnett (7.5 sacks) and Dan Footman (5 sacks) in the hopes of improving on their lackluster 29 sack total of '95. Pepper Johnson is still tough and will simply not allow the rest of his defensive mates not to be. McCardell averaged a steady 7.2 yards per punt return while Earnest Hunter averaged over 22 yards per kickoff return.

Kicker—

Matt Stover was a perfect 26-for-26 on point-afters and missed only four field goals all season long. One-hundred and thirteen points are not to be sneezed at, but he failed on his only attempt greater than 50 yards. ★

By Larry Weisman
Sports Columnist
USA Today

Buffalo Bills

4 TM

Projected Starters:

QB *Jim Kelly*
RB *Thurman Thomas*
WR *Quinn Early*
WR *Russell Copeland*
WR *Eric Moulds*
WR *Andre Reed*
K *Steve Christie*

Buffalo's resurgence last year surprised nearly everybody. The Bills, coming off a 7-9 season, seemed headed for that inevitable cycle of rebuilding and some years of obscurity. Instead, with its defense roaring to life under a new coordinator (Wade Phillips) and with some new talent on board (Bryce Paup, Ted Washington, Jim Jeffcoat), the Bills won 10 games and the AFC East division title. The Bills keep blending fresh talent with their core group of their Super Bowl years but time seems to be catching up a bit with Jim Kelly's arm and knees. How well he holds up may determine how far the Bills can go.

Quarterback—

Jim Kelly's numbers are a model of consistency. In 1994 he threw 22 touchdown passes and passed for 3,114 yards. Last year he matched the TD total and added 3,381 yards. He was hurt by the loss for much of the season of Andre Reed and the Bills hope to offset that with the addition of free-agent Quinn Early. Kelly's 35 and the arm isn't what it was. That could show up late in the season when fatigue and harsh weather become factors. Expect the Bills to start getting a look at second-year backup Todd Collins. He played very little as a rookie. The nominal #2 is Alex Van Pelt but the future is Collins.

Running Back—

Thurman Thomas remains a good fantasy choice but he can't be expected to match his numbers of old. He broke 1,000 yards rushing again and scored six TDs on the ground but his receptions dropped by nearly half, to 26 (two for scores). At 30 he can't be expected to be the every-down threat but he should duplicate his '95 figures. That means Darick Holmes can be an interesting player. As an unheralded #7 pick, he broke in with 698 rushing yards and four touchdowns. He's a power back, which means he could see more extensive use around the goal line. Don't overlook him really emerging, if not as a starter then as a substitute who gets plenty of playing time. Thomas and Holmes will get the work. No other Bills back will be worth drafting.

Wide Receiver—

Bill Brooks had a great year once the Bills re-signed him after releasing him. But he's not going to catch 11 TD passes for them again as he signed in May with the 'Skins. He'll be missed. The guy to watch is Quinn Early, signed from New Orleans. He'll put some outside speed on the field and give Kelly an excellent deep target. He'll prosper in this offensive scheme. Russell Copeland could step forward as the other starter, although he will compete in camp against Andre Reed, whom they re-signed in May. He's not really a burner, though he did have a 77-yard TD catch (his only one) last season. Certain to see plenty of time, as coach Marv Levy softens his anti-rookie stance, is #1 pick Eric Moulds. He's big, strong, explosive after the catch and able to make the acrobatic grabs. He'll get on-the-job training and should challenge for the starting job by late in the season. Look for 45 catches, maybe five TDs. Lonnie Johnson has started to look the part of a Bills tight end. He caught 49 passes but only one for a touchdown and is not a guy the Bills look for around the goal line.

Defense/Special Teams—

Buffalo had the lowest average return on kickoffs in the NFL last season at 18.6 yards. They don't really have a breakaway return artist. Punt returner Jeff Burris has some nice moves but comes off a knee injury. Moulds might be interesting if he handles kickoffs. He led the nation in 1994 at Mississippi State.

The Bills played very well on defense last year, based on their league-leading sack total of 49. Leagues that score points for sacks will take notice. Turnovers, however, is not the strength of the Bills' game, though a rash of injuries in their secondary held down interceptions to 17, only one more than the previous year. They scored twice on interception returns.

The Bills' defense is effective at stopping the other team, less stunning at making the big play that becomes immediate points. The combined sack/turnover ratio is positive if your league counts those figures. Looking for that individual player? Bryce Paup led the NFL with 17.5 sacks and Bruce Smith had 10.5. Paup probably won't match that number with more attention from blockers but Smith, who had an all-around great year, might add a sack or two if he can escape double- and triple-teams.

Kicker—

Steve Christie made 31 of 40 field goal tries last year but that .775 percentage ranked him 12th in the AFC alone. He made 25 of those at distances of 39 yards or less and was only 6 of 11 from 40 and out. He scored 126 points, however, fifth best in the NFL. The Bills move the ball well and Christie gets his shots. He may not make the booming 50-yarders much any more but he's very consistent in the shorter range. ★

By Kevin Lynch
Pro Sports Xchange

Carolina Panthers

Projected Starters:

QB Kerry Collins
RB Bob Christian
RB Tim Biakabutuka
WR Willie Green
WR Mark Carrier
WR Mushin Muhammad
TE Wesley Walls
K John Kasay

Many are still marveling at the Panthers' 7-9 record in their inaugural season last year. Here's an expansion team that wasn't out of the playoff chase until the dying weeks of the season. They have an outstanding coach, an aggressive owner, a big-time defense, and a young budding QB. They are also a treasure trove for potential fantasy football finds. In the off-season, the Panthers turned their attention to offense, choosing three offensive skill players with their first three selections in the draft, and going after more offensive help in free agency. The Panthers are a team to watch, especially if fantasy football owners are willing to draft on potential.

Quarterback—

Frank Reich was supposed to be the starter last year, but after a miserable beginning, he gave way to rookie Kerry Collins. Now, the team seems fully satisfied and confident with Collins, who compiled a winning record of 7-6 in his first season. Collins appears to have it all: size, smarts, arm strength, and amazing composure. His stats last season were possibly the worst in football, with the exception of Buccaneer Trent Dilfer. He was the only starter to complete less than 50% of his passes (49.4) and he threw 19 INTs and 14 TDs. But, with a year's seasoning, better protection and more talent around him, expect those figures to rise dramatically. Reich was scared off by Collins' potential and has since signed a free agent deal with the Jets to back up Neil O'Donnell. The Panthers didn't want to take any chances so they signed veteran Steve Beuerlein, who lost his job in Jacksonville. Former top round washout Kelly Stouffer will battle veteran Jack Trudeau for the third spot.

Running Back—

The Panthers were elated with the pickup of former Michigan RB Tim Biakabutuka in the first round of the draft. They've handed him the starting job and expect him to have impact his rookie season. The conservative Dom Capers will love to revolve his team around a potent ground game, and he thinks he now has his runner. The only concern is Biakabutuka's lack of receiving in college, where he only caught 12 passes. However, he did well receiving in a workout before the draft. The all-time leading receiver for RBs (Roger Craig) also caught just 12 passes in college. The Panthers dipped into the third round to pick up blindingly quick Winslow Oliver who could become the next Dave Meggett. Last season, Derrick Moore was the leading ground gainer. He did a serviceable job, and the Panthers would like to re-sign him. FB Bob Christian was a powerful blocker when healthy. Howard Griffith is also likely to see some playing time at that spot. Tony Smith spent most of the season on the IR. He showed flashes of brilliance in his early career with the Falcons and could compete if he gets off to a good start in camp. The Panthers also drafted Marquette Smith and Scott Greene who are ticketed for backup duty. The FA acquisition of massive T Greg Skrepenak will help open holes for RBs and add extra protection for Collins at QB.

Wide Receiver—

The Panthers hope another rookie will figure prominently in their receiving plans. Michigan State's Mushin Muhammad was drafted for the express purpose of starting at flanker. He's an extremely aggressive receiver with his size, and he can and will be used on punt coverage teams. Muhammad is also said to be lethal after the catch. Veteran WRs Mark Carrier and Don Beebe were supposed to come in last year and show the way. Beebe has already left the team. Carrier proved there was still some power left in his 30-year-old legs. He led the Panther receivers with 66 catches for 1,002 yards and three TDs. Willie Green was a starter beside Carrier, is under contract, and will probably return. He was a deep threat, catching six TD passes including one of 89 yards. He also had a 18.8 yard average, which was the highest in the conference. Eric Guliford was effective as the team's third WR, playing mostly in the slot on third downs (29 catches, 444 yards, 3 TDs). The Panthers signed former Saint/49er Wesley Walls, who will likely be their starting TE. Walls set the team record last year in New Orleans with 57 catches, and has amazing speed for his size. His height, 6'5", makes him a perfect target for the end zone when the Panthers are in the *Red Zone*. Walls could be an excellent pick to fill the TE spot and he will probably be the only one in that role this season, as Pete Metzelaars high-tailed it to the high-powered Lions den!

Defense/Special Teams—

The Panthers' seventh-ranked DT caused 37 turnovers, the third-best in the league. That total is likely to go up. Players have had a year to get used to one another, and Carolina added former 49er Eric Davis, a gambling CB with incredibly quick feet. The combination of him and Tyrone Poole on the other side give the Panthers two of the best turnover players in the league. Poole not only makes INTs, but causes fumbles. The Panthers collected 36 sacks last year, which was about in the middle of pack. They were disappointed in their two OLBs Lamar Lathon and Darion Connor, despite the fact that both combined for 15 sacks. They are committed to Lathon, who is getting a $3 million salary. There's a possibility Connor will not return to the team. A nagging knee injury hampered him last year. ILB Sam Mills is an ageless marvel at 37, and the Panthers hope he has one more year left. Carlton Bailey did a credible job beside him. The Panthers hope to wreak even more havoc with their complicated set of blitzes this season. Eric Guliford was a very capable punt return man, but Tyrone Poole is probably more talented. Capers is reluctant to use him because he's so valuable on defense. If rookie Winslow Oliver shows well in training camp he could become the main return man.

Kicker—

John Kasay is the highest paid kicker in the league but had a slight problem converting to kicking outdoors on grass (he came from Seattle) He was still solid, making 26 of 33 kicks. Kasay was actually better making kicks over 40 yards (9 of 12) than he was kicking in the 30 to 39 yard range (10 of 14). ★

By Kevin Lynch
Pro Sports Xchange

Chicago Bears

Projected Starters:

QB Erik Kramer
RB Rashaan Salaam
RB Raymont Harris
WR Curtis Conway
WR Michael Timpson
TE Keith Jennings
K Kevin Butler

After being the Cinderella team that eked into the playoffs in 1994, Bear fans were expecting marked improvement over last year. They got it, statistically, but couldn't improve in the win column and were left out of the playoff chase. Bears fans are likely to get downright ornery with HC Dave Wannstedt if he doesn't lead the beloved Bears into the playoffs this time. The pressure is on, and unlike last year, the Bears look like they have some talented players who can help them (and fantasy football owners). Unlike the year before, the Bears now have a legitimate QB in Erik Kramer, a potentially high scoring RB in Rashaan Salaam, and Curtis Conway—an emerging big-play WR. Offensively, the only things that could prevent these players from posting big points are injuries to the *Big Three*, or an offensive line unfamiliar with one another. The Bears let C Jerry Fontenot go, and signed former Cardinal Ed Cunningham who isn't considered as talented.

Quarterback—

Erik Kramer made Wannstedt look like a genius after posting the best season ever by a Bears QB. Kramer won the job in training camp away from Steve Walsh and never missed a snap during the regular season while compiling a 93.5 QB rating, which was fourth highest in the league. He threw 29 TDs and only 10 INTs while completing 60.3 percent of his passes. However, gone is favorite WR Jeff Graham and Kramer is left with an offensive line that might not protect nearly as well. The line allowed only 15 sacks last year, which was tied for second best in the league. Kramer played well enough to chase Walsh south to St. Louis, where he signed with the Rams. Dave Krieg signed as the backup, but the Bears could be in trouble if Kramer gets hurt.

Running Back—

Expect Salaam to get a real workout this year. Wannstedt didn't like the pass happy Bears last year and he wants to return to the Bears' tough running roots. Salaam carried the ball 276 times for 1,074 yards and ten TDs, but had a disappointing 3.6 yard average. The Bears would like to see all those numbers go up, which is why Salaam might be a solid pick for RB. The only problem is his constant fumbling. The Bears feel they can solve his fumbilitis with a full training camp (which Salaam missed last year with a contract hold-out). However, there's always the possibility that Salaam could be the next Cleveland Gary. But, hey, let's go easy on the guy—he was just a rookie last year. The return of Raymont Harris (who missed 15 games last year) will bode well for the running game. He was the Bears most valuable offensive player in 1994. Fantasy owners should keep in mind that Chicago FBs catch a lot of passes. Last year, as the starter, Tony Carter caught 40 balls for 329 yards and a TD. Robert Green is anxiously waiting on the sidelines. He had a 5.3 yard average with only 107 carries last year, and may be a hard guy to keep on the bench.

Wide Receiver—

The Bears tried to hold on to last year's leading receiver Jeff Graham but they simply couldn't afford to pay both Graham and Curtis Conway, whose contracts were both up this year. Graham took his 82 catches, 1,301 yards, and four TDs to the Jets for a cool $5.4 million contract over three years. While Graham was a smooth-running veteran, Conway is an undisciplined player bristling with talent. Last year, he was the Bears' leading TD scorer with 12. He also caught 62 passes for 1,037 yards. Now he'll be depended on to be the deep threat and clutch third-down receiver, and it appears Conway is ready to break into the upper echelon of receivers. Conway had a better third year than many other NFL receivers, and got a four-year, $10 million deal out of the Bears in the offseason. Michael Timpson didn't get much work as the Bears third WR (24 catches, 289 yards, two TDs) but that will all change now that Graham is gone. However, Timpson will have to fend off rookie Bobby Engram, who comes highly recommended from none other than Joe Paterno. The Bears were, however, disappointed that they didn't snag a tight end in the draft. They will once again have to depend on Keith Jennings and Chris Gedney, who's well-liked but can't stay healthy. Wannstedt believes Gedney can do it all, but he needs to put three injury-plagued seasons behind him. Gedney could be a good gamble as a late round TE.

Defense/Special Teams—

Defensively, the Bears ended up last season in the middle of the pack in turnovers with 29. They hope to improve upon their 16 INTs with the drafting of Mississippi State CB Walt Harris. Although he doesn't expect to start right away, Harris could overtake Jeremy Lincoln at one corner spot as the year wears on. Coaches seem satisfied with safeties Marty Carter and Mark Carrier. The only significant player the Bears lost on defense was LB Ron Cox, but they replaced him with the fiery Bryan Cox, who will man the storied middle linebacker spot. After signing DE Alonzo Spellman to a $12 million four-year deal, the Bears will expect big things out of him. They also hope that former top round pick John Thierry picks it up at the other end spot. If so, the Bears could have two pass rush threats at DE, which could help pass rushing terror Jim Flanigan on the inside. He came out of nowhere to notch 11 sacks last season. In all, the Bears' 35 sacks was just under the league average, and is a number they could certainly improve upon next year. In losing Graham, the Bears also lose their lead punt returner, but that's not a significant loss. He averaged just 8 yards a return last year. Nate Lewis, if he's re-signed, could slide over from kickoff returns and take on punt return duties as well. As the kick returner, Lewis averaged 21.5 yards with a long of 52.

Kicker—

Kevin Butler, the lone holdover from the Bears 1985 Super Bowl team, might have a tough time making it through training camp. He only converted eight of 15 field goals down the stretch and a few of those misses might have won an all-important 10th game for the Bears last year. Canadian League kicker Carlos Huerta was signed over the offseason and might have the inside track. ★

By Dave Douglas
NFL Films

Cincinnati Bengals

4 TM

Projected Starters:

QB *Jeff Blake*
RB *Ki-Jana Carter*
WR *Carl Pickens*
WR *Darnay Scott*
TE *Tony McGee*
TE *Marco Battaglia*
K   *Doug Pelfrey*

The Bengals more than doubled their 1994 win total last year and stayed in the playoff hunt until late in the season. Dave Shula guided the NFL's second youngest team to a 7 and 9 finish highlighted by victories over contenders like the Colts, Bears and AFC champion Pittsburgh. They were sparked by their dynamic duo, Jeff Blake and Carl Pickens, and to be sure there are some fantasy gems to be mined in the Queen City.

Quarterback—

Jeff Blake is a dead-solid first round pick. He loves to go deep which means big bonus points for those wise enough to snatch him up early...and do that because he won't last long and the quarterback position is as thin as it has been for some time. Blake led the AFC in touchdown passes while shattering team records in completions and TD passes in consecutive games. Blake fired it up 567 times, and with the Bengals likely to be trailing in many of their games, he'll keep tossing it up this season.

He completed 326 passes for a whopping 3,822 yards and 28 touchdowns. He also rushed for a pair of scores. He has a gun of an arm and plenty of big play targets. To the endzone and in the first round he'll go. The only way Erik Wilhelm, the backup, takes a snap is if Blake is injured or they need someone to mop up.

Running Back—

As a Penn Stater, I couldn't wait to watch Ki-Jana Carter light it up in the NFL. His preseason injury was painful to watch— *over and over*. In the off-season, the Bengals hired a personal trainer to oversee Carter's long road back.

How far has he come? The preseason will be the true test. If he plays like the back who cracked the 100 yard mark nine times in his senior year, consider him a steal in the fourth round of your fantasy draft. Harold Green (661 yards, 2 TDs) is still a solid back but could easily go undrafted.

Eric Bienemy (381 yards, 3 TDs), James Joseph, and Jeff Cothran simply don't get enough carries to be considered.

Wide Receiver—

99 catches! 1,234 yards! 17 touchdowns! The preceding eye-popping numbers were brought to you by Carl Pickens. He is now a playmaking machine in absolute synergy with his quarterback. From the slot, he runs the slants, curls, posts and bonus-bringing "go" routes. He's Blake's third down target nearly every time and if he's still there in the second round you should pull the trigger without batting an eye. He is the third best fantasy receiver in the game right now and he could be a counted-on cornerstone of your squad.

Darnay Scott is a home run hitter as well but he's a notch below Pickens. Scott (52 catches for 821 yards and 5 TDs) seems to put up huge numbers one week then vanish the next.

He is a perfect third receiver in fantasy football terms. Tight end Tony McGee was second on the team with 55 catches and scored four touchdowns but with the drafting of Marco Battaglia, keep an eye on both in the preseason to see who emerges as the projected starter. Battaglia doesn't have blazing speed but his Mark Bavaro-like strength after the catch will make him a factor in the passing game in the near future.

Defense/Special Teams—

The Bengal defense is young and raw. It's a unit that shows flashes of brilliance but doesn't have the continuity to be a force week in and week out. One thing they do well is sack the quarterback…42 times last year. Big John Copeland paced the team with 9 while Dan "Big Daddy" Wilkinson finished a close second with 8. Wilkinson improved in his second season and in his third year, he could be truly dominant.

Safety Bracey Walker topped the team with only 4 interceptions but the addition of Ashley Ambrose and Bo Orlando will strengthen the final line of defense.

Rookie David Dunn averaged nearly 22 yards per kickoff return while Corey Sawyer handled the punt returns.

Kicker—

Doug Pelfrey has a huge leg, drilling one from 51 yards out on his way to 121 points. He was 29 of 36 in the field goal department and is a top ten fantasy football kicker to be sure.

The Bengals will score often and Pelfrey will be a big contributor. ★

By Larry Weisman
Sports Columnist
USA Today

Dallas Cowboys

Projected Starters:

QB *Troy Aikman*
RB *Emmitt Smith*
RB *Daryl Johnston*
WR *Michael Irvin*
WR *Kevin Williams*
WR *Stepfret Williams*
TE *Jay Novacek*
K *Chris Boniol*

Start with an offensive line as big on savvy and smarts as size. Factor in outstanding players at the skill positions. Throw in an overlooked defense. *Voila!* The Dallas Cowboys. Super Bowl champions three times in four seasons. Face it. They're good. When the stars don't make plays, that strong second tier of players steps it up. Not that the Cowboys are without some worries. Free agency strafed them again, Michael Irvin's legal problems might jeopardize his status, and some of those wide bodies on the offensive line could start to show their age. That said, they're probably still the NFL's best team counting only the 22 starters.

Quarterback—

Because Dallas' ground game is so strong, Troy Aikman won't rank with the top passers in fantasy football. He's just not going to throw enough touchdown passes. He tossed 16 last year, 13 the year before and 20 is an optimistic target. Face it, Dallas would rather run the ball into the end zone and they certainly can do it. Aikman is a safe pick because he won't turn the ball over. But his percentage of touchdown passes last year, 2.7%, is marginal. Don't be surprised if Jason Garrett supplants aging Wade Wilson as the #2. Wilson has done little in his few chances. Garrett's the more exciting player.

Running Back—

Take Emmitt Smith. *Please!*
Even if he holds out into the regular season he will still be among the league's most productive running backs. He led the NFL in scoring last year with 150 points, on 25 rushing touchdowns. Though he's under contract for 1996, he wants a new deal and the Cowboys have serious salary cap concerns.

Sherman Williams showed some flashes as a rookie in the very limited role of backing up Smith. If Smith holds out, Williams gets the nod but won't be anything like Smith. FB Daryl Johnston is a great player in the real world but no factor in fantasy football.

Wide Receiver—

Irvin answered the challenge last year when the Cowboys lost Alvin Harper. He had 111 catches and 10 touchdowns. But his off-season run-in with the law could put him on the wrong side of the NFL's substance abuse policy. So could the courts. Keep scanning the legal notices and police blotter. Other than his off-the-field worries, he should be very productive once again.

The x factor here is Deion Sanders. Having given up baseball, at least temporarily, he's expected to get a full training camp and extensive work at receiver, as well as cornerback. How much Dallas can milk from him playing two ways is an interesting question. If Sanders appears to be close to getting half the snaps on offense, grab him. When he makes catches, things can and do happen.

Kevin Williams was about adequate and not much more in replacing Harper. He caught 38 passes, two for touchdowns, and could be replaced by a draft choice. He doesn't have that great downfield explosion and more or less fills the role of a possession receiver. He could be pushed a bit by rookie Stepfret Williams.

Tight end Jay Novacek can usually be counted on for five to seven TDs. He's consistent. The *Pokes* have no notable backup.

Defense/Special Teams—

Dallas didn't score on punt or kick returns last season. If Sanders plays receiver, Williams probably moves back into the return role. He's better on punts than kickoffs. Sanders probably won't handle any kicks until late in the season or even the playoffs.

The Cowboys forced a modest 25 turnovers and clocked in with 36 sacks. They have to replace four starters—CB Larry Brown, T Russell Maryland, and LBS Robert Jones and Dixon Edwards.

But the Cowboys did return four interceptions for touchdowns. They're weaker at cornerback without Brown, Kevin Smith coming off a ruptured Achilles' tendon, and Sanders playing more on offense.

Kicker—

Chris Boniol led all kickers last year by making 27 of 28 field goals and scored 127 points. He's a good choice because Dallas moves the ball well and gives him opportunities to try makeable kicks.

He attempted only three field goals longer than 40 yards and made them all. He also kicks plenty of PATS. ★

By John Weiss
NFL Films

Denver Broncos

Projected Starters:

QB John Elway
RB Terrell Davis
RB Aaron Craver
WR Anthony Miller
WR Mike Sherrard
TE Shannon Sharpe
K Jason Elam

Once a playoff regular, the Broncos have been just another NFL also-ran the past two seasons. Denver finished 8-8 last year and failed to make the playoffs for the second straight season, the first time they've missed the post-season in back-to-back years since 1981 and 1982.

But don't blame the offense. Last season, the Broncos set franchise records for points scored (388), passing yards (4,260) and total yards (6,040). The offense ranked #1 in the AFC and third in the NFL, and could light it up against just about anyone. Head coach Mike Shanahan needs to shore up a defense that ranked 15th in the league, and 23rd against the run, before Denver can once again make a run at the playoffs.

Quarterback—

With a contract extension that ensures he'll finish his career as a Bronco, John Elway shows no signs of slowing down, as he's putting up the best statistics of his career. At one time, Elway was much more valuable in the NFL than the FFL. But he's changed all that the past few years by putting up some big numbers, and he should certainly be among the top 10 passers drafted in your league.

Last year, Elway aired it out for 3,970 yards (best in the AFC), and completed 316-of-542 passes (58.3%) for a career-high 26 touchdowns and 14 interceptions. If his 36-year-old body can withstand another season of punishment, he should be piling up the fantasy points once again.

Running Back—

No rookie had a more surprising season in 1995 than Terrell Davis, a sixth-round draft pick out of Georgia who came out of nowhere to re-energize the Denver ground game. Davis led the team with 1,117 yards (4.7 average) and seven touchdowns, becoming the lowest draft choice in NFL history to rush for 1,000 yards in his rookie season. He added 49 catches for 367 yards and a score. He may have slipped through the cracks in last year's fantasy draft, but he won't this year. His versatility makes him a great #1 back for your offense. Look for him to go in the second or early third round.

Aaron Craver was second on the team in rushing with 333 yards (4.6 average) and five scores. He also had 43 catches for 369 yards and one touchdown. Denver added muscle to the ground game by drafting Texas A&M fullback Detron Smith in the third round.

Wide Receiver—

Elway spread the ball around to so many backs and receivers last season (six players caught more than 30 passes), that no Bronco put up the huge numbers that others boasted around the league. If you're going to bet on anyone, it would once again be Anthony Miller. The pluses on Miller are that he had 1,079 receiving yards and a whopping 14 TD catches, tying him for the fourth highest total in the league. The big minus is he had just 59 receptions, and with WRs routinely catching 90 and 100 passes a season, Miller will have to significantly raise his total to be among the elite fantasy pass catchers. He's probably a third or early fourth-round pick.

On the other hand, if you're looking for a tight end, Shannon Sharpe is among the top guys around. Last year, he led the Broncos in receiving for the fourth straight season with 63 catches for 756 yards and four touchdowns. He ranked second among all tight ends in both catches and yards. Since 1990, Sharpe leads all tight ends in receiving yards and ranks behind only Jay Novacek in catches. He's as sure a thing as there is at the position.

Mike Pritchard had a disappointing season with 33 catches for 441 yards and three scores.

Defense/Special Teams—

The Bronco defense needs to work on a couple important things in 1996—getting to the quarterback and creating more turnovers. Denver recorded just 30 sacks and 21 takeaways last season. The takeaway total was the second worst in the league. Needless to say, they weren't much help to fantasy owners. The team's all-time sack leader, Simon Fletcher, retired after last season, and the Broncos need someone to step up and fill the void. They signed defensive end Alfred Williams, who recorded 4.5 sacks last season for the 49ers and 9.5 in 1994 with the Bengals. Last season, defensive tackle Michael Dean Perry led the Broncos with only six sacks.

Another problem for the defense was that three of its top four tacklers were in the secondary. Pro Bowl safety Steve Atwater led the team with 148 tackles (107 solo) and also had a team-high three interceptions. Safety Tyrone Braxton tied for second with 110 tackles (77 solo) and cornerback Ray Crockett was fourth with 78 (61 solo). Amazingly, no Denver cornerback had an interception last season. They selected LSU cornerback Tory James in the second round of the draft.

The Broncos needed to bolster their LB corps, and they started by signing linebacker Bill Romanowski away from the Eagles. They also got help in the draft by selecting Kutztown's John Mobley in the first round. Mobley, who wowed scouts in the Senior Bowl, is a terrific athlete with great quickness, lateral range, and the ability to blitz and cover. Third-year linebacker Allen Aldridge made an impact last season with 110 tackles (77 solo).

On special teams, record-setting returner Glyn Milburn was traded to Detroit, leaving the return duties to Rod Smith, who averaged 13.5 yards on just four kick returns last season.

Kicker—

Jason Elam is now established as one of the league's top fantasy kickers. Last year, Elam racked up 132 points, tying him for the second highest total in the NFL. He connected on 31-of-38 field goals, including a terrific 5-of-7 from 50-plus yards, and 39-of-39 extra points. If the Broncos continue to put big points on the board, Elam will once again be one of the top two or three fantasy kickers in 1996. ★

By Kevin Lynch
Pro Sports Xchange

Detroit Lions

Projected Starters:

QB Scott Mitchell
RB Barry Sanders
WR Herman Moore
WR Brett Perriman
WR Johnnie Morton
TE David Sloan
K Jason Hanson

After inputting all the relevant information on all playoff teams last year, a computer spit out the Lions as the team that should win Super Bowl XXX. They certainly looked like contenders after winning their last seven games to finish the season. They beat their last two opponents (Jacksonville and Tampa Bay) by a combined score of 81-10. They were then waxed by the untalented Eagles 58-37 in the Wildcard playoff. So which team will show up for 1996, the club overflowing with offensive firepower and brimming with confidence, or the one that got its butt handed to them in the playoffs? The answer is probably both. The Lions will likely suffer through some rough spots, and then raise up like a phoenix just in time to save HC Wayne Fontes' job. Whatever their record, fantasy football owners will fawn over their talented offensive players. The Lions added a few more over this past season to go with Herman Moore and Barry Sanders. QB Scott Mitchell shook off a poor first season as the Lions' starter to become a passing marvel. WR Johnnie Morton also emerged. Owners should try to draft as many Lions as possible, and even might want to take a chance on their unpredictable defense.

Quarterback—

The fabled Black and Blue division is starting to lose that label. Four of the top ten QBs came out of the NFC Central, and Scott Mitchell was one of them. Mitchell's 32 TDs were third in the league right behind Favre and Marino, and with the Lions' incredible corps of talented WRs, there's no reason to believe Mitchell can't repeat this performance. The only problem might be the upheaval the Lions experienced on the offensive line. Their best lineman, Lomas Brown, was signed by the Cardinals and starting guard Dave Widell signed with the Colts. The Lions signed Seahawk Ray Roberts to take Brown's spot, but he isn't nearly as talented. They also drafted Penn State guard Jeff Hartings, and they expect him to start. Even with last year's line, the immobile Mitchell was sacked 31 times. Journeyman veteran Don Majkowski is the backup.

Running Back—

Sanders continues to amaze, and there's no reason to believe he's still not the best RB in the game. While Emmitt Smith gained more yards and scored more TDs, Smith has (or at least had) a much better offensive line. Sanders gained an even 1500 yards on 314 carries (a 4.8 average, highest in the NFC among those with over 100 carries). He also scored 11 TDs. He was also the Lions' third leading receiver (48 receptions, 283 yards, 1 TD). He also has gained at least 1,000 yards in the last seven seasons, which ties him for the all-time record with Eric Dickerson. The Lions also picked up former Bronco Glyn Milburn who's in the Sanders mode—short stature and great quickness.

Wide Receiver—

The Lions have possibly the best trio of WRs in the league. In a year highlighting the WR, Moore might have been the league's best. He set the NFL single season record with 123 catches for 1,686 yards and 14 TDs. By definition it doesn't seem possible that Moore could repeat that performance. He'll also get plenty of competition for the football. Brett Perriman had 108 catches for 1,488 yards and 9 TDs. Perriman was tremendous in the clutch and incredibly tough going over the middle. If Moore becomes complacent after his big year, Perriman could over take him for the team lead. Morton was probably the most productive third WR in the game with 44 catches for 590 yards and 8 TDs.

Morton is already complaining that he doesn't see the ball enough. If any of these players get hurt the speedy Aubrey Matthews is waiting in the wings.

With the Lions three WR set, it doesn't leave much room for a TE. However, rookie David Sloan played well after starter Ron Hall broke his leg, and he might have too much potential to ignore. He's a bruising runner after the catch and is talented in catching the ball. But, drafting a TE in the Lions WR-laden offense is risky. Hall is still on the team but was unsigned late in the off season, and the Lions signed Pete Metzelaars, so those two will likely battle for the backup position.

Defense/Special Teams—

The Lions suffered some significant player losses in a defense that ranked 23rd in the league and completely collapsed in the playoff loss to the Eagles. MLB, and some say the soul of the team, Chris Spielman signed a $8 million deal with the Bills, where he'll be more comfortable as a true MLB. Meanwhile the Lions signed productive middle man Michael Brooks as his replacement. First round rookie Reggie Brown gives the Lions some needed speed at LB. He's a player who can stay with tight ends and backs out of the backfield, something the Lions had trouble with last year. The Lions' 22 INTs was among the best in the league. They seemed satisfied at CB with Corey Raymond and Ryan McNeil. However, there will be some shifting at safety, where Willie Clay has accepted a free agent offer from the Patriots, and Bennie Blades' situation is unclear.

Should Blades leave, third round rookie Ryan Stewart may be asked to start. He's a great hitter, but only had three interceptions in his college career. The Lions ranked fourth in the conference in sacks with 42. Tracy Scroggins and Antonio London brought good heat from the outside, (9.5 and 7 sacks respectively). They were a good complement to Henry Thomas who was tremendous in his first season since coming over from the Vikings (10.5 sacks). The Lions spent a bundle to keep defensive tackle Robert Porcher. By trading for Glyn Milburn, the Lions solved their kick and punt return problems. Last year, it was a fumble-marred mess. Behind Milburn, the Broncos were the best punt returning team in the AFC last year. Milburn was ranked second in kick returns as well.

Kicker—

Jason Hanson's booming leg was a great asset to the Lions last year. Nothing like having an accurate kicker perform in at least nine games indoors. ★

By Kevin Lynch
Pro Sports Xchange

Green Bay Packers

Projected Starters:

QB Brett Favre
RB Edgar Bennett
RB Dorsey Levens
WR Robert Brooks
WR Anthony Morgan
TE Mark Chmura
K Chris Jacke

How confident are the Packers heading into the 1996 season? General manager Ron Wolf was asked what the Packers needed as they headed into last April's draft. "The biggest gaps on our football team?" Wolf asked, "I don't think we have any gaps on our team." Certainly there are many aspects of the Packers that would dazzle the fantasy football owner. Quarterback Brett Favre, TE Mark Chmura, WR Robert Brooks are all players who will be highly sought after. At the beginning of last season, it certainly didn't look like the Packers would land in the NFC Championship for the first time since winning their last Super Bowl. Last year at this time they were disappointed with the free agent losses of pass rusher Bryce Paup and TE Jackie Harris. Wide receiver Sterling Sharpe was bringing a $9.6 million suit against them, and free agent tight end Keith Jackson refused to report to the team. Now the Packers are one of the best teams in the NFL, not only in the standings, but in fantasy football as well.

Quarterback—

Assuming he recovers from his off-season dependency on painkillers, Brett Favre will be at the top of everyone's fantasy football draft charts, and for good reason. He's a young, strong-armed QB, playing for a well-coached, pass-oriented offense. What more could a fantasy owner want? They may want Favre to improve last year's MVP-winning performance. It is possible for Favre to improve upon his 38 touchdown performance? Certainly. He's only 26, and even though this is the fourth year as the Packers starter, there's still more he can learn. He also underwent arthroscopic ankle surgery in the off-season which hampered him for half the season last year. The only thing that could doom the Packers is if Favre gets injured. In the last two seasons, the Packers have lost two talented backups in Mark Brunell and Ty Detmer. The main backup will be Jim McMahon, the player most people thought retired a few years ago. The third QB will be determined in training camp, with the main combatants being Kyle Warholtz and Doug Pederson.

Running Back—

Edgar Bennett successfully switched from FB to HB a few seasons ago, but yards were tough to come by in Green Bay. True, he did gain 1,070 yards, but he needed 316 carries to do it (a 3.4 yard average). Despite the tough sledding, HC Mike Holmgren refuses to abandon the run, seeing it as essential to winning. Bennett is a fine runner, but often has nowhere to run. The Packers' aging offensive line has trouble run-blocking. That's part of the reason they took three offensive linemen in their first six picks during this year's draft. However, none of those players is likely to crack the starting lineup this year. When considering Bennett, also remember that he catches an amazing number of passes—61 last year (648 yards, 4 TDs)—bringing his TD total to seven. Look for Dorsey Levens to get more carries.

Wide Receiver—

Robert Brooks was the biggest surprise for the Packers last year. With everyone concerned how the Packers were going to make up for the loss of Sterling Sharpe, Brooks stepped up with 102 receptions for 1,497 yards and a whopping 13 TDs. They were Sharpe-like numbers and Favre felt more comfortable with Brooks because he didn't feel a pressure to get him the ball like he did with Sterling. The Packers would like to get a little more production out of second receiver Anthony Morgan, whom they re-signed in the offseason. He used to be the Packers' leading receiver despite being a part-time starter. The Packers also have a promising receiver in Antonio Freeman, who should see more time, particularly if the team doesn't re-sign Mark Ingram which is a distinct possibility.

The Pack drafted Notre Dame receiver Derrick Mayes with their second round choice, and he could play a key role depending on his training camp performance. Mark Chmura seemed to take the signing of Keith Jackson as a personal affront. He went out and caught 54 balls (679 yards, 7 TDs). For his efforts he was awarded a three-year $4.8 million contract. Undoubtedly, he will continue to be one of Favre's best targets, as well as best friends, and the perfect player to fill that tight end slot.

Defense/Special Teams—

Their DT is solid although unspectacular. Remarkably, the Packers were dead last in the league in turnovers (13 INTs, 3 fumbles recovered). The Packers did nothing to address their lack of turnovers—they didn't sign a monster pass rusher, or ball hawking DB. In fact in the draft, they chose mostly offensive players. Defensive end Reggie White returns for his 12th season. Despite being hampered by a hamstring injury, White finished just one shy of the NFC lead in sacks with 12. The menacing Sean Jones started slow but finished strong on the other side. The Packers certainly need more INTs, meaning they need more players like FS LeRoy Butler, whose five picks came at the most opportune times. Last year's rookie CB Craig Newsome allowed 10 TDs, but was downright brilliant in the playoff win against the 49ers. The Packers are in the market for a kick and punt returner. Charles Jordan left the team through free agency. It's possible that fourth round rookie RB Chris Darkins will get a shot at the job. He might also get some opportunities from scrimmage. Antonio Freeman subbed for Jordan last year, and is the lead candidate to replace him.

Kicker—

Chris Jacke did a serviceable job in converting 17 of 23 kicks, including three of four from 50+ or more yards. But he did miss a crucial kick against the Buccaneers which lead to defeat. Still, he will get a lot of chances, so you could do a lot worse than this cold-weather blaster. ★

By Dave Douglas
NFL *Films*

Houston Oilers

Projected Starters:

QB *Chris Chandler*
RB *Rodney Thomas*
RB *Eddie George*
WR *Chris Sanders*
WR *Willie Davis*
TE *Frank Wycheck*
K *Al Del Greco*

You have to give a lot of credit to General Manager Floyd Reese and Head Coach Jeff Fisher. How did the talent-stripped Oilers turn around a dismal 2 and 14 mark and manage to finish at a respectable 7 and 9 last season? They stayed focused and they never quit and despite Nashville rumors and a half-empty Astrodome, they fought to the finish in 1995. Fisher was tough but fair. Newcomers contributed. Their defense was one of the NFL's best kept secrets last season. Heisman Trophy winner Eddie George is in town and so is a renewed sense of commitment.

Quarterback—

Chris Chandler is the starter. Steve McNair will be brought along slowly. Chandler (225 of 356, 2,460 yards, 17 TDs) rebounded quite nicely from injury and played steadily. He is not a top fantasy signal caller but he is a reliable backup. The Oilers will trail often in a wide-open division so he'll have to throw. Steve McNair (41 of 80, 569 yards, 3 TDs) is as green as they come and like all second year QBs he has much to learn. His college experience at Alcorn State and his few NFL starts last season leave him ill-prepared to take over an NFL offense, but if he is nurtured and the Oilers are patient he could really be something special in the years to come. It is not entirely impossible that he'll start this season but he is too inexperienced to hang your hat on.

Running Back—

Gary Brown was cut! Lorenzo White is long gone! Veteran Marion Butts (185 yards and 4 TDs) was acquired last season and he may or may not make the team! Last season, rookie Rodney Thomas really turned some heads by rushing for nearly 1,000 yards and scoring 5 touchdowns. Thomas and first round pick Eddie George will give them some real backfield depth. George will more than likely be their prime weapon by mid-season and he's a perfect fit for Houston's one back attack. He has that rare blend of speed and power and is a fine pass catcher out of the backfield. I hate to draft rookies in my league but Marshall Faulk and Rashaan Salaam proved that you could be smart by picking a talented star like Eddie George. Houston also gave themselves some experience in the backfield with the free agent signing of Ronnie Harmon.

Wide Receiver—

The best is second-year stud Chris Sanders. When you think of Ohio State receivers the names Joey Galloway and Terry Glenn come to mind. Chris Sanders is worthy of consideration too. Last season, as a rookie, he came on big time by catching 35 passes for 823 yards. Yes, that's 23.5 yards per catch. He scored 9 times and he loves to go long. Is he this year's Isaac Bruce? Well, don't go overboard but if he's there late, give him a shot. Haywood Jeffires' best years are behind him and he was let go, but could be back. His 61 catches for 684 yards and 8 TDs are great late-round numbers. Former Chief Willie Davis was signed and should see some action.

Defense/Special Teams—

Believe it or not, the Oiler defense was the NFL's fifth best. HC Jeff Fisher knows defense. He knows how to heat up the pocket, stuff the run, and cover. Last season he did all three with a pretty anonymous group. No one had 5 sacks but everybody chipped in. Safety Blaine Bishop and interception leader Darryll Lewis made the Pro Bowl and they set the tone for a secondary that loves to blitz and hit. Chris Dishman is one of the best defenders in the game when he really wants to play. This is a unit that will force turnovers this season, and leading the charge will be veteran Ray Childress and hit-man Michael Barrow. A key loss to free agency was LB Eddie Robinson (Jaguars).

Mel Gray returned both punts and kicks and he's still the best...end of discussion.

Kicker—

Al Del Greco didn't let those Nike ads go to his head last season. He was 27 of 31 on field goals and drilled 3 out of 5 from 50 yards or more. You'd like a bit more than 114 points out of your kicker but *"Little Al"* will do you just fine. ★

Indianapolis Colts

By Dave Douglas
NFL Films

Projected Starters:

QB *Jim Harbaugh*
RB *Marshall Faulk*
RB *Zack Crockett*
WR *Sean Dawkins*
WR *Marvin Harrison*
WR *Floyd Turner*
TE *Ken Dilger*
K *Cary Blanchard*

For the first time in twenty years, the Colts made it all the way to the AFC championship game and within one final play of Super Bowl 30. What did they do to celebrate? They got rid of their head coach. Go figure. Twelve of their 16 regular season games were decided by 7 points or less as the Colts walked the high wire to a terrific season. Hats off to General Manager Bill Tobin and comeback kid Jim Harbaugh.

Quarterback—

Jim Harbaugh was a real miracle worker and new head coach Lindy Infante hopes he still has some more tricks up his sleeve. Harbaugh (200 of 314, 2,575 yards, 17 TDS) threw only five interceptions all season long and seemed to come up with the big play right when the Colts needed one. He's a great competitor but he is an average at best fantasy QB. He rushed for a couple of scores as well but he still doesn't crack the top ten list of NFL signal callers. Is he a solid backup? You bet. Craig Erickson (50 of 83, 586 yards, 3 TDS) saw limited action and will only start if Indy fails to resign Harbaugh.

Running Back—

Marshall Faulk was named to the Pro Bowl despite a late season injury. He should be totally healed and if that's the case, he's a very early second-round pick. Fourteen TDS, 1,078 rushing yards, and 475 receiving yards last year are three prime reasons why you want him on your team. Roosevelt Potts (309 yards, but no TDS) is unsigned and will go undrafted. Big Zack Crockett came on strong in the playoffs but will do little more than spell Faulk from time to time. In this town there may be lots of sheriffs but there's only one Marshall.

Wide Receiver—

The Colts made Marvin Harrison (Syracuse) the 19th pick overall in this year's draft. He is the future, not the present, on your fantasy team. If Flipper Anderson can bounce back from injury he could be a factor. Sean Dawkins really turned it on toward the end of last season and I believe he could be ready for his finest year. He caught 52 balls for 784 yards and scored three touchdowns but those numbers should improve. Floyd Turner (35 catches, 431 yards, 4 TDS) will compete with Flipper and Marvin for the starting job. Dawkins is the choice here in the late rounds. Ken Dilger figures to be starting at tight end.

Defense/Special Teams—

It starts with Tony Bennett and Quentin Coryatt…a hard-hitting, play making unit that was the real reason why the Colts astonished so many so-called experts last season.

Tony Bennett was brought in to sack the quarterback, and he did so a team leading 10 and a half times. Quentin Coryatt was the hit man and now that he's signed a new bazillion dollar deal he should be a very happy hitter. Eugene Daniel and Ray Buchanan are the big play men in the secondary.

The loss of DB Ashley Ambrose to free agency is eased somewhat by the drafting of Dedric Mathis (Houston). Unsung hero Tony "The Goose" Siragusa mans the center of the line, a line that must heat up their pass rush if the Colts are to repeat their heroics of last season. Ray Buchanan returned punts while Aaron Bailey returned kicks including one for a score.

Kicker—

Cary Blanchard was acquired to replace Mike Cofer and was solid but not spectacular. Faulk led the team in scoring as Blanchard totalled a mere 82 points. He was 19 of only 24 attempts so he's not a top flight fantasy kicker. ★

By Kevin Lynch
Pro Sports Xchange

Jacksonville Jaguars

Projected Starters:

QB Mark Brunell
RB Natrone Means
RB James Stewart
WR Willie Jackson
WR Keenan McCardell
TE Pete Mitchell
K Mike Hollis

If it wasn't for the Carolina Panthers, people might have been marveling over the Jaguars' first-year record of 4-12 which included an October 8 win over the eventual AFC Champion Steelers. And despite having the most hard-nosed coach in the league, the Jaguars are almost surely going to improve upon last year's record. Jacksonville may have been the most aggressive team in offseason free agency. They had a goal of signing 10 free agents and two or three premier guys. However, they were thwarted at nearly every turn. They were on the verge of signing Rams CB Todd Lyght, Cardinals CB Aeneas Williams, Colts LB Quentin Coryatt, and Bears DE Alonzo Spellman and every team matched, or the player settled for less money from their original team. The Jaguars might not be a great team to pick up fantasy players next season, but they almost certainly will be in the future.

Quarterback—

Mark Brunell was the team's first and, so far, their best trade. They surrendered third- and fifth-round picks to the Packers for the rights to Brunell last season. When Steve Beuerlein didn't take as the starter, Brunell was right there. He brings RB speed and moves to the position but, sometimes, that obscures his value as a pocket passer. He threw 15 TDs and just 7 INTs while completing 58% of his passes. Those are remarkable stats when you consider that Brunell plays a daring style that would get most QBs in turnover trouble. He also had little talent to throw or hand off to, while was running for his life most of the time. Only Seattle's Rick Mirer, who doesn't run nearly as well, was sacked more in the AFC. Brunell, however, should get much better protection. The Jaguars paid former Steeler Leon Searcy $17 million over five years to become one of the tackles. The other is Tony Boselli, who already looked like one of the best as a rookie last year.

Running Back—

Natrone Means should excel in the Jaguars' two back set, which is different from what he played in San Diego. Means seems to be thankful that the Jaguars picked him up on waivers and thus saved his hefty contract. He's already made a commitment by agreeing to be less hefty once the season starts and has been working out regularly in the team's rigorous off-season conditioning program. He was supposedly 15 pounds above his playing weight in April. HC Tom Coughlin wants Means to play under the 245 pounds he played at in San Diego last year when he racked up 730 yards (186 carries, 3.9 average). He missed several games with a pulled hamstring. Means figures to be spelled often by last year's rookie James Stewart, whom the Jaguars like very much. Stewart was the *Jags*' leading rusher (525 yards, 137 carries, 3.8 yard average). The team is probably going to hang on to former Saint Vaughn Dunbar, who is a quick changeup from bangers Means and Stewart.

Wide Receiver—

Keenan McCardell was the Browns' third WR last year, and yet he led the team in receptions, with 56 receptions for 709 yards and four TDs. What sold the Jaguars more than anything was McCardell's seven-catch performance against the *Jags* on Christmas Eve last year. McCardell isn't a burner, but he should help the Jaguars with big plays, as they had only one over 40 yards last year. Jackson was the Jags' leading receiver last year with 53 receptions and 589 yards. But the Jaguars are not wedded to any of their WRs, including former Heisman trophy winner Desmond Howard who checked in with 26 catches for 276 yards and a TD last year.

That's one reason Jacksonville drafted a slew of receivers with their late round picks. If Reggie Barlow (*fourth round*), Greg Spann (*seventh round*), Clarence Jones (*seventh round*), or Chris Doering (*sixth round*) emerge, they could get some significant time. Pete Mitchell looked like the real deal as the rookie tight end. He hauled in 41 passes for 527 yards and two TDs. He'll only get better!

Defense/Special Teams—

It's amazing that the Jaguars were able to win four games with a defense that got only 17 sacks all year, eight less than the Buccaneers, who were second to last. They also had just 72 yards in losses, and Tampa Bay at number 29 had 140 yards. Jacksonville also had just 24 total turnovers—another frightfully low figure. They did spend some draft time and free agent money to improve themselves. In the linebacking corps, they signed Eddie Robinson ($10.4 million, four years) and drafted Kevin Hardy with their first round pick. Those players coupled with middle LB Bryan Schwartz give the Jaguars one of the best young trios in the league. They also signed defensive tackle John Jurkovic, cornerback Robert Massey and safety Dana Hall. In the second round they picked defensive end Tony Brackens who could become an instant starter.

The special teams were undistinguished at best. Desmond Howard was tried at punt returner and did a serviceable job, although there's a concern he won't be back. Jimmy Smith was the kick returner and had an 89-yard TD but there's a question as to whether he'll return to the team.

Kicker—

Mike Hollis did make 20 of his 27 attempts, but his kickoffs were weak, and he was ineffective overall. That's why former Penn State kicker Craig Kayak could challenge him in training camp. ★

By Dave Douglas
NFL Films

Kansas City Chiefs

Projected Starters:

QB Steve Bono
RB Marcus Allen
RB Kimble Anders
WR Lake Dawson
WR Tamarick Vanover
TE Keith Cash
K Bjorn Nittmo

The Kansas City Chiefs earned a trip to the playoffs for an unprecedented sixth straight season. They accomplished it by compiling the best record in the entire league, winning 13 of 16 games. They came up short in the playoffs when the upstart Colts knocked them off at Arrowhead, denying Marty Schottenheimer yet another opportunity to make it to the big dance. From a fantasy standpoint, the Chiefs offer a few players that could help solidify your team if you choose wisely.

Quarterback—

Steve Bono found himself in a tough spot in 1995. He had to replace the legendary Joe Montana and lead a team that some skeptics picked to finish sixth in a five team division. He responded with an excellent season that included three pulsating overtime victories in the clutch. Bono is a calm leader and last year he posted the big numbers you want from your fantasy QB starter. Bono (293 of 520, 3,121 yards, 21 TDs) rushed for five touchdowns in addition to his 21 scoring passes, so he is a bonus baby. Pick him late because he'll be there. Rich Gannon saw practically no playing time last season.

Running Back—

The cupboard is bare here because Marcus Allen is just too old to carry a full load and the rest all share the work. Allen is still the best but 890 yards and only five touchdowns are not enough to make the NFL's 8th all-time leading rusher an early pick. He's a perfect third back when your starters are banged up or in a bye week. He does get the ball in close but how much longer can he do it? Greg Hill (667 yards and 1 TD) and Kimble Anders (398 yards and 2 TDs) are the other two backfield weapons but Hill has yet to break a long one and Anders is used mostly as a receiver. Hill might be ready to assert himself and if he has a sparkling pre-season, he could move up on your list of draftable backs. Marty loves to substitute liberally in the backfield in the course of a game... a curse in the fantasy world.

Wide Receiver—

Running back Kimble Anders was the Chiefs' leading receiver last year so that's an indication of how the wide outs were used, or more appropriately, under-used. Willie Davis (33 catches for 527 yards and 5 TDs.) was lost to the Oilers in free agency. The best two for the upcoming season are Lake Dawson and Tamarick Vanover. Dawson will be the go-to guy for Bono this season and I think he could catch 70 balls.

Last season he hauled in 40, but of those 40, only 5 were for scores. Vanover lit it up on special teams and this season he should replace Davis at receiver. He only caught 6 passes as a rookie so he's still one season away from making your first-team fantasy roster. Tight end Keith Cash had a solid year with 42 catches but he scored only once, leaving a hole for Johnny Mitchell to possibly be signed.

Defense/Special Teams—

The Chief defense has been a hot commodity in leagues around the country for quite a while and the unit will be again in '96. The reason is simply that they take the ball away. Schottenheimer and his defensive staff stress this from the first mini camp through the final game of the year. Turnovers mean points for the Chiefs and for the fantasy owner smart enough to capitalize on their thievery.

Last year, Kansas City rang up 47 sacks. Neil Smith logged 12 to lead the team while Derrick Thomas (8) and Dan Saleaumua (7) helped drill passers as well. A minor loss on the front line was Darren Mickell, but Marty will find a replacement somehow and some way. Dale Carter picked off 4 passes while Brian Washington and James Hasty added 3 apiece. The Chief secondary is physical and opportunistic and one of the finest in the game. Drafting Jerome Woods (Safety/Memphis) will only strengthen them there.

On special teams, the story was rookie Tamarick Vanover. The Florida State flyer returned 2 kicks and 1 punt for long distance scores and he is a threat to do so at anytime.

Kicker—

Lin Elliott totalled a respectable 106 points, hitting on 24 of 30 attempts. There are some kickers you just know will make the clutch kick just about everytime…Elliott is not one of them. He missed three PATs last year and attempted no kicks of 50 yards or more! HC Marty Schottenheimer has the sense to look elsewhere for his kicking needs, and going into camp it appears to be a contest between Roman Anderson, Scott Szeredy, and Bjorn Nittmo. ★

By Larry Weisman
Sports Columnist
USA Today

Miami Dolphins

Projected Starters:

QB Dan Marino
RB Bernie Parmalee
RB Keith Byars
WR Fred Barnett
WR O.J. McDuffie
TE Eric Green
K Pete Stoyanovich

The Miami Dolphins stocked their roster with high-priced free agents last year in a desperate bid for the Super Bowl. It proved to be money badly spent. A 4-0 start turned sour, the club's discipline and work ethic was openly questioned, and ultimately Don Shula either jumped or was pushed into retirement. Thus begins the Jimmy Johnson Era. He won a national college title just down the road at the University of Miami and two Super Bowls with Dallas. Neither his hunger nor his aim diminished during his two years parked in various television studios. Johnson must remake a defense strafed by free agency and try to generate the running game Shula overlooked year after year. At the very least this is going to be awfully interesting.

Quarterback—

Dan Marino isn't coming off one of his better years but that's such a ridiculous standard to measure anyone, even him, against. If he's available in the draft, take him. He threw 24 touchdown passes last year and probably will find a way to do at least that again. But he won't be throwing 600 times as he did in 1994 and he loses Irving Fryar, his favorite receiver. The early games could be rocky as he and the club adjust to Johnson's ways.
The danger here is if he gets hurt. The pass rush found him 22 times last year and the offensive line is getting a makeover.

Backing him likely will be Bernie Kosar, the one quarterback in the league less mobile than Marino. Kosar can finish well in relief but won't get it done as a starter.

Running Back—

Bernie Parmalee had a pretty good season, scoring nine touchdowns and rushing for 878 yards. He'll probably still figure in the ground game, in short yardage and goal-line situations, and that makes him an interesting pick.

Terry Kirby gets fewer carries but catches lots of passes. He scored four times rushing, three times by reception, and he's also a decent choice as a second or third running back. Keith Byars, released and then re-signed, looks more and more like a blocking fullback who will see the ball less. Miami didn't get to running backs until its back-to-back picks in the third round. They selected Karim Abdul-Jabbar of UCLA and FB Stanley Pritchett (South Carolina). Neither looks like he'll unseat the incumbents but Johnson doesn't waste draft picks. He must see something he likes.

Wide Receiver—

With Fryar moving on to Philadelphia, the Dolphins hope Fred Barnett, signed away from the Eagles, can still make the acrobatic catches he patented fielding Randall Cunningham's tosses. He should emerge as the go-to guy. Look for 70 catches and seven to 10 touchdowns. The other starter is O.J. McDuffie. He has Barnett's touch for going up and getting the ball and played well last year, with 62 catches, eight for scores. He can duplicate those numbers. Randal Hill, who did nothing with Arizona and not much more last year with Miami, says he's reborn through reunification with Johnson, for whom he played two years with the Hurricanes. He's the fastest receiver on a team with a coach that loves receiver speed. He won't catch 50 passes but he'll hit some home runs. Think of him as a third receiver. The mystery guest is tight end Eric Green. His prolonged absences from practice last year was quickly noted by Johnson, who won't tolerate the same. If he gets Green to work to his capabilities, the big guy's production will improve. He caught only three TD passes last year and should double that—unless Johnson benches him.

Defense/Special Teams—

Miami lost its three top players to free agency—defensive end Marco Coleman, cornerback Troy Vincent and linebacker Bryan Cox. The Dolphins must try younger players as they implement a new scheme. There are too many "*ifs*" involved here—*if* Steve Emtman can rush the passer, *if* Terrell Buckley can survive as a starting cornerback, *if* rookie defensive tackle Daryl Gardener emerges as an interior force. Don't gamble!

Johnson always has stressed special teams and Miami has a way to go to meet his exacting standards. The Dolphins didn't score on any kick or punt returns and McDuffie averaged only 6.8 yards per punt return. He'll probably be replaced by a specialist.

Kicker—

Pete Stoyanovich had an odd year. He missed three of 10 field goals between 20-29 yards but was 17 of 18 from 30-49. Stoyanovich has a strong leg but every year seems to falter in one particular range. Because the Dolphins move the ball decently, he gets plenty of chances but he's no longer in the upper echelon of kickers. ★

By Kevin Lynch
Pro Sports Xchange

Minnesota Vikings

Projected Starters:
QB Warren Moon
RB Robert Smith
RB Amp Lee
WR Cris Carter
WR Jake Reed
WR Qadry Ismail
TE Andrew Jordan
K Fuad Reveiz

HC Dennis Green is definitely on the hot seat after the Vikings finished 8-8 and out of the playoff running. There have already been rumors that Green has lost a lot of his decision-making power. Part of the problem is that other teams are constantly raiding Green's coaching staff. Last year DB coach Willie Shaw went to the Rams; this year defensive coordinator Tony Dungy was named HC of the Buccaneers. Still, the Vikings are left with plenty of talent, even if they don't know quite how to coach it. They also play in one of the toughest divisions in football. Don't look for them to make any marked improvement in the standings or in their standing with fantasy football owners. They didn't make any free agent moves on offense, and only one on defense. Meanwhile, they lost three defensive starters.

Quarterback—

At 40, Warren Moon will be back as the Vikings starting QB, although the man seems impervious to age. Last year, he once again passed for over 4,000 yards. Moon completed 377 passes in 606 attempts for 4,228 yards, 33 TDs and only 14 interceptions. He did all of it despite having to contend with the very public domestic violence charge that was brought by the state of Texas. (Moon was exonerated in an off-season trial.) While Moon has had 180 starts in his career, the Vikings are hoping he stays healthy. Backups Chad May and Brad Johnson don't have a start between them. Their play this year will be key, seeing as Moon is in the last year of his Vikings contract.

Running Back—

Robert Smith missed half the season last year with a sprained ankle and management appears fed up with his attitude. There's a good chance he won't be on the team when the season begins. Amp Lee played extremely well in Smith's stead. Even though he got only 69 carries, he averaged 5.4 yards per carry. Scottie Graham also picked up the slack getting more carries, but not many yards with a 3.7 yard average. Lee was also used as a third down back and corralled 71 passes for 558 yards. But, the Vikings aren't likely to have him be in on every down. In fact, that's the problem with the Vikings—no one's sure who will become an every down back. The Vikings wouldn't mind seeing second year man James Stewart win the job in training camp. They also drafted highly touted Kentucky rookie Moe Williams in the third round. He's equally adept at running and receiving which is perfect for the Vikings system. Those prone to gambling might want to take Stewart over Smith, Graham, or Lee.

Wide Receiver—

Cris Carter and Warren Moon have proven to be one of the most lethal quarterback-receiver combos in NFL history. No one has caught more passes in the last two seasons than Carter, and no one has thrown for more yards in a professional career than Moon. Carter got a lot more credit for his 122 catches in '94. At the time, it was an NFL record. This year, he equaled that amount, but Lion Herman Moore caught one more pass to snatch the record away. However, Carter did more with his 122 catches than he did the year before, gaining more yards and—more importantly—more than doubling his TD total to 17 for 1995. Even though Carter is entering his tenth season, he'll tell you he's better with age—in the early part of his career he was released by the Eagles.

As a second receiver, no one could do much better than the steady Jake Reed. He caught 72 balls for 1,167 yards and nine TDs—numbers usually reserved for a team's leading receiver. Qadry Ismail is the third WR and designated deep threat. He has great running ability, but often drops passes. Last season, he caught 32 passes for 597 yards and three TDs. Andrew Jordan is the underused TE, catching only 27 balls last year.

Defense/Special Teams—

While yielding a lot of yards, the Viking defense is the kind that should be attractive to fantasy players. They were second in the league in interceptions with 25 and recovered a whopping 40 turnovers overall. It will be up to the new defensive coordinator to keep the Vikings' turnover-minded defense sharp. Rookie safety Orlando Thomas made the biggest splash on defense, grabbing a league-leading nine passes and returning one of them 45 yards for a TD. He's in the same secondary as promising young players Dewayne Washington and Corey Fuller. The Vikings have the potential to be one of the best secondaries in the league, but they'll need to decrease their mistakes and keep their interception tally high. Last year, the Vikings were ranked 28th against the pass.

The acquisition of LB Dixon Edwards and the drafting of pass rusher Duane Clemons should make up for the loss of Broderick Thomas, who ran afoul with the law and was released. Middle LB Jack Del Rio was also released and will be replaced by either Jeff Brady or Ed McDaniel. David Palmer was the best punt returner in the league with a 13.2-yard average and a 74-yard return for a TD. Ismail also ranked highly, but there are some who believe he won't return to the team, much less return kicks.

Kicker—

Fuad Reveiz seemed to lose the long touch last year. He was one of four in kicks over 50 yards and missed three attempts in 12 tries in the 40 to 49 yard range. But he did convert 26 of 36 kicks, and could always revert back to his Pro Bowl form of 1994. ★

By Dave Douglas
NFL Films

New England Patriots

Projected Starters:

QB Drew Bledsoe
RB Curtis Martin
RB Sam Gash
WR Vincent Brisby
WR Will Moore
WR Terry Glenn
TE Ben Coates
K Matt Bahr

The Patriots' seven game winning streak and playoff appearance in 1994 created great expectations for 1995. But in a complete reversal of fortune, they followed up their 10 and 6 season with a 6 and 10 year. Bill Parcells was frustrated. Quarterback Drew Bledsoe played tentatively. The defense couldn't make the plays when they were needed. What does this season hold? I think they'll return to their winning ways led by Bledsoe and AFC rookie-of-the-year Curtis Martin. Parcells is a winner and New England will bounce back in 1996.

Quarterback—

Last year, Drew Bledsoe was one of the top five players taken in many FFL drafts. He won't be this year but he is still a top flight fantasy performer. He was stripped of many weapons last season and his huge contract seemed to make him a little complacent, but this season he has something to prove. Bledsoe still threw for over 3,500 yards but a slow start and an injury netted him only 13 touchdown passes. The numbers (323 of 636, 3,507 yards, 13 TDs) will be up this year. Just look at those attempts. That's what you look for in a fantasy QB and Bledsoe fills the bill. Scott Zolak will once again handle the clipboard duties.

Running Back—

Curtis Martin! Grab him in the second round. Don't hesitate! Pull the trigger and sit back and watch him run up a zillion fantasy points for you! There will be no sophomore jinx and Parcells will unleash him early, often and near the goal line. Martin (1,487 yards rushing and 261 receiving) scored 15 touchdowns last year. He runs over linebackers and carries safeties. He is a horse who gets stronger as the game wears on.

Dave Meggett (250 yards and 2 TDs) is purely a third down specialist and no other backs are worth drafting. Martin is *the man* in New England and he'd look great in your opening day lineup.

Wide Receiver—

New England's leading receiver was tight end Ben Coates. Defenses tried to take him away from Bledsoe with double teams and rotating coverages. They were not very successful as Coates hauled in 84 passes for 915 yards and 6 touchdowns. As tight ends go, he's right there near the top. Vincent Brisby is one of the best of the second tier of fantasy wide outs. He finished with 66 receptions good for a team best 974 yards but only scored three touchdowns. Will Moore made some spectacular catches last season on his way to 43 for 502 yards and a touchdown. He's a great one-game replacement guy during a bye week.

The *Pats* drafted Ohio State WR Terry Glenn with their first pick to provide Bledsoe with a home run threat. He has been compared to ex-Buckeye teammate Joey Galloway, who put up great fantasy numbers for the *Seahawks* last season. Watch these three wideouts in preseason. It will be interesting to see if the *Pats* are looking to reassert Bledsoe and the passing game or rely on Martin. *Stay tuned!*

Defense/Special Teams—

Last season, the Patriot defense couldn't slam the door and force a punt on third down. This concerns Parcells and you know he'll be working to tighten things up on defense. He is one of the most innovative defensive coaches in the business and as the head man, he'll insist on improvement.

Sacks were not the problem. New England nailed passers 37 times which is a respectable total. Willie McGinest led the charge with 11 and linebackers like Vincent Brown and Chris Slade blew in often on blitzes. McGinest is an all pro waiting in the wings and this could be his explosive season. In addition to his 4 sacks, Vincent Brown paced the team with 4 picks and had perhaps the best year of any Patriot defender.

Dave Meggett returned no punts or kicks for touchdowns but nearly always gave the Patriots outstanding field position.

Kicker—

Matt Bahr is two years younger than Bob Dole. He's been kicking since 1979 and you have to wonder how much leg he has left. He was only 23 of 33 on field goals but one of them was good from 55 yards out. It would not be surprising if Bill Parcells brought in an army of kickers to try and replace his veteran in the pre-season. ★

By Kevin Lynch
Pro Sports Xchange

New Orleans Saints

Projected Starters:

QB *Jim Everett*
RB *Mario Bates*
RB *Lorenzo Neal*
WR *Michael Haynes*
WR *Torrance Small*
TE *Irv Smith*
K *Doug Brien*

The Saints have experienced an offensive explosion like no other in their history, and they don't like it. Since QB Jim Everett joined the team in 1994, the Saints have been one of the best passing teams in the league. They've also had identical 7-9 records the last two years and have been left out of the playoffs. Long time HC Jim Mora wants to solve the problem by going back to the philosophy that brought the Saints unprecedented success in the late 1980's and early '90's. Those Saint teams were built on a low-risk offense and a rugged defense. However, Mora wants to tailor his team to the mid '90's which means stopping the opposition's passing game. That's why the Saints have laid out an unspeakable amount of money drafting and signing secondary players. Even though he has turned his attention to defense, Mora still has a high-functioning offense, which could draw some fantasy owner interest.

Quarterback—

Jim Everett was just 30 yards shy of 4,000 yards but still set team records for yardage and TDs (26). Don't expect Everett to return to those levels. He's getting older, but more importantly, he no longer has the weapons. Two of his favorite receivers (TE Wesley Walls and WR Quinn Early) left through free agency, a development Everett has been highly critical of. Still, there's enough talent around to post some pretty good numbers. Hopefully for fantasy players, Mora will back off the passing pedal slowly.

What would really make the Saints slow up is if Everett gets hurt. In his two years with the Saints he has stayed remarkably healthy. The signing of Hugh Millen doesn't bode well for journeyman backup Tommy Hodson. Millen is a creditable QB, but the Saints would certainly be in trouble without Everett. Young Doug Nussmeier hasn't played at all in the last three seasons.

Running Back—

Saints coach Jim Mora doesn't have confidence in starting RB Mario Bates, and he's said as much. In the offseason he challenged Bates to do better. Bates was just 49 yards shy of gaining 1,000 yards last year, he had a 3.9 yard average and seven TDs.

The Saints were so unimpressed with Bates they tried to trade a few their draft picks to the Patriots so they could move up in the draft to grab Tim Biakabutuka. Since that didn't happen, the Saints might try to augment their running game by playing former Notre Dame FB Ray Zellars. He might over take Neal at FB, but that means losing a powerful blocker in Neal. Derek Brown will likely get some spot time at HB.

Wide Receiver—

Quinn Early hit the free agent high road after the Saints didn't meet his contract demands. Securing a four-year $8.8 million contract from the Bills. He was one of only five WRs to catch at least 80 passes in the last two seasons. With Early gone, Michael Haynes is going to have to justify his $2 million salary, something he has failed to do the last two seasons with the Saints. Last year, Haynes caught 41 passes for 597 yards and four TDs. Early nearly doubled his production (81 catches, 1087 yards, 8 TDs). Now, it will be up to Haynes to take up the slack. Torrance Small will now move into the starting line-up. He had a productive go of it in limited minutes (38 catches for 461 yards and 5 TDs). In fact, Small may became the go-to guy. QB Jim Everett was critical of management when they didn't make more an effort to re-sign tight end Wesley Walls, who signed a $4 million three year deal with the rival Panthers. Now, it's up to Irv Smith to try and make up Walls' franchise record 57 catches. Smith was not that far behind with 45 receptions, and he's a better blocker. The loss of Early and Walls might mean that rookie wideout Terry Guess could get some significant time.

Defense/Special Teams—

The Saints lavished some of the money they had earmarked for offense on their secondary. Joining CB Eric Allen in the high-rent category is CB Mark McMillian (3 years, $5.175 million). Soon to join these two is rookie CB Alex Molden, the first DB taken in the draft. He'll start in the nickel package. With their second pick, the Saints went out and got safety Je'Rod Cherry from Cal-Berkeley. Their rationale was the NFC West is a passing conference. Even without most of this rich secondary help the Saints checked in with 29 turnovers, which isn't bad. If they can keep LBs Rufus Porter and Brian Jones healthy they could be a draftable defense. They certainly get after people, they finished with 44 sacks, which tied them for second in the NFC. Defensive tackle Wayne Martin had 13, which tied him for the lead in the conference. Tyrone Hughes might be the most talented returner in the league, and the records prove it. In '95, Hughes broke his own NFL record in kickoff returns (63) and kickoff return yards (1,556 yards). His 24.5 yard average on those returns was third in the conference. He is equally adept at returning punts.

Kicker—

Doug Brien was picked up after Chip Lohmiller was released in the early going. In his second game, Brien booted four field goals, including two over 40 yards. But later he was dogged by the inconsistency that cost him his job with the 49ers. In all, he was 19 of 29, but could be better seeing as he's kicking indoors. ★

By Larry Weisman
Sports Columnist
USA Today

New York Giants

Projected Starters:

QB Dave Brown
RB Rodney Hampton
RB Charles Way
WR Thomas Lewis
WR Chris Calloway
WR Amani Toomer
TE Howard Cross
K Brad Daluiso

What a year! The New York Giants slid backwards, bickered among themselves and with coaches, endured benchings and personnel shifts. When it was over they were 5-11, second-to-last in the league in total offense and facing a change at the top.

But Dan Reeves couldn't get himself fired. Not with two years left on his contract. Management wouldn't budge. This team should be a beauty with so much unhappiness rampant and free agent departures taking a continuing toll. We said last year Dave Brown would improve at quarterback, the defense would generate more pressure and the interceptions would come. We seem to have lied. Brown leveled off and was briefly replaced by Tommy Maddox, whose one fan is Reeves. The defense never rushed the passer with authority and remained stuck at 16 interceptions. This team has a long way to go but appears directionless.

Quarterback—

Few teams threw the ball less effectively than the Giants, no matter which stat you turn to. Let's say this for Brown—he did throw more touchdown passes (11) than interceptions (10). That's just not enough for a fantasy league starter. He's in a run-first offense and that hasn't changed. Tommy Maddox is the nominal backup. His one disastrous appearance last year netted him a passer rating of zero, which is almost unheard of for a quarterback. This starter-backup tandem may be the worst in the league. The Giants drafted Florida State's Danny Kanell but probably won't let him do more than chart plays. He's smart and may pick up Reeves' system but Brown is the future and needs all the playing time he can get.

Running Back—

San Francisco made a big offer to pry Rodney Hampton from the Giants but they retained their all-time leading rusher. Hampton is a very steady performer and a good choice, even though he runs against stacked defenses. He won't break long runs but he's the man at the goal line. He's a 1,000-yard rusher and worth 8-10 touchdowns. Tyrone Wheatley, the Giants' top pick in 1995, impressed no one as a rookie. Not with his performance, and certainly not with his attitude. There were questions about whether he really wanted to play football when he entered the draft and he failed to answer them positively. The Giants may give him some extended looks in the middle of the field where he can be the breakaway runner Hampton isn't. But don't expect him to replace Hampton. Herschel Walker did nothing and probably won't be back. Keith Elias plays mostly on special teams.

Wide Receiver—

The Giants showed no interest in bringing back Mike Sherrard, leaving them with Chris Calloway and Thomas Lewis as potential starters. Calloway is a good player with mid-range skills but no burner. Lewis can get deep but he always seems to be hurt. He was a #1 pick in 1994 and needs to begin showing something other than bandages. Rookie Amani Toomer might be an interesting selection. He's big, strong, will go down the middle, and can get open deep. The Giants need such a target for Brown.

Tight end Howard Cross is an excellent player but saw very little of the ball last year. He scored four times in '94, not at all last year. The Giants, when they want a big receiver in the red zone, lean toward H-back Aaron Pierce, but he too was shut out last year. It doesn't seem like the Giants see their tight ends as go-to guys on money downs.

Defense/Special Teams—

Only three teams managed fewer than the 29 sacks the Giants put up. That's where rookie defensive end Cedric Jones is supposed to fit in. But first-year pass rushers rarely make a big impact, so don't get too excited. The Giants' 31 takeaways put them in the middle of the pack. Nothing here to warrant a party. The Giants were the NFC's worst punt returning team and handled the job by committee last year. That's a bad sign. With the exception of Lewis' 91-yard touchdown return, they didn't fare very well on kickoffs either. The return game has yet to recover from the loss of David Meggett.

Kicker—

Brad Daluiso has a great leg for kickoffs and some problems with accuracy as a field goal kicker. He was 20 for 28 last year but a weird two for nine from 40-49 yards. The way the Giants move the ball in their snail-like style, he simply cannot miss that many when that's as close as he's going to get. This looks like it could be a problem position, both in terms of accuracy and number of opportunities to make scoring kicks. Back off. ★

*By Larry Weisman
Sports Columnist
USA Today*

New York Jets

Projected Starters:

QB Neil O'Donnell
RB Adrian Murrell
RB Brad Baxter
WR Keyshawn Johnson
WR Jeff Graham
TE Kyle Brady
K Nick Lowery

Hey, who are these guys? Meet the new New York Jets. Neil O'Donnell. Keyshawn Johnson. Jeff Graham. Jumbo Elliott. Certainly not yesterday's stumblebums.

The Jets went nuts in the off-season after a 3-13 horror show in 1995 and spent an estimated $70 million to reconfigure the team. A pretty solid defense gets a rebuilt offense with some high-profile players and a new offensive coordinator in Ron Erhardt. If this doesn't help, there's definitely a curse on the franchise. At long last the club seems to be moving in the right direction.

Quarterback—

Here's the problem with Neil O'Donnell—the Jets paid him so much money ($25 million for five years, $7 million to sign) that people expect him to be Elway, Marino and Namath. He's O'Donnell, whose greatest talent in Pittsburgh was not turning the ball over. Can he lead? Can he make big plays? How fast can he get to know his receivers? And what about the pressure of playing before the hometown crowd with such high expectations? The betting here is the early part of the season looks nasty and then things tick upwards. Don't jump on him too early in your draft.

The backup is Frank Reich, who excelled in that role with Buffalo and bombed as a starter with Carolina. He needs to resurrect his game but O'Donnell figures to get every snap unless he's badly damaged. Promising Glenn Foley seriously injured his throwing shoulder last season and is a question mark.

Running Back—

The Jets seem convinced Adrian Murrell can be their every-down player. We're not. The whole running game needs to be rethought. The Jets scored two rushing touchdowns last season, so even massive improvement won't be enough. Murrell caught 71 passes to lead the team.

A curious play might be fullback Brad Baxter. He has been effective around the goal line but an afterthought in the offense the last two years. Erhardt likes power and Baxter is a smash-mouth player. There's not much depth here. Murrell's a gamble but his offensive line will be better.

Wide Receiver—

A distinct weakness last year that is really on the upswing. Jeff Graham had an outstanding year with Chicago, but only four of his 82 grabs went for touchdowns. He's the established pro and you can expect O'Donnell to look for him.

Keyshawn Johnson, the first player picked in the draft, is a big, strong receiver and he'll start from day one. Expect 50 catches and a couple of touchdowns but he'll struggle at times against the bump at the line of scrimmage. Wayne Chrebet could be the odd man out or the third receiver. As a rookie free agent he caught 66 passes, four for TDS. But he's smallish and not a burner. The Jets drafted Alex Van Dyke with their second pick so he should see some time at the third wide receiver slot. Ryan Yarborough might not fit in.

The Jets waived Johnny Mitchell, leaving the tight end position to Kyle Brady. They coached him almost not at all last season but this year have an excellent position coach in Pat Hodgson. Erhardt has always liked to go to the tight end, so Brady bears watching.

Defense/Special Teams—

The Jets ranked sixth in defense, first against the pass. That's not bad considering how sorry the offense was. Hugh Douglas emerged as a standout pass rusher and middle linebacker Marvin Jones can be a star if he ever stays healthy. Mo Lewis will bounce back after a disastrous experiment moving inside.

The Jets had 43 sacks and 34 takeaways, not bad numbers for a team that played from behind a lot. If the offense holds up its end, this group can be for real.

Rob Carpenter did a decent job running back kickoffs but the Jets got no touchdowns that way. They need to find a punt returner. Maybe they can go back to speedy cornerback Aaron Glenn. They tried him as a rookie and he dropped nearly everything.

Kicker—

Nick Lowery lacks the booming leg and won't make many long-distance field goals. He's accurate from the shorter ranges. The problem is opportunities. The Jets didn't score a lot last year and certainly didn't need late field goals when they trailed by big margins. He'll get more shots this year but not enough to be a week-in, week-out fantasy standout. ★

By Kevin Lynch
Pro Sports Xchange

Oakland Raiders

Projected Starters:

QB Jeff Hostetler
RB Harvey Williams
RB Napoleon Kaufman
WR Tim Brown
WR Rocket Ismail
TE Rickey Dudley
K Jeff Jaeger

An enigma, that's what the Raiders have become. They changed head coaches, returned to their ancestral home, and tinkered with varying offensive philosophies—all in an effort to wake their slumbering and immense talent. The only thing the Raiders haven't changed is owners. Last year was a classic example. The Raiders flew through the first 10 weeks of the season, compiling an 8-2 record, before they went into an utter nose dive. They lost their last six to finish 8-8 and out of the playoffs. It's frustrating to Raiders fans, but shouldn't be of much alarm to fantasy owners. The Raiders are stocked with talented players who could carry the day. They might do better now that the organization has moved completely back to Oakland. No team has done well practicing in one city and then playing their games hundreds of miles away. Players are also trying to get acclimated to HC Mike White. If the Raiders become a playoff team, they would break the seal on their talent all that much more.

Quarterback—

When Hostetler was dumped on his shoulder against the Cowboys, that precipitated the Raiders' six-game slide. He never returned, and the Raiders couldn't find an adequate signal caller between 40-year-old Vince Evans and young Billy Joe Hobert. The Raiders re-signed the 35-year-old Hostetler who completed 172 passes in 286 attempts for 1,998 yards, 12 TDs, and nine INTs.

There's no question Hostetler can get the job done, but can the Raiders keep him healthy? Their best tackle, Gerald Perry, was unsigned in late spring and he plays the crucial left tackle position. Hostetler will also have to get used to throwing the ball deep again, something coach Mike White said they are committed to after flirting with a short passing game last year.

Running Back—

Even in the bad times, there seemed to be nothing wrong with the Raiders' running game. While the oft-injured offensive line had trouble pass protecting, their run blocking never wavered, which was of great benefit to RB Harvey Williams, the Raiders' leading rusher. He had the best rushing year of his career (1,114 yards, 255 carries, a 4.4 yard average, 9 TDs). If he stays healthy, those numbers are certainly obtainable again this year. Williams was also the Raiders second leading receiver with 54 catches for 375 yards and no TDs. It looks like Harvey will be around for quite a while after signing a six-year $11 million deal. The Raiders have found the perfect complement to Williams in speedster Napoleon Kaufman, who lugged the ball 108 times for 490 yards and broke several long runs. He also catches the ball. Fenner is uncomfortable with his job as the blocking FB and may want more carries from scrimmage. Last year he carried the ball 39 time for only 110 yards, but many of those situations where short yardage downs.

Wide Receiver—

The quest for the Raiders last year was to find someone who could relieve the pressure from Tim Brown, a perennial fantasy football favorite. By year's end, Brown was the only reliable WR, and since the Raiders did little to improve their WR corps, expect that to happen again. Despite dropping a number of passes, Brown was the AFC's third leading receiver with 89 catches, 1,342 yards and 10 TDs. The Raiders tried to groom Rocket Ismail to be the long-ball threat. He had a career game against the Colts and then faded into obscurity. For the year, Ismail caught 28 passes for 491 yards, a 17.5 yard average per catch, and three TDs. In fact, possession receiver Daryl Hobbs surpassed Ismail as the third WR with 38 catches, 612 yards and three TDs. With the Raiders saying they want to re-establish the long game don't expect Hobbs to start, even though he probably should. The Raiders hoped they helped themselves immensely, with the drafting tight end Rickey Dudley out of Ohio State. HC Mike White said the offense was not aggressive enough in attacking the middle of the opposition's defense. Dudley has the speed (4.49 in the 40-yard dash) to split the seam, but he still has a lot to learn.

Defense/Special Teams—

The Raiders were playing solid team defense until they suddenly got tired right before the six-game losing streak. The middle of their defense was exploited for rushing yards towards the end of the year. They finished 11th in overall defense—17th against the run and 10th against the pass. They led the AFC by recovering 22 fumbles but had only 11 INTs. They helped themselves in this area by signing CB Larry Brown, who was the Super Bowl MVP last year with the Cowboys. That probably means the end to Albert Lewis' days as a starter. They also signed two safeties, former Cardinal Lorenzo Lynch, and former Jaguar/Charger Darren Carrington. Those moves plus the addition of Cowboys defensive tackle Russell Maryland should improve their overall defense. Tim Brown was unspectacular as the punt returner with a 10.1 yard average and a long of 38 yards. Napoleon Kaufman split duties as kick returner with Rocket Ismail. Kaufman's 26-yard average was much better than Ismail's 19.6. He also had an 84-yard TD return last year.

Kicker—

Veteran Jeff Jaeger sprained his knee late in the preseason and had an off year. He's a better kicker than his 13 for 18 showed last year, and he'll probably prove it. ★

By Dave Douglas
NFL Films

Philadelphia Eagles

Projected Starters:

QB Ty Detmer
RB Ricky Watters
RB Kevin Turner
WR Irving Fryar
WR Calvin Williams
TE Jason Dunn
K Gary Anderson

In sports today, it seems that eccentricity has taken the place of performance, celebrity the place of character. In Philly, that was certainly not the case. One look at Ray Rhodes tells you why. The NFL coach of the year in his rookie season with the Eagles, Rhodes demanded and got the very best his players had to give. He forced the likes of Ricky Watters, Rodney Peete, his unsung heroes on defense and 30 new players to fight to the finish. In the draft, the first four players he selected all have something to prove. He likes lunch pail guys. Unselfish guys. Team first guys. Guys that know what it takes to win championships. This season, Rhodes will drive them on once again.

Quarterback—

Randall Cunningham was benched last season and his days of starting for the Eagles are over. The best they have is Rodney Peete. He doesn't throw deep. He doesn't break the 300 yard mark very often. But he doesn't throw costly interceptions that lose games. That's good enough for Ray Rhodes for the present but it's not quite good enough in the fantasy world. Peete (215 of 375, 2,326 yards, only 8 TDs) simply doesn't throw enough and he rarely connects deep.

Is he a good back up? Yes. Ty Detmer could very easily win the job in the preseason and might be just the West Coast offensive QB they need. Bobby Hoying (Ohio State) was drafted as their QB of the future but he will wait and watch this season.

Running Back—

Ricky Watters...boy did he surprise a lot of experts and FFL owners last season. They said he wasn't tough enough to run hard between the tackles and that the Eagle offensive line couldn't open enough holes for him. They said he was too egocentric to mesh with Rhodes' approach to the game. Instead he was a perfect fit and perhaps the single best free agent acquisition next to Bryce Paup in the league last year. Watters (1,273 yards rushing, 434 receiving) scored 11 touchdowns and this season he'll be in high demand in your league. Unlike last year, he won't be there in the third round of your draft. Charlie Garner is one of the most electrifying backs in the game, but he only carried the ball 108 times last year. He's too small and Watters too strong to be the main man. Garner scored 6 touchdowns though, so if Watters goes down, he'll be a guy to pick up.

Wide Receiver—

Calvin Williams hauled in 63 passes for 768 yards but he scored only twice. He's a late round pick at best. Freddie Barnett is off to hook up with Dan Marino down in Miami so the second receiver spot is up for grabs. Irving Fryar (62 catches, 910 yards, 8 TDS) was acquired from the Dolphins and will more than likely replace Barnett.

Rob Carpenter and Chris T. Jones will vie for the third receiver spot but will not be on any fantasy rosters to start the season. The Eagles' starting tight end should be draft pick Jason Dunn from Eastern Kentucky.

Defense/Special Teams—

The *Birds* won 9 of their final 12 regular season games and the big reason was their "bend but don't break" defense. If you can stuff Emmitt Smith twice on third and fourth downs...that's saying something and not just about Barry Switzer. You have to start with 48 sacks and their two biggest sackers, William Fuller (13) and Andy Harmon (11). Mike Mamula will come on at defensive end and Rhodes will certainly field a consistent pass rush. Linebackers Kurt Gouveia and Bill Romanowski were lost to free agency but they still have William Thomas, whose 7 interceptions from the linebacker position were remarkable indeed. The biggest addition to the defense was the signing of cornerback Troy Vincent. Vincent grew up near Philly and could have a super homecoming season. The Eagle defense is in the NFL's top ten.

Kicker—

Gary Anderson was brought in from Pittsburgh and he was steady and solid. 98 points aren't quite what you'd like to see but he has the big leg and Rhodes will not hesitate to use him.

He was 22 of 30 on field goal attempts but, uncharacteristically, he misfired on all three of his kicks longer than 50 yards. ★

By Dave Douglas
NFL Films

Pittsburgh Steelers

Projected Starters:
QB *Jim Miller*
RB *Jerome Bettis*
FB *Tim Lester*
WR *Yancey Thigpen*
WR *Ernie Mills*
TE *Mark Bruener*
K *Norm Johnson*

Halfway through the 1995 season no one thought that the Pittsburgh Steelers were on their way to Super Bowl 30. They were three and four, out of sync and struggling. But head coach Bill Cowher refused to let his team quit and the result was eight straight victories and their third AFC Central Division title in four years. On offense, Neil O'Donnell, Kordell Stewart, Bam Morris and Yancey Thigpen rose to the occasion while hitmen Greg Lloyd, Kevin Greene and Carnell Lake smashed the enemy on defense. But the off-season was filled with storm clouds as Neil O'Donnell took off for the bright lights and big money of the Big Apple, Leon Searcy signed with Jacksonville and Bam Morris was arrested on a drug charge. How will the Steelers respond? That's what Bill Cowher is wondering!

Quarterback—

The loss of Neil O'Donnell is huge. He proved himself a gritty, clutch leader last season and his nearly 3000 passing yards and 17 touchdown passes will be sorely missed this season. What the Steelers are left with is journeyman Mike Tomczak, former world-leaguer Jim Miller and the raw, jack of all trades Kordell "*Slash*" Stewart. Tomczak and Miller have met with new offensive coordinator Chan Gailey regularly in the off season while Slash reportedly has not shown the same dedication.

In the preseason, it is believed that either Miller or Tomczak will step up and earn the job. If the two are even when it all settles out, then Miller will likely get the nod. Stewart is the offensive spark that ignited the Steelers last season so somehow or another, Cowher and Gailey will get his talented hands on the ball. Obviously, from a fantasy standpoint, the quarterback situation has to be monitored carefully in training camp.

Running Back—

The good news is that the signing of veteran lineman Will Wolford will make up for the loss of Leon Searcy. The bad news is that Bam Morris's future is in doubt because of his run-in with the Texas police. Pittsburgh acted on draft day to solidify their backfield by trading for Jerome Bettis (637 yards and 3 TDs). Bettis may flourish behind Pittsburgh's outstanding offensive line and I think he could have a rebound season. Erric Pegram led the team in rushing with 813 yards but his five touchdowns are far short of what you want from a fantasy back and he seemed to be worn down a bit by the end of the season. Fullback Jon Wittman (Penn State) was drafted to be a tough lead blocker and Jamain Stephens (N.C. A&T) is a monster of a lineman. Bam is the wildcard but the likely starting backfield will be Bettis and blocking back Tim Lester.

Wide Receiver—

As the season progressed, the Steelers found that they were most effective when operating in the four receiver set. Defenses couldn't double anybody and gang up on the run and it allowed the Steelers, especially with Slash in there, to mix things up and make big plays. The biggest of the playmakers was Yancey Thigpen (85 catches, 1,307 yards, 5 touchdowns) who turned in a sensational year. He is the best of the second level of NFL receivers. He's not your ace but he's a super second guy.

Andre Hastings (48 catches, 502 yards, 1 TD), Ernie Mills (39 catches, 679 yards, 8 TDS) and Charles Johnson (38 catches, 432 yards, 0 TDS but hurt last year) are basically interchangeable parts and it's a crapshoot as to who's going to have the best fantasy season. I think Thigpen is a certain middle-round fantasy pick and that Mills is the best of the rest. If Pittsburgh pounds the ball on the ground without O'Donnell around, all bets are off.

Defense/Special Teams—

Today's Steel Curtain is as good as it gets and with Rod Woodson healed, they'll be better than ever. They stuff the run like no other and they can cover. They don't give up many big plays and they get to the quarterback. Last season, Pittsburgh blitzed their way to 42 sacks as Kevin Greene (9), Ray Seals (8.5) and Greg Lloyd (6.5) spearheaded the defensive onslaught.

Green is gone, but Lloyd is simply the best all around linebacker in the game and his intensity is infectious.

In Woodson, Carnell Lake, Darren Perry, and Willie Williams, the Steelers boast one of the AFC's top secondaries. The entire defense senses blood and the feeding frenzy begins. Especially when it's cold... at Three Rivers...in the playoffs.

Ernie Mills did an outstanding job of returning kickoffs while Andre Hastings returned punts, including one for a touchdown.

Kicker—

Norm Johnson was an awesome fantasy kicker last season. He banged out an amazing 141 points. He was a perfect 39 for 39 on PATS and was 34 of 41 in the field goal department. He'll be one of the top three fantasy kickers taken in this year's draft. ★

By John Weiss
NFL Films

St. Louis Rams

Projected Starters:

QB Steve Walsh
RB Lawrence Phillips
RB Jerald Moore
WR Isaac Bruce
WR Todd Kinchen
WR Eddie Kennison
TE Troy Drayton
K Chip Lohmiller

Remember when the Rams started last season 4-0 and everyone talked about the wonders a change of scenery can do a team? They then dropped nine of their last 12 games and finished 7-9. I guess the novelty of moving to St. Louis wore off real quick.

Actually the Rams just lost their grip—literally. After not committing a single turnover in their first four games, the team finished with 39, the fourth worst total in the league. Despite the freefall, it was the Rams' best season since 1989, and they accomplished it with the NFL's youngest team. To improve this year, they'll have to adapt to an uncertain quarterback situation and a brand new running game. Second-year head coach Rich Brooks has his work cut out for him in a division that doesn't include any pushovers.

Quarterback—

After sustaining yet another concussion that sidelined him the final three games of last year, Chris Miller is sitting out this season to avoid further injury. So who does that leave at quarterback? Well, veteran Mark Rypien stepped in the final three weeks last season and recorded a personal-best three consecutive 300-yard passing games. He finished 129-of-217 (59.4%), with nine touchdowns and eight interceptions. If he's given a shot, who knows, maybe he can rekindle the magic that made him a Super Bowl MVP with the Redskins in '91.

The Rams also signed Steve Walsh away from the Bears, though he didn't throw a pass as a backup last season. As a starter most of the 1994 season in Chicago, Walsh passed for 2,078 yards and 10 touchdowns. With Walsh and Rypien battling for the job, neither should go very high on your quarterback wish list. St. Louis added depth by making Michigan State's Tony Banks the top quarterback picked in the '96 draft.

Running Back—

The Rams weren't scared away by the questions about his character and the concern over his past assault charges, and so they decided to take a chance on Nebraska's Lawrence Phillips, the best running back in the '96 draft. The Rams are counting on Phillips to rejuvenate a rushing attack that ranked 25th in the league last season. With Jerome Bettis traded to Pittsburgh, and the quarterbacking shaky, Phillips will be counted on heavily in the offense, and could pile up the yards and the points. If he can control his temper off the field, he can become a star on it. He should be among the top 12 or 15 runners on your draft list, and, depending on the size of your league, could make a nice #1 back. Greg Robinson joined the Rams in the middle of last season and rushed for 165 yards (4.1) average and no scores.

Wide Receiver—

No receiver ever had a bigger breakout year than Isaac Bruce did in 1995. In his second season, Bruce took the NFL by storm as he finished with 119 catches, 1,781 yards and 13 TDs. The yardage total was the 2nd highest in NFL history, bettered only by Jerry Rice's total last season, and the reception total was 5th best in history. He posted nine 100-yard receiving games and was the first player in history to record three straight at 170+ yards.

The only concern is the QB situation. Most of Bruce's numbers were put up with Chris Miller behind center. He now has to adapt to a new passer, and it seems he'd have a better chance to put up big numbers with Rypien, who can air it out, rather than Walsh, who is more conservative and efficient. Even if Bruce's numbers suffer, he should have a good enough season to make him a #1 fantasy receiver.

Tight end Troy Drayton was second on the team with 47 catches for 458 yards and four TDs. Todd Kinchen had 36 catches for 419 yards and four scores, Jessie Hester added 30 catches for 399 yards and three TDs, and Alexander Wright had 23 receptions for 368 yards and two scores. With their second first-round pick in the '96 draft, the Rams selected LSU's Eddie Kennison, a real speed-burner with 4.45 speed who is still a raw talent as a receiver but is a dangerous return man.

Defense/Special Teams—

The Rams have some good talent on defense, but played pretty average most of last season. They finished 12th in the league, and 13th against both the rush and the pass. They did, however, produce some fantasy points with five defensive TDs, tying the team record set in 1978. Their 36 takeaways ranked 6th in the NFL. And they've added a few new faces to try to bolster the unit. The signing of free agent DE Leslie O'Neal will certainly strengthen a pass rush that already improved from 26 sacks in '94 to 36 in '95. O'Neal led the Chargers in sacks the past six seasons, including last year's 12.5. He'll make up for the loss of Sean Gilbert, who was traded to the Redskins. The addition of O'Neal should help further free up third-year DT D'Marco Farr, who led the Rams with 11.5 sacks last year. In his rookie season, DE Kevin Carter was second on the team with six sacks.

LB Roman Phifer was the man around the ball last season, pacing the team with a career-high 149 tackles (106 solo). He also posted personal bests in sacks and interceptions with three apiece. Shane Conlan started 11 games before suffering a season-ending knee injury. The Rams added to their LB corps by signing Robert Jones away from Dallas. Safety Toby Wright led the team in INTs last season with six, and was also second in tackles with 126 (100 solo). CB Todd Lyght added four INTs.

On special teams, J.T. Thomas was fourth in the NFC with a 23.5-yard kick return average. Todd Kinchen averaged 7.8 yards per punt return and 21.2 per kick return. This season, look for rookie receiver Eddie Kennison to make a big impact on returns.

Kicker—

Last year, the Rams replaced Steve McLaughlin in mid-season with longtime Colt Dean Biasucci, who connected on 9-of-12 field goals and 13-of-14 extra points for 40 total points. Overall, the two kickers combined for just 81 points, a number you can't afford to keep on your fantasy team. Avoid this unstable situation altogether and look elsewhere for your kicker. ★

By John Weiss
NFL Films

San Diego Chargers

Projected Starters:

QB Stan Humphries
RB Aaron Hayden
RB Terrell Fletcher
WR Tony Martin
WR Jimmy Oliver
TE Alfred Pupunu
K John Carney

By the middle of last season, it appeared the good fortune that had escorted the Chargers to Super Bowl 29 had finally abandoned them. At 4-7 they were headed nowhere, with nothing left to play for but pride. But give head coach Bobby Ross credit. His gritty Chargers put together five straight wins, including a season finale amidst a snowball barrage at Giants Stadium, and managed to reach the playoffs as a wildcard. Where does that leave them for 1996?

With the right breaks, the Chargers could once again challenge for the AFC West title. With the wrong ones, they could end up near the cellar. They're really that unpredictable. My guess is they'll end up closer to the top of the division than the bottom. Their defense is still one of the better units in the league, their offense is functional, and they have one of the game's great motivators in Ross. In a wide-open AFC playoff race, who knows how far that can take them.

Quarterback—

When you think of middle-of-the-road fantasy quarterbacks, Stan Humphries is the guy that comes to mind. He's not going to kill you, but he's also not going to carry you by himself to an FFL championship. Humphries should once again be rated in the middle of your '96 quarterback prospects. Last season, he passed for a career-high 3,381 yards, completing 282-of-478 (59%). However, he's never been a big touchdown producer. His 17 scoring passes last year tied a personal best. He also threw 14 interceptions. If he's your quarterback you'd better surround him with some big-time fantasy weapons. Perennial backup Sean Salisbury was signed as just that.

Running Back—

The 'Bolts waived Natrone Means, a guy who looked like he'd be piling up yards in San Diego for years. However, 1995 was a disappointing season for the big back, who was hobbled by a groin injury the last half of the season. He finished with 730 yards (3.9 average) and five TDs. That leaves the bulk of the running duties to second-year back Aaron Hayden, who was on the active roster for just the last six games of the '95 season. But the fourth-round pick led the team in rushing the last five regular-season games and in the playoffs, finishing with 470 yards (3.7 average) and three TDs. With a full season to work with, Hayden should be a 1,000-yard performer. Another second-year man, Terrell Fletcher, should see more playing time as a third-down back and pass catcher, taking the role of the now-departed Ronnie Harmon. Last year, Fletcher rushed for just 140 yards (5.4 average) and one TD, and caught three passes for 26 yards. Rodney Culver ran for 155 yards (3.3 average) and three touchdowns, but was killed in a tragic plane crash this spring. He will be missed by Charger fans and players alike.

Receiver—

With all the huge numbers put up by receivers around the league last year, it was easy to overlook the season put together by Tony Martin. Martin set a team record with 90 catches (that's right, better than anyone in the Air Coryell era), and racked up 1,224 yards and six TDs. His catch total ranked second in the AFC, and his yardage total was fourth in the conference. With Shawn Jefferson and Mark Seay now gone, Martin is the Chargers' go-to guy more than ever. And he's now a bonafide #1 receiver for your fantasy depth chart. He may go overlooked in your draft, so maybe you could steal him with a third or fourth round pick, but don't be afraid to take him higher. Second-year man 'OMar Ellison will see more playing time at the other receiver spot. The Chargers used their first pick of this year's draft on University of Virginia receiver Bryan Still.

Tight end/H-back Alfred Pupunu had a career-high 35 catches for 315 yards and no touchdowns last year. Shannon Mitchell will step into the other tight end/H-back slot and should improve on last year's numbers (three catches, 31 yards, one TD).

Defense/Special Teams—

The Chargers' defense hopes to be more opportunistic than it was a year ago, when the unit forced just 27 takeaways, ranking 22nd in the league. A few new faces have been added to a unit that finished 10th overall last season (14th rushing, 12th passing). The Chargers must make up for the loss of free agent defensive end Leslie O'Neal, who signed with the Rams. O'Neal led the team in sacks each of the last six seasons, and was third in the AFC last year with 12.5. To fill his spot, San Diego signed Marco Coleman away from Miami, where he recorded 6.5 sacks last season. Defensive tackle Shawn Lee was second for the Chargers last year with a career-high eight sacks.

Linebacker Junior Seau continues to be the team leader and most destructive force on defense. Last season he led the Chargers in tackles for the fifth straight season (129 total, 111 solo). Free agent Kurt Gouveia was signed away from Philadelphia. In the secondary, cornerback Dwayne Harper had four interceptions, while safety Shaun Gayle recorded two. Free agent Kevin Ross was signed from the Falcons, and makes up for the free agent loss of Bo Orlando. On special teams, Andre Coleman is one of the most dangerous return men in the game. He led the AFC in punt return average (11.6) last season, and returned one for a TD. He averaged 22.8 yards per kick return and brought back two for scores.

Kicker—

John Carney remains one of the best kickers in the league, but he certainly wasn't a big fantasy point producer last season. Carney hit a respectable 21-of-26 field goals and 32-of-33 extra points, but his 95 total points ranked 20th overall among kickers. It goes to show you that from year to year, you never know who will be the hot fantasy kickers.

Carney is certainly one of the top kickers for you to consider in '96. You just have to hope the Chargers get him more opportunities. ★

By Larry Weisman
Sports Columnist
USA Today

San Francisco 49ers

4 TM

Projected Starters:

QB *Steve Young*
RB *Johnny Johnson*
RB *Tommy Vardell*
WR *Jerry Rice*
WR *J.J. Stokes*
TE *Brent Jones*
K *Jeff Wilkins*

San Francisco started to break down late last year just when they should have been taking off. Poor pass protection and a running game that never clicked did the 'Niners in and they seemed to suffer a crisis of confidence when Green Bay smacked them around in the playoffs. Former coach Bill Walsh returns to advise the offense, which had its moments but struggled under new coordinator Marc Trestman. The offensive line is in transition with left tackle Steve Wallace and center Bart Oates gone. The defense led the NFL but lost cornerback Eric Davis as a free agent. This season could be an experiment in chemistry again. The 'Niners can't let Steve Young get pounded, must run more effectively, and need a big season from J.J. Stokes.

Quarterback—

Young missed a lot of time with shoulder injuries and that cut his numbers down. When healthy he's the most dangerous fantasy quarterback. He's certainly worth considering among the top picks based on years of consistency. Young threw for 20 touchdowns and rushed for three, poor figures for him. With Walsh tweaking the offense, his numbers should head upwards.

Backup Elvis Grbac played very well in relief and answered the question about whether he belonged in the NFL. That makes the San Francisco QB combination a good one.

Running Back—

Derek Loville scored 10 rushing touchdowns and that's good. But he averaged 3.3 yards a carry and that's bad. He also caught 87 passes, three for touchdowns, and that's good. Yet the 'Niners sought an upgrade at this position through free agency.

They pitched hard to sign Rodney Hampton but couldn't get him, then signed Tommy Vardell and Johnny Johnson. Vardell hasn't played much because of knee injuries and figures at fullback while William Floyd bounces back from knee surgery of his own. Johnson didn't play last season. The sleeper in the bunch is Johnson, a tough but slow inside runner who has fair hands. The 49ers really need Floyd but even he would not be a big numbers guy in fantasy play.

Wide Receiver—

The untouchable Jerry Rice belongs at the top of any draft list. He caught 122 passes—tying him for second in the NFL—for a league-high 1,848 yards and 15 touchdowns. Don't even hesitate!

Stokes must become the #2 guy with John Taylor retired. He had big problems after a holdout and couldn't get off the line. But he picked it up late in the season and four of his 38 catches went for touchdowns. He can easily double those numbers.

Tight end Brent Jones had an off year, scoring only three touchdowns. Defenses drove him toward the sidelines and manhandled him late in the year. He seems to be a declining player. Ted Popson is not the receiver Jones is.

Defense/Special Teams—

San Francisco played very well on defense and made big plays. They notched 40 sacks and hope for more with signing of defensive end Chris Doleman. They're strong at linebacker, a little shaky in the secondary if Marquez Pope and Tyronne Drakeford are the starting cornerbacks. That's a far cry from the days of Deion Sanders and Eric Davis. The 49ers are tough to run on and force teams to throw. That creates the possibility of turnovers. They made a league-high 26 interceptions last year.

The 49ers ranked near the bottom of the league in kickoff returns though they perked up when they reacquired Dexter Carter. He can break 'em. Carter also hauls the punts and scored once on a 78-yard return. With him around for a full season, this unit might be worth a look.

Kicker—

A perennial weakness! After ditching erratic Doug Brien, the 49ers settled on Jeff Wilkins. He made 12 of 13 field goals but remains an unknown quantity. Oddly, he missed more extra points (two) than field goals.

How he stands the rigors of a full season is anybody's guess. The only certainty is that a 49ers kicker should get lots of shots at the uprights behind that scary offense. ★

By John Weiss
NFL Films

Seattle Seahawks

Projected Starters:
QB *Rick Mirer*
RB *Chris Warren*
RB *Mack Strong*
WR *Brian Blades*
WR *Joey Galloway*
TE *Christian Fauria*
K *Todd Peterson*

It's been another off-season filled with off-field distractions for the Seahawks, with the team forced to deal with the uncertainty of moving to Los Angeles. It appears that the Seahawks will stay put for now, and if the players can keep their mind on football they might be able to put together a decent season.

Head coach Dennis Erickson did a better job in his first year than many people noticed. After stumbling to a 2-6 start, the Seahawks went 6-2 in the second half of the season to finish at 8-8. And their turnaround came thanks more to their offense than defense. Their 363 points were the fourth highest total in the AFC, and was the team's best output since 1987, despite ranking just 22nd in passing. They'll need to improve their air attack and shore up their defense if they hope to reach the playoffs for the first time since 1988.

Quarterback—

The Seahawks are hoping this is the season Rick Mirer finally breaks out. The fourth-year quarterback hasn't done anything special thus far in his career, and he may be facing a make-or-break year.

Last season, Mirer started 13 games and completed 209-of-391 (53.5%) for 2,564 yards, 13 touchdowns and 20 interceptions. His 63.7 quarterback rating tied him with Drew Bledsoe for lowest in the AFC. A separated left shoulder in Week 15 sidelined Mirer, and he was replaced with John Friesz for the remainder of the season. Friesz, who some Seahawks' fans may prefer as the starter, completed 64-of-120 (53.3%), six touchdowns and three interceptions.

Unless you're desperate, don't look to Mirer as your top quarterback. He should strictly be considered as a backup for your roster. He's too inconsistent, and if he struggles he may get yanked for Friesz.

Running Back—

After Emmitt Smith and Barry Sanders, there's no fantasy back clearly better than Chris Warren. He should be a definite first-round pick in your '96 draft. Not only does he pile up the yardage, but he's the clear go-to guy when the Seahawks are close to the endzone. In 1995, Warren registered his fourth straight 1,000-yard season with 1,346 yards (second in the AFC), a 4.3-yard average, and 15 rushing touchdowns (second only to Smith). He set a team record with eight 100-yard rushing games, and twice rushed for three touchdowns in a game. He also had 35 catches for 247 yards and a score. He's emerged as a true franchise running back to build your fantasy team around. Mack Strong will spell Warren, but could go undrafted in your league.

Wide Receiver—

The Seahawks have two great targets in Brian Blades and Joey Galloway, both of whom should be ranked fairly high on your receivers list. I'd rate Galloway slightly higher because of his potential.

In a terrific rookie season last year, Galloway had 67 catches for 1,039 yards and seven touchdowns. He was the first rookie receiver to surpass 1,000 yards since 1986. His lightning speed makes him one of the NFL's most dangerous deep threats, and one would expect he'll only get better.

Blades led the team in catches (77) last season, and also had 1,001 yards and five touchdowns. He's become a consistent performer in the offense.

At tight end, Carlester Crumpler had 23 catches for 254 yards and a touchdown, while rookie Christian Fauria had 17 receptions for 181 yards and a score.

Defense/Special Teams—

The Seahawks need to tighten up a defense that ranked 25th in the league last season, 28th against the run. Seattle also needs to create more opportunities. Their unit forced just 25 takeaways, tying them for 24th in the league.

Defensive tackle Cortez Kennedy is still a force in the middle. Last year, Kennedy was named to his fifth straight Pro Bowl and tied for the team lead with 6.5 sacks. Due to constant double and triple teaming, however, his tackle stats (54 total, 40 solo) weren't as high as you'd like. Defensive end Antonio Edwards tied Kennedy with 6.5 sacks, while Michael Sinclair added 5.5.

Linebacker Terry Wooden is the team's big tackler. Last year, he led Seattle with a personal best 135 (114 solo), marking the third straight year he's gone over 100 tackles. He had seven games with at least 10 tackles. He did not, however, record a sack.

Safety Eugene Robinson had more than 100 tackles for the fourth straight season, with 105 (79 solo). Safety Robert Blackmon led the team with five interceptions and cornerback Carlton Gray added four. The Seahawks reinforced their secondary by signing safety Darryl Williams away from Cincinnati.

On special teams, Steve Broussard was the team's leading kick returner with a 24.7-yard average, ranking sixth in the AFC. Joey Galloway averaged 10.0 yards per punt return, eighth in the AFC, and had one return for a touchdown.

Kicker—

Todd Peterson made a good showing in his first full season in the league, hitting 23-of-28 field goals and 40-of-40 extra points. He was 0-for-2 on 50-plus yarders. He hit 16 of his last 17 field goals, and his last 11 in a row.

His 109 points tied him for 14th among kickers. He's like any number of kickers whose fantasy production will depend on the opportunities he's given. ★

By Kevin Lynch
Pro Sports Xchange

Tampa Bay Buccaneers

Projected Starters:
QB Trent Dilfer
RB Errict Rhett
RB Mike Alstott
WR Alvin Harper
WR Lawrence Dawsey
WR Courtney Hawkins
TE Jackie Harris
K Michael Husted

A new coach, a new owner, and a new attitude is pervading down in Tampa. Something needs to happen to the horrendous *'Bucs* who are battling the NBA's Los Angeles Clippers to become the worst professional sports team of the last 20 years. Up until last year, the *'Bucs* had suffered through 12 seasons of double digit losses, finishing last season at a barely-better 7-9. New owner Malcom Glazer, who bought the team in January of 1995, hopes the Tony Dungy era will be different. He takes over for the ever-earnest Sam Wyche and inherits the horrendous legacy. The *'Bucs* appeared headed for promising things after thumping the Panthers, Bengals, Vikings, and Falcons in successive games in the middle of the season last year. Things began to unravel when they lost to the lowly Oilers and then lost their next four. They do have some talent, but drafting off the *'Bucs* roster is always a risky proposition.

Quarterback—

QBs have always found Tampa Bay to be a huge black hole. Last year, starter Trent Dilfer soared to new highs in lowness. He tossed 18 INTs and a mere four TDs. He made a huge leap from Fresno State to the pros and is only in his third season. He also left school as a junior. Part of Dilfer's problem was his mercurial relationship with HC Sam Wyche. By the end of the season, the two weren't even talking. New offensive coordinator Mike Shula might make an immediate impact in Dilfer's confidence. There's no question Dilfer has talent but will he be able to tap it in a place that couldn't even make Steve Young a star? Casey Weldon got plenty of time subbing for an ineffective Dilfer last year, but couldn't do much with it. In fact his 58.8 quarterback rating was actually below Dilfer's 60.1. The *'Bucs* are fully committed to Dilfer, the only question is whether he can produce.

Running Back—

The *'Bucs* have found themselves a jewel of a RB in the hard-charging Errict Rhett. Unfortunately, he's also a hard-charger when it comes to contract negotiations. Rhett, who became only the 12th player in NFL history to rush for over 1,000 yards in each of his first two seasons, is due to make $336,000 this year. He wants a new contract and negotiations haven't gone well. If he does re-sign and isn't soured by the process, he would be a solid pick. He gained 1,207 yards last year behind the *'Bucs'* line, which is saying something. He also tied with three other players for second in the conference in rushing TDs with eleven. Should negotiations bog down, Jerry Ellison played remarkably well as the backup, averaging an amazing 8.4 yards per carry. He had all of the *'Bucs'* four longest runs from scrimmage. Second round rookie Mike Alstott also may get a look as a ball carrier if Rhett's situation isn't resolved. But the *'Bucs* would rather use him as the blocker for Rhett.

Wide Receiver—

If the 'Bucs could get their QBs cranked up, their receivers could then realize some of their talents. As it was, TE Jackie Harris was the 'Bucs leading receiver with 62 catches for 751 yards and a TD. It's a ringing endorsement for Harris, who proved he could be a good receiver no matter what the QB situation. Courtney Hawkins continues to be a flash-in-the-pan kind of guy—one week he is everywhere, the next week it's as if he is absent. All in all, I would proceed with caution. Tampa Bay dished out big dollars for former Cowboy WR Alvin Harper, who started the season with a sprained knee and never got on track. In all, he finished with 46 catches, a 13.8 average and two TDS. He wasn't nearly the deep threat he was as a Cowboy. Some say that's because he doesn't have Michael Irvin on the other side, although others believe he just needs a consistent QB and a healthy knee to be effective. Dawsey missed the last four games with an infected finger, but he should be back. Horace Copeland proved to be a solid option as the third WR (35 catches for 605 yards).

Defense/Special Teams—

The 'Bucs made a serious financial commitment to middle LB Hardy Nickerson, who may be the best in the game. He secured a four-year $12.8 million contract. There was much upheaval on the defensive line, as both Mark Wheeler and Santana Dotson left through free agency. But the 'Bucs feel they have more than made up for their loss by re-signing Chidi Ahanotu and drafting former Cal-Berkeley star Regan Upshaw. With their second first round choice, they took Marcus Jones, a defensive tackle who should start along with last year's top rounder Warren Sapp. Tony Dungy's overall aggressive style should increase the Bucs' ability to induce turnovers. Tampa Bay is in great need of increasing their sacks and INTs; they had only 16 of the latter and 25 of the former. Only expansion Jacksonville had fewer sacks. Returner Bobby Joe Edmonds was released. opening the door for 'Bucs' sixth round draft choice Nilo Silvan. He's a 5'8", 175-pound speed burner (4.4 in the 40-yard dash) who could open some eyes.

Kicker—

Probably the biggest compliment paid to Buccaneer kicker Michael Husted was the $2.4 million four-year offer he received from the 49ers. The 'Bucs matched and the 'Niners tried to trade for him, but Dungy rejected their offers. Husted won three games with last minute kicks, but had the opportunity to win two others and didn't. For the year, he made 19 of 26 attempts. ★

By Larry Weisman
Sports Columnist
USA Today

Washington Redskins

Projected Starters:

QB Heath Shuler
RB Terry Allen
RB Marc Logan
WR Henry Ellard
WR Michael Westbrook
WR Bill Brooks
TE Scott Galbraith
K Scott Blanton

Washington loves a good quarterback controversy! Sonny or Billy? Jay Schroeder or Doug Williams? Now Heath Shuler vs. Gus Frerotte. Where the Redskins are going and how they'll get there revolve around the two young QBs and their development. The supporting cast keeps improving but the guy pulling the trigger makes the most difference.

Coach Norv Turner enters the third year of his rebuilding plan. The six wins in 1995 doubled his initial season's output. If the QB situation doesn't crystallize early, progress could halt. His other big problem early in camp will be reshaping the offensive line. Left tackle Jim Lachey might not be kept around and guard Ray Brown signed with San Francisco. Rookie Andre Johnson could start at left tackle with Joe Patton moving inside.

Quarterback—

The Redskins say it's an open competition but they have to give Shuler the edge, just based on their investment in him and his long-term contract. Frerotte had the better numbers and the seeming faith of his teammates. Shuler performed adequately late in the season in an offensive scheme tailored down to his knowledge of the playbook and confidence. Look for Shuler to win the job. Then stay away from him. Cut the legs out from under one of your opponents by grabbing Frerotte as a backup. He'll probably relieve Shuler by midseason, then lose the job late as the Redskins try to salvage their bonus baby.

Running Back—

Terry Allen had an outstanding year for the Redskins, often carrying the offense. He ran for 1,309 yards and 10 touchdowns. The Redskins didn't rush to re-sign him but he's not going anywhere. He'll be the starter again. Rookie Stephen Davis might bear a good look. He didn't have a great senior year at Auburn but that offense put the ball in the air a lot.

Reggie Brooks disappeared two years ago and has barely been seen since. Don't count on him. FB Marc Logan lends veteran savvy but doesn't see the ball much. He gets a smattering of rushes and a few passes. Brian Mitchell is productive in spots but more valuable for his kick and punt returns and doesn't get enough opportunities in the offense for fantasy purposes.

Wide Receiver—

The Redskins liked what they saw in limited exposure to big rookie receiver Michael Westbrook. He caught 34 passes, one for a touchdown, and has the look of a player on the cusp of big-time numbers. Westbrook can also be dangerous running the reverses Turner loves. Ageless Henry Ellard remains the go-to guy and five of his 56 catches were for touchdowns. He's capable of more, but are the quarterbacks?

Leslie Shepherd is sneaky fast and potentially explosive. Look for him as the #3 receiver, although the signing of Bill Brooks could threaten that. Tydus Winans could be fighting for a job. The Redskins employ a number of tight ends. They like Scott Galbraith around the end zone but also use Coleman Bell. Neither will do you a world of good!

Defense/Special Teams—

The Redskins improved defensively last year and should be bigger and better this year. One reason they didn't get fried by the pass was that they couldn't stop the run (29th in the league). Defensive tackle Sean Gilbert, acquired in a trade for their #1 draft choice, ought to help plug those leaks. At linebacker, the Redskins boast Ken Harvey, a top pass rusher. The secondary is sound, though Darrell Green is getting up there in years. The Redskins came up with 35 takeaways—not bad considering a mediocre 30 sacks. They'll be better against the run and stronger with the pass rush but need to make more big plays.

The special teams are a selling point because of Mitchell. He led the NFC but didn't score on kickoff returns. He did add a touchdown on punt returns. He alone makes this group worth considering. If the defense pins teams back and gives him a decent shot, he can bring it back to the end zone.

Kicker—

Eddie Murray has a limited leg left. He converted 27 of 36 field goals but was 6 of 13 from 40 yards or further. He made all 10 tries under 30 yards. He just can't bang it that far any more. Think of him as a backup kicker for that bye week. Looks like Scott Blanton will assume the *'Skins'* kicking duties. ★

4
TM

5 Quarterbacks

Drafting Quarterbacks—

In most fantasy football scoring systems, quarterbacks generally are among the top producers. There are a few exceptions to this rule (i.e., Emmitt Smith, Jerry Rice, Carl Pickens, etc.), but generally in the first round the top selections tend to be quarterbacks.

Why, you absurdly yawn? Look, the QB spot is the *hot zone* of your franchise. This spot *has* to pump out points each week. An FFL franchise with key scoring out of its QB will have an advantage over the other franchises. The quarterback position has the opportunity to deliver a whopping 4-5 TDs in a game any given week. Therefore, I like the idea of selecting a solid quality quarterback for my first pick.

However let me reiterate one *key* point—if drafting later in the first round (and Steve Young and Brett Favre are off the board), and Mr. Emmitt Smith is *still* there, I immediately jump *all over* Emmitt as my pick! *Whew*, I had to get that off my chest!

Drafting Backup Quarterbacks—

Psst...a little tip for you draftniks: if you draft a quality quarterback from a quality team, it makes good sense to draft that team's backup QB. For example, last season we saw Steve Young go down and out with injuries. Yet due to a solid offensive game plan, his backup, Elvis Grbac, actually performed well. Coupled with this experience and additional offensive help for '96, Elvis will be a solid backup selection for anyone who drafts Steve Young.

Let's take the case of the Washington Redskins' quarterbacks. Let's say your draft strategy enabled you to draft Emmitt Smith (*first round*), Errict Rhett (*second round*), and you scarfed up Heath Shuler (*third round*). Obviously you would then focus in on receivers for your *fourth* and *fifth* round picks. By the *sixth* round, you would be smart to pounce on QB Gus Frerotte. Why? Simple, this summer either Heath or Gus will win the starting job, and the other will be the backup. For three years there has been always the quirky question with these two, *"Who will win the job, and how long will he hold it?"* HC Norv Turner has a propensity for switching the two out, so keep focused on the nation's capital this summer. Also, with the ever-present injury bug running rampant in the NFL, it makes sense to draft both QBs.

How about in Atlanta?
As of this writing Jeff George hasn't signed. Although I feel strongly that by the time you read this, *Boy Georgie* has signed and is ready to play. So if you draft the irksome George, what happens if he gets hit with something heavier than his ego (*such as a 300-pound*

5 QB

defensive end) and he gets planted on the disabled list, as he waits for his head (*and ego*) to be reattached to his body? What happens to you and your miserable FFL franchise? Well, if you were completely prepared on *Draft Day* (see Martha Stewart for tips on preparation, and Miss Manners for draft etiquette), you would have neatly picked Bobby Hebert as your backup. You see, fiery Bobby may not have Jeff's cannon or his money, but he can lead the Falcons and he *can score!*

Okay, Mr. Smarty Pants, should we draft the backup for just any *quarterback that we draft?* Hey, good question. Answer: *No!* For example, Jeff Blake is a solid draft pick and he will score several zillion points this season, but his backup Erik Wilhelm is not known as "*Air Erik*". Therefore my second QB selection would be to grab a Rick Mirer (*later in the draft*) and then selecting Mirer's backup John Friesz (*much later in the draft*). If this scenario actually happened, I would be on my knees weekly praying that Blake has a *verrry* healthy season!

Starter:	Backup:	Team:
Steve Young	Elvis Grbac, Gino Torretta	*San Francisco 49ers*
Brett Favre	Jim McMahon, Kyle Wacholtz	*Green Bay Packers*
Scott Mitchell	Don Majkowski, Donald Hollas	*Detroit Lions*
Dan Marino	Bernie Kosar, Dan McGwire	*Miami Dolphins*
Jeff George	Bobby Hebert, Perry Klein	*Atlanta Falcons*
Jeff Blake	Erik Wilhelm	*Cincinnati Bengals*
Drew Bledsoe	Scott Zolak, Jay Barker	*New England Patriots*
John Elway	Bill Musgrave, Jeff Lewis	*Denver Broncos*
Neil O'Donnell	Frank Reich, Glenn Foley	*New York Jets*
Jim Kelly	Alex Van Pelt, Todd Collins	*Buffalo Bills*
Erik Kramer	Dave Krieg, Shane Matthews	*Chicago Bears*
Mark Brunell	Rob Johnson	*Jacksonville Jaguars*
Jim Everett	Doug Nussmeier, Hugh Millen	*New Orleans Saints*
Jeff Hostetler	Billy Joe Hobert, Vince Evans	*Oakland Raiders*
Warren Moon	Brad Johnson, Chad May	*Minnesota Vikings*
Steve Bono	Rich Gannon, Matt Blundin	*Kansas City Chiefs*
Stan Humphries	Sean Salisbury, Gale Gilbert	*San Diego Chargers*
Vinny Testaverde	Eric Zeier	*Baltimore Ravens*
Troy Aikman	Wade Wilson, Jason Garrett	*Dallas Cowboys*
Jim Harbaugh	Craig Erickson, Paul Justin	*Indianapolis Colts*
Kerry Collins	Steve Beuerlein, Kelly Stouffer	*Carolina Panthers*
Heath Shuler	Gus Frerotte, Trent Green	*Washington Redskins*
Rick Mirer	John Friesz, Stan Gelbaugh	*Seattle Seahawks*
Chris Chandler	Steve McNair, Will Furrer	*Houston Oilers*
Boomer Esiason	Stoney Case, Kent Graham	*Arizona Cardinals*
Steve Walsh	Mark Rypien, Tony Banks	*St. Louis Rams*
Ty Detmer	Rodney Peete, Bobby Hoying	*Philadelphia Eagles*
Jim Miller	Mike Tomczak, Kordell Stewart	*Pittsburgh Steelers*
Dave Brown	Danny Kanell, Tommy Maddox	*New York Giants*
Trent Dilfer	Casey Weldon, Scott Milanovich	*Tampa Bay Buccaneers*

Free Agent Quarterbacks— A quick tidbit and tip—keep your eyes on free agent QBs that will be gobbled up during training camp and the exhibition season. No, these players won't make or break your franchsie, but they could latch on as a backup and *may* backup your star QB! For example, there is great interest in Indianapolis for Kerwin Bell, and in Miami for Mike Buck.

Player:	Old Team:
Randall Cunningham	*Philadelphia Eagles*
Bubby Brister	*New York Jets*
David Klingler	*Cincinnati Bengals*
Kerwin Bell	*Indianapolis Colts*
Mike Buck	*Arizona Cardinals*

Speaking of Randall Cunningham, I can't believe *some* team out there can't use *"Too Hot To Handle Randall!"* Sure, Randall is a blowhard, malcontent, selfish, bonehead who takes himself *way too seriously*, but he has always possessed incredible talent.

Couldn't a player's coach like Bill '*I love ya man*' Cowher reign in Randall? Couldn't Randall perhaps stand a better chance than Mike Tomczak, Jim Miller (*Who?*) and second year all-everything Kordell '*Slash*' Stewart? Couldn't those outlaws in Oakland use a deep long ball thrower *a la Jim Plunkett*? Wouldn't Randall look groovy in the black and silver? If Rick Mirer falters, instead of John Friesz replacing the *ex-Domer*, how about Randall? Can you imagine Randall throwing long to Joey Galloway? Is Randall any worse of a gamble than, say, Vinny Testaverde? Couldn't grandfatherly Teddy Marchibroda perhaps be the coach to teach Randall how to quarterback in Baltimore? Of course, the scary thought of Randall and Andre Rison together could age even Dick Clark, but still, is *Vinny Testaverde* the *answer*? Finally, please tell me that Randall couldn't help the Tampa Bay *'Bucs*! Trent Dilfer tossed something like 3 TDs in '95. Heck, Randall could do that in a half with the current *'Bucs* receiving corps.

So here's a vote for Randall Cunningham landing in a new city, with a new attitude, and a new mission: finally living up to his immense talent. *If this happens, maybe Randall will appreciate the value of teamwork.* ★

Quarterback Question Marks—

Jeff George	Will he sign a contract? Is he just going to play this season and bolt?
Jim Kelly	Word is that he is feeling great. If this is so '*Machine Gun*' could be a steal for '96.
Drew Bledsoe (5 QB)	Is he completely healed (*mentally and physically*)? Did last season do a number to his pysche? Will he hook up with Jefferson and Brisby this season?
John Elway	Word is that '*Long John*' is back to form! Is this his year for 30 TDs? Will Sherrard, Sharpe and Miller stay healthy?
Jeff Hostetler	Can '*Hoss*' develop a long bombing style? Can he stay alive and well in '96? Can he play a full season?
Warren Moon	No one was hotter than Warren the last 6 weeks of '95, but can he remain error-free and healthy at 40?
Heath Shuler	Who starts and sticks in Washington, Heath or Gus? Will the proposed shotgun offense help deliver '*Baby Heath*' to stardom?
Neil O'Donnell	Can Neil shake off the memories of Larry Brown and the Super Bowl loss? Can he prove to be a top-5 type QB with leadership, receivers, and an improved Jets offensive game plan?
Ty Detmer	Can Ty really take the NFL punishment? Can he finally shuck that Heisman curse and develop into another Jeff Blake?
Stan Humphries	Cutting loose WRs Shawn Jefferson and Mark Seay, Ronnie Harmon (3rd down backfield receiver), TE Duane Young and Natrone Means—not to mention the untimely death of Rodney Culver—has to have a negative effect on "*Stan-Diego.*" *Yeah, yeah,* Jefferson and Seay bobbled and dropped as many as they caught, but *wow*, that's a full chunk of offense to replace!
Brett Favre	Will just *aspirin* keep him together?

'95 Official Bombers (Two or More TDS Over 40 Yards)—

Player:	Team:	TDS:	Total TDS:
Erik Kramer	CHI	8	30
John Elway	DEN	8	27
Warren Moon	MIN	6	33
Jeff Blake	CIN	6	30
Brett Favre	GB	5	41
Scott Mitchell	DET	5	36
Jeff George	ATL	5	24
Jim Kelly	BUF	5	22
Rick Mirer	SEA	5	14
Jim Everett	NO	4	26
Chris Chandler	HOU	4	19
Kerry Collins	CAR	4	17
Steve Bono	KC	3	26
Dan Marino	MIA	3	24
Troy Aikman	DAL	3	17
Neil O'Donnell	PIT	3	17
Dave Brown	NYG	3	15
Gus Frerotte	WAS	3	14
Jeff Hostetler	RAI	3	12
Elvis Grbac	SF	3	10
Vince Evans	RAI	3	6
Steve Young	SF	2	23
Jim Harbaugh	IND	2	19
Stan Humphries	SD	2	18
Chris Miller	RAM	2	18
Boomer Esiason	NYJ	2	16
Billy Joe Hobert	RAI	2	6

1994 TDS, 40+ YDS: 85
1995 TDS, 40+ YDS: 112

Fast Feet Feats ('95 Quarterback Rushing Stats)—

Player:	Team:	Yards:	Average:	TDS:
Mark Brunell	JAX	480	36.9	4
Jeff Blake	CIN	311	19.4	2
Steve Young	SF	250	22.7	3
Dave Brown	NYG	228	14.3	4
Jim Harbaugh	IND	208	13.9	2
Rick Mirer	SEA	191	12.7	1
Brett Favre	GB	183	11.4	3
John Elway	DEN	179	11.2	1
Rodney Peete	PHI	147	9.8	1
Jeff Hostetler	RAI	119	10.8	0
Trent Dilfer	TB	115	7.2	2
Steve Bono	KC	113	7.1	5

'96 Pre-Season Quarterback Review—

Steve Young
San Francisco 49ers

	1995:	1994:	1993:
Passing TDs	20	35	29
Rushing TDs	3	7	2
TDs over 40 Yards	2	5	5
Total Passing Yards	3,200	2,969	4,023
Total Completions/Attempts	299/447	324/461	314/462
Average Yards per Game	290.9	185.6	251.4
Interceptions Thrown	11	10	16
Times Sacked	25	31	31
Games Played	11	16	16

I know a lot of folks that drafted Steve Young, expected to coast to an easy victory last season, and winced with pain when he went down! Don't expect Young to suddenly become a member of Blue Cross yet; he can still be the best and most explosive guy in the NFL on any given Sunday. I am making him my number one fantasy pick due to his incredible numbers the past three years, an improved San Francisco offensive running game, and—most importantly—his durability, mental toughness, and a strong desire to return his team to greatness.

Brett Favre
Green Bay Packers

	1995:	1994:	1993:
Passing TDs	38	33	17
Rushing TDs	3	2	1
TDs over 40 Yards	5	1	2
Total Passing Yards	4,413	3,882	3,303
Total Completions/Attempts	359/570	363/582	318/522
Average Yards per Game	275.8	242.6	206.4
Interceptions Thrown	13	14	24
Times Sacked	30	31	30
Games Played	16	16	16

If there are any believers out there that felt that Favre was nothing without Sterling Sharpe, they were silenced in a wild, NFL MVP 1995 season. He is the prototypical commanding field general, as he showed in snubbing the 49ers in the playoffs. In May, he announced that he was participating in the NFL's Voluntary Substance Abuse Program for treatment to an addiction to painkillers. If Favre is healthy and happy, the *Pack* will continue to cruise! The question has to be asked, though, *"Can an NFL QB survive a season on just aspirin?"*

		1995:	1994:	1993:
Scott Mitchell *Detroit Lions*	Passing TDS	32	10	12
	Rushing TDS	4	1	0
	TDS over 40 Yards	5	0	3
	Total Passing Yards	4,338	1,456	1,773
	Total Completions/Attempts	346/583	119/246	133/233
	Average Yards per Game	271.1	161.8	253.3
	Interceptions Thrown	12	11	8
	Times Sacked	31	12	7
	Games Played	16	9	7

A lot of draft wizards will shy away from the Scottster due to his awful showing against the Eagles in the playoffs. Look, Mitchell will run up some quality numbers in '96—don't be a putz and overlook him. Just look at the offensive weapons he's got. You can't lose! Honest!

		1995:	1994:	1993:
Dan Marino *Miami Dolphins*	Passing TDS	24	30	8
	Rushing TDS	0	1	1
	TDS over 40 Yards	3	4	3
	Total Passing Yards	3,668	4,453	1,218
	Total Completions/Attempts	309/482	385/615	91/150
	Average Yards per Game	275.8	278.3	243.6
	Interceptions Thrown	15	17	3
	Times Sacked	22	17	7
	Games Played	14	16	5

With a new sheriff in town (Jimmy Johnson), I expect that the offense will shape up and *Dan-de-roo* will not have to bark at his offense as much, because J.J. will supply the bite. Wakeup calls will be officially issued to Keith Byars and Eric Green. Freddy Barnett gives Dan a great receiver and O.J. McDuffie is entering the top echelon of receivers. Marino signed an off-season deal that will keep him a *'Fin* well into 2000, so you can expect similar numbers, and a better system, thanks to Jimmy J.

		1995:	1994:
Jeff Blake *Cincinnati Bengals*	Passing TDS	28	14
	Rushing TDS	2	1
	TDS over 40 Yards	6	4
	Total Passing Yards	3,822	2,154
	Total Completions/Attempts	326/567	156/306
	Average Yards per Game	238.9	239.3
	Interceptions Thrown	17	9
	Times Sacked	25	19
	Games Played	16	9

Forget the knock that he is only 6'0" and that some skeptics feel that he was worn out by season's end—Blake is a scorer and can launch bombs to receivers like Carl Pickens and Darnay Scott. Expect a healthy Ki-Jana Carter to add to (*not take away from*) his production.

	1995:	1994:	1993:

Jeff George
Atlanta Falcons

	1995:	1994:	1993:
Passing TDs	24	23	8
Rushing TDs	0	0	0
TDs over 40 Yards	5	4	1
Total Passing Yards	4,143	3,734	2,526
Total Completions/Attempts	336/557	322/524	234/407
Average Yards per Game	258.9	233.4	229.6
Interceptions Thrown	11	18	6
Times Sacked	42	32	26
Games Played	16	16	11

As I write this George is still a Falcon. I am also suffering from the delusion that no one else will sign him and once again we will see him wearing Falcon black. Plus, the good news is that Terance Mathis re-signed and will be joining Eric Metcalf and Bert Emanuel streaking down the field for bombs. George could have a great season if he stays put and continues to get comfortable with his receivers.

Jim Kelly
Buffalo Bills

	1995:	1994:	1993:
Passing TDs	22	22	18
Rushing TDs	0	1	0
TDs over 40 Yards	5	2	3
Total Passing Yards	3,130	3,114	3,382
Total Completions/Attempts	255/458	285/448	288/470
Average Yards per Game	208.7	222.4	211.4
Interceptions Thrown	13	17	18
Times Sacked	25	34	25
Games Played	15	14	16

Sure the knees are gone, the arm is not getting any younger, and he is not the Kelly of old. But he hangs in there and fights with the best of them! Let's also not forget that many of the numbers he has posted are played in weather that makes penguins chilly. Until time or injury claim him, he's on my list of top guys, and should be on yours too.

John Elway
Denver Broncos

	1995:	1994:	1993:
Passing TDs	26	16	25
Rushing TDs	1	4	0
TDs over 40 Yards	8	3	2
Total Passing Yards	4,413	3,490	4,030
Total Completions/Attempts	316/542	307/494	348/551
Average Yards per Game	248.1	249.3	251.9
Interceptions Thrown	14	10	10
Times Sacked	23	46	39
Games Played	16	14	16

Okay, so what if Big John is no longer a dashing young QB with a cannon for an arm? He is now a hobbling older QB, but still has the arm and he is still dangerous! Want more? Well, he played in 16 games and tossed 26 TDs in '95.

		1995:	*1994:*	*1993:*
Neil O'Donnell *New York Jets*	Passing TDS	17	13	14
	Rushing TDS	0	1	0
	TDS over 40 Yards	3	2	1
	Total Passing Yards	2,970	2,443	3,208
	Total Completions/Attempts	246/416	212/370	270/486
	Average Yards per Game	247.5	174.5	213.9
	Interceptions Thrown	7	9	7
	Times Sacked	15	35	41
	Games Played	12	14	15

If I hear another bonehead explain that Neil is an overrated choker, I will personally begin a Neil O'Donnell *'Feel Good Club'*. O'Donnell will blossom with ex-Steeler Jeff Graham, hotshot rookie WR Keyshawn Johnson, steady-handed second-year WR Wayne Chrebet and sophomore TE Kyle Brady. *For my sake, give him a break!*

		1995:	*1994:*	*1993:*
Erik Kramer *Chicago Bears*	Passing TDS	29	8	8
	Rushing TDS	1	0	0
	TDS over 40 Yards	8	2	1
	Total Passing Yards	3,838	1,129	1,002
	Total Completions/Attempts	315/522	99/158	87/138
	Average Yards per Game	239.9	225.8	250.5
	Interceptions Thrown	10	8	3
	Times Sacked	15	14	5
	Games Played	16	5	4

Okay draftniks, which Kramer shows up in '96?
The guy who transformed into Broadway Joe Namath for the first 11 games, or the chump that barely showed up in the last five games? Personally I have always been in Kramer's corner, but to be a complete QB, he needs to add a finish to his game and season.

	1995:	1994:	1993:
Passing TDs	13	25	15
Rushing TDs	0	0	0
TDs over 40 Yards	1	1	2
Total Passing Yards	3,507	4,555	2,494
Total Completions/Attempts	323/636	400/691	214/429
Average Yards per Game	233.8	284.7	249.4
Interceptions Thrown	16	27	15
Times Sacked	23	22	16
Games Played	15	16	12

Drew Bledsoe
New England Patriots

Break out the bumper stickers—I am backing Drew Bledsoe in '96! Despite getting hurt in '95, he still had a miserable year when he was healthy. Perhaps he got his sophomore jinx a year late. Whatever the case, adding WR Shawn Jefferson to TE Ben Coates and WR Vincent Brisby should bolster that offense. Bullrusher Curtis Martin should continue to take the heat off Bledsoe. *Memo to Parcells: Can we expect to see David Meggett more in that offensive scheme?*

Mark Brunell
Jacksonville Jaguars

Passing TDs	15	0
Rushing TDs	4	1
TDs over 40 Yards	0	0
Total Passing Yards	2,168	95
Total Completions/Attempts	201/346	12/27
Average Yards per Game	166.8	47.5
Interceptions Thrown	7	0
Times Sacked	39	5
Games Played	13	2

Okay, I've long said that Brett Favre is a poor man's Steve Young. Therefore, Mark Brunell is a poorer man's Brett Favre. The upside on Brunell is that he is fearless, steady, and has a knack for scoring. The downside is that he has a penchant for getting dinged-up due to his carefree, swashbuckling style. That said, if he is given receivers with clear vision and two good hands, we should continue to see him posting bigger and better numbers.

	1995:	1994:	1993:
Jim Everett			
New Orleans Saints			
Passing TDS	26	22	8
Rushing TDS	0	0	0
TDS over 40 Yards	4	2	4
Total Passing Yards	3,970	3,855	1,652
Total Completions/Attempts	345/567	346/540	135/274
Average Yards per Game	248.1	240.9	183.6
Interceptions Thrown	14	18	12
Times Sacked	27	21	18
Games Played	16	16	9

I like the fact that Everett seems to actually be enjoying himself and although his passing footwork is still poor, he does have serious striking ability. The big loss for Jimbo is that Quinn Early's top quality receiving workmanship is heading north to Buffalo.

	1995:	1994:	1993:
Warren Moon			
Minnesota Vikings			
Passing TDS	33	18	21
Rushing TDS	0	0	1
TDS over 40 Yards	6	4	2
Total Passing Yards	4,228	4,264	3,485
Total Completions/Attempts	359/570	363/582	318/522
Average Yards per Game	264.3	284.3	248.9
Interceptions Thrown	14	19	21
Times Sacked	39	29	34
Games Played	16	15	14

In the prior two years combined, ('93 and '94), MoonMan only threw 39 TDS. Yet in '95, instead of showing his age he fired 33 TDS. The big question in my mind is if Moon can remain healthy and competitive!

	1995:	1994:	1993:
Jeff Hostetler			
Oakland Raiders			
Passing TDS	12	20	14
Rushing TDS	0	2	5
TDS over 40 Yards	3	4	3
Total Passing Yards	1,998	3,334	3,242
Total Completions/Attempts	172/286	263/454	236/419
Average Yards per Game	181.6	208.4	216.1
Interceptions Thrown	9	12	10
Times Sacked	22	25	38
Games Played	11	16	15

I really thought that Hoss may have gone to Pittsburgh, but he will be sticking with the Raiders. I question this since the Raiders claim that they want to stretch the field out in '96. Hoss is more of a pick-and-shoot type of passer. Health now plays a role when selecting Hostetler as your QB! *Can he survive a season?*

5 QB

		1995:	1994:	1993:
Stan Humphries *San Diego Chargers*	Passing TDS	17	17	12
	Rushing TDS	1	0	0
	TDS over 40 Yards	2	6	2
	Total Passing Yards	3,381	3,209	1,981
	Total Completions/Attempts	282/478	264/453	173/324
	Average Yards per Game	225.4	213.9	198.1
	Interceptions Thrown	14	12	10
	Times Sacked	23	25	18
	Games Played	15	15	10

Humphries has proven himself over the last few years to be a consummate pro, with the field presence of a gritty veteran. He always throws a few bombs each year, but serious questions exist about the receivers. Still, I like *"Stan, the Man!"*

		1995:	1994:	1993:
Troy Aikman *Dallas Cowboys*	Passing TDS	16	13	15
	Rushing TDS	1	1	0
	TDS over 40 Yards	3	1	4
	Total Passing Yards	3,304	2,676	3,100
	Total Completions/Attempts	280/432	233/361	271/392
	Average Yards per Game	206.5	191.1	221.4
	Interceptions Thrown	7	12	6
	Times Sacked	15	14	26
	Games Played	16	14	14

Hmmm, look at the past three year stats—15, 13, and 16 TDS! No argument here that Aikman is a great NFL QB, but as a fantasy scorer, he is just average. Frankly, since the *'Pokes* offense hasn't changed much, why would we expect Aikman to produce any more than 20 TDS?

		1995:	1994:	1993:
Vinny Testaverde *Baltimore Ravens*	Passing TDS	17	16	14
	Rushing TDS	2	2	0
	TDS over 40 Yards	1	3	2
	Total Passing Yards	2,883	2,575	1,797
	Total Completions/Attempts	241/392	207/376	130/230
	Average Yards per Game	221.8	198.1	179.7
	Interceptions Thrown	10	18	9
	Times Sacked	18	12	17
	Games Played	13	13	10

The question in everyone's mind is how much Vinny will improve with friendly, offensive-minded Teddy Marchibroda, instead of grimacing, defensive-minded Bill Belichick! I believe Vinny will win over the Baltimore fans with steady play under the kind direction of a man who can befriend any QB.

	1995:	1994:	1993:

Steve Bono
Kansas City Chiefs

	1995:	1994:
Passing TDS	21	4
Rushing TDS	5	0
TDS over 40 Yards	3	1
Total Passing Yards	3,121	796
Total Completions/Attempts	293/520	66/117
Average Yards per Game	195.1	132.7
Interceptions Thrown	10	4
Times Sacked	21	0
Games Played	16	6

I am still trying to figure out how a slow-moving mass like Bono can score 5 TDS! I really hate to rain on Bono's parade, but I think he is strictly a backup QB masquerading as a starter. The telling sign was how he crumbled by the end of the season and flaked-out in the playoffs. Bono could lead to greatness, but be warned: have a good backup!

Jim Harbaugh
Indianapolis Colts

	1995:	1994:	1993:
Passing TDS	17	9	7
Rushing TDS	2	0	4
TDS over 40 Yards	2	1	1
Total Passing Yards	2,575	1,440	2,002
Total Completions/Attempts	200/314	125/202	200/325
Average Yards per Game	171.6	160.0	133.5
Interceptions Thrown	5	6	11
Times Sacked	35	17	43
Games Played	15	9	15

Harbaugh was last season's feel-good story. This year, I'm sure he will produce, but 17 passing TDS is not the thing that makes fantasy championships. He should be relegated to the role of an offical backup guy!

Kerry Collins
Carolina Panthers

	1995:
Passing TDS	14
Rushing TDS	3
TDS over 40 Yards	4
Total Passing Yards	2,717
Total Completions/Attempts	214/433
Average Yards per Game	181.1
Interceptions Thrown	19
Times Sacked	24
Games Played	15

Collins was a surprise for such a young player on an expansion team. He performed exceptionally well and produced some solid numbers. Paterno loved him at the State Penn, and you should love him too. I rank him higher than more experienced young QBs such as Shuler, Frerotte, and especially Dilfer, simply because Carolina is tailoring their offense around him, and he has a great head for the game.

5 QB

Rick Mirer
Seattle Seahawks

	1995:	1994:	1993:
Passing TDs	13	11	12
Rushing TDs	1	0	3
TDs over 40 Yards	5	1	1
Total Passing Yards	2,564	2,151	2,833
Total Completions/Attempts	209/391	195/381	274/486
Average Yards per Game	170.9	165.5	177.1
Interceptions Thrown	20	7	17
Times Sacked	41	27	47
Games Played	15	13	16

Mirer appears to be on his way as a major bust for the *S'hawks*. Something has gone awry in his game—he stinks. It is crucial for Mirer to take charge of this team and produce! One guy I would search for on every passing down would be that toe-dancing speedster Joey (*Beep-Beep*) Galloway.

Heath Shuler
Washington Redskins

	1995:	1994:
Passing TDs	3	10
Rushing TDs	0	0
TDs over 40 Yards	0	5
Total Passing Yards	745	1,658
Total Completions/Attempts	66/125	120/265
Average Yards per Game	106.4	207.3
Interceptions Thrown	7	12
Times Sacked	13	12
Games Played	7	8

Baby Heath has heard a lot of cheers and praises during his high school and college days. In 1995, he heard something else from the fans in RFK—*boos*! This is his "make it or break it" opportunity this summer. Gus Frerotte was not traded and if Shuler falters, the job's Frerotte's—maybe for good!

Ty Detmer
Philadelphia Eagles

	1995:	1994:	1993:
Passing TDs	8	4	6
Rushing TDs	1	0	1
TDs over 40 Yards	0	1	1
Total Passing Yards	2,326	470	1,670
Total Completions/Attempts	215/375	33/56	157/252
Average Yards per Game	155.1	78.3	167.0
Interceptions Thrown	14	1	14
Times Sacked	30	4	34
Games Played	15	6	10

Detmer joins his second team in five years, hoping to break into a starting role. With Peete in front of him, and Randall out of work, this could be the year the *Ty-man* sees some playing time, and the NFL learns why he has a Heisman on the mantle!

Dave Brown
New York Giants

	1995:	1994:	1993:
Passing TDS	11	12	
Rushing TDS	4	2	
TDS over 40 Yards	3	2	
Total Passing Yards	2,814	2,536	
Total Completions/Attempts	254/456	201/350	
Average Yards per Game	175.9	169.1	
Interceptions Thrown	10	16	
Times Sacked	44	42	
Games Played	16	15	

Dave Brown is not exactly busting the graphs on the infamous FFL score-o-meter! He is kinda suffering from that same boring status of Vinny Testaverde—I mean, they look great in uniform, but they really don't shake out the stats the way you need your starters to!

Best of the Rest—

Chris Chandler
Houston Oilers

	1995:	1994:	1993:
Passing TDS	17	7	3
Rushing TDS	2	1	0
TDS over 40 Yards	4	2	0
Total Passing Yards	2,460	1,352	471
Total Completions/Attempts	225/356	108/176	52/103
Average Yards per Game	189.2	225.3	235.5
Interceptions Thrown	10	2	2
Times Sacked	21	7	4
Games Played	13	6	2

Ah, Mr. Chandler—how would you have done with an offensive line? I expect Chris Chandler to be the man, but the Oilers have an explosive backup in Steve McNair, and we could see Chandler yanked if he does not perform.

Chris Miller
St. Louis Rams

Passing TDS	18	16	1
Rushing TDS	0	0	0
TDS over 40 Yards	2	2	0
Total Passing Yards	2,623	2,104	345
Total Completions/Attempts	232/405	173/317	32/66
Average Yards per Game	201.8	210.4	172.5
Interceptions Thrown	15	14	3
Times Sacked	31	28	8
Games Played	13	10	2

Chris Miller has wisely chosen to retire (at least for now). It is my hope that Chris realizes that he doesn't have to play ball—he needs to stay healthy for his family. I applaud Miller's toughness but injuries and concussions have diminished his great talent.

Rodney Peete
Philadelphia Eagles

Passing TDS	8	4	6
Rushing TDS	1	0	1
TDS over 40 Yards	0	1	1
Total Passing Yards	2,326	470	1,670
Total Completions/Attempts	215/375	33/56	157/252
Average Yards per Game	155.1	78.3	167.0
Interceptions Thrown	14	1	14
Times Sacked	30	4	34
Games Played	15	6	10

I wouldn't place all my stock in Peete this season. Losing the quality pro Fred Barnett to Miami will hurt, even though Irving Fryar will be his replacement. Calvin Williams has been a disappointment and Peete could easily be the Detmer clipboard holder this year! ★

'96 Pre-Season Quarterback Ranking—

	Player:	Team:
1	Steve Young	San Francisco 49ers
2	Brett Favre	Green Bay Packers
3	Scott Mitchell	Detroit Lions
4	Dan Marino	Miami Dolphins
5	Jeff Blake	Cincinnati Bengals
6	Jeff George	Atlanta Falcons
7	Jim Kelly	Buffalo Bills
8	John Elway	Denver Broncos
9	Neil O'Donnell	New York Jets
10	Erik Kramer	Chicago Bears
11	Drew Bledsoe	New England Patriots
12	Mark Brunell	Jacksonville Jaguars
13	Jim Everett	New Orleans Saints
14	Jeff Hostetler	Oakland Raiders
15	Warren Moon	Minnesota Vikings
16	Stan Humphries	San Diego Chargers
17	Troy Aikman	Dallas Cowboys
18	Vinny Testaverde	Baltimore Ravens
19	Steve Bono	Kansas City Chiefs
20	Jim Harbaugh	Indianapolis Colts
21	Kerry Collins	Carolina Panthers
22	Rick Mirer	Seattle Seahawks
23	Heath Shuler	Washington Redskins
24	Ty Detmer	Philadelphia Eagles
25	Dave Brown	New York Giants
26	Boomer Esiason	Arizona Cardinals
27	Chris Chandler	Houston Oilers
28	Steve Walsh	St. Louis Rams
29	Trent Dilfer	Tampa Bay Buccaneers
30	Jim Miller	Pittsburgh Steelers
31	Gus Frerotte	Washington Redskins
32	Steve McNair	Houston Oilers
33	Kordell Stewart	Pittsburgh Steelers
34	Rodney Peete	Philadelphia Eagles
35	Randall Cunningham	Free Agent
36	Bobby Hebert	Atlanta Falcons
37	Craig Erickson	Indianapolis Colts
38	Elvis Grbac	San Francisco 49ers
39	Dave Krieg	Chicago Bears
40	Mike Tomczak	Pittsburgh Steelers
41	Frank Reich	New York Jets
42	Don Majkowski	Detroit Lions
43	Bernie Kosar	Miami Dolphins
44	Billy Joe Hobert	Oakland Raiders
45	Eric Zeier	Baltimore Ravens
46	Mark Rypien	St. Louis Rams
47	Alex Van Pelt	Buffalo Bills
48	John Friesz	Seattle Seahawks
49	Casey Weldon	Tampa Bay Buccaneers
50	Sean Salisbury	San Diego Chargers

5 QB

5
QB

6 Running Backs

Drafting Running Backs—

Your running back is always key in fantasy football. Face it, you get to start two players—so you have additional scoring opportunities. With this in mind, you really need to get at least two scores per week from running backs. Now add to this equation—if your league includes rushing stats, then it is imperative that you draft quality *full-time* backs that not only score, but can gain gobs of yards!

Obviously, the best performances for major *scoring* and *yardage* will come from guys like Emmitt Smith, Curtis Martin, Chris Warren, Marshall Faulk, Ricky Watters, Ki-Jana Carter, and Barry Sanders. These are *gimme picks* and all should have double-digit scoring barrages *and* 1,200-plus yard rushing seasons. That's a no-brainer. The key is being able to draft these guys before the rest of your league jumps in and ruins your draft plans.

The Running Back Draft Plan—

Okay, genius, you drafted Errict Rhett and Rodney Hampton early in the draft. You are feeling smug because you just know that they both will gain over 1,000 yards and score an easy dozen TDs each! So as the draft proceeds, you select receivers, kickers, etc., and suddenly you get that sickening feeling—what if either Rhett or Hampton go down with injuries? *Ugh*, you need to a grab some more capable running backs, but who the heck do you draft? Don't sweat the details, it's time to kick in with a running back draft plan!

Look, there are loads of running backs just waiting to bust loose, the trick is to find 'em and be lucky enough to have 'em perform well. Many players are going to be overlooked and underrated—i.e., Adrian Murrell, Mario Bates, Bernie Parmalee, Erric Pegram, etc. What about second year young bloods like Terrell Davis, Aaron Hayden, Napoleon Kaufman, Rodney Thomas, Ray Zellars, Jamal Anderson, or Darick Holmes? How about hot rookies like Lawrence Phillips, Eddie George, and Tim Biakabutuka? What about guys with bad reps but new homes: Natrone Means, Jerome Bettis, and Johnny Johnson? What if you opted to draft some of those *"catch a million passes"* type of running backs like Larry Centers, Kimble Anders, Brian Mitchell, Ronnie Harmon, Derek Loville, Amp Lee, and Aaron Craver?

So you see, there are plenty of good solid options to take when drafting your running backs. One of my friends will draft two players from the same team (i.e., Eddie George and Rodney Thomas) and see which player turns out to be the workhorse. Another league member likes to grab a backup to his key starter (i.e., Rodney Hampton and Tyrone Wheatley) and if Hampton goes out with an injury, he can scoot in Ty and not lose too much.

Bonus Scoring— In most FFL leagues, policy allows for bonus scoring. The bonus is based on distance scoring. The FFL suggests 40 yards as a distance barometer. Therefore, if a running back romps off for a 40-yard-plus TD run, he would receive double points. Another bonus comes when a running back catches a pass and scores a TD. If the yardage distance was 39 yards or under, the running back gets double points. If the pass play TD was 40 yards or more, the running back gets the famous "DOUBLE/DOUBLE!" The DOUBLE/DOUBLE is a rarity, but when it happens, it is *sooo sweet* and it's a back breaker for the other teams in your league!

Example Point System:

RB scores on a TD run 39 yards or less:	6 PTS
RB scores on a TD pass reception 39 yards or less:	12 PTS
RB scores on a TD run 40 yards or more:	12 PTS
RB scores on a TD pass 40 yards or more:	24 PTS

'95 DOUBLE/DOUBLES (40+ YD TDS)—

Player:	Team:	40+TDS:	Total TDS:
Barry Sanders	*Detroit Lions*	4	12
Emmitt Smith	*Dallas Cowboys*	1	25
Terrell Davis	*Denver Broncos*	1	8
Rodney Thomas	*Houston Oilers*	1	7
Mario Bates	*New Orleans Saints*	1	7
Charlie Garner	*Philadelphia Eagles*	1	6
Ronnie Harmon	*San Diego Chargers*	1	6
Robert Smith	*Minnesota Vikings*	1	5
Derrick Moore	*Carolina Panthers*	1	4
Kimble Anders	*Kansas City Chiefs*	1	3
Amp Lee	*Minnesota Vikings*	1	3
Sherman Williams	*Dallas Cowboys*	1	1

Free Agent Running Backs— This is a quirky situation, but there unfortunately will be running backs that get injured during the exhibition season. That will open the door for free agent running backs that are not on rosters due to the salary cap. Last season, for example, free agent runners like Barry Foster and Johnny Johnson completely blew opportunities to re-enter the league with the Bengals and 'Niners. Both would have pumped in some points for any franchise that may have gambled and selected them (in the late rounds, or in supplemental drafts). Unfortunately these two smart guys decided to spend the year in a hot tub watching their careers dwindle.

The key here is to watch where these players end up—some may sign prior to camp while others may sign during the exhibition or regular season. Players like Terry Allen, Robert Smith, and Lorenzo White could decide to sign with their old clubs if there are no takers. Do your homework and find out!

Player:	*Old Team:*
Terry Allen	*Washington Redskins*
Robert Smith	*Minnesota Vikings*
Gary Brown	*Houston Oilers*
Lorenzo White	*Baltimore Ravens*
Barry Foster	*Carolina Panthers/Cincinnati Bengals*
Todd McNair	*Houston Oilers*

Who are these guys? The True Sleepers—

Player:	*Team:*
Adrian Murrell	*New York Jets*
Darick Holmes	*Buffalo Bills*
Jamal Anderson	*Atlanta Falcons*
Zack Crockett	*Indianapolis Colts*
Dorsey Levens	*Green Bay Packers*
Tim Lester	*Pittsburgh Steelers*
James Stewart	*Jacksonville Jaguars*
Detron Smith	*Denver Broncos*

Question Marks at Running Back—

Marshall Faulk	Will he keep Zack Crockett and Lamont Warren on the bench *all game?* Is there really interest by Jimmy Johnson in trading for Marshall? *Wow!*
Ki-Jana Carter	Is he fully healed? If healthy, I say watch out!
Lawrence Phillips	Can this talent *run* straight and *stay* straight? No question on the talent meter—he will dominate now!
Errict Rhett	Is he going to freak out over the money situation? He wants more…*hey, that's a new concept!* Is he really going to hold out?
Terrell Davis	Is this 6th round '95 draft pick really that good? Will he *slide* or continue to *ride* in '96?
Tim Biakabutuka	*Wow, what wheels!* But will that groin pull cause problems in the future? Can he catch? We know he can run!
Jerome Bettis	Can Jerome take the hint that after two mediocre seasons, his career is on the line? Can Cowher spread his '*I love ya, man*' enthusiasm to Bettis?
Johnny Johnson	Talented and a bull lugging the football, but also can be poison in the locker room. Team game, J.J.—better join in or soon you'll be catching games on the tube.
William Floyd	Gutsy guy but many think he will not be ready at start of the season. I expect mid-season! Watch for his progress.
Aaron Hayden	He was all-world last season but now—without Natrone— can he blast up big numbers? It sure appears so!
Adrian Murrell	Finally Murrell gets his shot. I think he's a real sleeper and will be a steady producer. Still, he has zippo of a big time record.

Bernie Parmalee	Look, the guy can run, but will he *still* have to share the ball with 3-4 other running backs?
Terry Allen	Will he hold out too long? Will the *'Skins* eye rookie back Stephen Davis in the one back offense? Don't wait too long, Terry, Davis is a perfect fit!
Robert Smith	Quick feet, and super intelligence. Therefore Rob babe, be quick and use *da brain*! You're going to be replaced soon—wake up, genius!!!
David Meggett	Expect to see Meggett play better or, if not, look for him to be the Patriots' mascot next season!
Bam Morris	Put an "x" through this joker—for now, it appears that he will be tied up in legal matters. Cross him off!
Garrison Hearst	Supposedly he will play out this season on a one-year deal and bolt next season. He needs to produce because rookie Leland McElroy and ex-Packer LeShon Johnson are awfully hungry.
Tommy Vardell	With William Floyd out perhaps until midseason, the value of Tommy Vardell should be evident early. If healthy (*and that's a big if*), his receiving skills should be a plus.
Terry Kirby	The question is where does Kirby fit into Jimmy Johnson's game plans? Remember that J.J. has added rookies Karim Abdul-Jabbar and Stanley Pritchett.
Leroy Hoard	Okay, I am willing to give credit to HC Teddy Marchibroda that he will figure Leroy is a complete back and will play him full time. Still, I can guarantee that most members of your FFL league will back away from Hoard. ★

6
RB

'95 Top Receiving Running Backs—

Player:	Team:	RECEP:	YDS:	TDS:	GP:
Larry Centers	Arizona Cardinals	101	962	2	16
Derek Loville	San Francisco 49ers	87	662	3	16
Amp Lee	Minnesota Vikings	71	558	1	16
Adrian Murrell	New York Jets	71	465	2	15
Terry Kirby	Miami Dolphins	66	618	3	16
Ronnie Harmon	San Diego Chargers	62	662	5	16
Ricky Watters	Philadelphia Eagles	62	434	1	16
Emmitt Smith	Dallas Cowboys	62	375	0	16
Edgar Bennett	Green Bay Packers	61	648	4	16
Earnest Byner	Cleveland Browns	61	494	2	16
Todd McNair	Houston Oilers	60	501	1	15
Marshall Faulk	Indianapolis Colts	56	475	3	16
Harvey Williams	Oakland Raiders	55	375	0	16
Kimble Anders	Kansas City Chiefs	55	349	1	16
Dave Meggett	New England Patriots	52	334	0	16
Keith Byars	Miami Dolphins	51	362	2	16
Terrell Davis	Denver Broncos	49	367	1	14
Dorsey Levens	Green Bay Packers	48	434	4	15
Barry Sanders	Detroit Lions	48	398	1	16
William Floyd	San Francisco 49ers	47	348	1	8
Eric Bienemy	Cincinnati Bengals	43	424	0	16
Aaron Craver	Denver Broncos	43	369	1	16
Bernie Parmalee	Miami Dolphins	39	345	1	16
Rodney Thomas	Houston Oilers	39	204	2	16
Brian Mitchell	Washington Redskins	38	324	1	16
Johnny Bailey	St. Louis Rams	38	265	0	12
Craig Heyward	Atlanta Falcons	37	350	2	16
Derek Brown	New Orleans Saints	35	266	1	16
Derrick Fenner	Oakland Raiders	35	252	3	16
Chris Warren	Seattle Seahawks	35	247	1	16
Herschel Walker	New York Giants	31	234	1	16
Terry Allen	Washington Redskins	31	232	1	16
Curtis Martin	New England Patriots	30	261	1	16
Daryl Johnston	Dallas Cowboys	30	248	1	16
Bob Christian	Carolina Panthers	29	255	1	15
Garrison Hearst	Arizona Cardinals	29	243	1	16
Anthony Johnson	Carolina Panthers	29	207	0	15
Robert Green	Chicago Bears	28	246	0	12
Marcus Allen	Kansas City Chiefs	27	210	0	16
Harold Green	Cincinnati Bengals	27	182	1	15
Sam Gash	New England Patriots	26	242	1	15
Thurman Thomas	Buffalo Bills	26	220	2	14
Erric Pegram	Pittsburgh Steelers	26	206	1	15
Marc Logan	Washington Redskins	25	276	2	16
Darick Holmes	Buffalo Bills	24	214	0	16
Rodney Hampton	New York Giants	24	142	0	16
John L. Williams	Pittsburgh Steelers	24	127	1	12
Glyn Milburn	Denver Broncos	22	191	10	16

Player:	Team:	RECEP:	YDS:	TDS:	GP:
Roosevelt Potts	Indianapolis Colts	21	228	1	15
James Stewart	Jacksonville Jaguars	21	190	1	14
James Joseph	Cincinnati Bengals	20	118	0	16
Leshai Maston	Jacksonville Jaguars	18	131	0	16
Mario Bates	New Orleans Saints	18	114	0	16
Jerome Bettis	St. Louis Rams	18	106	0	15
Lamont Warren	Indianapolis Colts	17	159	0	12
Leonard Russell	St. Louis Rams	16	89	0	13
Fred Mcafee	Pittsburgh Steelers	15	88	0	16
Errict Rhett	Tampa Bay Buccaneers	14	110	0	16
Leroy Hoard	Cleveland Browns	13	103	0	12
Vince Workman	Indianapolis Colts	13	74	0	10
Adam Walker	San Francisco 49ers	11	78	0	14
Steve Broussard	Seattle Seahawks	10	94	0	15
Charlie Garner	Philadelphia Eagles	10	61	0	15
Keith Elias	New York Jets	9	69	0	15
Napoleon Kaufman	Oakland Raiders	9	62	0	16
Leroy Thompson	Kansas City Chiefs	9	37	0	16
Lorenzo White	Cleveland Browns	8	64	0	13
Ronald Moore	New York Jets	8	50	0	15
Jeff Cothran	Cincinnati Bengals	8	44	0	15
Bam Morris	Pittsburgh Steelers	8	36	0	13
Rashaan Salaam	Chicago Bears	7	56	0	16
Natrone Means	San Diego Chargers	7	46	0	10
Greg Hill	Kansas City Chiefs	7	45	0	16
Jerry Ellison	Tampa Bay Buccaneers	7	44	0	16
Robert Smith	Minnesota Vikings	7	35	0	9
Charles Way	New York Giants	6	65	1	16
Tommy Vardell	Cleveland Browns	6	18	0	5
Gary Brown	Houston Oilers	6	16	0	9
Randy Jordan	Jacksonville Jaguars	5	89	1	12
Rod Bernstine	Denver Broncos	5	54	0	3
Aaron Hayden	San Diego Chargers	5	53	0	6
Earnest Hunter	Cleveland Browns	5	42	0	10
Tyrone Wheatley	New York Giants	5	27	0	13
Richie Anderson	New York Jets	5	26	0	10
Rodney Culver	San Diego Chargers	5	21	0	8
Irving Spikes	Miami Dolphins	5	18	1	9
Derrick Moore	Carolina Panthers	5	11	0	13
Jamal Anderson	Atlanta Falcons	4	42	0	16
Scottie Graham	Minnesota Vikings	4	30	0	16
Reggie Rivers	Denver Broncos	3	32	0	16
Sherman Williams	Dallas Cowboys	3	28	0	11
Terrell Fletcher	San Diego Chargers	3	26	0	16
Blair Thomas	Carolina Panthers	3	24	0	7
William Henderson	Green Bay Packers	3	21	0	15
Derrick Ned	New Orleans Saints	3	9	0	12
Jamal Willis	San Francisco 49ers	3	8	0	12

6 RB

'96 Running Back Review—

Emmitt Smith
Dallas Cowboys

	1995:	1994:	1993:
Rushing TDS	25	21	9
Receiving TDS	0	1	1
TDS over 10 Yards	7	1	3
Total Rushing Yards	1,773	1,484	1,486
Total Receiving Yards	375	341	414
Total Attempts	377	368	283
Average Rush Yards/Game	110.8	98.9	106.1
Average Receiving Yards/Game	23.4	22.7	26.9
Games Played	16	15	14

Stick with Emmitt!
Stick with Emmitt until he shows signs of slowing down! The guy is a fierce competitor and he is on a level all by himself. What other RB is going to get your team 25 TDS? *Emmitt is the Michael Jordan of football*—downright serious, capable of growing with his immense talent, and possesses the knowledge of *what it takes to win!* Even with an aging offensive line and the off-the-field troubles of his teammates, *you gotta expect a mid-20's-TD performance from this guy!*

Curtis Martin
New England Patriots

Rushing TDS	14
Receiving TDS	1
TDS over 10 Yards	1
Total Rushing Yards	1,487
Total Receiving Yards	261
Total Attempts	368
Average Rush Yards/Game	92.9
Average Receiving Yards/Game	16.3
Games Played	16

Curtis Martin was a third round pick and he has proven to be invaluable already. I kept expecting Martin to fizzle out, but he really blasted through! According to inside sources, Martin has a burning desire to enter the top echelon of NFL backs currently presided over by *Sir Emmitt Smith*. The word "*quit*" is not in Curtis Martin's vocabulary! You can expect similar results this year, with an up side of HC Parcells *inventing new ways to get this guy scores!*

		1995:	1994:	1993:
Chris Warren	Rushing TDS	15	9	7
Seattle Seahawks	Receiving TDS	1	2	0
	TDS over 10 Yards	7	6	3
	Total Rushing Yards	1,346	1,545	1,072
	Total Receiving Yards	247	323	99
	Total Attempts	310	333	273
	Average Rush Yards/Game	84.1	96.6	7.1
	Average Receiving Yards/Game	15.4	20.2	26.9
	Games Played	16	16	14

You can't go wrong with Chris Warren and it's great to see this solid RB finally achieve recognition! Warren is a *stud* and with an im-proved offensive scheme, he should continue to flourish. There were a ton of distractions for the Seahawks last season and hopefully second year HC Dennis Erickson can quell the storm. Warren is set for another 15 TDS!

Ki-Jana Carter	Rushing TDS	*(Injured)*		
Cincinnati Bengals	Receiving TDS			
	TDS over 10 Yards			
	Total Rushing Yards			
	Total Receiving Yards			
	Total Attempts			
	Average Rush Yards/Game			
	Average Receiving Yards/Game			
	Games Played			

I fully expect Ki-Jana to be ready this season and crunch out some hefty numbers. This Bengal offense lacks only a punishing runner and Carter fits this description to the "T." Ki-Jana is not a "*take-the-money-and-run*" kind of guy and he will want to show the NFL that he is a legitimate superstar worthy of the hype.

		1995:	1994:
Marshall Faulk	Rushing TDs	11	11
Indianapolis Colts	Receiving TDs	3	1
	TDs over 10 Yards	6	4
	Total Rushing Yards	1,073	1,282
	Total Receiving Yards	475	522
	Total Attempts	289	314
	Average Rush Yards/Game	67.4	80.1
	Average Receiving Yards/Game	29.7	32.6
	Games Played	16	16

Wow, how can so many folks so suddenly begin to doubt Marshall Faulk's drive and ability? Critics are now sniping at "*the Marshall*" for suddenly becoming injury-prone and losing his desire. Keep this point in the back of your mind—no less than the talented guru, HC Jimmy Johnson, has been drooling over the prospect of trading for Faulk! What a perfect marriage! We could call it, "*In search of Emmitt Smith!*"

Ricky Watters	Rushing TDs	11	6	10
Philadelphia Eagles	Receiving TDs	1	5	1
	TDs over 10 Yards	0	4	3
	Total Rushing Yards	1,273	877	950
	Total Receiving Yards	434	719	326
	Total Attempts	337	239	208
	Average Rush Yards/Game	79.6	54.8	73.1
	Average Receiving Yards/Game	27.1	44.9	25.1
	Games Played	16	16	13

All right now, will someone kindly explain to me how the '*Niners* didn't miss Ricky in '95? After "*Runnin*" Watters' initial self-serving week one outbreak, he finally woke up and realized, "*Hey, I am no longer in 'Frisco! These Philly fans will stomp me if I don't grow up and deliver!*" Deliver he did and he should fare even better with Kevin Turner returning as a blocking backs.

		1995:	1994:	1993:
Barry Sanders *Detroit Lions*	Rushing TDS	11	7	3
	Receiving TDS	1	1	0
	TDS over 10 Yards	6	5	2
	Total Rushing Yards	1,500	1,883	1,115
	Total Receiving Yards	398	283	205
	Total Attempts	314	331	243
	Average Rush Yards/Game	93.8	117.7	79.6
	Average Receiving Yards/Game	24.9	17.7	18.6
	Games Played	16	16	11

Someone must have whispered rather loudly into Wayne Fontes' ear to "*Let Barry Score!*" I figure that Fontes is running out of time and Barry ain't getting any younger, so expect to see Barry carry an *Emmitt Smith* type of workload!

Lawrence Phillips *St. Louis Rams*	Rushing TDS	(Rookie)
	Receiving TDS	
	TDS over 10 Yards	
	Total Rushing Yards	
	Total Receiving Yards	
	Total Attempts	
	Average Rush Yards/Game	
	Average Receiving Yards/Game	
	Games Played	

Two years ago I was predicting that Jerome Bettis would be the *king of the road* in the Rams organization. Bettis is now back east, thanks to a draft-day trade with Pittsburgh. Well, here I am this year predicting that if Lawrence Phillips can put his troublesome past behind him and concentrate on the NFL, he has the potential to be the big, bruising back the Rams so desperately want and need!

	1995:	1994:	1993:

Errict Rhett
Tampa Bay Buccaneers

	1995:	1994:
Rushing TDS	11	7
Receiving TDS	0	0
TDS over 10 Yards	2	0
Total Rushing Yards	1,207	1,011
Total Receiving Yards	110	119
Total Attempts	334	284
Average Rush Yards/Game	75.4	63.2
Average Receiving Yards/Game	6.9	7.4
Games Played	16	16

As I am writing this section, the word out of Tampa is that Rhett is not a happy man over the amount of money that he is making! A content Rhett would be worth a sizable dozen TDs. If he holds out for more money, expect rookie FB Mike Alstott and/or Jerry Ellison—who spelled Rhett last season and looked good—to step in, although I look for Rhett to be back no later than the second game to help his poor *Buckaroos* out.

Terrell Davis
Denver Broncos

	1995:
Rushing TDS	7
Receiving TDS	1
TDS over 10 Yards	1
Total Rushing Yards	1,117
Total Receiving Yards	367
Total Attempts	237
Average Rush Yards/Game	79.8
Average Receiving Yards/Game	26.2
Games Played	14

Okay, quick...how many of us expected a sixth-round pick to carry the Broncos ground game in '95? Davis was much like fellow rookie Curtis Martin, as he was a surprise to many experts. They were so impressed with Davis that Rod Bernstine went bye-bye before the season was over. As for scoring, my only question would be will Davis carry the ball on the goal line or will rookie FB Detron Smith? And how does Aaron Craver fit into the picture?

	1995:	1994:	1993:

Edgar Bennett
Green Bay Packers

	1995:	1994:	1993:
Rushing TDS	3	5	9
Receiving TDS	4	4	1
TDS over 10 Yards	4	3	2
Total Rushing Yards	1,067	623	550
Total Receiving Yards	648	546	457
Total Attempts	316	178	159
Average Rush Yards/Game	66.7	38.9	34.3
Average Receiving Yards/Game	40.5	34.1	28.6
Games Played	16	16	16

6 RB

Bennett will never be Emmitt Smith, but he can do two things exceptionally well—catch the ball from out of the backfield and score! Bennett is the kind of player that can easily score 5-6 TDS on pass plays—and in FFL scoring, *that's double points, gang*! You can't go wrong making him your second back!

Tim Biakabutuka
Carolina Panthers

Rushing TDS		(Rookie)	
Receiving TDS			
TDS over 10 Yards			
Total Rushing Yards			
Total Receiving Yards			
Total Attempts			
Average Rush Yards/Game			
Average Receiving Yards/Game			
Games Played			

The Panthers, who are bringing as many RBS into camp as they are water bottles, are really high on this draft choice from Michigan. Expect him to start, expect him to post good numbers, and expect Chris Berman to have a *cool nickname* for him by August! I wouldn't be surprised if he did a *Terrell Davis* or a *Curtis Martin*, and pounded out 10 or more TDS.

Eddie George
Houston Oilers

Rushing TDS		(Rookie)	
Receiving TDS			
TDS over 10 Yards			
Total Rushing Yards			
Total Receiving Yards			
Total Attempts			
Average Rush Yards/Game			
Average Receiving Yards/Game			
Games Played			

This young player has a Heisman to show for his excellent work at Ohio State, but can he turn that into NFL success? My bet is *yes*! Look for him to start within a month, and I can't wait for him to settle in and blow'em away in Houston/Nashville, *a la Earl Campbell*.

		1995:	1994:	1993:
Aaron Hayden *San Diego Chargers*	Rushing TDS	3		
	Receiving TDS	0		
	TDS over 10 Yards	0		
	Total Rushing Yards	470		
	Total Receiving Yards	53		
	Total Attempts	128		
	Average Rush Yards/Game	78.3		
	Average Receiving Yards/Game	8.8		
	Games Played	6		

The *Lightning Bolts* made several changes in the offense, one being Aaron Hayden replacing Natrone Means. Hayden is another in the long line of Bobby Beathard gems. His slashing, bull-rushing style will equate into a ton of yards and scores!

		1995:	1994:	1993:
Rashaan Salaam *Chicago Bears*	Rushing TDS	10		
	Receiving TDS	0		
	TDS over 10 Yards	1		
	Total Rushing Yards	1,074		
	Total Receiving Yards	56		
	Total Attempts	296		
	Average Rush Yards/Game	67.1		
	Average Receiving Yards/Game	3.5		
	Games Played	16		

Here's another guy that can easily blow you away! Wannstedt likes him, and the Bears have a long history of great RBs, so you can feel warm and fuzzy drafting him as your second or third back, as he gets over last year's rookie jitters and pounds home 9-12 scores.

		1995:	1994:	1993:
Rodney Hampton *New York Giants*	Rushing TDS	10	6	5
	Receiving TDS	0	0	0
	TDS over 10 Yards	0	1	1
	Total Rushing Yards	1,182	1,075	1,007
	Total Receiving Yards	142	546	210
	Total Attempts	306	327	292
	Average Rush Yards/Game	73.9	76.8	83.9
	Average Receiving Yards/Game	8.9	23.4	17.5
	Games Played	16	14	12

I really thought that this season he would be playing on the *Left Coast* with the *'Niners*, especially since Tyrone Wheatley was a number one pick and appears ready for prime time. I expect Hampton to continue to dominate, but could be used more and more around the goal line, with Reeves using Wheatley as the mid-field burner.

		1995:	1994:	1993:
Mario Bates	Rushing TDS	7	6	
New Orleans Saints	Receiving TDS	0	0	
	TDS over 10 Yards	2	2	
	Total Rushing Yards	951	579	
	Total Receiving Yards	114	62	
	Total Attempts	245	151	
	Average Rush Yards/Game	59.4	52.6	
	Average Receiving Yards/Game	7.1	6.0	
	Games Played	16	11	

Bates appears to have Jim Mora's confidence, and could be in store for a 1,000-yard season. He is young, tough, and not a bad second RB pick.

6
RB

		1995:	1994:	1993:
Adrian Murrell	Rushing TDS	1	0	1
New York Jets	Receiving TDS	2	0	0
	TDS over 10 Yards	1	0	1
	Total Rushing Yards	795	160	157
	Total Receiving Yards	465	76	0
	Total Attempts	192	32	34
	Average Rush Yards/Game	53.0	17.8	13.1
	Average Receiving Yards/Game	31.0	8.4	0.0
	Games Played	15	9	12

I put this guy in my sleeper category, and he could easily become another Edgar Bennett—just a steady work horse that *double-dips*, catching balls out of the backfield as well as pounding out the yards on the ground. Keep your eyes on this one!

		1995:	1994:	1993:
Johnny Johnson	Rushing TDS	*(Did not*	3	3
San Francisco 49ers	Receiving TDS	*play)*	2	1
	TDS over 10 Yards		0	2
	Total Rushing Yards		931	821
	Total Receiving Yards		303	641
	Total Attempts		240	198
	Average Rush Yards/Game		58.2	54.7
	Average Receiving Yards/Game		18.9	13.2
	Games Played		16	15

Johnson steps into the perfect opportunity at '*Frisco*: William Floyd is recovering from a major knee injury, Ricky Watters is sorely missed, and Derek Loville is an underachiever! If Johnson is going to make it anywhere, it will be here. The above numbers came from a poorly schemed Jets offense; look for Seifert to bring him into the fold *quickly*.

		1995:	1994:	1993:
Harvey Williams *Oakland Raiders*	Rushing TDs	9	4	
	Receiving TDs	0	3	
	TDs over 10 Yards	1	1	
	Total Rushing Yards	1,114	983	
	Total Receiving Yards	375	391	
	Total Attempts	255	282	
	Average Rush Yards/Game	69.6	61.4	
	Average Receiving Yards/Game	23.4	24.4	
	Games Played	16	16	

I have finally been vindicated! For several years I had promoted Williams as a *can't-miss* scorer and a quality player. And each season he played as if he was standing in an elevator! He was a major bust at best! But just when I said, *"A pox on his career,"* he played this past season as if his name was *Rocky*. The Raiders will use Williams and Kaufman to tear up the field in Oakland.

		1995:	1994:	1993:
Terry Allen *Washington Redskins*	Rushing TDs	10	8	*(Injured)*
	Receiving TDs	1	0	
	TDs over 10 Yards	0	2	
	Total Rushing Yards	1,309	1,031	
	Total Receiving Yards	232	148	
	Total Attempts	338	368	
	Average Rush Yards/Game	81.8	64.4	
	Average Receiving Yards/Game	14.5	9.3	
	Games Played	16	16	

Terry Allen truly had a solid season and is playing on *two surgically-repaired knees!* He is holding out, and if he fails to come to terms could see his job fall to Stephen Davis. However, if he signs, I expect another 1,000-yard, 10-12 TD season for Allen in '96 and for Terry to remain the key component of the *'Skins* offense!

		1995:	1994:	1993:
Bernie Parmalee *Miami Dolphins*	Rushing TDs	9	6	
	Receiving TDs	1	1	
	TDs over 10 Yards	3	2	
	Total Rushing Yards	878	868	
	Total Receiving Yards	345	249	
	Total Attempts	236	216	
	Average Rush Yards/Game	54.9	66.8	
	Average Receiving Yards/Game	21.6	19.2	
	Games Played	16	13	

I don't think that Jimmy Johnson will be using a dozen RBs like Don Shula did. Johnson really would like to swing a deal to grab Marshall Faulk, but that may not happen. I think Bernie Parmalee would be closer to the mark as a 22-25 carry per game kind of back that J.J. would prefer!

		1995:	1994:	1993:
Natrone Means *Jacksonville Jaguars*	Rushing TDs	5	12	8
	Receiving TDs	0	0	0
	TDs over 10 Yards	1	3	2
	Total Rushing Yards	730	1,350	645
	Total Receiving Yards	46	235	59
	Total Attempts	186	343	160
	Average Rush Yards/Game	73.0	84.4	40.3
	Average Receiving Yards/Game	4.6	14.7	3.7
	Games Played	10	16	16

What a major disappointment last season. His injury, coupled with a bad attitude, cost Natrone a job with the Chargers. He was plucked off the waiver wire by the *Jags* and at only 24 years old, he should have plenty of power to rumble. My question is what happens to James Stewart? Can Means handle boot camp with HC Tom Coughlin? If so, look for him to pound out 10-12 TDs and 1,000 yards.

		1995:	1994:	1993:
Craig Heyward *Atlanta Falcons*	Rushing TDs	6	7	0
	Receiving TDs	2	1	0
	TDs over 10 Yards	0	0	0
	Total Rushing Yards	1,083	779	206
	Total Receiving Yards	350	335	0
	Total Attempts	236	183	68
	Average Rush Yards/Game	67.7	48.7	12.9
	Average Receiving Yards/Game	21.9	20.9	0
	Games Played	16	16	16

Ironhead has slimmed that 300 LB weight down to a *svelte* 260 and his hard work is paying off. Expect another solid season, but keep a left eye open and watch out for Jamal Anderson—he could steal some playing time from *Ironhead*.

		1995:	1994:	1993:
Thurman Thomas *Buffalo Bills*	Rushing TDs	6	7	6
	Receiving TDs	2	2	0
	TDs over 10 Yards	2	3	0
	Total Rushing Yards	1,005	1,093	1,315
	Total Receiving Yards	220	349	387
	Total Attempts	267	287	355
	Average Rush Yards/Game	71.8	72.9	82.2
	Average Receiving Yards/Game	15.7	23.3	24.2
	Games Played	14	15	16

Thermal is nearing the end of a successful career and is no longer the head-of-steam that he once was. He has mellowed out a bit and actually seems to be enjoying Buffalo and playing. A hot-handed Jim Kelly and relief from second-year RB Darick Holmes could extend his career and help him snatch 9-10 TDs.

	1995:	1994:	1993:
Jerome Bettis — *Pittsburgh Steelers*			
Rushing TDs	3	3	7
Receiving TDs	0	1	0
TDs over 10 Yards	0	0	2
Total Rushing Yards	637	1,025	1,429
Total Receiving Yards	106	293	244
Total Attempts	183	319	294
Average Rush Yards/Game	42.5	64.1	89.3
Average Receiving Yards/Game	7.1	18.3	15.3
Games Played	15	16	16

6 RB

Even though Bettis performed *well under expectations* with the Rams, he should get quite a bit of playing time, since the fate of Bam Morris is currently unknown! True, he will contend with Erric Pegram for the starting role, but look for Bettis to do great things in Pittsburgh under HC Bill Cowher.

James Stewart — *Jacksonville Jaguars*	
Rushing TDs	2
Receiving TDs	1
TDs over 10 Yards	0
Total Rushing Yards	525
Total Receiving Yards	190
Total Attempts	137
Average Rush Yards/Game	37.5
Average Receiving Yards/Game	13.6
Games Played	14

Stewart has to be scratching his head over the '*Jags* grabbing Natrone Means. After all, Stewart was being groomed to tote the pigskin this season. If Means shows up in shape and ready to play—Stewart will be strictly backup material. I would wait until the eleventh hour to make up your mind on Stewart.

Greg Hill — *Kansas City Chiefs*		
Rushing TDs	1	1
Receiving TDs	0	0
TDs over 10 Yards	0	0
Total Rushing Yards	667	574
Total Receiving Yards	45	92
Total Attempts	155	141
Average Rush Yards/Game	41.7	35.9
Average Receiving Yards/Game	2.8	5.8
Games Played	16	16

Memo to KC: Turn Greg Hill loose and see if he can play!
Placing the rushing hopes on the shoulders of a 35 year-old RB is not wise. Greg Hill has performed well in mop-up time and has gained over 1,200 yards in his first two seasons. I say with a fulltime job in the Chiefs' offense, he could rush for 1,200 yards in *one* season.

		1995:	1994:	1993:
William Floyd *San Francisco 49ers*	Rushing TDS	2	6	
	Receiving TDS	1	0	
	TDS over 10 Yards	0	1	
	Total Rushing Yards	237	305	
	Total Receiving Yards	348	196	
	Total Attempts	64	87	
	Average Rush Yards/Game	29.6	20.3	
	Average Receiving Yards/Game	43.5	13.1	
	Games Played	8	15	

I don't expect to see much of Floyd in the summer, but I do expect this hard-working fullback to make a solid recovery and by mid-season play a pivotal role in the *'Niner* offense. After last season, the *'Niners* will cherish the opportunity to use Floyd, Johnny Johnson, and Tommy Vardell to pound the ball around the goal line.

Rodney Thomas *Houston Oilers*	Rushing TDS	5		
	Receiving TDS	2		
	TDS over 10 Yards	2		
	Total Rushing Yards	947		
	Total Receiving Yards	204		
	Total Attempts	251		
	Average Rush Yards/Game	59.2		
	Average Receiving Yards/Game	12.8		
	Games Played	16		

Last season it was "*Move over Gary Brown, here comes Rodney Thomas!*" This year it should be "*Move over Rodney Thomas*" with the entrance of Eddie George. Still, I am intrigued with how the Oilers may use Thomas around the goal line. One concern with *Hot Rod* is fumbles, but expect him to show up ready to play and do battle with George.

Darick Holmes *Buffalo Bills*	Rushing TDS	4		
	Receiving TDS	0		
	TDS over 10 Yards	1		
	Total Rushing Yards	698		
	Total Receiving Yards	214		
	Total Attempts	172		
	Average Rush Yards/Game	43.6		
	Average Receiving Yards/Game	13.4		
	Games Played	16		

I am crazy about this guy! Expect more involvement and more carries and the job as designated goal line scorer. With Jim Kelly *nickle-and-diming* opposing offenses, Darick will be a welcome relief for the 30-year-old Thurman Thomas.

Napoleon Kaufman
Oakland Raiders

	1995:
Rushing TDS	1
Receiving TDS	0
TDS over 10 Yards	2
Total Rushing Yards	490
Total Receiving Yards	62
Total Attempts	108
Average Rush Yards/Game	30.6
Average Receiving Yards/Game	3.9
Games Played	16

Throw out last season! Hostetler was injured and the Raiders seemed confused on how they wanted to use Nap Kaufman. I expect that a healthy *Hoss* will hit him swinging out of the backfield and he should carry the ball 10-12 times a game. Whenever Nap touches the ball, he will be a threat to score.

Brian Mitchell
Washington Redskins

	1995:	1994:	1993:
Rushing TDS	1	0	3
Receiving TDS	1	1	0
TDS over 10 Yards	3	3	1
Total Rushing Yards	301	311	246
Total Receiving Yards	324	236	157
Total Attempts	46	78	63
Average Rush Yards/Game	18.8	19.4	15.4
Average Receiving Yards/Game	20.2	14.8	9.8
Games Played	16	16	16

Brian Mitchell has firmly established himself in D.C. as a fan favorite—a guy that can hurt a defense in a variety of interesting ways. Trouble is, the *'Skins* have about four full-time RBS ahead of him, and he does not play from the backfield as much as he would like.
One thing that worked last year was using him as a decoy, as a receiver out of the backfield, and as a recipient of the Shuler special—a shovel pass. Nevertheless, HC Norv Turner realizes what a treasure Mitchell really is! You will continue to see him used as the *ultimate utility player*! Plus, he remains one of the best punt and kick returners in the league—if your league scores points for a RB returning kicks or punts, then you are in for a trip to *Bonus City*!

	1995:	1994:	1993:
Leroy Hoard — *Baltimore Ravens*			
Rushing TDS	0	5	0
Receiving TDS	0	4	0
TDS over 10 Yards	0	4	0
Total Rushing Yards	547	890	227
Total Receiving Yards	103	445	351
Total Attempts	136	209	56
Average Rush Yards/Game	45.6	55.6	15.1
Average Receiving Yards/Game	8.6	27.8	21.9
Games Played	12	16	15

While checking the above numbers on Leroy, note that *he performs well every other year*—therefore, this will be an "*on*" year. HC Teddy Marchibroda will focus on Hoard and I predict that his numbers will rise. Why Bill Belichick ignored Hoard last season is a mystery! Sure, Earnest Byner is still in the picture, but he isn't the banger or receiver that Hoard is!

	1995:	1994:	1993:
Robert Smith — *Minnesota Vikings*			
Rushing TDS	5	1	2
Receiving TDS	0	0	0
TDS over 10 Yards	2	1	1
Total Rushing Yards	632	106	399
Total Receiving Yards	35	105	111
Total Attempts	139	31	82
Average Rush Yards/Game	70.2	8.2	49.9
Average Receiving Yards/Game	3.9	8.1	13.9
Games Played	9	13	8

Hmmm—the Vikings stable is jammed with a zillion RBS! *Soooo*—where does smart guy Robert Smith fit in? Good question, since the *Vikes*' patience with Smith and all his nagging injuries is very thin. But Smith is a gamebreaker and frankly better than anyone else in the *Vikes*' stable!

6 RB

6 RB

Terry Kirby
Miami Dolphins

	1995:	1994:	1993:
Rushing TDs	3	2	3
Receiving TDs	3	0	3
TDs over 10 Yards	4	0	4
Total Rushing Yards	414	233	390
Total Receiving Yards	618	154	874
Total Attempts	108	60	119
Average Rush Yards/Game	25.9	58.3	24.4
Average Receiving Yards/Game	38.6	38.5	54.6
Games Played	16	4	16

We've already said that we don't think Jimmy Johnson will use the "*RB by committee*" approach that Shula used. That said, I still feel that Kirby, teamed up with Parmalee, is a dynamite combo. Look for him to continue to be used to spell Parmalee, plus catch balls out of the backfield.

Leland McElroy
Arizona Cardinals

Rushing TDs	(Rookie)		
Receiving TDs			
TDs over 10 Yards			
Total Rushing Yards			
Total Receiving Yards			
Total Attempts			
Average Rush Yards/Game			
Average Receiving Yards/Game			
Games Played			

This guy tore up the Lone Star State at Texas A&M, and will compete against tough-minded Larry Centers and Garrison Hearst for the backfield job.

Erric Pegram
Pittsburgh Steelers

	1995:	1994:	1993:
Rushing TDs	5	1	3
Receiving TDs	1	0	0
TDs over 10 Yards	0	0	1
Total Rushing Yards	813	358	1,185
Total Receiving Yards	206	76	302
Total Attempts	213	103	292
Average Rush Yards/Game	54.2	27.5	79.0
Average Receiving Yards/Game	13.7	5.8	20.1
Games Played	15	13	15

Erric Pegram may see plenty of action because he will compete with that load Jerome Bettis. Pegram can deliver, and Bettis is a major question mark—this should prove interesting with HC Bill Cowher. Cowher is a blood-and-guts guy and he won't appreciate any display of laziness or malcontent. Look for Pegram to improve in the heat of increased competition.

	1995:	1994:	1993:
Larry Centers — *Arizona Cardinals*			
Rushing TDS	2	5	2
Receiving TDS	2	2	0
TDS over 10 Yards	2	1	3
Total Rushing Yards	254	336	152
Total Receiving Yards	962	647	603
Total Attempts	78	115	25
Average Rush Yards/Game	15.9	21.0	10.1
Average Receiving Yards/Game	60.1	40.4	40.2
Games Played	16	16	15

With Boomer at the controls, Larry should see plenty of short passes and opportunities to set himself up to score. He faced some personal problems and skipped the Pro Bowl, but he should regroup and have a terrific season.

Charlie Garner — *Philadelphia Eagles*

	1995	1994
Rushing TDS	6	3
Receiving TDS	0	0
TDS over 10 Yards	2	1
Total Rushing Yards	588	399
Total Receiving Yards	242	74
Total Attempts	108	5
Average Rush Yards/Game	39.2	39.9
Average Receiving Yards/Game	4.1	7.4
Games Played	15	10

Philly will be using a good RB field of Ricky Watters, Kevin Turner and Charlie Garner. Watters runs and catches well, Turner blocks and catches well, and Garner simply rushes very well. Charlie showed himself to be a great, explosive runner, and I feel that he could start as the main guy on a team without Watters. Give Garner a shot as your third back, and sit back and watch how he is used in camp and during the preseason.

Tyrone Wheatley — *New York Giants*

	1995
Rushing TDS	1
Receiving TDS	0
TDS over 10 Yards	1
Total Rushing Yards	245
Total Receiving Yards	27
Total Attempts	78
Average Rush Yards/Game	18.8
Average Receiving Yards/Game	2.1
Games Played	13

After signing that contract, Hampton is clearly the man in New York. However, last season the Giants used him every third series and they plan on doing the same this season. The talent is there, so keep an eye on how he looks in training camp. He could be worth taking as your last running back.

	1995:	1994:	1993:
Garrison Hearst *Arizona Cardinals*			
Rushing TDs	1	1	1
Receiving TDs	1	0	0
TDs over 10 Yards	0	1	0
Total Rushing Yards	1,070	169	264
Total Receiving Yards	243	49	18
Total Attempts	284	37	76
Average Rush Yards/Game	66.9	21.1	44.0
Average Receiving Yards/Game	15.2	6.1	3.0
Games Played	16	8	6

6 RB

By this point in Hearst's career, we should be comparing him to Emmitt Smith. Unfortunately we still don't know if Hearst can play at this level. The shame for Hearst is that the Cards drafted Leland McElroy and he will surpass Hearst in 1996. I think that Hearst will be peddled off to someone else by the summer—I see no room in Arizona for him.

Zack Crockett
Indianapolis Colts

Rushing TDs	0
Receiving TDs	0
TDs over 10 Yards	0
Total Rushing Yards	0
Total Receiving Yards	35
Total Attempts	2
Average Rush Yards/Game	0
Average Receiving Yards/Game	2.2
Games Played	16

Crockett is a sensational back who never plays, because he is playing behind a legitimate superstar. This guy only plays when Marshall Faulk is tired or hurt, so don't waste your time!

Dorsey Levens
Green Bay Packers

Rushing TDs	3	0
Receiving TDs	4	0
TDs over 10 Yards	0	0
Total Rushing Yards	120	15
Total Receiving Yards	434	0
Total Attempts	36	5
Average Rush Yards/Game	8.0	3.0
Average Receiving Yards/Game	28.9	0
Games Played	15	2

Nobody talks about this guy, but he is a terrific fantasy footballer. Hey, four receiving TDs (*double points*) and three rushing scores in '95 makes one take notice. Bennett is still the main man in Green Bay, but there is no denying that Favre and Holmgren have good things in store for this young, dynamic guy.

		1995:	1994:	1993:
Jamal Anderson	Rushing TDs	1		
Atlanta Falcons	Receiving TDs	0		
	TDs over 10 Yards	1		
	Total Rushing Yards	161		
	Total Receiving Yards	42		
	Total Attempts	39		
	Average Rush Yards/Game	10.1		
	Average Receiving Yards/Game	2.6		
	Games Played	16		

He is the #2 back in Atlanta, but running backs in Atlanta *don't touch the ball often*. If Heyward goes down he is worth grabbing, otherwise, he is not going to score any points!

6 RB

		1995:	1994:	1993:
Kimble Anders	Rushing TDs	1	2	0
Kansas City Chiefs	Receiving TDs	2	1	1
	TDs over 10 Yards	2	0	1
	Total Rushing Yards	398	231	291
	Total Receiving Yards	349	525	326
	Total Attempts	58	62	75
	Average Rush Yards/Game	24.9	14.4	18.2
	Average Receiving Yards/Game	21.8	32.8	20.3
	Games Played	16	16	16

Kimble Anders is not a bad RB, but I have to think Greg Hill and Marcus Allen are the main backs in Kansas City. You could take him as a late round or *Bye Week* pick.

		1995:	1994:	1993:
Stephen Davis	Rushing TDs	*(Rookie)*		
Washington Redskins	Receiving TDs			
	TDs over 10 Yards			
	Total Rushing Yards			
	Total Receiving Yards			
	Total Attempts			
	Average Rush Yards/Game			
	Average Receiving Yards/Game			
	Games Played			

At the Redskins' minicamp in May, Davis was the most impressive guy out there! As this is written, Terry Allen is still a holdout, and Reggie Brooks is done, so Davis could have a real shot at a spot in the lineup.

	1995:	1994:	1993:
Lorenzo Neal — *New Orleans Saints*			
Rushing TDS	0	1	1
Receiving TDS	1	0	0
TDS over 10 Yards	1	0	0
Total Rushing Yards	3	90	175
Total Receiving Yards	123	9	0
Total Attempts	5	30	21
Average Rush Yards/Game	0.2	6.9	87.5
Average Receiving Yards/Game	7.7	0.7	0.0
Games Played	16	13	2

6 RB

Neal is a guy that really seemed to be headed in the right direction in '93. He has done virtually nothing the last two years, and has Mario Bates ahead of him in the depth chart. This is not a good combination, and I would take a pass on him until he bears fruit!

	1995:	1994:	1993:
Tommy Vardell — *San Francisco 49ers*			
Rushing TDS	0	0	3
Receiving TDS	0	1	1
TDS over 10 Yards	0	1	1
Total Rushing Yards	9	48	644
Total Receiving Yards	18	137	151
Total Attempts	4	24	171
Average Rush Yards/Game	1.8	12.0	40.3
Average Receiving Yards/Game	3.6	34.3	9.4
Games Played	5	4	16

Well, well, well—"*Touchdown*" Tommy might actually get one or two or three this year. For years his performance on the field has made a mockery out of his nickname. This is the year that he competes with Loville, Floyd and Johnson for a piece of the 49er legacy and glory.

	1995:	1994:	1993:
Marcus Allen — *Kansas City Chiefs*			
Rushing TDS	5	7	12
Receiving TDS	0	0	3
TDS over 10 Yards	0	1	4
Total Rushing Yards	890	709	764
Total Receiving Yards	210	349	238
Total Attempts	207	189	206
Average Rush Yards/Game	55.6	54.5	47.8
Average Receiving Yards/Game	13.1	21.8	14.9
Games Played	16	13	16

Marcus is truly a well-conditioned back, but he is slipping in the stat column. Check above and note that the TD production has gradually dipped from 12 to 7 to 5. Personally if I were KC, I would dust off Marcus when the Chiefs hit the red zone (*inside the twenty*) and let him bust those patented one- and two-yard, high-vaulting plunges! If I were Marty, I'd start third-year runner Greg Hill.

Dave Meggett
New England Patriots

	1995:	1994:	1993:
Rushing TDS	2	4	0
Receiving TDS	0	1	0
TDS over 10 Yards	1	4	3
Total Rushing Yards	250	298	329
Total Receiving Yards	334	293	319
Total Attempts	60	91	69
Average Rush Yards/Game	15.6	18.6	20.6
Average Receiving Yards/Game	20.9	18.3	19.9
Games Played	16	16	16

6
RB

Meggett, long a Giant fan favorite and team playmaker, seemed to get lost up in New England in the roar of the Curtis Martin frenzy, and the rush to fix what was wrong with Bledsoe and the *Pats* last season. I know that Parcells will reassess Meggett's skills, and use him more as he should be used—as a receiver out of the backfield, as a passer on the halfback option, and as an all-around utility player extraordinaire! Fear not, and take this guy with a later round pick.

Best of the Rest—

	1995:	1994:	1993:

Ronnie Harmon
Houston Oilers

	1995:	1994:	1993:
Rushing TDs	1	1	0
Receiving TDs	5	1	2
TDs over 10 Yards	5	2	2
Total Rushing Yards	187	94	216
Total Receiving Yards	662	615	671
Total Attempts	51	25	46
Average Rush Yards/Game	11.7	5.9	13.5
Average Receiving Yards/Game	41.4	38.4	41.9
Games Played	16	16	16

If your league gives extra points for a running back catching the ball, you want to take Harmon. He is not going to carry the ball much, but he will basically be another receiver, a la Eric Metcalf. He is still one of the top five return men in the league.

Glyn Milburn
Detroit Lions

	1995:	1994:	1993:
Rushing TDs	0	1	0
Receiving TDs	0	3	3
TDs over 10 Yards	0	3	1
Total Rushing Yards	266	201	231
Total Receiving Yards	191	549	300
Total Attempts	49	58	52
Average Rush Yards/Game	16.6	12.6	14.4
Average Receiving Yards/Game	11.9	34.3	18.8
Games Played	16	16	16

Check Milburn out this season—I see another Eric Metcalf brewing in the Detroit offense. Milburn gives Detroit a return man that they desperately need and will likely line him up as a receiver *a la Metcalf.* Imagine an offense with Barry Sanders running and Herman Moore, Brett Perriman, Johnnie Morton and Glyn Milburn receiving—I see *scores-a-plenty.*

Derek Loville
San Francisco 49ers

	1995:	1994:
Rushing TDs	10	0
Receiving TDs	3	0
TDs over 10 Yards	1	0
Total Rushing Yards	723	99
Total Receiving Yards	662	12
Total Attempts	218	31
Average Rush Yards/Game	45.2	14.1
Average Receiving Yards/Game	41.4	1.7
Games Played	16	7

The honeymoon is over for Loville, as Johnny Johnson and Tommy Vardell enter the scene. Loville squeezed everything he could out of his average game but he is purely a backup player. Loville will still be capable of scoring and causing havoc as a third down back and with the improved offense in *'Frisco* this season, expect Loville to do some scoring. This time, however, he won't be the featured back.

	1995:	1994:	1993:
Byron "Bam" Morris — *Pittsburgh Steelers*			
Rushing TDs	9	7	
Receiving TDs	0	0	
TDs over 10 Yards	1	1	
Total Rushing Yards	559	836	
Total Receiving Yards	36	204	
Total Attempts	148	198	
Average Rush Yards/Game	43.0	64.3	
Average Receiving Yards/Game	2.8	15.7	
Games Played	13	13	

What a bonehead! Just when you thought Bam would break free from under Barry Foster's shadow and knock heads in Pittsburgh, he goes and does something stupid that could possibly land him in jail. Even if he is free and clear with the law, I expect that Bam Morris will not be much of a significance in 1996.
The big question here is what the heck was he thinking?
Who's his advisor, '60s pop icon Timothy Leary?

	1995:	1994:	1993:
Ron Moore — *New York Jets*			
Rushing TDs	0	4	9
Receiving TDs	0	1	0
TDs over 10 Yards	0	1	3
Total Rushing Yards	121	780	1,018
Total Receiving Yards	50	52	16
Total Attempts	43	232	263
Average Rush Yards/Game	8.1	48.8	67.9
Average Receiving Yards/Game	3.3	3.3	1.1
Games Played	15	16	15

Goodbye, it was nice knowin' ya! Ron Moore is another in a long line of players that have *one good season* and suddenly think that they no longer have to work out and strive to improve! Adrian Murrell is the horse that has the Jets excited!

	1995:	1994:	1993:
Derrick Moore — *Detroit Lions*			
Rushing TDs	4	4	3
Receiving TDs	0	0	1
TDs over 10 Yards	1	0	1
Total Rushing Yards	740	52	405
Total Receiving Yards	11	6	63
Total Attempts	195	27	88
Average Rush Yards/Game	56.9	3.5	31.2
Average Receiving Yards/Game	0.8	0.4	4.8
Games Played	13	15	13

The drafting of Tim Biakabutuka meant Derrick Moore was up for grabs, and he re-signed with Detroit. Look for him to be a goal-line puncher and a backup to Sanders.

Pre-Season Running Back Ranking—

	Player:	Team:
1	Emmitt Smith	*Dallas Cowboys*
2	Curtis Martin	*New England Patriots*
3	Chris Warren	*Seattle Seahawks*
4	Ki-Jana Carter	*Cincinnati Bengals*
5	Marshall Faulk	*Indianapolis Colts*
6	Ricky Watters	*Philadelphia Eagles*
7	Barry Sanders	*Detroit Lions*
8	Lawrence Phillips	*St. Louis Rams*
9	Errict Rhett	*Tampa Bay Buccaneers*
10	Terrell Davis	*Denver Broncos*
11	Tim Biakabutuka	*Carolina Panthers*
12	Eddie George	*Houston Oilers*
13	Aaron Hayden	*San Diego Chargers*
14	Rashaan Salaam	*Chicago Bears*
15	Rodney Hampton	*New York Giants*
16	Mario Bates	*New Orleans Saints*
17	Adrian Murrell	*New York Jets*
18	Johnny Johnson	*San Francisco 49ers*
19	Harvey Williams	*Oakland Raiders*
20	Terry Allen	*Washington Redskins*
21	Bernie Parmalee	*Miami Dolphins*
22	Natrone Means	*Jacksonville Jaguars*
23	Craig Heyward	*Atlanta Falcons*
24	Thurman Thomas	*Buffalo Bills*
25	Jerome Bettis	*Pittsburgh Steelers*
26	James Stewart	*Minnesota Vikings*
27	Greg Hill	*Kansas City Chiefs*
28	William Floyd	*San Francisco 49ers*
29	Rodney Thomas	*Houston Oilers*
30	Darick Holmes	*Buffalo Bills*
31	Napoleon Kaufman	*Oakland Raiders*
32	Brian Mitchell	*Washington Redskins*
33	Leroy Hoard	*Baltimore Ravens*
34	Robert Smith	*Minnesota Vikings*
35	Terry Kirby	*Miami Dolphins*
36	Leland McElroy	*Arizona Cardinals*
37	Erric Pegram	*Pittsburgh Steelers*
38	Larry Centers	*Arizona Cardinals*
39	Charlie Garner	*Philadelphia Eagles*
40	Tyrone Wheatley	*New York Giants*
41	Garrison Hearst	*Arizona Cardinals*
42	Zack Crockett	*Indianapolis Colts*
43	Dorsey Levens	*Green Bay Packers*
44	Jamal Anderson	*Atlanta Falcons*
45	Kimble Anders	*Kansas City Chiefs*
46	Stephen Davis	*Washington Redskins*
47	Lorenzo Neal	*New Orleans Saints*
48	Tommy Vardell	*San Francisco 49ers*
49	Marcus Allen	*Kansas City Chiefs*
50	David Meggett	*New England Patriots*

	Player:	Team:
51	Terrell Fletcher	San Diego Chargers
52	James Stewart	Jacksonville Jaguars
53	Derek Loville	San Francisco 49ers
54	Amp Lee	Minnesota Vikings
55	Jerry Ellison	Tampa Bay Buccaneers
56	Earnest Byner	Baltimore Ravens
57	Ray Zellars	New Orleans Saints
58	Aaron Craver	Denver Broncos
59	Daryl Johnston	Dallas Cowboys
60	Kevin Turner	Philadelphia Eagles
61	Raymont Harris	Chicago Bears
62	Mike Alstott	Tampa Bay Buccaneers
63	Karim Abdul-Jabbar	Miami Dolphins
64	Gary Brown	Free Agent
65	Lamont Warren	Indianapolis Colts
66	Keith Byars	Miami Dolphins
67	Ronnie Harmon	Houston Oilers
68	Derrick Fenner	Oakland Raiders
69	Eric Bienemy	Cincinnati Bengals
70	Robert Green	Chicago Bears
71	Sherman Williams	Dallas Cowboys
72	Mack Strong	Seattle Seahawks
73	Bam Morris	Pittsburgh Steelers
74	Antonio Carter	Chicago Bears
75	Detron Smith	Denver Broncos
76	Scottie Graham	Minnesota Vikings
77	Marc Logan	Washington Redskins
78	Chris Darkins	Green Bay Packers
79	Moe Williams	Minnesota Vikings
80	Derek Brown	New Orleans Saints
81	Larry Jones	Washington Redskins
82	Chuck Levy	Arizona Cardinals
83	Herschel Walker	New York Giants
84	Steve Broussard	Seattle Seahawks
85	Lorenzo White	Houston Oilers
86	Fred McAfee	Pittsburgh Steelers
87	Fred McCrary	Philadelphia Eagles
88	John L. Williams	Free Agent
89	Harold Green	Cincinnati Bengals
90	Ryan Christopherson	Jacksonville Jaguars
91	Bob Christian	Carolina Panthers
92	Ron Moore	New York Jets
93	Jerald Moore	St. Louis Rams
94	Vaughn Dunbar	Free Agent
95	Brad Baxter	New York Jets
96	Charles Way	New York Giants
97	Travis Jervey	Green Bay Packers
98	Carwell Gardner	Buffalo Bills
99	Irving Spikes	Miami Dolphins
100	Calvin Jones	Oakland Raiders

6
RB

7 Wide Receivers

Drafting Wide Receivers—

The wide receiver position is perhaps the most perplexing position to draft. First of all, you get to start three wide receivers in your FFL fantasy football lineup. The problem is selecting the potentially hot receivers.

In leagues that count pass receptions as points, receiver selection is fairly easy. For example, Jeff Graham caught 83 passes and that would excite FFLers who count receptions as points. But, for leagues that count only scores, Jeff Graham comes up as a big lightweight since he scored only 4 TDs.

Now, what I find interesting is how drafting strategy for wide receivers is changing. Several years ago, you would only think of drafting Jerry Rice or Michael Irvin in the *first* round. Generally, receivers would be nabbed in *third*, *fourth* and *fifth* rounds. That used to work well, but today we are seeing some eye-popping stats from wide receivers. Last season *eight* wide receivers caught over 100 passes: Herman Moore, Jerry Rice, Cris Carter, Isaac Bruce, Michael Irvin, Brett Perriman, Eric Metcalf, and Robert Brooks. *Wow*, and Carl Pickens just missed as he finished with 99! *Eleven* wide receivers scored 10 TDs or better in '95: Carl Pickens, Cris Carter, Jerry Rice, Anthony Miller, Herman Moore, Robert Brooks, Isaac Bruce, Curtis Conway, Bill Brooks, Tim Brown, and Michael Irvin.

How about the Eric Metcalf craze? Metcalf gets moved from running back to wide receiver. *Wham, bam*—huge success and everyone has a major headache attempting to cover the guy! Now we see Detroit trade Denver for Glyn Milburn and are moving him to a wideout slot. Minnesota is grooming David Palmer for a similar role. You see, Metcalf has opened the door for smallish, physical players. Let Metcalf, Milburn, or Palmer get loose with a quick-out slant pass and no one will catch 'em. Watch for other teams to develop similar strategies.

Therefore, due to this offensive surge in the wide receivers overall stats, draft strategy has changed. You cannot afford now to wait until the later rounds to scarf up receivers. And remember, these NFL speedsters can turn a short pass into a 40-plus yard TD and give all FFL owners *double points!*

Who are these guys? The True Sleepers—

Player:	Team:
Tamarick Vanover	*Kansas City Chiefs*
Torrance Small	*New Orleans Saints*
Glyn Milburn	*Detroit Lions*
David Palmer	*Minnesota Vikings*
Keenan McCardell	*Jacksonville Jaguars*
Jimmy Oliver	*San Diego Chargers*
Charles Jordan	*Miami Dolphins*
Derrick Alexander	*Baltimore Ravens*
Ed McCaffrey	*Denver Broncos*
Chris T. Jones	*Philadelphia Eagles*

What about Deion Sanders?

7 WR

We all know that Deion has been bugging about playing wide receiver, but last season all we saw was a few tosses and one long pass through the outstretched arms of Deion. Does this signal the end of the experiment of Deion as a receiver? *Heck No!* During the spring workouts, Troy Aikman and Deion were hooking up and connecting almost like that twin-headed Cowboy nemesis Steve and Jerry. Add to the Deion receiver equation that Michael Irvin is lost in space and may be preoccupied this fall with Perry Mason.

Kevin Williams sure isn't going to scare any first rate cornerbacks, so yes I believe that we will see Deion as a DB/WR. And the hits just keep on coming—follow me on this, because when Deion enters the game *he will* be the main target. No more of this Barry Switzer *peek-a-boo-fake'em-out-strategy*. Deion is really needed to step up like Michael Jordan and take over on defense and offense. Therefore, I think Deion would be a good FFL draft pick, because sooner or later he *will* be included in the Cowboys offense!

He's worth the gamble. A word of advice is to check with your league rules and see if you can establish that by drafting a Deion you get him for *everything*—punt returns and receiving.
One pick, two players, all in one!

Question Marks at Wide Receiver—

Michael Irvin	How will Michael's '96 off-season problems affect his upcoming season? What a disappointment! Now he wants to play with J.J. in Miami. Bad news, gang: I think Mike needs a reality check.
Andre Rison	Pass the attitude, here comes Andre. This season will Rison exert himself and show up to play like a Jerry Rice, Herman Moore, or Irvin? Rison *must* deliver now or he will be the next Vance Johnson.
Irving Fryar	This could be the last hurrah for Irving Fryar. How do you go from Dan Marino to Ty Detmer and Rodney Peete and pretend it's a career move? *Gee, it is*…the *end* of a career move!
Curtis Conway	Conway was super hot and suddenly cooled at the end of the season. Can't question his speed, but one wonders if he has that *total drive* to take over a game? He could be a Carl Pickens if he would add some grit to his game.
Alvin Harper	Gee, Mr. Harper, how was your *vacation* last season? A real bust last year and still a major question mark going into this year. Maybe Irvin could end up in Tampa and let Harper pretend *he* is the reason the offense clicks!
Brett Perriman	Take him out of Detroit's offensive system and he becomes very average. I will credit Perriman for achieving *way above* his ability. That and it sure doesn't hurt to have Herman Moore play the opposite side (and receive all the defensive attention). I think Glyn Milburn will replace him *ala Eric Metcalf.*
Calvin Williams	Calvin, what happened? Three years ago he appeared to be another Cris Carter. The past two seasons he has disappeared during crucial stretches. Can he work well with Ty Detmer? Can Rodney Peete's throws even reach him?
J.J. Stokes	J.J. has been ready for the pro game for the past two years. Unfortunately for him last season as a rookie everyone else in the league was ready for him as well. Let's wave off last year— I think he will shine this season with Steve Young and Jerry Rice's help.

	Kevin Williams	I am always waiting for Kevin to explode onto the scene and become a solid star. It's been three years, and I am still waiting. Here is the question, grasshopper…can he play like he did at the very end of the season (*untouchable*) or will he dweeb it out?
	Rocket Ismail	Go for it Rocket, or you will be gone! In the decade of the salary cap no team can afford to pay millions for a *maybe* or an *almost*. Coach Mike White needs to motivate and utilize Rocket's skills.
	Brian Blades	Heartbroken after his involvement in his cousin's accidental death, life has obviously done a number on Brian. Can he find a zone and heal or will he simply just be too overcome? Expect the Florida court to give him probation, therefore allowing him to play this season.
7 WR	*Andre Reed*	Can Andre overcome last season's injuries and teammates questions concerning his desire to play hard in the '95 playoffs? The good news is that Jim Kelly, Thurman Thomas, and Bruce Smith each personally contacted Reed and convinced him to come back for '96. *Good move!*
	Fred Barnett	Okay, Freddy has gone through several operations and plays a bit in pain. But, he now will be playing with Dan Marino and Jimmy Johnson's game plan. I like it. I question only how many TDS he can score.
	Mike Sherrard	Another receiver who has aches, pains, broken bones, etc., but he finds a reprieve with John Elway. Like Barnett, Sherrard will see his season lift and reach some great stats. Sherrard and Anthony Miller will cause havoc. Only question, can he play injury-free?
	Thomas Lewis	I am really tired hearing about how fast and good Lewis is. *Let's see it!* Make Lewis an integral part of the offense.
	David Palmer	Who? Look gang, Eric Metcalf is all the rage, and everyone will attempt to strike with a clone. David Palmer is *verrrry clone-able*! Watch for development on Palmer during exhibition games.
	Bill Brooks	Great move for the Washington Redskins! But who will be the QB—Shuler or Frerotte? Still, as a third receiver, Brooks will fit in well with Coach Norv Turner's aggressive game plans. Brooks and Henry Ellard (and maybe Terry Allen if re-signed) will give the *'Skins* some great veterans!

Quarterback/Wide Receivers Listing—

Quarterback:	1ST Receiver:	2ND Receiver:	3RD Receiver:	Team:
Steve Young	Jerry Rice	J.J. Stokes	Nate Singleton	SF
Brett Favre	Robert Brooks	Anthony Morgan	Antonio Freeman	GB
Scott Mitchell	Herman Moore	Brett Perriman	Johnnie Morton	DET
Dan Marino	Fred Barnett	O.J. McDuffie	Randal Hill	MIA
Jeff Blake	Carl Pickens	Darnay Scott	David Dunn	CIN
Jeff George	Eric Metcalf	Terance Mathis	Bert Emanuel	ATL
Jim Kelly	Quinn Early	Andre Reed	Eric Moulds	BUF
John Elway	Anthony Miller	Mike Sherrard	Ed McCaffrey	DEN
Neil O'Donnell	Jeff Graham	Keyshawn Johnson	Alex Van Dyke	NYJ
Erik Kramer	Curtis Conway	Michael Timpson	Bobby Engram	CHI
Drew Bledsoe	Vincent Brisby	Shawn Jefferson	Terry Glenn	NE
Mark Brunell	Keenan McCardell	Cedric Tillman	Willie Jackson	JAX
Jim Everett	Michael Haynes	Torrance Small	Mercury Hayes	NO
Warren Moon	Cris Carter	Jake Reed	Qadry Ismail	MIN
Jeff Hostetler	Tim Brown	Raghib Ismail	Daryl Hobbs	RAI
Stan Humphries	Tony Martin	Andre Coleman	Jimmy Oliver	SD
Troy Aikman	Michael Irvin	Kevin Williams	Stepfret Williams	DAL
Vinnie Testaverde	Andre Rison	Michael Jackson	Derrick Alexander	BAL
Steve Bono	Lake Dawson	Tamarick Vanover	Danan Hughes	KC
Jim Harbaugh	Sean Dawkins	Floyd Turner	Marvin Harrison	IND
Kerry Collins	Willie Green	Mark Carrier	Mushin Muhammad	CAR
Rick Mirer	Brian Blades	Joey Galloway	Ricky Proehl	SEA
Heath Shuler	Henry Ellard	Michael Westbrook	Bill Brooks	WAS
Ty Detmer	Irving Fryar	Calvin Williams	Mark Seay	PHI
Dave Brown	Chris Calloway	Thomas Lewis	Amani Toomer	NYG
Jim Miller	Yancey Thigpen	Ernie Mills	Andre Hastings	PIT
Boomer Esiason	Rob Moore	Frank Sanders	Anthony Edwards	AZ
Trent Dilfer	Courtney Hawkins	Alvin Harper	Horace Copeland	TB
Chris Chandler	Chris Sanders	Willie Davis	Derrick Russell	HOU
Steve Walsh	Isaac Bruce	Todd Kinchen	Eddie Kennison	RAM

'96 Wide Receiver Review—

Jerry Rice
San Francisco 49ers

	1995:	1994:	1993:
Receiving TDS	15	13	15
TDS over 40 Yards	6	2	3
Total Receiving Yards	1,848	1,499	1,503
Total Receptions	122	112	98
Average Receiving Yards/Game	115.5	93.7	93.9
Games Played	16	16	16

Jerry Rice is so special, and just look at those numbers! What can you say about him that has not been said? The guy is the consummate big game player, a true gamer, he never gets injured, and trains like a madman in the offseason. Oh, and let's give him Steve Young for a complete season and watch the numbers continue to spiral higher and higher! Rice is still the champion and a first-round lock until someone knocks him out!

Herman Moore
Detroit Lions

	1995:	1994:	1993:
Receiving TDS	14	11	6
TDS over 40 Yards	3	1	1
Total Receiving Yards	1,686	1,173	935
Total Receptions	123	72	61
Average Receiving Yards/Game	105.4	73.3	62.3
Games Played	16	16	15

Herman Moore is one of those young players who instead of punking out, follows a rigid training schedule! In fact, he trains a lot like Jerry Rice. The special talent Moore has besides speed and good hands, is his great jumping ability. I pity the short CB who must contend with this leaping 6'5" receiver in the endzone! Based on the last two years, he too is a first-rounder or possible high second-rounder! *Get him!*

Carl Pickens
Cincinnati Bengals

	1995:	1994:	1993:
Receiving TDS	17	11	6
TDS over 40 Yards	3	2	0
Total Receiving Yards	1,234	1,127	565
Total Receptions	99	71	43
Average Receiving Yards/Game	77.1	75.1	47.1
Games Played	16	15	12

Carl Pickens has entered the *trifecta level* with Jerry Rice and Herman Moore! Carl can easily nail 20 TDS in '96 and he, along with Darnay Scott and Tony McGee, will continue to thrive with the "*Air Force*" game of Jeff Blake!

		1995:	1994:	1993:
Isaac Bruce	Receiving TDS	13	3	
St. Louis Rams	TDS over 40 Yards	2	0	
	Total Receiving Yards	1,781	272	
	Total Receptions	119	21	
	Average Receiving Yards/Game	111.3	24.7	
	Games Played	16	11	

I really like the hard-working Isaac Bruce, but I can't help but wonder about the St. Louis quarterbacking (Steve Walsh and Mark Rypien). I am a bit surprised that Bruce doesn't have more 40-yard-plus TDS, but other than that Bruce is a solid pick. He is very explosive and somewhat reminds me of a young Jerry Rice!

		1995:	1994:	1993:
Robert Brooks	Receiving TDS	13	6	0
Green Bay Packers	TDS over 40 Yards	5	0	0
	Total Receiving Yards	1,497	648	180
	Total Receptions	102	58	20
	Average Receiving Yards/Game	93.6	40.5	16.4
	Games Played	16	16	11

Talk about doubling your stats!
Robert Brooks really came of age in the absence of Sterling Sharpe. For '96, all signs are a go for another great season! Unlike Isaac Bruce, Robert Brooks has a superstar QB in Brett Favre!

		1995:	1994:	1993:
Michael Irvin	Receiving TDS	10	6	7
Dallas Cowboys	TDS over 40 Yards	2	1	2
	Total Receiving Yards	1,603	1,241	1,330
	Total Receptions	111	79	88
	Average Receiving Yards/Game	100.2	77.6	83.1
	Games Played	16	16	16

Somehow, I feel that Michael Irvin will escape his judicial headaches and begin concentrating on his football responsibilities! His stats will still be in the nosebleed section, but he may lose some of his offensive pie to *Neon Deion*!

		1995:	1994:	1993:
Eric Metcalf *Atlanta Falcons* (RB in 1994 and 1993)	Receiving TDs	8	3	2
	TDs over 40 Yards	3	1	1
	Total Receiving Yards	1,189	436	539
	Total Receptions	104	47	63
	Average Receiving Yards/Game	74.3	27.3	33.7
	Games Played	16	16	16

Eric Metcalf—a RB in '94 and '93—is a dangerous guy and he may double his touchdown production if Jeff George is his QB in '96. Like Deion Sanders, he is a legitimate threat to score whenever he touches the ball! It took him a while to fit into that Falcon offense—now he *is* the offense!

7
WR Tim Brown
Oakland Raiders

		1995:	1994:	1993:
	Receiving TDs	10	9	8
	TDs over 40 Yards	4	2	1
	Total Receiving Yards	1,342	1,309	1,180
	Total Receptions	89	89	80
	Average Receiving Yards/Game	83.9	81.8	73.8
	Games Played	16	16	16

I imagine Tim Brown every now and then must daydream over what could have been! A couple of seasons ago, he signed with the Broncos and thought that he would be on the receiving end of John Elway's cannon arm. Instead, the Raiders matched the offer and Brown has had to watch Jeff Hostetler *suck it up* with major nagging injuries and a questionable offense! In '95, *Hoss* missed a large part of the season, yet Brown somehow scored 10 TDs with four over 40 yards!

Cris Carter
Minnesota Vikings

		1995:	1994:	1993:
	Receiving TDs	17	7	9
	TDs over 40 Yards	1	2	0
	Total Receiving Yards	1,371	1,256	1,071
	Total Receptions	122	122	86
	Average Receiving Yards/Game	85.7	78.5	66.9
	Games Played	16	16	16

The concern here is when will Carter begin to slide?
First of all, I will be surprised if he hits 17 TDs again in '96!
Why? I just doubt that Warren Moon will be able to launch another air attack like he did in '95. Carter is very capable of another 100+ catch season, but remember that Cris was upset that Moon wasn't going to him enough at the season's end! Also, note that over the past three seasons, Carter has only three TDs over 40 yards!

		1995:	1994:	1993:
Curtis Conway	Receiving TDS	12	3	2
Chicago Bears	TDS over 40 Yards	6	1	0
	Total Receiving Yards	1,037	546	231
	Total Receptions	62	39	19
	Average Receiving Yards/Game	64.8	42.0	14.4
	Games Played	15	13	16

Streaky guy, this Curtis Conway! He completely dominated the first half of the season and then suddenly disappeared during the last part of the season. Can he tough out a full season like a Michael Irvin, or will he be like Anthony Miller, who has a penchant for disappearing during the season? One thing to hook onto is Conway's ability to split defenses and run deep patterns for long scores! I like his chances for 14-15 TDS in '96!

Joey Galloway	Receiving TDS	7	
Seattle Seahawks	TDS over 40 Yards	4	
	Total Receiving Yards	1,039	
	Total Receptions	67	
	Average Receiving Yards/Game	64.9	
	Games Played	16	

Beep, beep! Here comes the *Roadrunner*. Expect major scores from the flashy second year pro. The only downfall on selecting Joey is that Rick Mirer is not renowned as a great passing QB. Still, a flyer like Galloway can make Mirer look great on quick-splitting fly patterns. Hit him 20 yards on the fly and let Joey's feet do the rest! Great pick and expect to double your pleasure with over 40 yard scores!

Andre Rison	Receiving TDS	3	8	15
Baltimore Ravens	TDS over 40 Yards	0	1	2
	Total Receiving Yards	701	1,088	1,242
	Total Receptions	47	81	86
	Average Receiving Yards/Game	43.8	77.7	77.6
	Games Played	16	14	16

Gee, nice effort in '95, Andre!
This is the final play for Andre this season if he flops! He has a wise, friendly, offensive-minded HC in Teddy Marchibroda, and an opportunity to silence all his critics. It's up to Andre—put up or shut up, babe! Since I am feeling generous, I predict that Andre will rebound in Baltimore, scoring 12 TDS and receiving for over 1,000 yards!

	1995:	1994:	1993:
Keyshawn Johnson — *New York Jets*		(Rookie)	
Receiving TDS			
TDS over 40 Yards			
Total Receiving Yards			
Total Receptions			
Average Receiving Yards/Game			
Games Played			

The Jets have their future pinned to the shirt of this lanky, cocky rookie. Keyshawn took USC by storm, and now hopes to do the same for the *Big Apple*! I think with the Jets' O'Donnell, Keyshawn has an excellent opportunity to create an offense from thin air in *Jetsville*, and prove to HC Rich Kotite that there is life beyond a two TE set. I'd say get him as a late-rounder, and hold on for a wild rookie-year ride!

7 WR

	1995:	1994:	1993:
Chris Sanders — *Houston Oilers*			
Receiving TDS	9		
TDS over 40 Yards	4		
Total Receiving Yards	823		
Total Receptions	35		
Average Receiving Yards/Game	51.4		
Games Played	16		

Wow, is this guy an eye popper! His ability will allow him to heap some major numbers this season, as he further learns the Houston offensive scheme. The big question here, is who will be quarterbacking—Chris Chandler or Steve McNair? Regardless, Chris Sanders is a solid pick and many draftniks are going to stare blankly and wonder, "*Who is he*"? Be smart and grab him if you can. I expect 12 TDS and plenty of 40+ scores!

	1995:	1994:	1993:
J.J. Stokes — *San Francisco 49ers*			
Receiving TDS	4		
TDS over 40 Yards	1		
Total Receiving Yards	517		
Total Receptions	38		
Average Receiving Yards/Game	43.1		
Games Played	12		

Last season J.J. showed up late, got injured, and never really was in the swing of things. He really needs to wake up and put away his old press clippings and learn under the tutelage of two surefire Hall of Famers (*Rice* and *Young*). With his natural ability, plus that kind of veteran leadership—look for him to excel this year. Expect J.J. to show his stuff this season and put up some great numbers. I am putting him in the

		1995:	1994:	1993:
Deion Sanders *Dallas Cowboys*	Receiving TDS	0	(Played Corner Back)	
	TDS over 40 Yards	0		
	Total Receiving Yards	25		
	Total Receptions	2		
	Average Receiving Yards/Game	2.8		
	Games Played	9		

Deion is going to do everything this year but clean up the stands after the game! Ernie Zampese, the *Pokes'* Offensive Coordinator, has already put in some plays that feature *Prime Time*, so expect to see him on all sides of the ball. He is one of the classic explosive, take-your-breath-away kind of players that can kill you every time they touch the ball. He's got great hands, incredible speed after the catch, and the "*Throw it to me*" attitude that wants the ball every down. Take him, but with the forewarning that Switzer will not senselessly risk his starting CB, and will be used sparingly but effectively, or as a decoy!

7 WR

Tamarick Vanover *Kansas City Chiefs*	Receiving TDS	2
	TDS over 40 Yards	0
	Total Receiving Yards	231
	Total Receptions	11
	Average Receiving Yards/Game	15.4
	Games Played	15

Book 'em Dano! Here is a guy that will excite and can score any time he touches the ball. Sure, he has that *Pro Bono, nolo contendre* QB Stevie-B throwing to him, but I think he is a legit to burst upon the scene and scare the wits out of opposing defenses! Vanover easily could score a dozen TDS in '96, if Bono can get the ball to him.

		1995:	1994:	1993:
Fred Barnett *Miami Dolphins*	Receiving TDS	5	5	0
	TDS over 40 Yards	0	4	0
	Total Receiving Yards	585	1,127	170
	Total Receptions	48	78	17
	Average Receiving Yards/Game	41.8	70.4	42.5
	Games Played	14	16	4

Double those numbers for 1996! Freddy Barnett now will be on the receiving end of Dan Marino's hard tosses (*and harder stares if he plays dropsies*). Forget playing spud with Rodney Peete, or bad karma head games with Randall! I really like this move and expect Fred to corral a dozen or more TDS!

	1995:	1994:	1993:
Quinn Early *Buffalo Bills*			
Receiving TDS	8	4	6
TDS over 40 Yards	3	0	2
Total Receiving Yards	1,087	894	670
Total Receptions	81	82	45
Average Receiving Yards/Game	67.9	59.6	44.7
Games Played	16	15	15

What a steal for the Bills! Completely underrated, Quinn Early has been the best receiver in the state of Louisiana for the last several years! Let me clue you in to the fact that if Bill Brooks can muster 11 scores in that Buffalo offense, just imagine Early playing catch with a healthy *Jimbo*. Look out! Look for 12-13 TDS and 90-100 receptions!

7 WR **Darnay Scott** *Cincinnati Bengals*

	1995:	1994:
Receiving TDS	5	5
TDS over 40 Yards	3	3
Total Receiving Yards	821	866
Total Receptions	52	46
Average Receiving Yards/Game	51.3	54.1
Games Played	16	16

Darnay Scott had back-to-back seasons that mirrored each other in the stat column. I really think that Scott is a dangerous deep threat and expect him to flourish in his third season with an improving Bengal offense. By adding Ki-Jana Carter, the offense will open up and be more consistent. With Carl Pickens seeing a lot of double teaming, I expect Scott to push bigger numbers and results. I have Scott collared for 10 TDS and as many as 6 of those TDS could be for over 40 yards, if Blake continues to bomb defenses with the long ball!

Brett Perriman *Detroit Lions*

	1995:	1994:	1993:
Receiving TDS	9	4	2
TDS over 40 Yards	2	0	0
Total Receiving Yards	1,488	761	496
Total Receptions	108	56	49
Average Receiving Yards/Game	93.0	47.6	35.4
Games Played	16	16	14

The key here is seeing if Perriman will play, demand to be traded, or hold out and renegotiate his contract. Frankly, I think Perriman is good, but not great and he should accept the Lions' offer and keep picking passes out of the air while being in single coverage! Herman Moore always receives the double coverage.

	1995:	1994:	1993:
O.J. McDuffie *Miami Dolphins*			
Receiving TDS	8	3	0
TDS over 40 Yards	0	0	0
Total Receiving Yards	819	488	197
Total Receptions	62	37	19
Average Receiving Yards/Game	51.2	32.5	12.3
Games Played	16	15	16

With Fred Barnett roaming loose on one side, I expect to see O.J. McDuffie to continue improving and putting up solid numbers. Jimmy Johnson will not overlook the steady McDuffie in his game plan! McDuffie will score 12 TDS and gain over 1,000 receiving yards!

	1995:	1994:	1993:
Michael Westbrook *Washington Redskins*			
Receiving TDS	2		
TDS over 40 Yards	0		
Total Receiving Yards	522		
Total Receptions	34		
Average Receiving Yards/Game	47.5		
Games Played	11		

Hopefully the talented Michael Westbrook will report to camp ready to go. Last season a late signing and early injuries robbed Westbrook of crucial on-the-job training. Physically, Westbrook is a Michael Irvin clone but he will need to develop Irvin's hard-nosed attitude to raise his level of play!

	1995:	1994:	1993:
Vincent Brisby *New England Patriots*			
Receiving TDS	3	5	2
TDS over 40 Yards	1	0	0
Total Receiving Yards	974	904	626
Total Receptions	66	58	45
Average Receiving Yards/Game	60.9	64.6	44.7
Games Played	16	14	14

Bledsoe-to-Brisby was suppose to be the cry in New England last season! Unfortunately, Drew Bledsoe developed shoulder and confidence problems and Vincent Brisby all but disappeared during parts of the season, leaving greater Boston metro area residents crying instead! With Shawn Jefferson latching onto the *Pats*, Brisby should open up and succeed in '96.

7 WR

	1995:	1994:	1993:

Terance Mathis
Atlanta Falcons

	1995:	1994:	1993:
Receiving TDS	9	11	1
TDS over 40 Yards	1	2	0
Total Receiving Yards	1,039	1,342	352
Total Receptions	78	111	24
Average Receiving Yards/Game	74.2	83.9	27.1
Games Played	14	16	13

For a while it appeared that Mathis would not be signed by the Falcons, but fortunately for Atlanta fans, he signed. I expect a 10-12 TD season and 90 receptions in '96, and you should too!

Jake Reed
Minnesota Vikings

	1995:	1994:	1993:
Receiving TDS	9	4	0
TDS over 40 Yards	2	0	0
Total Receiving Yards	1,167	1,175	65
Total Receptions	72	85	5
Average Receiving Yards/Game	72.9	73.4	16.3
Games Played	16	16	4

Jake Reed is a really solid player, but I haven't seen him attempt to step out of the huge shadow of Cris Carter! Reed is solid and reminds me a lot of John Taylor (another good receiver in the shadow of greatness). The question here is will Moon have the juice to hit both Carter and Reed with the same knack that he demonstrated in '95?

Rob Moore
Arizona Cardinals

	1995:	1994:	1993:
Receiving TDS	5	6	1
TDS over 40 Yards	0	1	0
Total Receiving Yards	907	1,010	843
Total Receptions	63	78	64
Average Receiving Yards/Game	60.5	63.1	64.8
Games Played	15	16	13

In '94, Esiason hit Rob for 6 TDS with the Jets. The knock on Moore by Boomer in '94 was that he was talented but lacked guts! Now both hook up again! I expect Boomer to successfully search out Moore.

Willie Davis
Houston Oilers

	1995:	1994:	1993:
Receiving TDS	5	5	7
TDS over 40 Yards	2	2	1
Total Receiving Yards	527	822	909
Total Receptions	33	51	52
Average Receiving Yards/Game	32.9	63.2	56.8
Games Played	16	13	16

Watch out—Willie Davis and Chris Sanders will be streaking down the sidelines for some Chris Chandler or perhaps Steve McNair bombs. Houston will be opening it up and Willie Davis should get an expanded role in this offense. I think he will be a 10 TD receiver!

		1995:	1994:	1993:
Shawn Jefferson *New England Patriots*	Receiving TDS	2	3	2
	TDS over 40 Yards	2	3	2
	Total Receiving Yards	621	627	391
	Total Receptions	48	43	30
	Average Receiving Yards/Game	38.8	39.2	26.1
	Games Played	06	16	15

Jefferson quickly became one of Humphries' favorite targets in '94, and is a super deep threat. He is now a Drew Bledsoe target, so the jury is still out!

		1995:	1994:	1993:
Tony Martin *San Diego Chargers*	Receiving TDS	6	7	3
	TDS over 40 Yards	2	3	1
	Total Receiving Yards	1,224	885	347
	Total Receptions	90	50	20
	Average Receiving Yards/Game	76.5	55.3	34.7
	Games Played	16	16	10

Tony Martin is a good but not great receiver. However, he and the other cast of butterfingered clowns, dropped *way* too many catchable balls. Now that Shawn Jefferson and Mark Seay are long gone, expect Tony Martin to become Humphries' "*Go-to guy*" in '96. I expect him to be in the 10-12 TD range with 110 receptions!

		1995:	1994:	1993:
Michael Jackson *Baltimore Ravens*	Receiving TDS	9	2	8
	TDS over 40 Yards	1	0	1
	Total Receiving Yards	714	304	756
	Total Receptions	44	21	41
	Average Receiving Yards/Game	54.9	43.4	50.4
	Games Played	13	7	15

Looking at '93 and '95, one could surmise that Michael "*Moonwalk*" Jackson scores every 5 receptions. That's the *good news*! The *bad news* is he has never grabbed more than 44 receptions! How come? Jackson also comes up with an assortment of nagging injuries, and that will drive you nuts constantly checking on his physical condition. I think Jackson will put up maybe 50-55 receptions and 10 TDS in '96, but I also expect him to play second fiddle to Andre Rison!

	1995:	1994:	1993:
Frank Sanders *Arizona Cardinals*			
Receiving TDS	2		
TDS over 40 Yards	0		
Total Receiving Yards	883		
Total Receptions	52		
Average Receiving Yards/Game	55.2		
Games Played	16		

Man, is Boomer Esiason going to like this receiver! Frank Sanders is one of those young polished players that will get better as he learns the *Cards* offensive system. Toss in Leland McElroy at RB and Johnny McWilliams at TE and this *kiddie corps* will excite! I like Sanders to pull in 10 scores, 75 receptions and break the 1,000 yard mark!

7 WR **Mike Sherrard** *Denver Broncos*

	1995:	1994:	1993:
Receiving TDS	4	6	2
TDS over 40 Yards	1	2	2
Total Receiving Yards	577	825	433
Total Receptions	44	53	24
Average Receiving Yards/Game	44.4	55.0	72.2
Games Played	13	15	6

Here is an interesting pick—the much injured, brittle Mike Sherrard playing in Denver. I like this gamble, despite the concern of injury, especially since John Elway is throwing the ball! That's a big difference over Dave Brown! Sherrard could be one of this season's best sleepers.

Jeff Graham *New York Jets*

	1995:	1994:	1993:
Receiving TDS	4	5	0
TDS over 40 Yards	2	1	0
Total Receiving Yards	1,301	944	579
Total Receptions	82	68	38
Average Receiving Yards/Game	81.3	59.0	48.3
Games Played	16	16	12

Jeff Graham is more of a possession receiver and to this point, he has not been a scorer. It is interesting that Graham and Neil O'Donnell were once Steeler teammates. Therefore they will not take forever to learn each other's game. *Ahhh*, familiarity—that is something necessary for any QB and receiver! Look for Graham to also play a role near the endzone, but the deep threat will be Keyshawn Johnson.

		1995:	1994:	1993:
Henry Ellard *Washington Redskins*	Receiving TDs	5	6	2
	TDs over 40 Yards	2	3	1
	Total Receiving Yards	1,005	1,397	945
	Total Receptions	56	74	61
	Average Receiving Yards/Game	67.0	93.1	59.1
	Games Played	15	15	16

Here is the consummate pro in the *Jerry Rice form*!
Henry Ellard could give a seminar on how to play in the NFL and succeed. Hard work and quality effort are the stories of this guy's life. True, he is 35 years old, but he has not shown a drop in performance, despite having to work with the differing styles of Heath Shuler and Gus Frerotte. I would expect 8-10 TDs in '96, as those young QBs gradually learn Michael Westbrook's style.

7 WR

Torrance Small *New Orleans Saints*	Receiving TDs	6	5	1
	TDs over 40 Yards	0	1	0
	Total Receiving Yards	461	719	164
	Total Receptions	38	49	16
	Average Receiving Yards/Game	28.8	51.4	23.4
	Games Played	16	14	7

With Quinn Early heading for the winterlands of Buffalo, the door opens up to Torrance Small and it's up to him to take the opportunity and make himself a success. Small has always been a solid performer as a backup and I think he will become a star in New Orleans.
I like him to score 9-10 TDs and catch 65-70 passes!

Bert Emanuel *Atlanta Falcons*	Receiving TDs	5	4	
	TDs over 40 Yards	0	1	
	Total Receiving Yards	1,039	649	
	Total Receptions	74	46	
	Average Receiving Yards/Game	64.9	46.4	
	Games Played	16	14	

The above are good stats for a third receiver in the Falcon offense. Expect similar numbers in '96 since Eric Metcalf and Terance Mathis will continue to get the bulk of Jeff George's passes!

	1995:	1994:	1993:
Johnnie Morton — *Detroit Lions*			
Receiving TDS	8	2	
TDS over 40 Yards	0	0	
Total Receiving Yards	590	39	
Total Receptions	44	3	
Average Receiving Yards/Game	36.9	7.8	
Games Played	16	5	

Just how good can Johnnie Morton become? For now he is the third receiver in the Lions' scheme. Personally I think he has the talent to surpass Brett Perriman and become the #2 guy. But Johnnie needs to grow up and toughen up, however, if he is going to become a top receiver. He should also be aware that Glyn Milburn may steal some time from him. Still, I think Morton has the talent for 10 TDs and 60 receptions.

	1995:	1994:	1993:
Andre Reed — *Buffalo Bills*			
Receiving TDS	3	8	6
TDS over 40 Yards	1	1	2
Total Receiving Yards	312	1,303	854
Total Receptions	24	90	52
Average Receiving Yards/Game	52.0	81.4	56.9
Games Played	6	16	15

A newly re-signed Andre Reed joins Quinn Early and rookie Eric Moulds at the heart of an exciting Bills receiving corps. If he is healthy, look for 6-8 TDs!

	1995:	1994:	1993:
Randal Hill — *Miami Dolphins*			
Receiving TDS	0	0	4
TDS over 40 Yards	0	0	1
Total Receiving Yards	260	544	519
Total Receptions	12	38	35
Average Receiving Yards/Game	37.1	41.8	37.0
Games Played	7	13	14

Hill went from being a key member of the *Cards'* offense to an also-ran in Miami. Will J.J. bring Hill into the mix as an Alvin Harper type receiver? We shall see!

	1995:	1994:	1993:
Michael Haynes — *New Orleans Saints*			
Receiving TDS	4	5	4
TDS over 40 Yards	0	1	1
Total Receiving Yards	597	985	778
Total Receptions	41	77	72
Average Receiving Yards/Game	39.8	61.6	51.9
Games Played	15	16	15

You know what shocks me? A speedster like Michael Haynes only has 2 TDS over 40 yards in three years! What gives here? All eyes have to be on Haynes now, since the reliable, underrated Quinn Early has hitched his sled to the Buffalo Bills. Hopefully Jim Everett and Haynes will work on the bomb this season.

	1995:	1994:	1993:
Yancey Thigpen — *Pittsburgh Steelers*			
Receiving TDS	5	4	3
TDS over 40 Yards	1	2	0
Total Receiving Yards	1,307	546	154
Total Receptions	85	36	9
Average Receiving Yards/Game	81.7	39.0	17.1
Games Played	16	14	8

Great story, great efforts, and great results in '95 for Yancey Thigpen. However, who will be heaving passes in Thigpen's direction? Tomczak, Miller, or Stewart? None of those guys are Neil O'Donnell!

	1995:	1994:	1993:
Keenan McCardell — *Carolina Panthers*			
Receiving TDS	4	0	0
TDS over 40 Yards	0	0	0
Total Receiving Yards	709	182	234
Total Receptions	56	10	13
Average Receiving Yards/Game	44.3	16.5	19.5
Games Played	16	11	12

McCardell will be a good player to pick up later in your draft, since he should be available. McCardell is a good player and will get the opportunity to play full-time in Carolina. I expect 8 TDS, 80 receptions, and 1,000 yards in '96.

	1995:	1994:	1993:
Courtney Hawkins			
Tampa Bay Buccaneers			
Receiving TDS	0	5	5
TDS over 40 Yards	0	0	1
Total Receiving Yards	493	438	933
Total Receptions	41	37	62
Average Receiving Yards/Game	30.8	39.8	58.3
Games Played	16	11	16

Hawkins was a guy that you really expected to go places with the addition of Trent Dilfer. Plus, with the deep threat of Harper, you had to figure the guy was a natural for a big season. Here we are in the harsh glare of daylight, and ya know what? His numbers really need to improve! You can still expect 6-8 TDS out of him, but I would take him as a third pick at best.

7 WR

	1995:	1994:	1993:
Irving Fryar			
Philadelphia Eagles			
Receiving TDS	8	7	5
TDS over 40 Yards	2	3	2
Total Receiving Yards	910	1,270	1,010
Total Receptions	62	73	64
Average Receiving Yards/Game	56.9	79.4	63.1
Games Played	16	16	16

You can look at Fryar signing with Philly and Fred Barnett signing with Miami as '96's version of a trade through free agency. This time Fryar will not have the fiery Dan Marino to push him. I think Fryar's stats will drop and I do not think he will show the brilliance that a healthy Fred Barnett can provide. I think he will become an Art Monk type of possession receiver (*good size, a drop in speed, and aging*). Fryar will greatly miss Marino's arm and fire!

	1995:	1994:	1993:
Sean Dawkins			
Indianapolis Colts			
Receiving TDS	3	5	1
TDS over 40 Yards	0	0	0
Total Receiving Yards	784	742	430
Total Receptions	52	51	26
Average Receiving Yards/Game	49.0	46.4	47.8
Games Played	16	16	9

You can't look at the success story of Jim Harbaugh in '95 without two other names appearing in the credits: Marshall Faulk and Sean Dawkins. Dawkins really stepped up last season, and you can expect him to continue to do so. Look for Harbaugh and Dawkins to starting making the long-distance connection more often.

	1995:	1994:	1993:
Brian Blades — *Seattle Seahawks*			
Receiving TDS	4	4	3
TDS over 40 Yards	2	0	0
Total Receiving Yards	1,001	1,086	945
Total Receptions	77	81	80
Average Receiving Yards/Game	62.6	67.9	59.1
Games Played	16	16	16

Let's be honest: Brian Blades has dealt with a major situation in his involvement with the accidental shooting death of his cousin in '95. The talent is there, but will Brian be able to overcome his emotions and concentrate on football?

	1995:	1994:
Thomas Lewis — *New York Giants*		
Receiving TDS	1	0
TDS over 40 Yards	1	0
Total Receiving Yards	208	46
Total Receptions	12	4
Average Receiving Yards/Game	26.0	5.1
Games Played	8	9

That lone touchdown in two years can not be what the Giants had in mind when they drafted Lewis in the first round several seasons ago. With Mike Sherrard hiking the Rockies in Denver, I'd say that this is as good a time as ever for Thomas Lewis to start paying dividends. He'd better hustle, because the Giants drafted WR Amani Toomer in the second round this year!

	1995:	1994:
Lake Dawson — *Kansas City Chiefs*		
Receiving TDS	5	2
TDS over 40 Yards	1	0
Total Receiving Yards	513	537
Total Receptions	40	37
Average Receiving Yards/Game	32.1	48.8
Games Played	16	11

Another O.J. McDuffie type receiver! Dawson is not a blazer, but he can make things happen in the open field. He is also developing some mental toughness and is becoming a gamer. The combination of Dawson and Tamarick Vanover should add some punch to that stilted, predictable Chief offense. I like Dawson to double his 1995 numbers!

7 WR

Best of the Rest—

	1995:	1994:	1993:
Anthony Miller — *Denver Broncos*			
Receiving TDS	14	5	7
TDS over 40 Yards	6	1	3
Total Receiving Yards	1,079	1,107	1,162
Total Receptions	59	60	84
Average Receiving Yards/Game	77.1	73.8	72.6
Games Played	14	15	16

Anthony Miller finally showed up in 1995 as the quality receiver that his talent yields. With John Elway and Anthony Miller on the same page, I expect Anthony Miller to continue progressing and scoring around 16-17 TDS. The big issue with Miller is if he can play tough through injuries—sometimes he is a bit of a crybaby!

7 WR **Bill Brooks** — *Washington Redskins*

	1995:	1994:	1993:
Receiving TDS	11	2	5
TDS over 40 Yards	3	0	0
Total Receiving Yards	763	482	714
Total Receptions	53	42	60
Average Receiving Yards/Game	50.9	30.1	44.6
Games Played	15	16	16

The addition of Bill Brooks to a Redskin lineup that includes Henry Ellard means that the *'Skins* are serious about putting a good quality team on the field, while giving their young receivers inspiration. Brooks might not duplicate his '95 numbers, but he certainly will be a great, experienced target for whoever the *'Skins* QB happens to be.

Willie Green — *Carolina Panthers*

	1995:	1994:	1993:
Receiving TDS	6	0	2
TDS over 40 Yards	3	0	1
Total Receiving Yards	882	150	462
Total Receptions	47	9	28
Average Receiving Yards/Game	55.1	37.5	38.5
Games Played	16	4	12

Willie Green is one of those guys who turn up on game highlights and you sit in your living room muttering *"I should get that guy for my team."* But reality should set in, and the follw-up question should be *"Do I really want this nobody named Willie Green"*? If you do, make him a later round selection—he'll still be there!

	1995:	1994:	1993:

Ernie Mills
Pittsburgh Steelers

	1995:	1994:	1993:
Receiving TDS	8	1	1
TDS over 40 Yards	2	0	0
Total Receiving Yards	679	384	386
Total Receptions	39	19	29
Average Receiving Yards/Game	42.4	24.0	24.1
Games Played	16	16	16

Ernie Mills really put his game together in '95 and will miss Neil O'Donnell. Still, if anyone in a Steeler uniform that is under center can get the ball downfield, Mills will be a *heckuva target* along with Yancey Thigpen, Andre Hastings, and Charles Johnson!

Mark Carrier
Carolina Panthers

	1995:	1994:	1993:
Receiving TDS	3	5	3
TDS over 40 Yards	2	0	0
Total Receiving Yards	1,002	452	746
Total Receptions	66	29	43
Average Receiving Yards/Game	62.6	34.8	49.7
Games Played	16	13	15

The key stat here is the 1,002 receiving yards! Carrier is a classy receiver but don't expect him to ever become a big producer in TDS. Steady production, good yardage and maybe 80 receptions.

Haywood Jeffires
Free Agent

	1995:	1994:	1993:
Receiving TDS	8	6	6
TDS over 40 Yards	0	0	1
Total Receiving Yards	684	783	753
Total Receptions	61	68	66
Average Receiving Yards/Game	42.8	48.9	50.2
Games Played	16	16	15

At this writing, Haywood Jeffires has been released by the Oilers due to the salary cap. I am somewhat surprised that Carolina hasn't made a move to sign him since he is a local guy. I think he will re-sign cheaply with the Oilers and be the third WR (after Willie Davis and Chris Sanders). Jeffires is a good complement to an offense with Chris Sanders streaking downfield and should garner 6-8 TDS in '96.

	1995:	1994:	1993:
Horace Copeland — *Tampa Bay Buccaneers*			
Receiving TDS	2	0	4
TDS over 40 Yards	1	0	3
Total Receiving Yards	605	633	308
Total Receptions	35	30	17
Average Receiving Yards/Game	40.3	39.6	25.7
Games Played	15	16	12

I am in a quandry here, just how do you rate Tampa Bay receivers? On the whole, the *Bucs* have a corps of some of the best receivers in the NFL: Copeland, Alvin Harper, and Courtney Hawkins. Yet, their stats are rather meager. Blame Trent Dilfer, blame Sam Wyche, blame it on Rio, or blame it on the bossa nova—but facts are facts! Copeland could be explosive, but will he be a primary target? As it is, Harper and Hawkins barely get noticed.

	1995:	1994:	1993:
Qadry Ismail — *Minnesota Vikings*			
Receiving TDS	3	5	1
TDS over 40 Yards	3	2	0
Total Receiving Yards	597	696	212
Total Receptions	32	45	19
Average Receiving Yards/Game	37.3	43.5	15.1
Games Played	16	16	14

In my mind, the '*Missile*' Qadry Ismail could be as effective as an O.J. McDuffie if he got the opportunity. At the moment he plays third fiddle to the likes of Cris Carter and Jake Reed, but he really can be utilized more as a returner. Unless Carter or Reed suffer an injury, I wouldn't expect more than 5 TDS and 50 receptions out of Qadry.

	1995:
Willie Jackson — *Jacksonville Jaguars*	
Receiving TDS	5
TDS over 40 Yards	0
Total Receiving Yards	589
Total Receptions	53
Average Receiving Yards/Game	42.1
Games Played	14

Let's look closely at the Jags, as they have signed Keenan McCardell (from Cleveland) and I think Keenan will become their top receiver. Willie Jackson will probably nose out Desmond Howard for the number two slot. With Mark Brunell at quarterback, I expect Willie Jackson to grab 7-8 TDS.

	1995:	1994:	1993:
Raghib Ismail *Oakland Raiders*			
Receiving TDS	3	5	1
TDS over 40 Yards	3	0	1
Total Receiving Yards	491	513	353
Total Receptions	28	34	26
Average Receiving Yards/Game	30.7	32.1	27.2
Games Played	16	16	13

Rocket Ismail may need another team to play for, because his numbers over the past three season are weak. This guy should be faring much better than just average "*Gee, I think I'm Desmond Howard*" type numbers. He does nothing to stretch out the field. Perhaps he has forgotten that he's supposed to be a *game breaker*, not just a *heart breaker*! With additional re-emphasis on the offense, expect 5-6 TDS and not much else unless he adds some grit to his game.

Leslie Shepherd *Washington Redskins*

Receiving TDS	3
TDS over 40 Yards	1
Total Receiving Yards	486
Total Receptions	29
Average Receiving Yards/Game	34.7
Games Played	14

Leslie Shepherd is a real gamer, but with the signing of Bill Brooks, at best he will be a fourth receiver in the Redskins game plan.
He does, however, possess some breakaway speed and the ability to come up with a big play. Definitely a late round selection!

Chris Calloway *New York Giants*

Receiving TDS	3	2	3
TDS over 40 Yards	1	1	0
Total Receiving Yards	796	666	513
Total Receptions	56	43	35
Average Receiving Yards/Game	49.8	41.6	39.5
Games Played	16	16	13

I have never been a big fan of Chris Calloway because his numbers are always so average. For years I have listened as experts have touted his ability, but frankly I don't see it and who needs a guy that scores only two or three times on your FFL roster?

	1995:	1994:	1993:
Daryl Hobbs *Oakland Raiders*			
Receiving TDS	3		
TDS over 40 Yards	1		
Total Receiving Yards	612		
Total Receptions	38		
Average Receiving Yards/Game	38.3		
Games Played	16		

Another in the long line of Raider backup receivers that look good in camp (i.e., Ismail, Jett, etc.) and then put up average numbers. In fairness to Hobbs, he is the fourth receiver and sees little action, but again, why draft a guy that can muster only 3 scores?

7 WR Floyd Turner *Indianapolis Colts*

	1995:	1994:	1993:
Receiving TDS	4	6	1
TDS over 40 Yards	1	0	0
Total Receiving Yards	431	593	163
Total Receptions	35	52	12
Average Receiving Yards/Game	30.8	37.1	20.4
Games Played	14	16	12

I really like Floyd Turner, but I don't see him benefitting from Jim Harbaugh's air game. Besides, the Colts made a super draft selection in wide receiver Marvin Harrison. That means that Turner now must compete with Marvin Harrison, Flipper Anderson, Aaron Bailey, and Sean Dawkins. I wouldn't expect a change in his stats for 1995; however, he may find another home!

Kevin Williams *Dallas Cowboys*

	1995:	1994:	1993:
Receiving TDS	2	0	2
TDS over 40 Yards	1	0	0
Total Receiving Yards	613	181	151
Total Receptions	38	13	20
Average Receiving Yards/Game	38.3	12.1	9.4
Games Played	16	15	16

Didn't Williams score those two *teeters* in the season finale? What a disappointment! That is why I am charged up over Neon Deion, because I think the *'Pokes* need another aggressive stud to play across from Michael Irvin. Williams just seems to disappear from time to time, and this is not acceptable to FFL franchise owners.

	1995:	1994:	1993:

Aaron Bailey
Indianapolis Colts

	1995:
Receiving TDS	3
TDS over 40 Yards	0
Total Receiving Yards	379
Total Receptions	21
Average Receiving Yards/Game	25.3
Games Played	15

I really like this second year player, but I wonder where and when he will find a home in this offense. Marvin Harrison is a #1 draft pick and he can start now. Flipper Anderson and Floyd Turner are vets and one or the other may get cut. Sean Dawkins is another former #1 pick and he has too much upside to be sent packing—so you tell me how Bailey will get effective playing time?

Mark Seay
Philadelphia Eagles

	1995:	1994:	1993:
Receiving TDS	3	6	*(Did not Play)*
TDS over 40 Yards	0	1	
Total Receiving Yards	537	645	
Total Receptions	45	58	
Average Receiving Yards/Game	33.6	40.3	
Games Played	16	16	

Mark Seay drops way too many passes, but he will stick around in Philadelphia in light of Fred Barnett moving onto Miami. Irving Fryar is in the fold, but he won't have Dan Marino passing the bullet. Calvin Williams has been a disappointment the past several seasons and that will open the competition up for Seay.

Anthony Morgan
Green Bay Packers

	1995:	1994:	1993:
Receiving TDS	4	4	0
TDS over 40 Yards	0	1	0
Total Receiving Yards	344	397	8
Total Receptions	31	28	1
Average Receiving Yards/Game	21.5	30.5	8.0
Games Played	16	13	1

Anthony Morgan is a speedster, but to date he has shown very little as a fulltime receiver. The *Pack* drafted Derrick Mayes and he may push Morgan out of the picture. Also, don't overlook the improving second year man Antonio Freeman. Therefore, I wouldn't expect Morgan's numbers to increase too much over 1995's production.

	1995:	1994:	1993:
Alvin Harper			
Tampa Bay Buccaneers			
Receiving TDS	2	8	5
TDS over 40 Yards	0	2	2
Total Receiving Yards	633	821	777
Total Receptions	46	33	36
Average Receiving Yards/Game	48.7	58.6	51.8
Games Played	13	14	15

What a bum!
He owes the *Bucs* fans some major effort (or else a refund on ticket prices) in '96. It appears that Alvin Harper took the money and ran. Unfortunately for the *Bucs*, he didn't run many post patterns and really was a flop! Perhaps Tony Dungy can get Harper to commit to football and perform.

	1995:	1994:	1993:
Calvin Williams			
Philadelphia Eagles			
Receiving TDS	2	3	10
TDS over 40 Yards	0	0	1
Total Receiving Yards	768	813	725
Total Receptions	63	58	60
Average Receiving Yards/Game	48.0	50.8	45.3
Games Played	16	16	16

Where is the Calvin Williams of 1993?
Who is this imposter?
In light of the questionable quarterbacking, I am curious if Ty Detmer or Rodney Peete can really get the job done. I say hold off on Williams and grab him in the later rounds!

Pre-Season Wide Receiver Ranking—

	Player:	Team:
1	Jerry Rice	San Francisco 49ers
2	Herman Moore	Detroit Lions
3	Carl Pickens	Cincinnati Bengals
4	Isaac Bruce	St. Louis Rams
5	Robert Brooks	Green Bay Packers
6	Michael Irvin	Dallas Cowboys
7	Eric Metcalf	Atlanta Falcons
8	Tim Brown	Oakland Raiders
9	Anthony Miller	Denver Broncos
10	Cris Carter	Minnesota Vikings
11	Curtis Conway	Chicago Bears
12	Joey Galloway	Seattle Seahawks
13	Andre Rison	Baltimore Ravens
14	Keyshawn Johnson	New York Jets
15	Chris Sanders	Houston Oilers
16	J.J. Stokes	San Francisco 49ers
17	Deion Sanders	Dallas Cowboys
18	Tamarick Vanover	Kansas City Chiefs
19	Fred Barnett	Miami Dolphins
20	Quinn Early	Buffalo Bills
21	Darnay Scott	Cincinnati Bengals
22	Brett Perriman	Detroit Lions
23	O.J. McDuffie	Miami Dolphins
24	Michael Westbrook	Washington Redskins
25	Vincent Brisby	New England Patriots
26	Terance Mathis	Atlanta Falcons
27	Jake Reed	Minnesota Vikings
28	Rob Moore	Arizona Cardinals
29	Willie Davis	Houston Oilers
30	Shawn Jefferson	New England Patriots
31	Tony Martin	San Diego Chargers
32	Michael Jackson	Baltimore Ravens
33	Frank Sanders	Arizona Cardinals
34	Mike Sherrard	Denver Broncos
35	Jeff Graham	New York Jets
36	Henry Ellard	Washington Redskins
37	Torrance Small	New Orleans Saints
38	Bert Emanuel	Atlanta Falcons
39	Johnnie Morton	Detroit Lions
40	Andre Reed	Buffalo Bills
41	Randal Hill	Miami Dolphins
42	Michael Haynes	New Orleans Saints
43	Yancey Thigpen	Pittsburgh Steelers
44	Keenan McCardell	Carolina Panthers
45	Courtney Hawkins	Tampa Bay Buccaneers
46	Irving Fryar	Philadelphia Eagles
47	Sean Dawkins	Indianapolis Colts
48	Brian Blades	Seattle Seahawks
49	Thomas Lewis	New York Giants
50	Lake Dawson	Kansas City Chiefs

7
WR

	Player:	Team:
51	Kevin Williams	Dallas Cowboys
52	Michael Haynes	New Orleans Saints
53	Calvin Williams	Philadelphia Eagles
54	Alvin Harper	Tampa Bay Buccaneers
55	Bill Brooks	Washington Redskins
56	Willie Green	Carolina Panthers
57	Mark Carrier	Carolina Panthers
58	Eric Moulds	Buffalo Bills
59	Michael Timpson	Chicago Bears
60	Marvin Harrison	Indianapolis Colts
61	J.J. Birden	Atlanta Falcons
62	Ernie Mills	Pittsburgh Steelers
63	Terry Glenn	New England Patriots
64	Chris T. Jones	Philadelphia Eagles
65	Alex Van Dyke	New York Jets
66	Raghib Ismail	Oakland Raiders
67	Glyn Milburn	Detroit Lions
68	David Palmer	Minnesota Vikings
69	Eddie Kennison	St. Louis Rams
70	Amani Toomer	New York Giants
71	Derrick Alexander	Baltimore Ravens
72	Wayne Chrebet	New York Jets
73	Charles Jordan	Miami Dolphins
74	Mushin Muhammed	Carolina Panthers
75	Daryl Hobbs	Oakland Raiders
76	Mark Seay	Philadelphia Eagles
77	Jimmy Oliver	San Diego Chargers
78	Floyd Turner	Indianapolis Colts
79	Lawrence Dawsey	Tampa Bay Buccaneers
80	Qadry Ismail	Minnesota Vikings
81	Willie Anderson	Indianapolis Colts
82	Will Moore	New England Patriots
83	Andre Coleman	San Diego Chargers
84	Todd Kinchen	St. Louis Rams
85	Ed McCaffrey	Denver Broncos
86	Willie Jackson	Jacksonville Jaguars
87	Horace Copeland	Tampa Bay Buccaneers
88	Antonio Freeman	Green Bay Packers
89	Leslie Shepherd	Washington Redskins
90	Steve Tasker	Buffalo Bills
91	Ricky Proehl	Seattle Seahawks
92	Chris Calloway	New York Giants
93	Mike Pritchard	Denver Broncos
94	Desmond Howard	Jacksonville Jaguars
95	Anthony Morgan	Green Bay Packers
96	Bryan Still	San Diego Chargers
97	Aaron Bailey	Indianapolis Colts
98	Haywood Jeffires	Free Agent
99	Olanda Truitt	Free Agent
100	Stepfret Williams	Dallas Cowboys

8 Tight Ends

Drafting Tight Ends—

If your league doesn't use tight ends, then you can pass up this piece of advice—if they do, listen up! The top TD producers at tight end generally max out at seven-eight TDs for a season; therefore, don't draft one in the early rounds. I suggest zoning in on Ben Coates, Mark Chmura, and maybe Brent Jones, Shannon Sharpe, Jay Novacek, and Wesley Walls. These are quality players that *can* score and receive a great deal of solid offensive attention.

But if your league doesn't designate a separate category for tight ends, are they worth drafting? Sure, but I wouldn't draft them early. Tight ends are more possession-type receivers and rarely streak for 70 yard TDs or pull in 100 receptions in a season. Still, I think that trend will be changing soon, due to a plethora of young talented tight ends.

The Oakland Raiders this year drafted Rickey Dudley out of Ohio State. Dudley is slated to become *the* next great tight end. The Raiders are already placing him in the same legendary status of Dave Caspar, Raymond Chester, and Todd Christensen. Look at the Jets—they are so intrigued with the prospective talent of second year man Kyle Brady that they released hard-headed Johnny Mitchell. Cincinnati has been concentrating on further opening up their offense. So besides finally unveiling running back Ki-Jana Carter this season, they will also send the *Marc Bavaro clone*...Marco Battaglia. This will match Marco up with another super bookend (Tony McGee). But the list of super athletic tight ends continues to grow. Look around in Pittsburgh (Mark Bruener), Indianapolis (Ken Dilger), Seattle (Christian Fauria), Philadelphia (Jason Dunn), Detroit (David Sloan), Jacksonville (Pete Mitchell), and Arizona (Johnny McWilliams). These players have exceptional receiving skills and will help transform the trend from the past decade, of tight ends performing as an extension of the offensive tackle for blocking purposes only.

Who are these guys? The True Sleepers—

Player:	Team:
David Sloan	Detroit Lions
Alfred Pupunu	San Diego Chargers
Pete Mitchell	Jacksonville Jaguars
Byron Chamberlain	Denver Broncos
Frank Wycheck	Houston Oilers
Shannon Mitchell	San Diego Chargers
Brian Kinchen	Baltimore Ravens

Questions Marks at Tight End—

Eric Green	Surprise here, huh? Will '*Big House*' survive Camp J.J.? If Eric '*Aches & Pains*' thinks he can skip practices to whirlpool away, dice that thought, *big guy*!
Shannon Sharpe	If Eric Green had Sharpe's guts, he'd be All-Pro! If Big Eric had Sharpe's injuries…he'd be on IR. Denver tried to trade Sharpe prior to draft—no takers. Can Shannon rebound with a healthy season?
Johnny Mitchell	Johnny, babe, we can't see the talent if you don't don't have the guts to show it. How about breaking a sweat out there and holding the ego and attitude in check? Great potential; too bad he hasn't stretched it out and delivered. Expect the Saints or Chiefs to leap for Johnny Mitchell.
Jay Novacek	If Michael Irvin doesn't juke his legal woes, Jay will have to be the go to guy (*please, don't say Kevin Williams*). The problem with Jay is that he has been pretty banged up. Can he stay healthy? How serious are his back/disc problems?
Keith Jackson	Once considered the prototype tight end. Once a real stud. Sorry folks, but when you continue to use the word '*once*' we ain't talking about *now*! If Jackson stays with the Pack, he could score a bit, but Chmura is much better…*now*!
Wesley Walls	Really an underrated player for years. I think he will get plenty of throws and TDS this season with the Panthers. Very solid!

Rickey Dudley	All systems go here, except for the fact that he is a rookie. I wonder if he will get the opportunity to shine. Remember how the Raiders kept last year's number one (*Napoleon Kaufman*) under wraps? Definitely a true talent.
Brent Jones	This is a *real* tough guy. Broken legs, knee problems…you name it, he doesn't flinch and he still delivers. A healthy Steve Young will mean plenty of action and scores for Brent.
Irv Smith	Irv came into the league with a big rep. Okay, Irv, Wesley Walls is gone and now the ball is yours. *Rock on…or move on!*
Troy Drayton	Known for playing in spurts. How about some consistency? The Rams were trying to peddle him—that's not much of an endorsement.

'96 Pre-Season Tight End Review—

		1995:	1994:	1993:
Ben Coates *New England Patriots*	Receiving TDs	6	7	8
	TDs over 40 Yards	0	1	1
	Total Receiving Yards	915	1,174	659
	Total Receptions	84	96	53
	Average Receiving Yards/Game	57.2	73.4	41.2
	Games Played	16	16	16

Throw out last season in New England—blame it on Bledsoe or Parcells or just bad luck! A healthy Drew Bledsoe will make a major difference in Ben Coates' production. Coates is a 1,000-yard receiver and can score 10-12 TDs and haul in 90-100 passes.

Mark Chmura *Green Bay Packers*	Receiving TDs	7	0	
	TDs over 40 Yards	0	0	
	Total Receiving Yards	679	165	
	Total Receptions	54	14	
	Average Receiving Yards/Game	42.4	33.0	
	Games Played	16	5	

If you need a quality tight end, grab this guy on the way up! Look at the increase in numbers from his rookie season in '94 to last season. Also remember that Chmura and Favre have developed a rapport and trust. Chmura is a legit 10-12 TD tight end!

Brent Jones *San Francisco 49ers*	Receiving TDs	3	9	3
	TDs over 40 Yards	0	1	0
	Total Receiving Yards	768	670	735
	Total Receptions	63	49	68
	Average Receiving Yards/Game	48.0	44.7	45.9
	Games Played	16	15	16

Critics of Brent Jones are now pointing out that he is not the player he was. *Bunk!* The guy played with injuries and played very well, in spite of Steve Young not being available for a chunk of the time. With a healthy Steve Young, expect Jones to score 8-9 TDs in '96.

		1995:	*1994:*	*1993:*
Eric Green	Receiving TDS	3	4	5
Miami Dolphins	TDS over 40 Yards	0	0	1
	Total Receiving Yards	499	618	942
	Total Receptions	43	46	63
	Average Receiving Yards/Game	35.6	44.1	62.8
	Games Played	14	14	15

No more excuses for nagging injuries in *Camp Von Jimmy Johnson!* Eric Green is in for a surprise this season. *No practice, no play!* Every year I sound like a broken record praising Green as a super tight end. And every year, Eric *'Big House'* Green is a *'big bust'*. If anyone is going to crank up Green, it will be Jimmy Johnson. Therefore (*here I go again*), I lay it on the line and rate Green as a 8-10 TD player!

Shannon Sharpe	Receiving TDS	4	4	9
Denver Broncos	TDS over 40 Yards	0	1	2
	Total Receiving Yards	756	1,010	995
	Total Receptions	63	87	81
	Average Receiving Yards/Game	58.2	72.1	62.2
	Games Played	13	14	16

Rumors were flying around during the spring that Shannon Sharpe was being offered around as trade bait. I think that's a mistake and hopefully a healthy Sharpe will help push the Broncos in '96. If healthy and still in Denver, Sharpe is worth 8 TDs!

Tony McGee	Receiving TDS	4	1	0
Cincinnati Bengals	TDS over 40 Yards	0	0	0
	Total Receiving Yards	768	492	525
	Total Receptions	63	40	44
	Average Receiving Yards/Game	48.0	35.1	37.5
	Games Played	16	14	14

Tony McGee started to find the endzone in 1995 and I expect him to double that production in '96! Jeff Blake has proven to be a solid quarterback and McGee has continued to improve and deliver.

			1995:	1994:	1993:
Johnny Mitchell *Free Agent*		Receiving TDs	5	4	6
		TDs over 40 Yards	1	0	1
		Total Receiving Yards	497	749	630
		Total Receptions	45	58	39
		Average Receiving Yards/Game	41.4	49.9	48.5
		Games Played	12	15	13

So much talent, so little gumption and drive! Hey Johnny, catch a clue! This is the NFL! How about a little hustle and some toughness? Mitchell should be a 10-12 TD player, not a name on the waiver wires.

			1995:	1994:
Wesley Walls *Carolina Panthers*		Receiving TDs	4	4
		TDs over 40 Yards	0	0
		Total Receiving Yards	694	406
		Total Receptions	57	38
		Average Receiving Yards/Game	43.4	31.2
		Games Played	16	13

8
TE

With the departure of WR Quinn Early, Walls could be a newfound favorite target of Jim Everett. I could see him making or even besting his usual 4-5 TDs.

			1995:
Ken Dilger *Indianapolis Colts*		Receiving TDs	4
		TDs over 40 Yards	0
		Total Receiving Yards	635
		Total Receptions	42
		Average Receiving Yards/Game	39.7
		Games Played	16

Ken is a steady player, much like Mark Chmura and with additional work in the offensive scheme, he can score 8 TDs! Jim Harbaugh likes Dilger and he looks for him around the endzone. Good solid player and pick!

Rickey Dudley *Oakland Raiders*		Receiving TDs	*(Rookie)*
		TDs over 40 Yards	
		Total Receiving Yards	
		Total Receptions	
		Average Receiving Yards/Game	
		Games Played	

Dudley appears poised to break it wide open this season. While he may be a rookie, the Raiders are committed to airing it out more this season, and Kerry Cash is getting creaky. Look for good things from this guy this season.

	1995:	1994:	1993:
Kyle Brady — *New York Jets*			
Receiving TDS	2		
TDS over 40 Yards	0		
Total Receiving Yards	262		
Total Receptions	26		
Average Receiving Yards/Game	16.8		
Games Played	15		

Kyle Brady is much better than his stats. I also think that he and the other Jets will benefit from Neil O'Donnell's presence. I like Brady even more since Johnny Mitchell has been released. Expect 5-6 TDS and 50 receptions!

	1995:	1994:	1993:
Troy Drayton — *St. Louis Rams*			
Receiving TDS	4	6	4
TDS over 40 Yards	0	0	0
Total Receiving Yards	458	276	319
Total Receptions	47	32	27
Average Receiving Yards/Game	28.6	21.2	26.6
Games Played	16	13	12

Troy Drayton is a talented tight end. However, in the spring he was being offered around as a tradeable option. If he stays in St. Louis, I can't see him scoring over 5-6 TDS!

	1995:	1994:	1993:
Jay Novacek — *Dallas Cowboys*			
Receiving TDS	5	2	2
TDS over 40 Yards	0	0	0
Total Receiving Yards	768	475	445
Total Receptions	63	47	44
Average Receiving Yards/Game	48.0	33.9	29.7
Games Played	15	14	15

Just when it appeared that Jay Novacek was fading out, he came back with a solid season in '95. The key is Novacek's health, because his hands are never in question! Probably maxed out in '95!

	1995:	1994:	1993:
Jackie Harris — *Tampa Bay Buccaneers*			
Receiving TDS	1	3	4
TDS over 40 Yards	0	1	1
Total Receiving Yards	751	337	604
Total Receptions	62	26	42
Average Receiving Yards/Game	46.9	37.4	50.3
Games Played	16	9	12

Although Jackie Harris didn't rip apart the scoring records (1 TD), he increased his receptions and yardage. The key to increased TD production is the maturing process of Trent Dilfer. Hey, to score you gotta have a QB that can fire the ball! Still, Harris is not going to score more than four TDS in '96!

			1995:	1994:	1993:
Mark Bruener *Pittsburgh Steelers*	Receiving TDS		3		
	TDS over 40 Yards		0		
	Total Receiving Yards		238		
	Total Receptions		26		
	Average Receiving Yards/Game		14.9		
	Games Played		16		

I really like Mark Bruener, but I am still questioning the Steelers' quarterbacking situation. Bruener however, could be a great secondary option in this offense. I'd be happy with 5-6 TDS in '96!

Jason Dunn *Philadelphia Eagles*	Receiving TDS		(Rookie)		
	TDS over 40 Yards				
	Total Receiving Yards				
	Total Receptions				
	Average Receiving Yards/Game				
	Games Played				

Should step in and start right away for Philadelphia. The Eagles were talking to Johnny Mitchell, until they drafted Dunn. This says what they think of him. Eagles Offensive Coordinator Jon Gruden is a product of Bill Walsh's offensive system where the TE plays a big part, so you can count on Dunn seeing the football.

Johnny McWilliams *Arizona Cardinals*	Receiving TDS		(Rookie)		
	TDS over 40 Yards				
	Total Receiving Yards				
	Total Receptions				
	Average Receiving Yards/Game				
	Games Played				

Was considered one of the best pass-catching tight ends in the draft and is going to a team in need of a tight end. However, tight ends get few opportunities to score—rookie tight ends even fewer!

			1995:	1994:	1993:
Irv Smith *New Orleans Saints*	Receiving TDS		3	3	2
	TDS over 40 Yards		0	0	0
	Total Receiving Yards		466	330	180
	Total Receptions		45	26	16
	Average Receiving Yards/Game		29.1	23.6	18.0
	Games Played		16	14	10

With Wesley Walls moving onto Carolina, the door may open wide for Irv Smith in the Saints offense. We could be talking about 5-6 TDS and 50-60 receptions!

	1995:	1994:	1993:
Pete Mitchell *Jacksonville Jaguars*			
Receiving TDS	2		
TDS over 40 Yards	0		
Total Receiving Yards	527		
Total Receptions	41		
Average Receiving Yards/Game	32.9		
Games Played	16		

Mitchell is as good a receiving tight end as there is in the league. However, he is not much of a blocker and with a Tom Coughlin offense the tight end has to block. The *Jags'* are weak at receiver, so Mitchell could end up being one of their top receiving threats.

	1995:	1994:	1993:
Frank Wycheck *Houston Oilers*			
Receiving TDS	2	1	0
TDS over 40 Yards	0	0	0
Total Receiving Yards	471	55	113
Total Receptions	40	6	8
Average Receiving Yards/Game	29.4	9.2	18.8
Games Played	16	6	6

Frank Wycheck is a talented receiver and may see his production rise in Houston this season. He has a great attitude and work ethic—plus the Oiler offense is making all the right moves. Expect Wycheck to catch 55 passes and 4-5 TDS!

	1995:
Christian Fauria *Seattle Seahawks*	
Receiving TDS	1
TDS over 40 Yards	0
Total Receiving Yards	181
Total Receptions	17
Average Receiving Yards/Game	12.9
Games Played	14

Fauria has great hands and hopefully in his second season he will get an opportunity to use 'em! Pencil Fauria in for 3-4 TDS in '96!

	1995:
Alfred Pupunu *San Diego Chargers*	
Receiving TDS	0
TDS over 40 Yards	0
Total Receiving Yards	315
Total Receptions	35
Average Receiving Yards/Game	21.0
Games Played	15

Pupunu started to become one of Stan Humphries' favorite targets down by the goal line last season, and there is no reason why this should not continue. The Chargers also cleared out most of their receiving staff, so Pupunu should be one option that Humphries is comfortable with. His numbers should only get better.

		1995:	1994:	1993:
David Sloan *Detroit Lions*	Receiving TDs	1		
	TDs over 40 Yards	1		
	Total Receiving Yards	184		
	Total Receptions	17		
	Average Receiving Yards/Game	11.5		
	Games Played	16		

David Sloan will compete with Ron Hall and the aging veteran Pete Metzelaars for the TE job in Detroit, so I only pencil him in for 2 TDs at best!

		1995:	1994:	1993:
Howard Cross *New York Giants*	Receiving TDs	0	4	5
	TDs over 40 Yards	0	0	0
	Total Receiving Yards	197	364	272
	Total Receptions	18	31	21
	Average Receiving Yards/Game	13.1	22.8	24.7
	Games Played	15	16	11

Howard Cross is still young enough (29), but will he get the scoring opportunities? The Giants like to punch that ball in and not pass. Cross is a solid player, that appears to be more of a blocking tight end! 2-3 TDs seems to be Cross' mark for '96!

		1995:	1994:	1993:
Andrew Jordan *Minnesota Vikings*	Receiving TDs	2	0	
	TDs over 40 Yards	0	0	
	Total Receiving Yards	185	336	
	Total Receptions	27	47	
	Average Receiving Yards/Game	14.2	25.8	
	Games Played	13	13	

Andrew Jordan is a decent tight end and he can grab decent numbers, but look, he is not going to score more than 4 TDs.

		1995:	1994:	1993:
Keith Jackson *Green Bay Packers*	Receiving TDs	1	7	6
	TDs over 40 Yards	0	0	2
	Total Receiving Yards	142	613	673
	Total Receptions	13	39	59
	Average Receiving Yards/Game	15.8	38.3	48.1
	Games Played	9	16	14

Keith Jackson may have worn out his welcome in the NFL. Once he was one of the great tight ends, but he has certainly appeared as a guy who has lost desire to play. He can still play but where and when? He is now only an average tight end and will never score more than 5 TDs (if that high) again!

	1995:	1994:	1993:
Keith Jennings — *Chicago Bears*			
Receiving TDS	6	3	0
TDS over 40 Yards	0	0	0
Total Receiving Yards	217	75	150
Total Receptions	25	9	16
Average Receiving Yards/Game	13.6	10.7	21.4
Games Played	16	7	7

Keith Jennings played perhaps his best season as a pro and he scored on every 4 passes. Can he keep up that production in '96? *Nah!* Look, be smart! Jennings is a decent but not a good receiving tight end. Expect 3-4 TDS in '96!

	1995:	1994:	1993:
Andrew Glover — *Oakland Raiders*			
Receiving TDS	3	2	1
TDS over 40 Yards	0	0	0
Total Receiving Yards	220	371	55
Total Receptions	26	33	6
Average Receiving Yards/Game	13.8	26.5	13.8
Games Played	16	14	4

Andrew Glover is a journeyman at best. He will soon be watching rookie Rickey Dudley take the job and TD production away!

	1995:	1994:	1993:
Keith Cash — *Kansas City Chiefs*			
Receiving TDS	1	2	4
TDS over 40 Yards	0	0	0
Total Receiving Yards	419	192	242
Total Receptions	42	12	16
Average Receiving Yards/Game	29.9	38.4	24.2
Games Played	14	5	10

Keith Cash has seen his best years and he is now on a downward slide. Sure, Cash can still score, but I just don't see that offense heating it up on the passing front. Three TDS would triple his production in '95!

	1995:
Brian Kinchen — *Baltimore Ravens*	
Receiving TDS	0
TDS over 40 Yards	0
Total Receiving Yards	216
Total Receptions	20
Average Receiving Yards/Game	16.6
Games Played	13

In Bill Belichick's offense, Kinchen was counted on to block first, block second, and catch the ball third! Marchibroda likes to use his tight ends more, but Kinchen should still only be a second or third tight end on your roster at best.

Best of the Rest—

		1995:	1994:	1993:
Kerry Cash	Receiving TDs	2	1	3
Oakland Raiders	TDs over 40 Yards	0	0	0
	Total Receiving Yards	254	190	402
	Total Receptions	25	13	38
	Average Receiving Yards/Game	15.9	17.3	26.8
	Games Played	16	11	15

If Rickey Dudley is as good as everyone says, I don't expect to see Kerry Cash and Andrew Glover to get much action. So don't knock yourself out and waste a draft choice!

		1995:	1994:	1993:
Pete Metzelaars	Receiving TDs	3	5	4
Detroit Lions	TDs over 40 Yards	0	0	0
	Total Receiving Yards	171	428	609
	Total Receptions	20	49	68
	Average Receiving Yards/Game	12.2	28.5	40.6
	Games Played	14	15	15

Metzelaars signed on with Detroit in the spring, and will likely knock Ron Hall out of the starting job. I like this guy playing in an offense with Sanders, Mitchell, Moore, and Milburn!

		1995:
Wendall Gaines	Receiving TDs	2
Arizona Cardinals	TDs over 40 Yards	0
	Total Receiving Yards	117
	Total Receptions	14
	Average Receiving Yards/Game	7.3
	Games Played	16

Move over Wendell Gaines, here comes Johnny McWilliams and some quality receiving skills. Gaines is strictly backup material!

		1995:	1994:	1993:
Ryan Wetnight *Chicago Bears*	Receiving TDS	2	1	1
	TDS over 40 Yards	0	0	0
	Total Receiving Yards	193	104	93
	Total Receptions	24	9	8
	Average Receiving Yards/Game	14.8	17.3	15.5
	Games Played	13	6	6

Ryan Wetnight is an average player and he will never do more than 3 TDS and 30-35 receptions.

		1995:	1994:	1993:
Aaron Pierce *New York Giants*	Receiving TDS	0	4	0
	TDS over 40 Yards	0	0	0
	Total Receiving Yards	310	214	212
	Total Receptions	33	16	15
	Average Receiving Yards/Game	19.4	21.4	30.3
	Games Played	16	10	7

Aaron Pierce is not as good as Howard Cross, yet his numbers overshadow Howard's. Just remember when drafting Cross or Pierce that neither scored in '95!

'96 Pre-Season Tight End Ranking—

	Player:	Team:
1	Ben Coates	New England Patriots
2	Mark Chmura	Green Bay Packers
3	Brent Jones	San Francisco 49ers
4	Eric Green	Miami Dolphins
5	Shannon Sharpe	Denver Broncos
6	Tony McGee	Cincinnati Bengals
7	Johnny Mitchell	Free Agent
8	Wesley Walls	Carolina Panthers
9	Ken Dilger	Indianapolis Colts
10	Rickey Dudley	Oakland Raiders
11	Kyle Brady	New York Jets
12	Troy Drayton	St. Louis Rams
13	Jay Novacek	Dallas Cowboys
14	Jackie Harris	Tampa Bay Buccaneers
15	Mark Bruener	Pittsburgh Steelers
16	Jason Dunn	Philadelphia Eagles
17	Johnny McWilliams	Arizona Cardinals
18	Irv Smith	New Orleans Saints
19	Pete Mitchell	Jacksonville Jaguars
20	Frank Wycheck	Houston Oilers
21	Christian Fauria	Seattle Seahawks
22	Alfred Pupunu	San Diego Chargers
23	David Sloan	Detroit Lions
24	Howard Cross	New York Giants
25	Andrew Jordan	Minnesota Vikings
26	Keith Jackson	Green Bay Packers
27	Keith Jennings	Chicago Bears
28	Andrew Glover	Oakland Raiders
29	Keith Cash	Kansas City Chiefs
30	Brian Kinchen	Baltimore Ravens
31	Pete Metzelaars	Carolina Panthers
32	Kerry Cash	Oakland Raiders
33	Brian Roche	San Diego Chargers
34	Derrick Walker	Kansas City Chiefs
35	Frank Hartley	Baltimore Ravens
36	Scott Galbraith	Washington Redskins
37	Ron Hall	Detroit Lions
38	Tracy Greene	Kansas City Chiefs
39	Aaron Pierce	New York Giants
40	Wendell Gaines	Arizona Cardinals
41	Jamie Asher	Washington Redskins
42	Ryan Wetnight	Chicago Bears
43	Jerry Evans	Denver Broncos
44	James Jenkins	Washington Redskins
45	Shannon Mitchell	San Diego Chargers
46	Carlester Crumpler	Seattle Seahawks
47	Oscar McBride	Arizona Cardinals
48	Fred Baxter	New York Jets
49	Chris Gedney	Chicago Bears
50	Coleman Bell	Washington Redskins

8 TE

9 Kickers and Punters

Please don't overlook this chapter!
In my opinion, the kicker is still a very crucial part of a solid FFL franchise. Who else scores every week? I say shame on you FFLers still wearing the leather helmets and treating the kicking game as if it is unimportant—*Wake Up!* A hot kicker playing for an offense that cruises up and down the field, can mean mega points for you and your greedy FFL team.

The point is you don't want to waffle on this pick and get stuck with some slug toiling for a team that finds itself behind by a bazillion points in the opening minutes of the game. A team regularly down 24-0, hardly is thinking *"Gee, a field goal about now would be nice!"* What you need is a kicker that can boot the 50-yard-plus kicks (i.e., indoor kickers) and one that is on a team that treats the guy like he is a major cog in their offense (i.e., Morten Andersen, Jason Elam, Steve Christie, etc.). These guys are clearly showcased by their head coaches. Heck, there isn't a doubt in June Jones' mind about trotting out Mort to attempt a 55-yarder. It's part of the Falcons offensive game plan—if *Boy George* can throw it in, or *Ironhead* can't run it in, then Mort will boot in through the cross bars. You got to like that attitude!

The opposite low down feeling is to see *your* franchise kicker, standing on the sidelines with his baseball cap turned backwards and watching the head coach decide not to attempt a 45- or 50-yarder because *your* guy might blow it! You don't see young guys like Chris Boniol (Cowboys) attempting those long jobbers. Boniol seems destined to punch the shorter ones for now. Even an indoors dude like Jason Hanson seems so solid and gets a ton of shots, but he doesn't respond well to the 50-plus yarders (despite spending at least half his games in a dome).

Questions Marks at Kicker—

Chip Lohmiller
Is he the old Chip, or the recent Chump?
A couple of years ago he was an untouchable franchise player. Now he can be reached on the waiver wire.

Pete Stoyanovich
Is he suffering from *Chip-itis*?
He hasn't really done as well as he should. *Stoy-o* should be knocking Mort off the top pedestal. Jimmy Johnson will surely point this fact out to him. We'll know if J.J. gets through, if *Stoy-o* begins lacquering his hair, and wears loud beach shirts over his uniform. *Fly, flamingo, fly!*

Fuad Reveiz
Reveiz has been an underrated kicker for years.
He is always selected in fantasy drafts late, but he always has heavy scoring binges. The drawback is he missed 10 field goals.
This gets kickers *shot* in Kansas City!

Norm Johnson
What a great season he had in '95 as he finished 2nd in the NFL in scoring with 141 points (for those of you scoring at home, a certain running back from Dallas had 150 points)! The question here is will the Steelers—minus O'Donnell—be able to move the ball into field goal range? Question number two: Can Norm quarterback?

Jeff Wilkins
Can this kid handle the swirling winds of Candlestick...*err...* 3COM park? *'Niner* kickers seem to have the career longevity of a school of guppies in a piranha tank!

Scott Blanton
The kid looked good during the exhibition season last year.
But Eddie Murray snatched the job until he mysteriously suffered a season ending cramp—or bad indigestion. Blanton could very well end up as the *Redskin* kicker in '96.

Jeff Jaeger	*Pssst*—Jeff, don't look now, but that kid who substituted for you last year (Cole *Porter*—no, Cole *Ford*) probably could outkick 90% of the current crop of NFL booters. But, *geez*, don't freak out, you've got a mildly understanding owner!
Kevin Butler	Is it me? I use to think that Kevin Butler was a 5'5" 155-pound guy because he seemed much better with those chip shots and *el stinko* with the long jobbers. But, whoa, he is 6'1" and 190-pounds. What's he kick with, his pinkie? Misses way too much.
Nick Lowery	He's a great guy and takes it on the chin when *both* Eddie Murray and Matt Bahr call him *gramps!* If Nick hangs onto the job, he will get a zillion chances to score with the *newfangled* high-powered offensive Jets.
Brad Daluiso	It's really bad, Brad, when even Lin Elliott laughs at your attempts at short field goals. The guy is amazing, he can blast a 56-yarder with precision (with 10 yards to spare), and then minutes later in the same game he can fire off a 23-yard sideways squib sailing into a hotdog vendor! *Ain't life grand?*

'96 Pre-Season Kicker Review—

Jason Elam
Denver Broncos

	1995:	1994:	1993:
Extra Points	33/33	29/29	41/42
Field Goals	31/38	30/37	26/35
10-29 Yard Field Goal	7/8	11/11	11/12
30-39 Yard Field Goal	14/15	11/11	7/7
40-49 Yard Field Goal	5/7	7/12	4/10
50+ Yard Field Goal	5/8	1/3	4/6
Points	126	119	119

Number one kicker (*in my eyes*) for this season!
You gotta love a guy that will get 40 cracks at field goals and can boot the 50+ in that thin Denver air!

Morten Andersen
Atlanta Falcons

	1995:	1994:	1993:
Extra Points	29/30	32/32	33/33
Field Goals	31/37	28/39	28/35
10-29 Yard Field Goal	9/9	9/9	9/9
30-39 Yard Field Goal	11/11	11/14	7/7
40-49 Yard Field Goal	3/8	8/10	11/14
50+ Yard Field Goal	8/9	0/6	1/5
Points	122	116	117

There have been plenty of gaffes in the NFL, but one of the biggest has to be the Saints letting Mort sign with Atlanta. As the hand played out, Mort had a great season and New Orleans spent the season sorting out a chorus line of kickers. Andersen nailed *eight* 50 yarders! That in itself warrants him as a terrific pick!!

Pete Stoyanovich
Miami Dolphins

	1995:	1994:	1993:
Extra Points	37/37	35/35	37/37
Field Goals	27/34	24/31	24/32
10-29 Yard Field Goal	8/11	9/9	11/11
30-39 Yard Field Goal	11/11	6/10	7/11
40-49 Yard Field Goal	7/8	8/10	4/7
50+ Yard Field Goal	1/4	1/2	2/2
Points	118	107	109

For some reason Stoyanovich had trouble inside the 29 yard line last season as he missed three *chippies*. For years I have felt that Stoyanovich was the most talented kicker in the NFL, but he seems to always fall short of the mark. Considering HC Jimmy Johnson's obsession for quality and hard work, Pete may settle in as a premier booter!

		1995:	1994:	1993:
Steve Christie *Buffalo Bills*	Extra Points	33/35	38/38	36/37
	Field Goals	31/40	24/28	23/32
	10-29 Yard Field Goal	10/11	11/12	4/5
	30-39 Yard Field Goal	15/18	6/7	12/12
	40-49 Yard Field Goal	4/6	5/7	6/9
	50+ Yard Field Goal	2/5	2/2	1/6
	Points	126	110	105

I really like the *new/old* Buffalo Bills' chances this season and Steve Christie is one of the reasons. Christie will benefit from this improved offense and a healthy Jim Kelly winging the ball. Last season Christie had 40 field goal attempts and he should be in that range again!

		1995:	1994:	1993:
Doug Pelfrey *Cincinnati Bengals*	Extra Points	34/34	24/25	13/16
	Field Goals	29/36	28/33	24/31
	10-29 Yard Field Goal	9/10	9/9	8/8
	30-39 Yard Field Goal	10/12	8/10	6/10
	40-49 Yard Field Goal	10/13	9/10	8/10
	50+ Yard Field Goal	0/1	2/4	2/3
	Points	121	108	85

Pelfrey is a guy that when he gets drafted onto an FFL team, half the league shouts "*who?*" I think after this season, everyone will be aware of his leg. Like the Lions, I believe that those other "*cats*" will score a ton in '96! Pelfrey needs to improve his distance kicking in order to become a all-around kicking weapon.

		1995:	1994:	1993:
Al Del Greco *Houston Oilers*	Extra Points	33/33	18/18	39/40
	Field Goals	27/31	16/20	29/34
	10-29 Yard Field Goal	6/6	4/5	13/13
	30-39 Yard Field Goal	8/8	4/4	8/9
	40-49 Yard Field Goal	10/12	7/8	4/5
	50+ Yard Field Goal	3/5	1/3	4/7
	Points	114	66	126

This is a good pick especially since the Oilers appear to be regrouped as an offensive unit. Del Greco is a polished kicker and this year he may make a move into the top echelon of kickers!

	1995:	1994:	1993:
Jason Hanson — *Detroit Lions*			
Extra Points	48/48	39/40	28/28
Field Goals	28/34	18/27	34/43
10-29 Yard Field Goal	6/6	6/7	9/9
30-39 Yard Field Goal	16/17	7/7	15/15
40-49 Yard Field Goal	5/10	5/8	7/12
50+ Yard Field Goal	1/1	0/5	3/7
Points	132	93	130

Hanson has everything: kicks for an explosive scoring machine, is consistent, and kicks *at home in a dome*. Hanson has everything *except* a powerful leg, as he is not a deep threat! Still, you have to like the fact that it will be rare to see the Lions deadlocked in the 4th quarter in a 7-7 game. Points will be a cinch for Hanson!

	1995:	1994:	1993:
Chris Jacke — *Green Bay Packers*			
Extra Points	43/43	41/43	35/35
Field Goals	17/23	19/26	31/37
10-29 Yard Field Goal	6/7	12/12	13/13
30-39 Yard Field Goal	1/3	4/6	6/10
40-49 Yard Field Goal	7/9	2/5	6/7
50+ Yard Field Goal	3/4	1/3	6/7
Points	94	98	128

Due to Brett Favre tossing a bazillion touchdowns, Jacke must have felt like the Maytag repair man with "*little to do*" but boot extra points! Still, he did manage to nail three 50+ yarders and is always a threat. Never rule out a kicker on a team favored to appear in the latter rounds of the playoffs! *Believe me*—Jacke will generate some points through the uprights!

	1995:	1994:	1993:
Fuad Reveiz — *Minnesota Vikings*			
Extra Points	44/44	30/30	27/28
Field Goals	26/36	34/39	26/35
10-29 Yard Field Goal	8/9	13/13	16/16
30-39 Yard Field Goal	8/11	12/13	6/6
40-49 Yard Field Goal	9/13	8/10	3/7
50+ Yard Field Goal	1/3	1/3	1/6
Points	122	132	105

The secret about Reveiz is that he will blow some kicks. However, he is streaky and capable of hitting 5 field goals in a game! I question whether Warren Moon can continue to move the Vikings with the ease he showed last season. I would expect more than three attempts at 50+ yard kicks, especially since the *Vikes* play inside in that '*Glad Bag*' of a stadium!

	1995:	1994:	1993:
Chris Boniol — *Dallas Cowboys*			
Extra Points	46/48	48/48	
Field Goals	27/28	22/29	
10-29 Yard Field Goal	11/12	6/7	
30-39 Yard Field Goal	13/13	10/12	
40-49 Yard Field Goal	3/3	6/9	
50+ Yard Field Goal	0/0	0/1	
Points	127	114	

Very, very accurate, but he hasn't really been challenged to boot 50-yarders with the game on the line. In fact, in two seasons he has only attempted one 50-yarder! Now if someone in the NFL could stop Emmitt Smith, Boniol's field goal production would increase!

	1995:	1994:	1993:
John Carney — *San Diego Chargers*			
Extra Points	32/33	33/33	31/33
Field Goals	21/26	34/38	31/40
10-29 Yard Field Goal	8/8	12/12	8/8
30-39 Yard Field Goal	10/11	15/15	14/17
40-49 Yard Field Goal	3/5	5/9	7/12
50+ Yard Field Goal	0/2	2/2	2/3
Points	95	135	124

What an *un-Carney* season for such a great kicker! John had solid seasons in '93 and '94, and I fully expect to see him back up with the Andersen's, Elam's, and Stoyanovich's for the '96 season. His stock will fall in most drafts! Therefore, you should be able to select him much later than his value belies!

	1995:
Jeff Wilkins — *San Francisco 49ers*	
Extra Points	27/29
Field Goals	12/13
10-29 Yard Field Goal	6/6
30-39 Yard Field Goal	5/5
40-49 Yard Field Goal	1/2
50+ Yard Field Goal	0/0
Points	63

Not bad for a rookie who kicked in the whipping, cold wind of Candlestick Park—*err*, make that 3COM Park. Wilkins will be brought along slowly, but he should kick a zillion extra points!

Jeff Jaeger
Oakland Raiders

	1995:	1994:	1993:
Extra Points	22/22	31/31	27/29
Field Goals	13/18	22/28	35/44
10-29 Yard Field Goal	4/5	6/6	12/12
30-39 Yard Field Goal	6/7	6/9	13/15
40-49 Yard Field Goal	3/5	8/11	6/10
50+ Yard Field Goal	0/1	2/2	4/7
Points	61	97	132

An injury in the summer of '95 really slowed Jeff Jaeger.
He may be pushed hard this season by Cole Ford for that kicking spot.
I think that Jaeger can get back to his '93 form!

Cary Blanchard
Indianapolis Colts

	1995:	1994:	1993:
Extra Points	22/22	(Did not	31/31
Field Goals	19/24	Play)	17/26
10-29 Yard Field Goal	5/5		8/9
30-39 Yard Field Goal	6/8		4/5
40-49 Yard Field Goal	7/10		5/10
50+ Yard Field Goal	1/1		0/2
Points	79		82

Blanchard was ripped off in New Orleans last season, as he appeared
to have easily won the Saints job. However, just as the season
was to start, he was released in favor of Chip Lohmiler. Lohmiller
bombed and Blanchard was finally rewarded by the Colts.
Good kicker, but how many points are the Colts capable of scoring?

Gary Anderson
Philadelphia Eagles

	1995:	1994:	1993:
Extra Points	32/33	32/32	32/32
Field Goals	22/30	24/29	28/30
10-29 Yard Field Goal	5/5	8/9	9/10
30-39 Yard Field Goal	9/10	8/9	14/14
40-49 Yard Field Goal	8/12	7/9	5/6
50+ Yard Field Goal	0/3	1/2	0/0
Points	98	104	116

Gary Anderson is a solid player, but his downside is age and distance
kicking. Just like Matt Bahr, Kevin Butler, and Eddie Murray, he is
fighting an inconsistent long game. Head coaches now no longer
gamble on these guys hitting long field goals (*since a miss puts the ball
at the spot*). Anderson is a solid pick as a *backup kicker* but you
won't win with him as your *lead kicker*!

		1995:	1994:	1993:
Norm Johnson *Pittsburgh Steelers*	Extra Points	39/39	32/32	34/34
	Field Goals	34/41	21/25	26/27
	10-29 Yard Field Goal	10/10	9/9	8/8
	30-39 Yard Field Goal	14/16	7/7	9/10
	40-49 Yard Field Goal	9/14	4/4	7/7
	50+ Yard Field Goal	1/1	1/5	2/2
	Points	141	95	112

The big question here is: Just how good will the quarterbacking be in Pittsburgh without Neil O'Donnell? Can Jerome Bettis move the piles on the ground? *'Stormin Norman'* will need to see the yardsticks move into scoring territory to be effective. Don't expect a ton of 50 yarders, because he no longer has the booming leg!

		1995:	1994:	1993:
Michael Husted *Tampa Bay Buccaneers*	Extra Points	25/25	20/20	27/27
	Field Goals	19/26	23/35	16/22
	10-29 Yard Field Goal	6/7	8/8	5/5
	30-39 Yard Field Goal	5/7	10/12	5/6
	40-49 Yard Field Goal	5/8	4/10	3/6
	50+ Yard Field Goal	3/4	1/5	3/5
	Points	82	89	75

Now please follow me on this one! The offense however has sputtered under Trent Dilfer and Husted can blast the long and short kicks. So what gives with this pick? I think HC Tony Dungy will shake up the *Bucs* and place Dilfer in a conservative *pick-pick-pick* offense. Husted is a solid selection! Watch him pile up the 50-yarders!

		1995:	1994:	1993:
John Kasay *Carolina Panthers*	Extra Points	27/28	25/26	29/29
	Field Goals	26/33	20/24	23/28
	10-29 Yard Field Goal	7/7	2/2	6/6
	30-39 Yard Field Goal	10/14	11/11	10/11
	40-49 Yard Field Goal	8/11	6/9	4/6
	50+ Yard Field Goal	1/1	1/2	3/5
	Points	105	85	98

John Kasay is a good kicker and now that the Panthers are looking to add some additional offensive punch, I expect Kasay's role to expand with increased field goal opportunities!

		1995:	1994:	1993:
Doug Brien *New Orleans Saints*	Extra Points	35/35	60/62	
	Field Goals	19/29	15/20	
	10-29 Yard Field Goal	7/8	5/5	
	30-39 Yard Field Goal	6/10	5/6	
	40-49 Yard Field Goal	5/9	5/8	
	50+ Yard Field Goal	1/2	0/1	
	Points	92	105	

A Tale of Two Cities! Brien has kicked in San Francisco and New Orleans and is faring much better in the dome versus the swirling winds of 3COM Park. Grab him as your second kicker and see if he *explodes* or just *glumps along*!

Nick Lowery *New York Jets*	Extra Points	24/24	26/27	37/37
	Field Goals	17/21	20/23	23/29
	10-29 Yard Field Goal	5/5	8/8	8/8
	30-39 Yard Field Goal	7/9	6/7	7/9
	40-49 Yard Field Goal	3/3	6/8	7/11
	50+ Yard Field Goal	2/4	0/0	1/1
	Points	75	86	106

Nick Lowery has been the consummate professional for years. Unfortunately, Lowery is at the end of his distinguished career. Now, having said that, as long as Lowery makes the team, expect a productive season because Neil O'Donnell will consistently push the Jets into a *kicker's delight*—the Red Zone!

Matt Stover *Baltimore Ravens*	Extra Points	26/26	32/32	36/36
	Field Goals	29/33	26/28	16/22
	10-29 Yard Field Goal	13/13	8/8	4/4
	30-39 Yard Field Goal	9/10	10/11	5/6
	40-49 Yard Field Goal	7/9	8/8	6/8
	50+ Yard Field Goal	0/1	0/1	1/4
	Points	113	110	84

Very consistent kicker, but he does not knock down the long kicks. I expect HC Teddy Marchibroda to open up the offense and move the ball much more than the conservative Bill Belichick. Yet, I don't foresee Stover banging out huge numbers, unless he makes some 50-yarders!

		1995:	1994:	1993:
Eddie Murray	Extra Points	33/33	33/33	38/38
Washington Redskins	Field Goals	27/36	21/25	28/33
	10-29 Yard Field Goal	10/10	9/9	8/8
	30-39 Yard Field Goal	10/13	10/10	9/12
	40-49 Yard Field Goal	6/11	2/6	8/8
	50+ Yard Field Goal	1/2	0/0	3/5
	Points	114	96	122

Eddie is no longer a sure bet to sign with Washington and may turn his spot over to Scott Blanton. Murray can still kick, but he no longer has the power in the foot to be a long distance power booter!

		1995:	1994:	1993:
Greg Davis	Extra Points	19/19	17/17	37/37
Arizona Cardinals	Field Goals	30/39	20/26	21/28
	10-29 Yard Field Goal	14/15	10/11	12/12
	30-39 Yard Field Goal	9/10	3/4	1/1
	40-49 Yard Field Goal	6/8	6/7	4/10
	50+ Yard Field Goal	1/6	1/4	4/5
	Points	109	77	100

I am hopeful that HC Vince Tobin will shake up the Cards and re-introduce the offense as a viable component of the overall game plan! Boomer Esiason will move the ball with some pretty decent offensive threats. This should provide Davis with many more opportunities to *shwak* the pigskin through the uprights!

		1995:	1994:
Todd Peterson	Extra Points	40/40	4/4
Seattle Seahawks	Field Goals	23/28	2/4
	10-29 Yard Field Goal	6/7	1/1
	30-39 Yard Field Goal	9/10	1/1
	40-49 Yard Field Goal	8/10	0/2
	50+ Yard Field Goal	0/1	0/0
	Points	109	10

Peterson has finally gotten a full year under his belt and I sense that he will continue to improve and impress. I also believe that QB Rick Mirer will leave a lot of scoring "*on the table.*" In other words, he will not consistently toss TDs and thus will provide Peterson with ample opportunities to kick field goals!

	1995:	1994:	1993:

Kevin Butler
Chicago Bears

	1995:	1994:	1993:
Extra Points	45/45	24/24	21/22
Field Goals	23/30	21/29	27/36
10-29 Yard Field Goal	16/19	8/8	7/8
30-39 Yard Field Goal	5/7	6/9	12/13
40-49 Yard Field Goal	2/2	5/8	3/7
50+ Yard Field Goal	0/2	2/4	5/8
Points	114	87	102

On paper, Butler had a good season due to all those extra points—48—but he made only 23 field goals and was zero-for-two attempting 50-yarders! He only had 2 cracks (and made 'em) on kicks over forty yards, therefore he wasn't much of a point producer. Expect similar numbers this season!

Lin Elliott
Free Agent

	1995:	1994:	1993:
Extra Points	34/37	30/30	2/3
Field Goals	24/30	25/30	2/4
10-29 Yard Field Goal	10/11	18/20	1/1
30-39 Yard Field Goal	7/9	4/6	0/1
40-49 Yard Field Goal	7/10	3/4	1/2
50+ Yard Field Goal	0/0	0/0	0/0
Points	106	105	8

Elliott had a decent season until that playoff game where he missed three chip shots and frankly, personally lost the game! In fact, if I was Elliott, I would have just left the field and headed to the parking lot in my uniform. Put his career in mothballs for now—maybe he will resurface six months from now in New Orleans, or St. Louis. Just keep him off your roster!

Michael Hollis
Jacksonville Jaguars

	1995:
Extra Points	27/28
Field Goals	20/27
10-29 Yard Field Goal	7/10
30-39 Yard Field Goal	7/8
40-49 Yard Field Goal	4/6
50+ Yard Field Goal	2/3
Points	87

Hey, who was this guy? Last season Hollis stepped in and performed very well. I like his leg strength and think he could blast 5 long balls (50-yards+), in '96! He can be a steal as a backup kicking selection. I doubt that anyone in an FFL league outside of Jacksonville will grab Hollis!

		1995:	1994:	1993:
Brad Daluiso	Extra Points	28/28	5/5	0/0
New York Giants	Field Goals	20/27	11/11	1/3
	10-29 Yard Field Goal	7/7	3/3	0/0
	30-39 Yard Field Goal	9/11	5/5	0/0
	40-49 Yard Field Goal	2/7	2/2	0/0
	50+ Yard Field Goal	2/2	1/1	1/3
	Points	88	55	3

Brad Daluiso is a success story only in the fact that he actually made it in the NFL! Daluiso was originally signed just to boot kickoffs and every once in a while attempt a *time-is-running-out, two-seconds-left-in-the-half, 60-yarder*! Daluiso in a dome would be illegal! The guy could hit a 65-70 yarder. That's great! But Daluiso on a chip shot can be a hair-raising (or hair-losing) experience! The other knock on Daluiso is that he plays for a very conservative offense.

		1995:	1994:	1993:
Matt Bahr	Extra Points	27/27	36/36	28/29
New England Patriots	Field Goals	23/33	27/34	13/18
	10-29 Yard Field Goal	12/13	14/14	6/8
	30-39 Yard Field Goal	3/8	9/12	5/5
	40-49 Yard Field Goal	6/7	4/8	2/5
	50+ Yard Field Goal	2/5	0/0	0/0
	Points	96	117	67

I am going to grade Matt low, due to his age and lack of consistency and leg strength. Bahr would be exceptional for extra points and *chippies*, but he no longer has the edge to be a huge scorer for a fantasy team!

		1995:	1994:	1993:
Dean Biasucci	Extra Points	13/14	37/37	15/16
St. Louis Rams	Field Goals	9/12	16/24	26/31
	10-29 Yard Field Goal	4/5	6/6	15/15
	30-39 Yard Field Goal	3/4	3/7	7/8
	40-49 Yard Field Goal	1/1	5/9	3/6
	50+ Yard Field Goal	1/2	2/2	1/2
	Points	40	85	93

I think Chip Lohmiller will beat out Biasucci for the St. Louis job. Biasucci was very consistent during his short stint with St. Louis, but he is beginning to fall into that aging kicker syndrome!

'96 Pre-Season Kicker Ranking—

	Player:	Team:
1	Jason Elam	*Denver Broncos*
2	Morten Andersen	*Atlanta Falcons*
3	Pete Stoyanovich	*Miami Dolphins*
4	Steve Christie	*Buffalo Bills*
5	Doug Pelfrey	*Cincinnati Bengals*
6	Al Del Greco	*Houston Oilers*
7	Jason Hanson	*Detroit Lions*
8	Chris Jacke	*Green Bay Packers*
9	Fuad Reveiz	*Minnesota Vikings*
10	Chris Boniol	*Dallas Cowboys*
11	John Carney	*San Diego Chargers*
12	Jeff Wilkins	*San Francisco 49ers*
13	Jeff Jaeger	*Oakland Raiders*
14	Cary Blanchard	*Indianapolis Colts*
15	Gary Anderson	*Philadelphia Eagles*
16	Norm Johnson	*Pittsburgh Steelers*
17	Michael Husted	*Tampa Bay Buccaneers*
18	John Kasay	*Carolina Panthers*
19	Doug Brien	*New Orleans Saints*
20	Nick Lowery	*New York Jets*
21	Matt Stover	*Baltimore Ravens*
22	Eddie Murray	*Washington Redskins*
23	Greg Davis	*Arizona Cardinals*
24	Todd Peterson	*Seattle Seahawks*
25	Kevin Butler	*Chicago Bears*
26	Chip Lohmiller	*St. Louis Rams*
27	Mike Hollis	*Jacksonville Jaguars*
28	Brad Daluiso	*New York Giants*
29	Scott Blanton	*Washington Redskins*
30	Matt Bahr	*New England Patriots*
31	Bjorn Nittmo	*Kansas City Chiefs*
32	Cole Ford	*Oakland Raiders*
33	Dean Biasucci	*St. Louis Rams*
34	Scott Szeredy	*Kansas City Chiefs*
35	Roman Anderson	*Kansas City Chiefs*

'95 Punter Review—

Punter:	Team:	Punts:	Yards:	Average:	Net:	Inside 20:
Rick Tuten	SEA	83	3,735	45.0	36.5	21
Darren Bennett	SD	72	3,221	44.7	36.6	28
Sean Landeta	RAM	83	3,679	44.3	36.7	23
Louis Aguiar	KC	91	3,990	43.8	36.5	29
Bryan Barker	JAX	82	3,591	43.8	38.6	19
Jeff Feagles	AZ	72	3,150	43.8	38.2	20
Tom Tupa	BAL	65	2,831	43.6	36.2	18
Tom Hutton	PHI	85	3,682	43.3	33.7	20
Reggie Roby	TB	77	3,296	42.8	36.2	23
John Kidd	MIA	57	2,433	42.7	36.3	15
Chris Gardocki	IND	63	2,681	42.6	33.4	16
Mike Horan	NYG	72	3,063	42.5	36.2	15
Matt Turk	WAS	74	3,140	42.4	37.7	29
Craig Hentrich	GB	65	2,740	42.2	34.6	26
Tom Rouen	DEN	52	2,192	42.2	37.6	22
Lee Johnson	CIN	68	2,861	42.1	38.6	26
Mark Royals	DET	57	2,393	42.0	31.0	15
Brian Hansen	NYJ	99	4,090	41.3	31.9	23
Jeff Gossett	RAI	75	3,089	41.2	34.7	22
Dan Stryzinski	ATL	67	2,759	41.2	36.2	21
Tommy Barnhardt	CAR	95	3,906	41.1	35.2	27
Rich Camarillo	HOU	77	3,165	41.1	34.8	26
Mike Saxon	MIN	72	2,948	40.9	33.1	21
John Jett	DAL	53	2,166	40.9	34.5	17
Klaus Wilmsmeyer	NO	73	2,965	40.6	35.6	21
Tommy Thompson	SF	57	2,312	40.6	33.7	13
Chris Mohr	BUF	86	3,473	40.4	36.2	23
Rohn Stark	PIT	59	2,368	40.1	33.3	20
Todd Sauerbrun	CHI	55	2,080	37.8	31.1	16
Pat O'Neill	NE	41	1,514	36.9	31.2	14

9
K

10 Defense and Special Teams

Ahhhh, defense! It's where experts say real NFL games are won. I am here to vouch for the fact that defenses can make or break your FFL team as well. When the FFL first came about, we would actually draft individual players. We would be allowed to start one linebacker and two defensive backs. In theory it seemed like a good idea, but in reality these individuals rarely scored. If you took a look at the NFL defensive scoring, it was always some guy you had never heard of. So we gradually decided that it was best if you picked an entire defensive team, thereby receiving points for plays made by anyone on that defensive team. Many leagues have decided to use this route, although some continue to use individual players. We feel that drafting a whole team gives you the opportunity to score points consistently each week.

The key to this is to set your scoring system up to reward the types of plays that defensive teams make, such as fumbles, interceptions, sacks, and even perhaps assists and tackles. More exciting are the defensive scores, those bold moves where a speedy linebacker or cat-quick cornerback steps in front of an errant QB pass and heads the other way—toward endzone bliss. We recommend that those types of plays follow the tradition of scoring plays, and be scored based on the yardage of the interception or fumble return. Some leagues, however, blow out those numbers to really reward the defenses that have those types of exciting players. No matter how you do it, adding the defensive perspective is an exciting and often breathtaking way to add depth to your roster and points to your team. ★

'95 Interception Leader Review—

	Team:	Position:	Games Played	INTS:	Return Yards:	TDS:
Orlando Thomas	MIN	DB	16	9	108	1
Willie Clay	DET	DB	16	8	173	0
Willie Williams	PIT	DB	16	7	122	1
William Thomas	PHI	LB	16	7	104	1
Larry Brown	RAI	DB	16	6	124	2
Aeneas Williams	RAI	DB	16	6	86	2
Daryll Lewis	HOU	DB	16	6	145	1
Otis Smith	NYJ	DB	11	6	101	1
Kurt Schulz	BUF	DB	13	6	48	1
Terry McDaniel	RAI	DB	16	6	46	1
Brock Marion	DAL	DB	16	6	40	1
Toby Wright	RAM	DB	16	6	79	0
Brett Maxie	CAR	DB	16	6	59	0
Corey Raymond	DET	DB	16	6	44	0
Troy Vincent	MIA	DB	16	5	95	1
Vencie Glenn	NYG	DB	15	5	91	1
Sam Mills	CAR	LB	16	5	58	1
Leroy Butler	GB	DB	16	5	105	0
Martin Mayhew	TB	DB	13	5	81	0
Stevon Moore	CLE	DB	16	5	55	0
Tyrone Drakeford	SF	DB	16	5	54	0
Robert Blackmon	SEA	DB	13	5	46	0
Merton Hanks	SF	DB	16	5	31	0
Rodney Harrison	SD	DB	11	5	22	0
Phillipi Sparks	NYG	DB	16	5	11	0
Tim McDonald	SF	DB	16	4	135	2
Tom Carter	WAS	DB	16	4	116	1
Todd Lyght	RAM	DB	16	4	34	1
Darren Perry	PIT	DB	16	4	71	0
Bracey Walker	CIN	DB	14	4	56	0
Dale Carter	KC	DB	16	4	45	0
Carlton Gray	SEA	DB	16	4	45	0
Donnell Woolford	CHI	DB	9	4	21	0
Dwayne Harper	SD	DB	16	4	12	0
Jimmy Spencer	NO	DB	16	4	11	0
Vincent Brown	NE	LB	16	4	1	0
Ken Norton	SF	LB	16	3	102	2
Eugene Daniel	IND	DB	16	3	142	1
Brian Washington	KC	DB	16	3	100	1
Tim McKeyer	CAR	DB	16	3	99	1
James Hasty	KC	DB	16	3	89	1
Jessie Tuggle	ATL	LB	16	3	84	1
Eric Davis	SF	DB	15	3	84	1
Darrell Green	WAS	DB	16	3	42	1
Chuck Cecil	HOU	DB	14	3	35	1

'95 Sack Leader Review—

Player:	Team:	Position:	Sacks:	Games Played:
Bryce Paup	BUF	LB	17.5	15
William Fuller	PHI	DL	13	14
Pat Swilling	RAI	DL	13	16
Wayne Martin	NO	DL	13	16
Leslie O'Neal	SD	DL	12.5	16
Reggie White	GB	DL	12	15
Neil Smith	KC	DL	12	16
D'Marco Farr	RAM	DL	11.5	16
Andy Harmon	PHI	DL	11	15
Clyde Simmons	AZ	DL	11	16
Jim Flanigan	CHI	DL	11	16
Willie McGinest	NE	LB	11	16
Charles Haley	DAL	DL	10.5	13
Bruce Smith	BUF	DL	10.5	15
Henry Thomas	DET	DL	10.5	16
John Randle	MIN	DL	10.5	16
Tony Bennett	IND	LB	10.5	16
Hugh Douglas	NYJ	DL	10	15
Phil Hansen	BUF	DL	10	16
Rickey Jackson	SF	LB	9.5	16
Tracy Scroggins	DET	LB	9.5	16
Chris Doleman	ATL	DL	9	16
John Copeland	CIN	DL	9	16
Sean Jones	GB	DL	9	16
Kevin Greene	PIT	LB	9	16
Eric Swann	AZ	DL	8.5	12
Ray Seals	PIT	DL	8.5	16
Alonzo Spellman	CHI	DL	8.5	16
Dan Wilkinson	CIN	DL	8	14
Lamar Lathon	CAR	LB	8	15
Derrick Thomas	KC	LB	8	15
Anthony Pleasant	CLE	DL	8	16
Shawn Lee	SD	DL	8	16
Michael Strahan	NYG	DL	7.5	15
Rob Burnett	CLE	DL	7.5	16
Chester McGlockton	RAI	DL	7.5	16
Bryan Cox	MIA	LB	7.5	16
Bryant Young	SF	DL	7	12
Renaldo Turnbull	NO	DL	7	15
Antonio London	DET	LB	7	15
Anthony Smith	RAI	DL	7	16
Dan Saleaumua	KC	DL	7	16
Darion Conner	CAR	LB	7	16
Marco Coleman	MIA	DL	6.5	16
Jumpy Geathers	ATL	DL	6.5	16
Cortez Kennedy	SEA	DL	6.5	16
Greg Lloyd	PIT	LB	6.5	16

'95 Defense Average Total Yards Allowed per Game—

Team:	Fumbles:*	Intercepts:*	Takeaways:*	Rushing Yards:	Passing Yards:	Total Yards:
Arizona Cardinals	23	19	42	139.9	216.1	346.0
Minnesota Vikings	14	24	40	83.1	247.7	340.8
Philadelphia Eagles	19	19	38	114.2	176.3	290.4
Houston Oilers	14	21	36	94.4	194.7	291.1
St. Louis Rams	14	22	36	104.7	214.7	319.4
Carolina Panthers	14	21	34	92.7	214.4	308.1
Detroit Lions	13	22	34	112.3	237.7	340.0
San Francisco 49ers	8	26	34	66.3	208.6	274.9
Pittsburgh Steelers	12	22	34	82.3	202.2	284.4
New York Jets	17	17	34	126.2	170.8	297.0
Oakland Raiders	23	11	34	111.6	207.1	318.7
Washington Redskins	18	16	34	133.3	204.3	337.6
Kansas City Chiefs	17	16	33	82.9	201.3	284.2
New York Giants	14	16	31	131.7	199.0	330.7
Miami Dolphins	16	14	30	103.9	223.6	327.4
Chicago Bears	14	16	30	89.9	249.4	339.3
Tampa Bay Buccaneers	16	14	30	109.7	247.4	347.2
Atlanta Falcons	12	18	30	96.7	283.8	380.4
New Orleans Saints	11	18	29	114.9	233.0	347.9
Buffalo Bills	11	17	28	101.7	218.9	320.6
New England Patriots	12	16	28	117.4	228.8	346.2
Indianapolis Colts	14	13	27	91.1	223.1	314.2
San Diego Chargers	10	17	27	104.6	211.3	314.9
Dallas Cowboys	6	19	24	110.7	204.6	314.3
Jacksonville Jaguars	12	13	24	124.1	219.4	344.6
Seattle Seahawks	9	16	24	133.2	221.2	344.4
Baltimore Ravens	6	18	24	114.3	239.1	343.4
Cincinnati Bengals	12	12	24	131.4	264.6	397.1
Denver Broncos	12	9	21	118.4	206.3	324.7
Green Bay Packers	3	13	16	93.9	228.6	322.4

* Season Totals

'96 Pre-Season Defensive Team Ranking—

Team:

1. San Francisco 49ers
2. Kansas City Chiefs
3. Arizona Cardinals
4. Buffalo Bills
5. Philadelphia Eagles
6. New York Jets
7. Cincinnati Bengals
8. Minnesota Vikings
9. St. Louis Rams
10. Pittsburgh Steelers
11. Oakland Raiders
12. Indianapolis Colts
13. San Diego Chargers
14. Houston Oilers
15. Dallas Cowboys
16. Denver Broncos
17. Green Bay Packers
18. Atlanta Falcons
19. Carolina Panthers
20. Washington Redskins
21. Miami Dolphins
22. Tampa Bay Buccaneers
23. Detroit Lions
24. Seattle Seahawks
25. New York Giants
26. New England Patriots
27. New Orleans Saints
28. Chicago Bears
29. Baltimore Ravens
30. Jacksonville Jaguars

'96 Pre-Season Defense/Special Team Review—

San Francisco 49ers

	1995:	1994:	1993:
Fumble Return/Touchdown	2	1	1
Interception Return/Touchdown	5	4	3
Block Return/Touchdown	0	0	0
Kick Return/Touchdown	0	1	0
Punt Return/Touchdown	1	0	1
Interceptions	26	23	19
Sacks	40	38	44

The Niners were as exciting defensively as they were offensively. Quietly over the winter they signed DE Chris Doleman, DE Roy Barker, and S Curtis Buckley. In the draft the 'Niners grabbed DE Israel Ifeanyi, and DE Daryl Price. Therefore, by adding 4 new defensive ends, I'd say that the 'Niners saw a problem! The return game was handled well by Dexter Carter.

Kansas City Chiefs

	1995:	1994:	1993:
Fumble Return/Touchdown	2	0	2
Interception Return/Touchdown	2	1	0
Block Return/Touchdown	0	0	1
Kick Return/Touchdown	2	1	0
Punt Return/Touchdown	1	0	0
Interceptions	16	12	21
Sacks	47	39	35

The Chiefs always play good defense and can shake the money tree, and add players and still stay under the cap. The Chiefs will be defensively irritating as all get out in '96! Good team to pick! With Tamarick Vanover returning kicks, a good guess would be that there are several scoring return opportunities here.

Arizona Cardinals

	1995:	1994:	1993:
Fumble Return/Touchdown	1	0	2
Interception Return/Touchdown	4	1	1
Block Return/Touchdown	1	0	0
Kick Return/Touchdown	0	0	0
Punt Return/Touchdown	0	0	1
Interceptions	19	23	9
Sacks	30	35	34

Buddy Ball is officially dead here but Vince Tobin is no slacker on the defensive front! I would expect—especially if he is able to keep Eric Swann—that the Cards will reap from the more even-handed Tobin. With less mental pressure on the defense to win *all* the games, I expect a much more cohesive team and scoring will still be a given. The return game gets a major lift with the fancy footing of rookie Leland McElroy who has the ability to be in the *Eric Metcalf mold*!

	1995:	1994:	1993:
Buffalo Bills			
Fumble Return/Touchdown	0	1	1
Interception Return/Touchdown	2	0	3
Block Return/Touchdown	1	0	0
Kick Return/Touchdown	0	0	0
Punt Return/Touchdown	0	0	1
Interceptions	17	17	23
Sacks	49	24	37

The Bills lost Cornelius Bennett, but they gained the always-tough LB Chris Spielman. With Bruce Smith, Bryce Paup, and Spielman, this will be an ornery group of guys! The defense should put pressure on QBs and expect some coughed-up fumbles and errant passes. Sack production in '95 was double that of '94. Good defensive pick! Jeff Burris is an adequate returner, but I expect to see rookie receiver Eric Moulds enter the picture!

	1995:	1994:	1993:
Philadelphia Eagles			
Fumble Return/Touchdown	3	0	1
Interception Return/Touchdown	1	2	4
Block Return/Touchdown	1	0	0
Kick Return/Touchdown	1	1	0
Punt Return/Touchdown	0	0	0
Interceptions	19	21	20
Sacks	48	42	36

Two words—Ray Rhodes! The man is an aggressive HC and will have his defense spanking folks! Rhodes also is one of those super coaches that can plug guys into open spots, such as linebacker. This is a super defensive team to pick. The return game is not scary, unless Chris T. Jones shows promise!

	1995:	1994:	1993:
New York Jets			
Fumble Return/Touchdown	1	0	0
Interception Return/Touchdown	3	3	1
Block Return/Touchdown	0	0	0
Kick Return/Touchdown	0	0	0
Punt Return/Touchdown	0	0	0
Interceptions	17	18	19
Sacks	43	29	32

Everyone enjoys dumping on head coach Rich Kotite, however, the guy is building a force with the Jets. The offense will keep opposing teams on their heels, and the Jets defense has a great enforcer in Hugh Douglas. Good pick! Rookies Keyhawn Johnson and Alex Van Dyke could see roles as return men!

	1995:	1994:	1993:
Cincinnati Bengals			
Fumble Return/Touchdown	0	0	0
Interception Return/Touchdown	1	0	2
Block Return/Touchdown	0	0	0
Kick Return/Touchdown	0	0	0
Punt Return/Touchdown	0	1	0
Interceptions	12	10	12
Sacks	42	31	22

The Bengals could be very lethal defensively this season! Dan Wilkinson is brute force if he puts his mind and body to it. Add All-Pro CB Ashley Ambrose, CB Jimmy Spencer, S Bo Orlando, and LB Gerald Dixon, and suddenly the defensive holes get filled! The return game was ranked last in the AFC for punt returns and will need to pump up the volume in '96!

	1995:	1994:	1993:
Minnesota Vikings			
Fumble Return/Touchdown	2	2	0
Interception Return/Touchdown	2	5	2
Block Return/Touchdown	0	0	0
Kick Return/Touchdown	0	0	0
Punt Return/Touchdown	1	0	0
Interceptions	25	18	24
Sacks	44	35	45

With HC Tony Dungy taking his aggressive defensive wizardry to Tampa Bay, just how will the 'Vikes play in '96? I still like the 'Vikes attitude and players, but due to the salary cap this isn't the same 'Vikes that dominated in '94! David Palmer averaged 13.2 yards per punt return and scored 1 TD in '95. Qadry Ismail was the kickoff return man and averaged 24.7 yards per return.

	1995:	1994:	1993:
St. Louis Rams			
Fumble Return/Touchdown	3	2	1
Interception Return/Touchdown	2	1	0
Block Return/Touchdown	0	0	0
Kick Return/Touchdown	0	0	0
Punt Return/Touchdown	0	1	0
Interceptions	22	14	11
Sacks	36	26	35

The Rams dipped into several teams (*Vikes*, etc.) in '95, and the defense improved. Despite trading Sean Gilbert to Washington, that defense will get added injections with ex-Charger DE Leslie O'Neal and ex-Cowboy LB Robert Jones. Rich Brooks has built a rocking defense. Great pick! As for the return game, expect Todd Kinchen (1 TD) and maybe rookies RB Lawrence Phillips and WR Eddie Kennison to add some pump and flair!

		1995:	1994:	1993:
Pittsburgh Steelers	Fumble Return/Touchdown	2	1	2
	Interception Return/Touchdown	3	2	1
	Block Return/Touchdown	0	0	0
	Kick Return/Touchdown	0	0	0
	Punt Return/Touchdown	1	0	0
	Interceptions	22	17	24
	Sacks	42	55	42

We all know how vital the Steelers offense is, but we overlook their defense and it's ability to score! Notch one-up for the Pittsburgh "D". Good solid defensive team to select! They will have opposing teams on the ropes all season and that means plenty of defensive scores. Look for Rod Woodson to be taken off the punt return team!

		1995:	1994:	1993:
Oakland Raiders	Fumble Return/Touchdown	3	2	0
	Interception Return/Touchdown	2	3	1
	Block Return/Touchdown	0	0	0
	Kick Return/Touchdown	1	0	0
	Punt Return/Touchdown	0	0	1
	Interceptions	11	12	14
	Sacks	43	38	45

The *Silver and Black* play in offensive and defensive spurts and this can drive you nuts! However, I wouldn't shy away from selecting the Raiders as a defensive fantasy team. *Why?* Simple—the Raiders always play aggressive, knockdown, kick-'em-in-the-butt type of football. The defense can be scary and quick. A tip is to always select quick, tough teams. The Raiders are such a pick! Tim Brown has been a mainstay as the punt returner, averaging 10.1 yards per return. *Nap* Kaufman was a dandy returning kickoffs with a 26.0-yard average return and 1 TD.

		1995:	1994:	1993:
Indianapolis Colts	Fumble Return/Touchdown	1	2	2
	Interception Return/Touchdown	1	3	0
	Block Return/Touchdown	0	0	0
	Kick Return/Touchdown	1	1	0
	Punt Return/Touchdown	0	1	0
	Interceptions	13	18	10
	Sacks	28	31	21

The Colts played solid defense in '95, but the scoring/fantasy stats were not so convincing! Still, Quentin Coryatt and Trev Alberts can rumble and shake loose many a bouncing ball. The return game is average, although Aaron Bailey did return a punt for a TD in '95.

	1995:	1994:	1993:
San Diego Chargers			
Fumble Return/Touchdown	1	0	0
Interception Return/Touchdown	1	3	1
Block Return/Touchdown	1	0	0
Kick Return/Touchdown	1	2	0
Punt Return/Touchdown	2	2	0
Interceptions	17	17	22
Sacks	35	43	32

Ouch, I have been disappointed in the Chargers defense from solely a scoring stand point. Bobby Ross is such a stickler for details that I know he can't be satisfied with the defensive results last season. Ross is doing an overhaul on the offense, and he will stand on top of that defense to ensure more production during '96. As for the return game, punt returner Andre Coleman was solid with a punt return *and* a kickoff return for touchdowns in '95.

	1995:	1994:	1993:
Houston Oilers			
Fumble Return/Touchdown	0	0	2
Interception Return/Touchdown	4	1	4
Block Return/Touchdown	0	0	0
Kick Return/Touchdown	0	0	0
Punt Return/Touchdown	0	1	0
Interceptions	21	14	26
Sacks	30	30	52

Never rule out a Jeff Fisher-coached team! The guy is a defensive wiz! Therefore, why not check out the Oilers for your defense? Don't look now, but slowly the Oilers are becoming a good young team. Good pick! Mel Gray is getting older, but still has the ability to scoot a return.

	1995:	1994:	1993:
Dallas Cowboys			
Fumble Return/Touchdown	0	0	0
Interception Return/Touchdown	4	3	1
Block Return/Touchdown	0	0	0
Kick Return/Touchdown	0	1	0
Punt Return/Touchdown	0	1	2
Interceptions	19	22	14
Sacks	35	46	34

Despite the exciting *Neon* Deion and his *score-whenever-he-touches-the-ball* ability, the 'Pokes are not a *strike-fear-in-your-heart* defensive team any longer! In fact, blame the cap or whatever, but this squad may have an Achilles' Heel beginning to show on defense due to player losses over the past two seasons. Still, where there is Deion—there are scores! Kevin Williams is a steady return man, and Deion always is a threat—if he gets the opportunity!

	1995:	1994:	1993:
Denver Broncos			
Fumble Return/Touchdown	1	0	0
Interception Return/Touchdown	0	0	1
Block Return/Touchdown	0	0	0
Kick Return/Touchdown	0	0	0
Punt Return/Touchdown	0	0	0
Interceptions	9	12	18
Sacks	29	23	46

Busy, busy, were those Denver Broncos as they signed several key players over winter: LB Bill Romanowski, and DE Alfred Williams. In the draft, the Bronc's tabbed LB John Mobley, DB Tory James, and DT Mark Campbell. Now, if you check the past three seasons, Denver ranks as a lousy choice—but they are heading in the right direction. The return game will suffer since Glyn Milburn has been traded. For now, Vance Johnson has requested a shot at the job.

	1995:	1994:	1993:
Green Bay Packers			
Fumble Return/Touchdown	0	0	1
Interception Return/Touchdown	0	1	0
Block Return/Touchdown	1	0	0
Kick Return/Touchdown	0	1	1
Punt Return/Touchdown	0	1	0
Interceptions	13	21	18
Sacks	39	36	46

Although the Packers have a solid defense, three defensive TDs in three years does not help us FFL'ers seal a championship! In the off-season, the pack added DT Santana Dotson and DB Marcus Turner. The return game could be exciting with second-year man Antonio Freeman handling the job!

	1995:	1994:	1993:
Atlanta Falcons			
Fumble Return/Touchdown	0	1	1
Interception Return/Touchdown	2	2	0
Block Return/Touchdown	1	0	0
Kick Return/Touchdown	0	0	1
Punt Return/Touchdown	1	0	0
Interceptions	18	22	13
Sacks	30	32	27

Cornelius Bennett will bolster an adequate Falcon defense. The Falcons have never been renowned as a tough defensive group, and I rate them as average. The return game is one of the best thanks to Eric Metcalf! Grab him if you can and relax as he will net you at least 2 return scores!!

	1995:	1994:	1993:
Carolina Panthers			
Fumble Return/Touchdown	1		
Interception Return/Touchdown	2		
Block Return/Touchdown	0		
Kick Return/Touchdown	0		
Punt Return/Touchdown	1		
Interceptions	21		
Sacks	35		

On paper the Panthers look good, especially with Kevin Greene departing Pittsburgh to sign with Carolina! Greene may be on the downslide of a fabulous career, but he is a force and his experience, attitude, and toughness will be a major plus. Eric Guilford handled the duties well in '95 and scored 1 TD.

	1995:	1994:	1993:
Washington Redskins			
Fumble Return/Touchdown	1	2	2
Interception Return/Touchdown	2	3	2
Block Return/Touchdown	0	0	0
Kick Return/Touchdown	0	0	0
Punt Return/Touchdown	1	2	0
Interceptions	16	17	17
Sacks	29	28	31

The addition of Sean Gilbert will add some teeth to the Redskins defense. Now if everyone can just remain healthy! I like Ken Harvey and his mentally and physically tough game. This squad will surprise in '96. Good pick! The return game is excellent with Brian Mitchell (1 TD return in '95) blasting through on punts and kicks!

	1995:	1994:	1993:
Miami Dolphins			
Fumble Return/Touchdown	1	0	0
Interception Return/Touchdown	1	1	1
Block Return/Touchdown	0	0	0
Kick Return/Touchdown	0	0	0
Punt Return/Touchdown	0	0	2
Interceptions	14	23	13
Sacks	29	29	29

I think it will be reasonable to presume and guess that the Jimmy Johnson era in Miami will start with some heavy hitting and much-ado about defensive takeways! J.J. is not a patient man and he will light a fire under the malcontent Dolphins—*It's J.J.'s way or the highway, babe!* The return game is effective with O.J. McDuffie; however, it wouldn't be a shock to see Jimmy put rookie Dorian Brew back there as well!

	1995:	1994:	1993:
Tampa Bay Buccaneers			
Fumble Return/Touchdown	1	0	0
Interception Return/Touchdown	1	0	2
Block Return/Touchdown	0	0	0
Kick Return/Touchdown	0	0	0
Punt Return/Touchdown	0	1	0
Interceptions	14	9	9
Sacks	25	20	29

Quick, someone find a pulse on the Tampa Bay defense! For the past three seasons these guys must have played *flag football*! All that will change with the smart, tough, take-away football of new HC Tony Dungy. Pack away those yawns—Dungy will shake up the *Tangerine Gang* although it may take a couple of years. Dungy did draft DE Regan Upshaw and DT Marcus Jones with the 12th and 22nd pick of the '96 draft. Another Dungy headache will be fixing the return game (*last in kickoff returns*). Bobby Joe Edmonds showed some ability in his comeback, but can he score for us FFL'ers?

	1995:	1994:	1993:
Detroit Lions			
Fumble Return/Touchdown	1	1	2
Interception Return/Touchdown	0	2	1
Block Return/Touchdown	0	0	0
Kick Return/Touchdown	0	4	1
Punt Return/Touchdown	0	0	0
Interceptions	22	12	19
Sacks	42	27	43

A ton of sacks last season—42—but only 1 defensive TD? *Hmmm*, that doesn't bode well for us FFL'ers. Still the *Silver* rush can cause havoc and force some scores. Great off-season move in trading for Glyn Milburn. Milburn is a double duty guy (punt and kickoff returns) and he should help ease Detroit's memories of Mel Gray! Milburn will pop 1 or 2 in '96!

	1995:	1994:	1993:
Seattle Seahawks			
Fumble Return/Touchdown	2	0	2
Interception Return/Touchdown	0	2	1
Block Return/Touchdown	0	0	0
Kick Return/Touchdown	0	1	0
Punt Return/Touchdown	1	0	0
Interceptions	16	19	22
Sacks	28	32	38

I can't get overly excited over the Seahawks defense, as it is really pretty average despite Cortez Kennedy. The return game is lethal whenever Joey Galloway touches the ball! I guarantee that he will steal at least 2 returns for TDs in '96!

	1995:	1994:	1993:
New York Giants			
Fumble Return/Touchdown	1	0	0
Interception Return/Touchdown	2	0	1
Block Return/Touchdown	1	0	0
Kick Return/Touchdown	1	0	0
Punt Return/Touchdown	0	2	1
Interceptions	16	16	18
Sacks	28	26	41

This has to be one of the most boring teams in the NFL! Other than Rodney Hampton, this squad doesn't glitter on offense or defense. FFL'ers still clamor and pick the *G-Men* because they think that LT, Carl Banks, Pepper Johnson, and Harry Carson are still there ripping off offensive players' heads! Very average defense gang. The return game is adequate at best although Thomas Lewis did score a TD in '95.

	1995:	1994:	1993:
New England Patriots			
Fumble Return/Touchdown	2	1	0
Interception Return/Touchdown	0	1	0
Block Return/Touchdown	0	0	0
Kick Return/Touchdown	0	0	0
Punt Return/Touchdown	0	0	0
Interceptions	16	22	13
Sacks	36	39	34

What's this? One stinking interception return for a TD in three years? Look, I love Bill Parcells and his *John Wayne defensive swagger*, but I don't see the *Pats* dominating anyone on defense. Yikes, *Cap'n Bill* even hired Bill Belichick (ex-Brown HC grump) as his defensive coordinator. Sorry gang, I just don't see Parcells' mojo working this year. The return game should have been a highlight last season with David Meggett; unfortunately it wasn't. Still, Meggett is a gamer and there is no shame in opting for him— he can still hit the holes!

	1995:	1994:	1993:
New Orleans Saints			
Fumble Return/Touchdown	0	2	2
Interception Return/Touchdown	1	1	0
Block Return/Touchdown	0	0	0
Kick Return/Touchdown	0	2	1
Punt Return/Touchdown	0	0	2
Interceptions	18	17	10
Sacks	43	36	51

Usually *'Dem Saints'* punch up good defensive and kickoff/punt return numbers—not so in '95! The good news is that this season the Saints added several decent defensive players and added two CB *beauts* in the draft (Alex Molden and Je'Rod Cherry). The return game didn't score in '95, but Tyrone Hughes is one of the NFL's most dangerous returners. I wouldn't shy from selecting Mr. Hughes!

		1995:	1994:	1993:
Chicago Bears	Fumble Return/Touchdown	0	0	2
	Interception Return/Touchdown	1	0	2
	Block Return/Touchdown	1	0	1
	Kick Return/Touchdown	0	0	0
	Punt Return/Touchdown	0	1	0
	Interceptions	16	12	18
	Sacks	34	29	46

The Bears defense *ain't* what it was two seasons ago and that is why HC Dave Wannstedt made several key moves over the winter and in the draft. He signed LB Bryan Cox and DE Alonzo Spellman, re-signed LB Barry Minter, and drafted CB Walt Harris. Also, a healthy Donnell Woolford will help everyone in Chicago breathe easier. I feel that the return game will get a major boost from Jack Jackson (*worth watching to see if he hits his stride during training camp*)!

Baltimore Ravens	Fumble Return/Touchdown	0	0	1
	Interception Return/Touchdown	2	1	1
	Block Return/Touchdown	0	1	0
	Kick Return/Touchdown	0	1	0
	Punt Return/Touchdown	1	2	3
	Interceptions	18	18	13
	Sacks	29	38	48

The Ravens seemed content in the off-season to not be aggressive in the free agent market, obviously still reeling after the Andre Rison fiasco. In the draft they added two rookies who may immediately help: LB Ray Lewis and DB DeRon Jenkins. Derrick Alexander—1 punt return for a TD—looked good last season when he was on special teams and should be slated for similar duties this season!

Jacksonville Jaguars	Fumble Return/Touchdown	0
	Interception Return/Touchdown	1
	Block Return/Touchdown	2
	Kick Return/Touchdown	0
	Punt Return/Touchdown	0
	Interceptions	13
	Sacks	17

Jacksonville is making all the right moves under HC Tom Coughlin by drafting LB Kevin Hardy, DE Tony Brackens, and DB Aaron Beasley. In the off-season, the *Jags* signed S Dana Hall and LB Eddie Robinson and now appear on their way to becoming a good defense. The return game may have Desmond Howard if he returns, but he really isn't the great shakes we all thought he was when he entered the league!

Drafting Special Team Returners—		Choosing a player or special team takes an equal mixture of research and luck, but if you hit it right—*bingo!* When drafting a fantasy team it is crucial that you fill your franchise's needs from top to bottom. Some franchises fall asleep and miss out on the extra points that a FFL franchise can get.
It is very frustrating to be neck-to-neck with another franchise in competition for winning the week, and you witness the *other* squad's punt returner leg out a broken field splurt for the endzone. Kiss it goodbye as the *other* lowlife squad takes the week, due to the points awarded for a punt/kickoff return.
Special Team Drafting Tips—	1	*When drafting a special team:*
If your league takes the approach of drafting a complete team, make sure it is a team with top-ranked return men. The team concept gives you the opportunity for multiple scores from multiple players—i.e., San Diego has 2-3 super returners, therefore great opportunities for scoring.
	2	*When drafting a return specialist (individual player):*
Select a full-time kick or punt returner. It simply makes more sense (and points) to select a player who will get many opportunities to "*handle*" the ball.
	3	*Stick with a consistent lineup:*
As long as your returner is healthy, do not develop the bad habit of flip-flopping return specialists. As a rule of thumb, you will get burned as the returner you benched will seemingly *always score!*
It's almost a given—don't tempt the curse!
	4	*Select a double-duty returner:*
There are a handful of players—like Brian Mitchell—who handle punt and kickoff duties. Guys like Mitchell have awesome value since they get *all* the opportunities to return and therefore become a double threat to score! Remember, gang, the more opportunities, the more scores.
	5	*Select a speedster:*
Sure there are returners who lack burning speed and do score (i.e., O.J. McDuffie), but your best bet for a return is with a player with lightning quick feet (i.e., Joey Galloway). Remember, a TD return is still a rarity. The guy with the best shot is the returner with the speed to break the crease and blast off!

What about Deion, Rod, and Tim?

You will never receive an argument from me that if Deion Sanders, Rod Woodson and Tim Brown were fulltime returners, they would be at the top of *any* fancy schmancy preseason ranking. But, the realistic side of my brain interrupts me with the cold facts—these guys are too valuable as cornerbacks and receivers.

Dallas, Pittsburgh and Oakland cannot afford to lose these gents to a knee injury, for example, on a punt return. Therefore I am shying away from adding their names to this list. Now I can't fault you for getting greedy and *after* initially selecting a returner (i.e., Napoleon Kaufman), and then reaching out wistfully and grabbing Deion, Rod or Tim. ★

'95 Punt Returner Review—

Player:	Team:	Position:	Returns:	Yards:	Return:	TDS:
David Palmer	MIN	WR	26	342	13.2	1
Brian Mitchell	WAS	RB	25	315	12.6	1
Andre Coleman	SD	WR	28	326	11.6	1
Jeff Burris	BUF	DB	20	229	11.5	0
Glyn Milburn	DEN	RB	31	354	11.4	0
Eric Guliford	CAR	WR	43	475	11.0	1
Tamarick Vanover	KC	WR	51	540	10.6	1
Dexter Carter	SF	RB	30	309	10.3	1
Desmond Howard	JAX	WR	24	246	10.3	0
Tim Brown	RAI	WR	36	364	10.1	0
Mel Gray	HOU	WR	30	303	10.1	0
Bobby Joe Edmonds	TB	RB	29	293	10.1	0
Charles Jordan	GB	WR	21	213	10.1	0
Joey Galloway	SEA	WR	36	360	10.0	1
Andre Hastings	PIT	WR	48	474	9.9	1
Eric Metcalf	ATL	WR	39	383	9.8	1
Tyrone Hughes	NO	DB	28	262	9.4	0
Dave Meggett	NE	RB	45	383	8.5	0
Jeff Graham	CHI	WR	23	183	8.0	0
Antonio Freeman	GB	WR	37	292	7.9	0

'95 Kick Returners Review—

Player:	Team:	Position:	Returns:	Yards:	Average:	TDS:
Glyn Milburn	DEN	RB	47	1,269	27.0	0
Ron Carpenter	NYJ	DB	21	553	26.3	0
Napoleon Kaufman	RAI	RB	22	572	26.0	1
Brian Mitchell	WAS	RB	55	1,408	25.6	0
Tamarick Vanover	KC	WR	43	1,095	25.5	2
Dave Meggett	NE	RB	38	964	25.4	0
Steve Broussard	SEA	RB	43	1,064	24.7	0
Qadry Ismail	MIN	WR	42	1,037	24.7	0
Tyrone Hughes	NO	DB	66	1,617	24.5	0
O. J. McDuffie	MIA	WR	23	564	24.5	0
Ernie Mills	PIT	WR	54	1,306	24.2	0
Aaron Bailey	IND	WR	21	495	23.6	1
Johnny Thomas	RAM	WR	32	752	23.5	0
Antonio Freeman	GB	WR	24	556	23.2	0
Andre Coleman	SD	WR	62	1,411	22.8	2
Kevin Williams	DAL	WR	49	1,108	22.6	0
Jamal Anderson	ATL	RB	24	541	22.5	0
Dexter Carter	SF	RB	56	1,227	21.9	0
Ryan Terry	AZ	RB	37	808	21.8	0
Nate Lewis	CHI	WR	42	904	21.5	0

'96 Pre-Season Special Team Returner Ranking—

	Player:	Team:
1	Eric Metcalf	Atlanta Falcons
2	Joey Galloway	Seattle Seahawks
3	Tamarick Vanover	Kansas City Chiefs
4	Brian Mitchell	Washington Redskins
5	Glyn Milburn	Detroit Lions
6	Tyrone Hughes	New Orleans Saints
7	Andre Coleman	San Diego Chargers
8	Napoleon Kaufman	Oakland Raiders
9	Kevin Williams	Dallas Cowboys
10	David Palmer	Minnesota Vikings
11	David Meggett	New England Patriots
12	Eric Guilford	Carolina Panthers
13	Antonio Freeman	Green Bay Packers
14	Bryan Still	San Diego Chargers
15	O.J. McDuffie	Miami Dolphins
16	Dexter Carter	San Francisco 49ers
17	Mel Gray	Houston Oilers
18	Leland McElroy	Arizona Carinals
19	Aaron Bailey	Indianapolis Colts
20	Nilo Silvan	Tampa Bay Buccaneers
21	Qadry Ismail	Minnesota Vikings
22	Ernie Mills	Pittsburgh Steelers
23	Mike Pringle	Denver Broncos
24	Kelvin Martin	Philadelphia Eagles
25	Jack Jackson	Chicago Bears
26	Bobby Joe Edmonds	Tampa Bay Buccaneers
27	Darrien Gordon	San Diego Chargers
28	Jeff Burris	Buffalo Bills
29	Derrick Mayes	Green Bay Packers
30	Desmond Howard	Jacksonville Jaguars
31	Jamal Anderson	Atlanta Falcons
32	Steve Broussard	Seattle Seahawks
33	Charles Jordan	Miami Dolphins
34	Aaron Glenn	New York Jets
35	Todd Kitchen	St. Louis Rams
36	Earnest Hunter	Baltimore Ravens
37	Jimmy Smith	Jacksonville Jaguars
38	Chuck Levy	Arizona Cardinals
39	Alex Van Dyke	New York Jets

11 *Offensive Teams*

This is a new chapter in the Journal this year, and can be very helpful when selecting a starting quarterback. Too often you draft what looks to be a great QB, only to see his butt on the turf due to a terribly ineffective offensive line. Therefore, you can use the *Offensive Line* stats in this chapter to determine which OLs get it done, and which could use some help. Remember, even the best NFL QB needs some 300+ pound big bad boys in front of him to get him some time to throw the ball—otherwise he is dead meat! The QB team stats are also great when you are looking for a quality backup QB, which we discussed further in the *Quarterbacks* chapter.

Even though most NFL teams have one defined starting quarterback who starts week in and week out, certain teams that have young quarterbacks, like Washington, might pull the starter due to ineffectiveness and go to his backup. I think it is always critical to know what the whole QB team unit does. In fact, this has been included in the book simply for the fact that some leagues now draft the entire QB unit from an NFL team.

Here's how it works: Let's say that you draft the Miami quarterback team unit. Let's say that Dan Marino, who is the everyday starter for the 'Fins, goes down with an injury in a game, and Bernie Kosar replaces him. Your franchise would get *both* Marino's and Kosar's stats for the week, since they are part of the QB team unit. Using that same scenario in the traditional way of drafting, if Marino were to get injured, if your franchise's backup QB was not an NFL starter, you are left hanging your head in shame. We have not yet incorporated this concept into the traditional FFL scoring system, but a lot of leagues are using this now, and I submit that it does shed a whole new light on the QB drafting philosophy. ★

3-Year Offensive Line Review—

		1995:	1994:	1993:
Chicago Bears	Rushing Yards Gained	1,930	1,588	1,677
	Average Yards Rushing	3.9	3.3	3.5
	Passing Yards Gained	3,743	3,230	2,270
	Sacks Allowed per Pass Attempt	2.9%	5.0%	12.4%
	Times Quarterback Sacked	15	25	48
Dallas Cowboys	Rushing Yards Gained	2,204	1,953	2,161
	Average Yards Rushing	4.5	3.6	4.4
	Passing Yards Gained	3,618	3,461	3,617
	Sacks Allowed per Pass Attempt	3.8%	4.5%	6.1%
	Times Quarterback Sacked	19	20	29
Kansas City Chiefs	Rushing Yards Gained	2,222	1,732	1,655
	Average Yards Rushing	4.4	3.7	3.7
	Passing Yards Gained	3,020	4,092	3,384
	Sacks Allowed per Pass Attempt	4.0%	3.1%	7.1%
	Times Quarterback Sacked	21	19	35
Pittsburgh Steelers	Rushing Yards Gained	1,842	2,180	2,003
	Average Yards Rushing	3.7	4.0	4.1
	Passing Yards Gained	3,925	3,247	3,606
	Sacks Allowed per Pass Attempt	4.0%	8.4%	7.8%
	Times Quarterback Sacked	24	39	42
Cincinnati Bengals	Rushing Yards Gained	1,441	1,556	1,511
	Average Yards Rushing	4.0	3.9	3.6
	Passing Yards Gained	3,752	3,541	2,830
	Sacks Allowed per Pass Attempt	4.4%	8.1%	10.4%
	Times Quarterback Sacked	26	44	53
Denver Broncos	Rushing Yards Gained	1,998	1,470	1,693
	Average Yards Rushing	4.6	3.4	3.6
	Passing Yards Gained	4,045	4,383	4,061
	Sacks Allowed per Pass Attempt	4.5%	8.8%	7.1%
	Times Quarterback Sacked	27	55	39
New England Patriots	Rushing Yards Gained	1,866	1,332	1,780
	Average Yards Rushing	3.9	2.8	3.5
	Passing Yards Gained	3,591	4,583	3,412
	Sacks Allowed per Pass Attempt	3.9%	3.1%	4.1%
	Times Quarterback Sacked	27	22	23

		1995:	1994:	1993:
New Orleans Saints	Rushing Yards Gained	1,386	1,336	1,766
	Average Yards Rushing	3.6	3.6	4.3
	Passing Yards Gained	3,787	4,027	3,183
	Sacks Allowed per Pass Attempt	4.9%	4.2%	8.3%
	Times Quarterback Sacked	28	24	40
Miami Dolphins	Rushing Yards Gained	1,509	1,658	1,459
	Average Yards Rushing	3.7	3.8	3.5
	Passing Yards Gained	4,207	4,533	4,564
	Sacks Allowed per Pass Attempt	4.9%	2.7%	5.2%
	Times Quarterback Sacked	29	17	30
Buffalo Bills	Rushing Yards Gained	1,993	1,831	1,943
	Average Yards Rushing	3.8	3.8	3.5
	Passing Yards Gained	3,125	3,714	3,535
	Sacks Allowed per Pass Attempt	5.9%	7.6%	6.2%
	Times Quarterback Sacked	30	41	31
Detroit Lions	Rushing Yards Gained	1,753	2,080	1,944
	Average Yards Rushing	4.5	5.1	4.3
	Passing Yards Gained	4,362	3,085	2,943
	Sacks Allowed per Pass Attempt	5.3%	5.7%	10.6%
	Times Quarterback Sacked	32	26	46
San Diego Chargers	Rushing Yards Gained	1,747	1,852	1,824
	Average Yards Rushing	3.6	3.8	4.0
	Passing Yards Gained	3,466	3,619	3,383
	Sacks Allowed per Pass Attempt	5.9%	5.6%	5.7%
	Times Quarterback Sacked	32	29	32
Baltimore Ravens	Rushing Yards Gained	1,482	1,657	1,701
	Average Yards Rushing	3.7	3.7	4.0
	Passing Yards Gained	3,594	3,269	3,328
	Sacks Allowed per Pass Attempt	5.8%	2.8%	9.4%
	Times Quarterback Sacked	32	14	45
Green Bay Packers	Rushing Yards Gained	1,430	1,543	1,619
	Average Yards Rushing	3.5	3.7	3.6
	Passing Yards Gained	4,326	3,977	3,330
	Sacks Allowed per Pass Attempt	5.4%	5.4%	5.7%
	Times Quarterback Sacked	32	33	30

		1995:	1994:	1993:
Houston Oilers	Rushing Yards Gained	1,659	1,682	1,792
	Average Yards Rushing	4.7	4.0	4.4
	Passing Yards Gained	3,236	3,216	4,145
	Sacks Allowed per Pass Attempt	6.2%	11.7%	7.0%
	Times Quarterback Sacked	33	65	43
San Francisco 49ers	Rushing Yards Gained	1,479	1,897	2,133
	Average Yards Rushing	3.6	3.9	4.6
	Passing Yards Gained	4,608	4,362	4,480
	Sacks Allowed per Pass Attempt	5.1%	6.8%	6.7%
	Times Quarterback Sacked	33	35	35
Washington Redskins	Rushing Yards Gained	1,951	1,415	1,726
	Average Yards Rushing	4.2	3.5	4.4
	Passing Yards Gained	3,230	3,524	2,764
	Sacks Allowed per Pass Attempt	6.9%	3.8%	7.5%
	Times Quarterback Sacked	36	21	40
Oakland Raiders	Rushing Yards Gained	1,932	1,512	1,425
	Average Yards Rushing	4.2	3.5	3.3
	Passing Yards Gained	3,570	3,556	3,882
	Sacks Allowed per Pass Attempt	6.6%	10.3%	10.1%
	Times Quarterback Sacked	36	50	50
Carolina Panthers	Rushing Yards Gained	1,570		
	Average Yards Rushing	3.5		
	Passing Yards Gained	3,040		
	Sacks Allowed per Pass Attempt	7.1%		
	Times Quarterback Sacked	38		
Minnesota Vikings	Rushing Yards Gained	1,730	1,524	1,623
	Average Yards Rushing	4.0	3.6	3.6
	Passing Yards Gained	4,203	4,570	3,380
	Sacks Allowed per Pass Attempt	6.2%	4.6%	6.7%
	Times Quarterback Sacked	40	31	35
Atlanta Falcons	Rushing Yards Gained	1,395	1,249	1,590
	Average Yards Rushing	4.1	3.8	4.0
	Passing Yards Gained	4,186	4,344	3,787
	Sacks Allowed per Pass Attempt	7.0%	5.9%	7.0%
	Times Quarterback Sacked	42	37	40

		1995:	1994:	1993:
Philadelphia Eagles	Rushing Yards Gained	2,121	1,761	1,761
	Average Yards Rushing	4.2	4.1	3.9
	Passing Yards Gained	2,693	3,736	3,463
	Sacks Allowed per Pass Attempt	8.7%	8.5%	7.6%
	Times Quarterback Sacked	43	48	42
St. Louis Rams	Rushing Yards Gained	1,431	1,389	2,014
	Average Yards Rushing	3.7	3.5	4.5
	Passing Yards Gained	3,807	3,597	3,021
	Sacks Allowed per Pass Attempt	6.8%	6.8%	6.6%
	Times Quarterback Sacked	43	35	31
Seattle Seahawks	Rushing Yards Gained	2,176	2,084	2,015
	Average Yards Rushing	4.6	4.3	4.3
	Passing Yards Gained	3,094	2,809	2,896
	Sacks Allowed per Pass Attempt	8.8%	8.0%	9.6%
	Times Quarterback Sacked	44	40	48
New York Giants	Rushing Yards Gained	1,833	1,754	2,210
	Average Yards Rushing	3.8	3.3	3.9
	Passing Yards Gained	2,652	2,847	3,180
	Sacks Allowed per Pass Attempt	9.6%	11.4%	9.4%
	Times Quarterback Sacked	46	46	40
New York Jets	Rushing Yards Gained	1,278	1,566	1,880
	Average Yards Rushing	3.5	3.8	3.6
	Passing Yards Gained	2,788	3,323	3,492
	Sacks Allowed per Pass Attempt	8.0%	5.2%	4.3%
	Times Quarterback Sacked	47	28	21
Indianapolis Colts	Rushing Yards Gained	1,830	2,060	1,288
	Average Yards Rushing	3.8	4.2	3.5
	Passing Yards Gained	3,064	2,519	3,623
	Sacks Allowed per Pass Attempt	11.1%	7.4%	4.9%
	Times Quarterback Sacked	48	28	29
Arizona Cardinals	Rushing Yards Gained	1,363	1,560	1,809
	Average Yards Rushing	3.5	3.3	4.0
	Passing Yards Gained	3,505	3,284	3,635
	Sacks Allowed per Pass Attempt	9.6%	6.3%	6.3%
	Times Quarterback Sacked	54	34	33

		1995:	1994:	1993:
Tampa Bay Buccaneers	Rushing Yards Gained	1,578	1,489	1,290
	Average Yards Rushing	4.0	3.5	3.2
	Passing Yards Gained	2,963	3,436	3,295
	Sacks Allowed per Pass Attempt	11.0%	6.1%	7.7%
	Times Quarterback Sacked	56	30	39
Jacksonville Jaguars	Rushing Yards Gained	1,702		
	Average Yards Rushing	4.2		
	Passing Yards Gained	2,800		
	Sacks Allowed per Pass Attempt	11.5%		
	Times Quarterback Sacked	57		

Quarterback Team Review—

		1995:	*1994:*	*1993:*
Green Bay Packers	Passing Touchdowns	39	33	19
	Rushing Touchdowns	3	3	1
	Total Passing Yards	4,539	3,977	3,330
	Total Completions/Attempts	372/593	375/609	322/528
	Average Yards per Game	283.7	248.6	208.1
	Interceptions Thrown	15	14	24
	Times Sacked	32	33	30
Minnesota Vikings	Passing Touchdowns	33	18	18
	Rushing Touchdowns	0	0	0
	Total Passing Yards	4,500	4,570	3,380
	Total Completions/Attempts	402/642	409/673	315/526
	Average Yards per Game	281.3	285.6	211.3
	Interceptions Thrown	16	20	14
	Times Sacked	40	31	35
Detroit Lions	Passing Touchdowns	33	24	15
	Rushing Touchdowns	4	1	0
	Total Passing Yards	4,499	3,085	2,943
	Total Completions/Attempts	361/603	250/459	264/435
	Average Yards per Game	281.2	192.8	183.9
	Interceptions Thrown	12	14	19
	Times Sacked	32	26	46
Cincinnati Bengals	Passing Touchdowns	29	21	11
	Rushing Touchdowns	2	1	0
	Total Passing Yards	3,910	3,541	2,830
	Total Completions/Attempts	333/582	289/542	272/510
	Average Yards per Game	244.4	221.3	176.9
	Interceptions Thrown	18	19	11
	Times Sacked	26	44	53
Chicago Bears	Passing Touchdowns	29	19	7
	Rushing Touchdowns	1	1	0
	Total Passing Yards	3,838	3,230	2,270
	Total Completions/Attempts	315/522	308/502	230/388
	Average Yards per Game	239.9	201.9	141.9
	Interceptions Thrown	10	16	16
	Times Sacked	15	25	48

11 OT

		1995:	1994:	1993:
San Francisco 49ers	Passing Touchdowns	28	37	29
	Rushing Touchdowns	5	7	1
	Total Passing Yards	4,717	4,362	4,480
	Total Completions/Attempts	430/642	322/524	354/524
	Average Yards per Game	294.8	272.6	280.0
	Interceptions Thrown	16	11	17
	Times Sacked	33	35	35
Miami Dolphins	Passing Touchdowns	27	31	27
	Rushing Touchdowns	1	1	0
	Total Passing Yards	4,367	4,533	4,564
	Total Completions/Attempts	383/591	392/627	342/581
	Average Yards per Game	272.9	283.3	285.3
	Interceptions Thrown	20	18	18
	Times Sacked	29	17	30
Denver Broncos	Passing Touchdowns	27	18	27
	Rushing Touchdowns	1	4	0
	Total Passing Yards	4,260	4,383	4,061
	Total Completions/Attempts	350/594	388/626	350/553
	Average Yards per Game	266.3	273.9	253.8
	Interceptions Thrown	14	13	10
	Times Sacked	27	55	39
St. Louis Rams	Passing Touchdowns	27	23	16
	Rushing Touchdowns	0	1	0
	Total Passing Yards	4,113	3,597	3,021
	Total Completions/Attempts	366/631	291/512	247/473
	Average Yards per Game	257.1	224.8	188.8
	Interceptions Thrown	23	18	19
	Times Sacked	43	35	31
Atlanta Falcons	Passing Touchdowns	26	25	28
	Rushing Touchdowns	0	0	0
	Total Passing Yards	4,456	4,344	3,787
	Total Completions/Attempts	364/602	374/629	334/573
	Average Yards per Game	278.5	271.5	236.7
	Interceptions Thrown	12	25	25
	Times Sacked	42	37	40

		1995:	1994:	1993:
New Orleans Saints	Passing Touchdowns	26	22	18
	Rushing Touchdowns	0	0	0
	Total Passing Yards	3,984	4,027	3,183
	Total Completions/Attempts	348/572	366/569	274/481
	Average Yards per Game	249.0	251.7	198.9
	Interceptions Thrown	14	18	21
	Times Sacked	27	24	40
Oakland Raiders	Passing Touchdowns	24	22	17
	Rushing Touchdowns	0	2	5
	Total Passing Yards	3,774	3,556	3,882
	Total Completions/Attempts	317/542	281/487	281/495
	Average Yards per Game	235.9	222.3	242.6
	Interceptions Thrown	21	16	14
	Times Sacked	36	50	50
Buffalo Bills	Passing Touchdowns	24	23	20
	Rushing Touchdowns	0	1	0
	Total Passing Yards	3,348	3,714	3,535
	Total Completions/Attempts	279/505	342/542	304/497
	Average Yards per Game	209.3	232.1	220.9
	Interceptions Thrown	14	21	18
	Times Sacked	31	41	31
Houston Oilers	Passing Touchdowns	22	13	23
	Rushing Touchdowns	2	3	1
	Total Passing Yards	3,512	3,216	4,145
	Total Completions/Attempts	314/535	274/554	357/614
	Average Yards per Game	219.5	201.0	259.1
	Interceptions Thrown	18	17	25
	Times Sacked	33	65	43
Pittsburgh Steelers	Passing Touchdowns	21	17	16
	Rushing Touchdowns	1	1	0
	Total Passing Yards	4,093	3,247	3,606
	Total Completions/Attempts	348/592	266/463	299/540
	Average Yards per Game	255.8	202.9	225.4
	Interceptions Thrown	21	9	12
	Times Sacked	24	39	42

		1995:	1994:	1993:
Baltimore Ravens	Passing Touchdowns	21	20	23
	Rushing Touchdowns	2	2	1
	Total Passing Yards	3,772	3,269	3,328
	Total Completions/Attempts	324/554	266/507	262/478
	Average Yards per Game	235.8	204.3	208.0
	Interceptions Thrown	19	21	19
	Times Sacked	32	14	45
Kansas City Chiefs	Passing Touchdowns	21	20	20
	Rushing Touchdowns	6	0	0
	Total Passing Yards	3,178	4,092	3,384
	Total Completions/Attempts	300/531	366/615	287/490
	Average Yards per Game	198.6	255.8	211.5
	Interceptions Thrown	10	14	10
	Times Sacked	21	19	35
Indianapolis Colts	Passing Touchdowns	20	15	10
	Rushing Touchdowns	2	3	0
	Total Passing Yards	3,373	2,519	3,623
	Total Completions/Attempts	270/433	217/376	332/594
	Average Yards per Game	210.8	157.4	226.4
	Interceptions Thrown	11	14	15
	Times Sacked	48	28	29
New York Jets	Passing Touchdowns	20	18	16
	Rushing Touchdowns	0	0	1
	Total Passing Yards	3,129	3,323	3,492
	Total Completions/Attempts	330/588	310/539	294/489
	Average Yards per Game	195.6	207.7	218.3
	Interceptions Thrown	24	18	12
	Times Sacked	47	28	21
Seattle Seahawks	Passing Touchdowns	19	13	13
	Rushing Touchdowns	1	0	3
	Total Passing Yards	3,359	2,809	2,896
	Total Completions/Attempts	273/511	253/498	280/498
	Average Yards per Game	209.9	175.6	181.0
	Interceptions Thrown	23	9	18
	Times Sacked	44	40	48

		1995:	1994:	1993:
Jacksonville Jaguars	Passing Touchdowns	19		
	Rushing Touchdowns	4		
	Total Passing Yards	3,144		
	Total Completions/Attempts	275/495		
	Average Yards per Game	196.5		
	Interceptions Thrown	15		
	Times Sacked	57		
Dallas Cowboys	Passing Touchdowns	18	19	18
	Rushing Touchdowns	1	1	0
	Total Passing Yards	3,741	3,461	3,617
	Total Completions/Attempts	322/494	282/448	317/475
	Average Yards per Game	233.8	216.3	226.1
	Interceptions Thrown	10	14	6
	Times Sacked	19	20	29
Arizona Cardinals	Passing Touchdowns	17	11	21
	Rushing Touchdowns	0	1	0
	Total Passing Yards	3,844	3,284	3,635
	Total Completions/Attempts	325/556	287/538	310/522
	Average Yards per Game	240.3	205.3	227.2
	Interceptions Thrown	23	19	20
	Times Sacked	54	34	33
San Diego Chargers	Passing Touchdowns	17	20	18
	Rushing Touchdowns	1	0	0
	Total Passing Yards	3,706	3,619	3,383
	Total Completions/Attempts	318/539	305/522	301/563
	Average Yards per Game	231.6	226.2	211.4
	Interceptions Thrown	18	14	14
	Times Sacked	32	29	32
Washington Redskins	Passing Touchdowns	16	25	11
	Rushing Touchdowns	1	0	3
	Total Passing Yards	3,496	3,524	2,764
	Total Completions/Attempts	265/521	271/546	287/533
	Average Yards per Game	218.5	220.3	172.8
	Interceptions Thrown	20	27	21
	Times Sacked	36	21	40

11 OT

		1995:	1994:	1993:
Carolina Panthers	Passing Touchdowns	16		
	Rushing Touchdowns	3		
	Total Passing Yards	3,258		
	Total Completions/Attempts	262/534		
	Average Yards per Game	203.6		
	Interceptions Thrown	24		
	Times Sacked	38		
New England Patriots	Passing Touchdowns	14	25	17
	Rushing Touchdowns	0	0	0
	Total Passing Yards	3,789	4,583	3,412
	Total Completions/Attempts	351/685	405/699	289/566
	Average Yards per Game	236.8	286.4	213.3
	Interceptions Thrown	16	27	24
	Times Sacked	27	22	23
Philadelphia Eagles	Passing Touchdowns	11	18	23
	Rushing Touchdowns	1	3	1
	Total Passing Yards	2,931	3,736	3,463
	Total Completions/Attempts	284/496	316/566	328/556
	Average Yards per Game	183.2	233.5	216.4
	Interceptions Thrown	19	14	13
	Times Sacked	43	48	42
New York Giants	Passing Touchdowns	11	16	17
	Rushing Touchdowns	4	2	0
	Total Passing Yards	2,863	2,847	3,180
	Total Completions/Attempts	260/479	226/405	257/424
	Average Yards per Game	178.9	177.9	198.8
	Interceptions Thrown	13	18	9
	Times Sacked	46	46	40
Tampa Bay Buccaneers	Passing Touchdowns	5	17	19
	Rushing Touchdowns	3	1	0
	Total Passing Yards	3,293	3,436	3,295
	Total Completions/Attempts	266/505	271/491	262/508
	Average Yards per Game	205.8	214.8	205.9
	Interceptions Thrown	20	16	25
	Times Sacked	56	30	39

12 Rookies and Free Agents

Drafting Rookies—

For this year's book, I have selected 30 offensive rookies that will have an impact on their teams. I purposely did not include the rookie quarterbacks, since none are ready to step in and start this season. However, there are several who will make an impact within the next several seasons:

Danny Kanell, *New York Giants*
Bobby Hoying, *Philadelphia Eagles*
Jeff Lewis, *Denver Broncos*
Tony Banks, *St. Louis Rams*
Scott Milanovich, *Tampa Bay Buccaneers*

This class will add some exciting players to the NFL this season and I would expect *all* 30 players to contribute. The top four (Phillips, Johnson, Biakabutuka, and George), are phenomenal and will provide immediate dividends. Receivers like Moulds, Harrison, and Glenn could take a little longer before they understand their pass routes, etc., but all three could be starting by midseason.

At tight end, I expect Dudley and Battaglia to start and produce this season (but remember, tight ends rarely hit double digits in the scoring column). My sleepers are Alstott, Davis, and McElroy at running back. All three are exceptional and will push for starting jobs. Keep an eye on these players during exhibition season—hopefully all will sign and be in camp. Some might warrant your consideration for drafting this season.

The Best of the New: The '96 Rookies—

Player:	Position:	Team:
Lawrence Phillips	RB	St. Louis Rams
Keyshawn Johnson	WR	New York Jets
Tim Biakabutuka	RB	Carolina Panthers
Eddie George	RB	Houston Oilers
Eric Moulds	WR	Buffalo Bills
Marvin Harrison	WR	Indianapolis Colts
Terry Glenn	WR	New England Patriots
Mike Alstott	RB	Tampa Bay Buccaneers
Rickey Dudley	TE	Oakland Raiders
Amani Toomer	WR	New York Giants
Leland McElroy	RB/RS	Arizona Cardinals
Bobby Engram	WR	Chicago Bears
Alex Van Dyke	WR	New York Jets
Eddie Kennison	WR	St. Louis Rams
Marco Battaglia	TE	Cincinnati Bengals
Detron Smith	RB	Denver Broncos
Stephen Davis	RB	Washington Redskins
Moe Williams	RB	Minnesota Vikings
Karim Abdul-Jabbar	RB	Miami Dolphins
Bryan Still	WR/RS	San Diego Chargers
Jason Dunn	TE	Philadelphia Eagles
Derrick Mayes	WR	Green Bay Packers
Johnny McWilliams	TE	Arizona Cardinals
Ernie Conwell	TE/RB	St. Louis Rams
Terrell Owens	WR	San Francisco 49ers
Stanley Pritchett	RB	Miami Dolphins
Brian Milne	RB	Indianapolis Colts
Brian Roche	TE	San Diego Chargers
Chris Darkins	RB	Green Bay Packers
Mercury Hayes	WR	New Orleans Saints

13 Dick's Picks

Here we are at my favorite part of the Journal: *Dick's Picks*. This is not my favorite part simply because it has my name on it; it is my favorite because it is the one thing that really distinguishes our Journal from all others out there, and the one piece I work the hardest on each year. This year you will notice there are more players on the list than ever before. In past years we have only listed the top 150 players; this year we blow that out and go all the way to the top 200 players. I feel that gives you the best, most complete listing of players to draft.

Many people write me online and wonder how it is that I come up with the *Dick's Pick's* section each year. Some suggest that I get it in a fortune cookie at Hunan Garden; other suggest that it comes to me in a dream! The truth is that I start compiling the list at the end of each NFL season, based on each players' stats and scoring, and adjust it over the offseason to account for the NFL draft, and any trades, injuries, legal problems, etc., that have occurred to the player or the NFL team. I also consider how they looked in the offseason, and other roster moves that might affect their stature.

For example, in the offseason Mark Seay and Shawn Jefferson left San Diego. This could affect Stan Humphries' season, as he adjusts to new receivers and the Chargers retool their offense. Therefore, he ranks a little lower than he might otherwise. Also, Brett Favre remains highly ranked on the list, despite his offseason entrance into the NFL's Substance Abuse Treatment Program. Similarly, Michael Irvin remains on the list, as it was rumored that he would avoid serious legal consequence and continue to play this season. So I try to take all these things into consideration, and put out a list that I feel is the best and most comprehensive list out there. Once again, you may want to shift players slightly based on your scoring system, but overall this should be all you need to do well in your fantasy draft this year. *Good Luck!* ★

Top 200 Scoring and Performance Picks—

	Player:	Position:	Team:
1	Steve Young	QB	San Francisco 49ers
2	Brett Favre	QB	Green Bay Packers
3	Emmitt Smith	RB	Dallas Cowboys
4	Jerry Rice	WR	San Francisco 49ers
5	Barry Sanders	RB	Detroit Lions
6	Scott Mitchell	QB	Detroit Lions
7	Dan Marino	QB	Miami Dolphins
8	Herman Moore	WR	Detroit Lions
9	Curtis Martin	RB	New England Patriots
10	Eric Metcalf	WR	Atlanta Falcons
11	Jeff George	QB	Atlanta Falcons
12	Jeff Blake	QB	Cincinnati Bengals
13	Chris Warren	RB	Seattle Seahawks
14	Carl Pickens	WR	Cincinnati Bengals
15	Marshall Faulk	RB	Indianapolis Colts
16	Ricky Watters	RB	Philadelphia Eagles
17	Ki-Jana Carter	RB	Cincinnati Bengals
18	Drew Bledsoe	QB	New England Patriots
19	John Elway	QB	Denver Broncos
20	Jim Kelly	QB	Buffalo Bills
21	Lawrence Phillips	RB	St. Louis Rams
22	Isaac Bruce	WR	St. Louis Rams
23	Robert Brooks	WR	Green Bay Packers
24	Cris Carter	WR	Minnesota Vikings
25	Tim Brown	WR	Oakland Raiders
26	Erik Kramer	QB	Chicago Bears
27	Errict Rhett	RB	Tampa Bay Buccaneers
28	Eddie George	RB	Houston Oilers
29	Michael Irvin	WR	Dallas Cowboys
30	Neil O'Donnell	QB	New York Jets
31	Rashaan Salaam	RB	Chicago Bears
32	Rodney Hampton	RB	New York Giants
33	Anthony Miller	WR	Denver Broncos
34	Edgar Bennett	RB	Green Bay Packers
35	Harvey Williams	RB	Kansas City Chiefs
36	Mario Bates	RB	New Orleans Saints
37	Johnny Johnson	RB	San Francisco 49ers
38	Aaron Hayden	RB	San Diego Chargers
39	Jim Everett	QB	New Orleans Saints
40	Tim Biakabutuka	RB	Carolina Panthers
41	Jeff Hostetler	QB	Oakland Raiders
42	Jason Elam	K	Denver Broncos
43	Morten Andersen	K	Atlanta Falcons
44	Warren Moon	QB	Minnesota Vikings
45	Mark Brunell	QB	Jacksonville Jaguars
46	Curtis Conway	WR	Chicago Bears
47	Terrell Davis	RB	Denver Broncos
48	Joey Galloway	WR	Seattle Seahawks
49	Adrian Murrell	RB	New York Jets
50	Bernie Parmalee	RB	Miami Dolphins

	Player:	Position:	Team:
51	Ironhead Heyward	RB	Atlanta Falcons
52	Terry Allen	RB	Washington Redskins
53	Pete Stoyanovich	K	Miami Dolphins
54	Jerome Bettis	RB	Pittsburgh Steelers
55	Natrone Means	RB	Jacksonville Jaguars
56	Vinny Testaverde	QB	Baltimore Ravens
57	Andre Rison	WR	Baltimore Ravens
58	Stan Humphries	QB	San Diego Chargers
59	Keyshawn Johnson	WR	New York Jets
60	Troy Aikman	QB	Dallas Cowboys
61	Steve Bono	QB	Kansas City Chiefs
62	Chris Boniol	K	Dallas Cowboys
63	Chris Sanders	WR	Houston Oilers
64	J.J. Stokes	WR	San Francisco 49ers
65	Steve Christie	K	Buffalo Bills
66	Fred Barnett	WR	Miami Dolphins
67	Jason Hanson	K	Detroit Lions
68	Quinn Early	WR	Buffalo Bills
69	Darnay Scott	WR	Cincinnati Bengals
70	O.J. McDuffie	WR	Miami Dolphins
71	Norm Johnson	K	Pittsburgh Steelers
72	Terance Mathis	WR	Atlanta Falcons
73	Jake Reed	WR	Minnesota Vikings
74	Al Del Greco	K	Houston Oilers
75	Brett Perriman	WR	Detroit Lions
76	Michael Jackson	WR	Baltimore Ravens
77	Tamarick Vanover	WR	Kansas City Chiefs
78	Michael Westbrook	WR	Washington Redskins
79	Deion Sanders	WR/CB	Dallas Cowboys
80	Ben Coates	TE	New England Patriots
81	Thurman Thomas	RB	Buffalo Bills
82	Willie Davis	WR	Houston Oilers
83	Jim Harbaugh	QB	Indianapolis Colts
84	Tony Martin	WR	San Diego Chargers
85	Michael Haynes	WR	New Orleans Saints
86	Bert Emanuel	WR	Atlanta Falcons
87	Shawn Jefferson	WR	New England Patriots
88	Kerry Collins	QB	Carolina Panthers
89	Chris Chandler	QB	Houston Oilers
90	Garrison Hearst	RB	Arizona Cardinals
91	Heath Shuler	QB	Washington Redskins
92	Henry Ellard	WR	Washington Redskins
93	Terry Kirby	RB	Miami Dolphins
94	Torrance Small	WR	New Orleans Saints
95	Mike Sherrard	WR	Denver Broncos
96	Andre Reed	WR	Buffalo Bills
97	Frank Sanders	WR	Arizona Cardinals
98	Charlie Garner	RB	Philadelphia Eagles
99	Tyrone Wheatley	RB	New York Giants
100	Doug Pelfrey	K	Cincinnati Bengals

	Player:	Position:	Team:
101	Yancey Thigpen	WR	Pittsburgh Steelers
102	Boomer Esiason	QB	Arizona Cardinals
103	Mark Chmura	TE	Green Bay Packers
104	Jeff Graham	WR	New York Jets
105	Fuad Reveiz	K	Minnesota Vikings
106	Brian Mitchell	RB	Washington Redskins
107	Leroy Hoard	RB	Baltimore Ravens
108	John Kasay	K	Carolina Panthers
109	Eric Green	TE	Miami Dolphins
110	Vincent Brisby	WR	New England Patriots
111	Ty Detmer	QB	Philadelphia Eagles
112	Larry Centers	RB	Arizona Cardinals
113	Chris Jacke	K	Green Bay Packers
114	Wesley Walls	TE	Carolina Panthers
115	Darick Holmes	RB	Buffalo Bills
116	Erric Pegram	RB	Pittsburgh Steelers
117	Napoleon Kaufman	RB	Oakland Raiders
118	James Stewart	RB	Minnesota Vikings
119	Rodney Thomas	RB	Houston Oilers
120	Calvin Williams	WR	Philadelphia Eagles
121	Greg Hill	RB	Kansas City Chiefs
122	Tommy Vardell	RB	San Francisco 49ers
123	Johnnie Morton	WR	Detroit Lions
124	Kevin Williams	WR	Dallas Cowboys
125	Irving Fryar	WR	Philadelphia Eagles
126	Brian Blades	WR	Seattle Seahawks
127	Brent Jones	TE	San Francisco 49ers
128	Steve Walsh	QB	St. Louis Rams
129	Rick Mirer	QB	Seattle Seahawks
130	Dorsey Levens	RB	Green Bay Packers
131	Leland McElroy	RB	Arizona Cardinals
132	Bill Brooks	WR	Washington Redskins
133	Alvin Harper	WR	Tampa Bay Buccaneers
134	Kimble Anders	RB	Kansas City Chiefs
135	Zack Crockett	RB	Indianapolis Colts
136	Thomas Lewis	WR	New York Giants
137	Mike Alstott	RB	Tampa Bay Buccaneers
138	Rocket Ismail	WR	Oakland Raiders
139	Ronnie Harmon	RB	Houston Oilers
140	Marcus Allen	RB	Kansas City Chiefs
141	Terry Glenn	WR	New England Patriots
142	Terrell Fletcher	RB	San Diego Chargers
143	William Floyd	RB	San Francisco 49ers
144	Eddie Kennison	WR	St. Louis Rams
145	Sean Dawkins	WR	Indianapolis Colts
146	Kyle Brady	TE	New York Jets
147	Courtney Hawkins	WR	Tampa Bay Buccaneers
148	Robert Smith	RB	Minnesota Vikings
149	Keenan McCardell	WR	Carolina Panthers
150	Michael Timpson	WR	Chicago Bears

Appendix A—1996 NFL Schedule

Week 1—

Sunday, September 1

Arizona	at	Indianapolis (FOX) 1:00	Pittsburgh	at	Jacksonville (NBC) 1:00
Atlanta	at	Carolina (FOX) 1:00	Green Bay	at	Tampa Bay (FOX) 4:00
Cincinnati	at	St. Louis (NBC) 1:00	New England	at	Miami (NBC) 4:00
Detroit	at	Minnesota (FOX) 1:00	New Orleans	at	San Francisco (FOX) 4:00
Kansas City	at	Houston (NBC) 1:00	NY Jets	at	Denver (NBC) 4:00
Oakland	at	Baltimore (NBC) 1:00	Seattle	at	San Diego (NBC) 4:00
Philadelphia	at	Washington (FOX) 1:00	Buffalo	at	NY Giants (TNT) 8:00

Monday, September 2
Dallas   at   Chicago (ABC) 9:00

Week 2—

Sunday, September 8

Baltimore	at	Pittsburgh (NBC) 1:00	Oakland	at	Kansas City (NBC) 1:00
Carolina	at	New Orleans (FOX) 1:00	Tampa Bay	at	Detroit (FOX) 1:00
Chicago	at	Washington (FOX) 1:00	Cincinnati	at	San Diego (NBC) 4:00
Houston	at	Jacksonville (NBC) 1:00	Denver	at	Seattle (NBC) 4:00
Indianapolis	at	NY Jets (NBC) 1:00	NY Giants	at	Dallas (FOX) 4:00
Minnesota	at	Atlanta (FOX) 1:00	St. Louis	at	San Francisco (FOX) 4:00
New England	at	Buffalo (NBC) 1:00	Miami	at	Arizona (TNT) 8:00

Monday, September 9
Philadelphia   at   Green Bay (ABC) 9:00

Week 3 —

Sunday, September 15

Arizona	at	New England (FOX) 1:00	San Diego	at	Green Bay (NBC) 1:00
Baltimore	at	Houston (NBC) 1:00	Indianapolis	at	Dallas (NBC) 4:00
Detroit	at	Philadelphia (FOX) 1:00	Jacksonville	at	Oakland (NBC) 4:00
Minnesota	at	Chicago (FOX) 1:00	Kansas City	at	Seattle (NBC) 4:00
New Orleans	at	Cincinnati (FOX) 1:00	Washington	at	NY Giants (FOX) 4:00
NY Jets	at	Miami (NBC) 1:00	Tampa Bay	at	Denver (TNT) 8:00

Monday, September 16
Buffalo   at   Pittsburgh (ABC) 9:00

Byes: Atlanta, Carolina, St. Louis, San Francisco

All game times are Eastern Standard Time.

Week 4—

Sunday, September 22

Arizona	at	New Orleans (FOX) 1:00	Washington	at	St. Louis (FOX) 1:00
Denver	at	Kansas City (NBC) 1:00	Chicago	at	Detroit (FOX) 4:00
Green Bay	at	Minnesota (FOX) 1:00	Dallas	at	Buffalo (FOX) 4:00
NY Giants	at	NY Jets (FOX) 1:00	Jacksonville	at	New England (NBC) 4:00
San Francisco	at	Carolina (FOX) 1:00	San Diego	at	Oakland (NBC) 4:00
Seattle	at	Tampa Bay (NBC) 1:00	Philadelphia	at	Atlanta (TNT) 8:00

Monday, September 23

Miami   at   Indianapolis (ABC) 9:00

Byes: Baltimore, Cincinnati, Houston, Pittsburgh

Week 5—

Sunday, September 29

Carolina	at	Jacksonville (FOX) 1:00	Oakland	at	Chicago (NBC) 1:00
Denver	at	Cincinnati (NBC) 1:00	Atlanta	at	San Francisco (FOX) 4:00
Detroit	at	Tampa Bay (FOX) 1:00	Green Bay	at	Seattle (FOX) 4:00
Houston	at	Pittsburgh (NBC) 1:00	Kansas City	at	San Diego (NBC) 4:00
Minnesota	at	NY Giants (FOX) 1:00	St. Louis	at	Arizona (FOX) 4:00
New Orleans	at	Baltimore (FOX) 1:00	NY Jets	at	Washington (TNT) 8:00

Monday, September 30

Dallas   at   Philadelphia (ABC) 9:00

Byes: Buffalo, Indianapolis, Miami, New England

Week 6—

Sunday, October 6

Atlanta	at	Detroit (FOX) 1:00	Indianapolis	at	Buffalo (NBC) 4:00
Carolina	at	Minnesota (FOX) 1:00	Jacksonville	at	New Orleans (NBC) 4:00
Green Bay	at	Chicago (FOX) 1:00	San Diego	at	Denver (NBC) 4:00
New England	at	Baltimore (NBC) 1:00	San Francisco	at	St. Louis (FOX) 4:00
Oakland	at	NY Jets (NBC) 1:00	Houston	at	Cincinnati (TNT) 8:00
Seattle	at	Miami (NBC) 1:00			

Monday, October 7

Pittsburgh   at   Kansas City (ABC) 9:00

Byes: Arizona, Dallas, NY Giants, Philadelphia, Tampa Bay, Washington

All game times are Eastern Standard Time.

Week 7—

Sunday, October 13

Arizona	at	Dallas (FOX) 1:00	NY Jets	at	Jacksonville (NBC) 1:00
Chicago	at	New Orleans (FOX) 1:00	St. Louis	at	Carolina (FOX) 1:00
Cincinnati	at	Pittsburgh (NBC) 1:00	Washington	at	New England (FOX) 1:00
Houston	at	Atlanta (NBC) 1:00	Detroit	at	Oakland (FOX) 4:00
Miami	at	Buffalo (NBC) 1:00	Philadelphia	at	NY Giants (FOX) 4:00
Minnesota	at	Tampa Bay (FOX) 1:00	Baltimore	at	Indianapolis (TNT) 8:00

Monday, October 14
San Francisco at Green Bay (ABC) 9:00

Byes: Denver, Kansas City, San Diego, Seattle

Week 8—

Thursday, October 17
Seattle at Kansas City (TNT) 8:00

Sunday, October 20

Atlanta	at	Dallas (FOX) 1:00	Buffalo	at	NY Jets (NBC) 4:00
Miami	at	Philadelphia (NBC) 1:00	Cincinnati	at	San Francisco (NBC) 4:00
New England	at	Indianapolis (NBC) 1:00	Jacksonville	at	St. Louis (NBC) 4:00
New Orleans	at	Carolina (FOX) 1:00	Pittsburgh	at	Houston (NBC) 4:00
NY Giants	at	Washington (FOX) 1:00	Tampa Bay	at	Arizona (FOX) 4:00
Baltimore	at	Denver (NBC) 4:00			

Monday, October 21
Oakland at San Diego (ABC) 9:00

Byes: Chicago, Detroit, Green Bay, Minnesota

Week 9—

Sunday, October 27

Carolina	at	Philadelphia (FOX) 1:00	Tampa Bay	at	Green Bay (FOX) 1:00
Indianapolis	at	Washington (NBC) 1:00	Dallas	at	Miami (FOX) 4:00
Jacksonville	at	Cincinnati (NBC) 1:00	Kansas City	at	Denver (NBC) 4:00
NY Giants	at	Detroit (FOX) 1:00	NY Jets	at	Arizona (NBC) 4:00
Pittsburgh	at	Atlanta (NBC) 1:00	San Diego	at	Seattle (NBC) 4:00
St. Louis	at	Baltimore (FOX) 1:00	Buffalo	at	New England (TNT) 8:00
San Francisco	at	Houston (FOX) 1:00			

Monday, October 28
Chicago at Minnesota (ABC) 9:00

Byes: New Orleans, Oakland

---

*All game times are
Eastern Standard Time.*

Week 10—

Sunday, November 3

Arizona	at	NY Giants (FOX) 1:00		San Diego	at	Indianapolis (NBC) 1:00
Carolina	at	Atlanta (FOX) 1:00		Tampa Bay	at	Chicago (FOX) 1:00
Cincinnati	at	Baltimore (NBC) 1:00		Houston	at	Seattle (NBC) 4:00
Detroit	at	Green Bay (FOX) 1:00		Miami	at	New England (NBC) 4:00
Kansas City	at	Minnesota (NBC) 1:00		Washington	at	Buffalo (FOX) 4:00
Philadelphia	at	Dallas (FOX) 1:00		San Francisco	at	New Orleans (ESPN) 8:00
St. Louis	at	Pittsburgh (FOX) 1:00				

Monday, November 4

Denver at Oakland (ABC) 9:00

Byes: Jacksonville, NY Jets

Week 11—

Sunday, November 10

Arizona	at	Washington (FOX) 1:00		Oakland	at	Tampa Bay (FOX) 1:00
Atlanta	at	St. Louis (FOX) 1:00		Pittsburgh	at	Cincinnati (NBC) 1:00
Buffalo	at	Philadelphia (NBC) 1:00		Baltimore	at	Jacksonville (NBC) 4:00
Green Bay	at	Kansas City (FOX) 1:00		Chicago	at	Denver (FOX) 4:00
Houston	at	New Orleans (NBC) 1:00		Dallas	at	San Francisco (FOX) 4:00
Indianapolis	at	Miami (NBC) 1:00		Minnesota	at	Seattle (FOX) 4:00
New England	at	NY Jets (NBC) 1:00		NY Giants	at	Carolina (ESPN) 8:00

Monday, November 11

Detroit at San Diego (ABC) 9:00

Week 12—

Sunday, November 17

Carolina	at	St. Louis (FOX) 1:00		Seattle	at	Detroit (NBC) 1:00
Chicago	at	Kansas City (FOX) 1:00		Washington	at	Philadelphia (FOX) 1:00
Cincinnati	at	Buffalo (NBC) 1:00		Baltimore	at	San Francisco (NBC) 4:00
Denver	at	New England (NBC) 1:00		Miami	at	Houston (NBC) 4:00
Jacksonville	at	Pittsburgh (NBC) 1:00		NY Giants	at	Arizona (FOX) 4:00
New Orleans	at	Atlanta (FOX) 1:00		Tampa Bay	at	San Diego (FOX) 4:00
NY Jets	at	Indianapolis (NBC) 1:00		Minnesota	at	Oakland (ESPN) 8:00

Monday, November 18

Green Bay at Dallas (ABC) 9:00

All game times are Eastern Standard Time.

Week 13—

Sunday, November 24

Atlanta	at	Cincinnati (FOX) 1:00		NY Jets	at	Buffalo (NBC) 1:00
Carolina	at	Houston (FOX) 1:00		San Diego	at	Kansas City (NBC) 1:00
Denver	at	Minnesota (NBC) 1:00		San Francisco	at	Washington (FOX) 1:00
Detroit	at	Chicago (FOX) 1:00		Dallas	at	NY Giants (FOX) 4:00
Indianapolis	at	New England (NBC) 1:00		Oakland	at	Seattle (NBC) 4:00
Jacksonville	at	Baltimore (NBC) 1:00		Philadelphia	at	Arizona (FOX) 4:00
New Orleans	at	Tampa Bay (FOX) 1:00		Green Bay	at	St. Louis (ESPN) 8:00

Monday, November 25
Pittsburgh   at   Miami (ABC) 9:00

Week 14—

Thursday, November 28
Kansas City   at   Detroit (NBC) 12:30
Washington   at   Dallas (FOX) 4:00

Sunday, December 1

Arizona	at	Minnesota (FOX) 1:00		Tampa Bay	at	Carolina (FOX) 1:00
Buffalo	at	Indianapolis (NBC) 1:00		Houston	at	NY Jets (NBC) 4:00
Chicago	at	Green Bay (FOX) 1:00		Miami	at	Oakland (NBC) 4:00
Cincinnati	at	Jacksonville (NBC) 1:00		St. Louis	at	New Orleans (FOX) 4:00
NY Giants	at	Philadelphia (FOX) 1:00		Seattle	at	Denver (NBC) 4:00
Pittsburgh	at	Baltimore (NBC) 1:00		New England	at	San Diego (ESPN) 8:00

Monday, December 2
San Francisco   at   Atlanta (ABC) 9:00

Week 15—

Thursday, December 5
Philadelphia   at   Indianapolis (ESPN) 8:00

Sunday, December 8

Atlanta	at	New Orleans (FOX) 1:00		Washington	at	Tampa Bay (FOX) 1:00
Baltimore	at	Cincinnati (NBC) 1:00		Buffalo	at	Seattle (NBC) 4:00
Denver	at	Green Bay (NBC) 1:00		Carolina	at	San Francisco (FOX) 4:00
Jacksonville	at	Houston (NBC) 1:00		Dallas	at	Arizona (FOX) 4:00
NY Giants	at	Miami (FOX) 1:00		NY Jets	at	New England (NBC) 4:00
St. Louis	at	Chicago (FOX) 1:00		Minnesota	at	Detroit (ESPN) 8:00
San Diego	at	Pittsburgh (NBC) 1:00				

Monday, December 9
Kansas City   at   Oakland (ABC) 9:00

All game times are Eastern Standard Time.

Week 16—

Saturday, December 14
Philadelphia	at	NY Jets (FOX) 12:30
San Diego	at	Chicago (NBC) 4:00

Sunday, December 15
Baltimore	at	Carolina (NBC) 1:00	St. Louis	at	Atlanta (FOX) 1:00
Cincinnati	at	Houston (NBC) 1:00	San Francisco	at	Pittsburgh (FOX) 1:00
Green Bay	at	Detroit (FOX) 1:00	Tampa Bay	at	Minnesota (FOX) 1:00
Indianapolis	at	Kansas City (NBC) 1:00	Oakland	at	Denver (NBC) 4:00
New England	at	Dallas (NBC) 1:00	Washington	at	Arizona (FOX) 4:00
New Orleans	at	NY Giants (FOX) 1:00	Seattle	at	Jacksonville (ESPN) 8:00

Monday, December 16
Buffalo	at	Miami (ABC) 9:00

Week 17—

Saturday, December 21
New England	at	NY Giants (NBC) 12:30
New Orleans	at	St. Louis (FOX) 4:00

Sunday, December 22
Arizona	at	Philadelphia (FOX) 1:00	Miami	at	NY Jets (NBC) 1:00
Atlanta	at	Jacksonville (FOX) 1:00	Minnesota	at	Green Bay (FOX) 1:00
Chicago	at	Tampa Bay (FOX) 1:00	Pittsburgh	at	Carolina (NBC) 1:00
Houston	at	Baltimore (NBC) 1:00	Dallas	at	Washingto (FOX) 4:00
Indianapolis	at	Cincinnati (NBC) 1:00	Seattle	at	Oakland (NBC) 4:00
Kansas City	at	Buffalo (NBC) 1:00	Denver	at	San Diego (ESPN) 8:00

Monday, December 23
Detroit	at	San Francisco (ABC) 9:00

All game times are Eastern Standard Time.

Appendix B— All-Fantasy '93-95 Dream Teams

If you could select nine players in a row on *Draft Day*, which would you pick?

We all know that isn't possible, since all FFL owners get only one pick per round. However, in this section we present for your review the FFL *Dream Teams*! These *Dream Teams* are comprised of the top players in the NFL over the last three seasons (1993-1995) based upon standard FFL scoring. The players are listed by position along with a summary of their incredible statistics. A *First Team* and a *Second Team* are shown for each of the last three years.

Do your homework prior to your league's *Draft Day* and then carefully make your selections. It is not unusual that the top team in any FFL league "*owned*" three or four of these players!

The abbreviations used within the tables are—

Passing Completions/Passing Attempts C/A
Yards (YDS)
Touchdowns (TDS)
Interceptions (INTS)
Carries (CARS)
Fumbles (FUMS)
Receptions (RECS)
Extra Points (XPTS)
Field Goals (FGS)
Points (PTS)
Sacks (SKS)
Fumbles Recovered (FUMS/R) ★

'95 All-Fantasy Dream Teams—

First Team:

QB Brett Favre	*Green Bay Packers*	359/570 C/A	4,413 YDS	41 TDS	13 INTS
RB Emmitt Smith	*Dallas Cowboys*	377 CARS	1,773 YDS	25 TDS	7 FUMS
RB Curtis Martin	*New England Patriots*	368 CARS	1,487 YDS	15 TDS	5 FUMS
WR Jerry Rice	*San Francisco 49ers*	122 RECS	1,848 YDS	17 TDS	3 FUMS
WR Herman Moore	*Detroit Lions*	123 RECS	1,686 YDS	14 TDS	2 FUMS
WR Isaac Bruce	*St. Louis Rams*	119 RECS	1,781 YDS	13 TDS	2 FUMS
TE Mark Chmura	*Green Bay Packers*	54 RECS	679 YDS	7 TDS	0 FUMS
K Morten Andersen	*Atlanta Falcons*	29/30 XPTS	31/37 FGS	122 PTS	
DT San Francisco 49ers		40 SKS	26 INTS	8 FUMS/R	8 TDS

Second Team:

QB Scott Mitchell	*Detroit Lions*	346/583 C/A	4,338 YDS	36 TDS	12 INTS
RB Chris Warren	*Seattle Seahawks*	310 CARS	1,346 YDS	16 TDS	5 FUMS
RB Barry Sanders	*Detroit Lions*	314 CARS	1,500 YDS	12 TDS	4 FUMS
WR Robert Brooks	*Green Bay Packers*	102 RECS	1,497 YDS	13 TDS	1 FUMS
WR Michael Irvin	*Dallas Cowboys*	111 RECS	1,603 YDS	10 TDS	1 FUMS
WR Cris Carter	*Minnesota Vikings*	122 RECS	1,371 YDS	17 TDS	0 FUMS
TE Shannon Sharpe	*Denver Broncos*	63 RECS	756 YDS	4 TDS	1 FUMS
K Norm Johnson	*Pittsburgh Steelers*	39/39 XPTS	34/41 FGS	141 PTS	
DT Kansas City Chiefs		47 SKS	16 INTS	17 FUMS/R	7 TDS

'94 All-Fantasy Dream Teams—

First Team:

QB Steve Young	*San Francisco 49ers*	324/461 C/A	3,969 YDS	42 TDS	10 INTS
RB Barry Sanders	*Detroit Lions*	331 CARS	1,883 YDS	8 TDS	5 FUMS
RB Emmitt Smith	*Dallas Cowboys*	368 CARS	1,484 YDS	22 TDS	4 FUMS
WR Jerry Rice	*San Francisco 49ers*	112 RECS	1,499 YDS	15 TDS	1 FUMS
WR Sterling Sharpe	*Green Bay Packers*	123 RECS	1,686 YDS	18 TDS	2 FUMS
WR Terance Mathis	*Atlanta Falcons*	111 RECS	1,342 YDS	11 TDS	3 FUMS
TE Ben Coates	*New England Patriots*	96 RECS	1,174 YDS	7 TDS	1 FUMS
K John Carney	*San Diego Chargers*	33/33 XPTS	34/38 FGS	135 PTS	
DT San Diego Chargers		43 SKS	17 INTS	16 FUMS/R	7 TDS

Second Team:

QB Dan Marino	*Miami Dolphins*	385/615 C/A	4,453 YDS	41 TDS	17 INTS
RB Chris Warren	*Seattle Seahawks*	333 CARS	1,545 YDS	11 TDS	3 FUMS
RB Ricky Watters	*San Francisco 49ers*	239 CARS	887 YDS	11 TDS	6 FUMS
WR Carl Pickens	*Cincinnati Bengals*	71 RECS	1,127 YDS	11 TDS	1 FUMS
WR Irving Fryar	*Miami Dolphins*	73 RECS	1,270 YDS	7 TDS	2 FUMS
WR Andre Reed	*Buffalo Bills*	90 RECS	1,303 YDS	8 TDS	1 FUMS
TE Brent Jones	*San Francisco 49ers*	49 RECS	670 YDS	9 TDS	2 FUMS
K Fuad Reveiz	*Minnesota Vikings*	30/30 XPTS	34/39 FGS	132 PTS	
DT Indianapolis Colts		29 SKS	18 INTS	11 FUMS/R	7 TDS

'93 All-Fantasy Dream Teams—

First Team:

QB Steve Young	San Francisco 49ers	314/462 C/A	4,023 YDS	31 TDS	16 INTS
RB Marcus Allen	Kansas City Chiefs	206 CARS	764 YDS	15 TDS	6 FUMS
RB Keith Byars	Miami Dolphins	64 CARS	269 YDS	7 TDS	6 FUMS
WR Jerry Rice	San Francisco 49ers	98 RECS	1,503 YDS	16 TDS	2 FUMS
WR Andre Rison	Atlanta Falcons	86 RECS	1,242 YDS	15 TDS	1 FUMS
WR Sterling Sharpe	Green Bay Packers	112 RECS	1,274 YDS	11 TDS	1 FUMS
TE Shannon Sharpe	Denver Broncos	81 RECS	995 YDS	9 TDS	1 FUMS
K Chris Jacke	Green Bay Packers	35/35 XPTS	31/37 FGS	128 PTS	
DT Houston Oilers		51 SKS	26 INTS	17 FUMS/R	6 TDS

Second Team:

QB John Elway	Denver Broncos	348/551 C/A	4,030 YDS	25 TDS	10 INTS
RB Ricky Watters	San Francisco 49ers	208 CARS	950 YDS	11 TDS	5 FUMS
RB Terry Kirby	Miami Dolphins	119 CARS	390 YDS	6 TDS	3 FUMS
WR Calvin Williams	Philadelphia Eagles	60 RECS	725 YDS	10 TDS	1 FUMS
WR Tim Brown	Los Angeles Raiders	80 RECS	1,180 YDS	8 TDS	2 FUMS
WR Anthony Miller	San Diego Chargers	84 RECS	1,162 YDS	7 TDS	2 FUMS
TE Ben Coates	New England Patriots	53 RECS	659 YDS	8 TDS	0 FUMS
K Jeff Jaeger	Los Angeles Raiders	27/29 XPTS	35/44 FGS	132 PTS	
DT Cleveland Browns		48 SKS	13 INTS	9 FUMS/R	5 TDS

Appendix C—
Three-Year
Fantasy Rankings

Presented in this section are tables presenting the *Top 25 Quarterbacks*, the *Top 50 Running Backs*, the *Top 50 Wide Receivers & Tight Ends*, the *Top 25 Kickers*, the *Top 25 Defenses & Special Teams*, the *Top 25 Linebackers*, the *Top 25 Defensive Backs*, and the *Top 25 Defensive Lines* in the NFL over the last three seasons (1993-1995) based upon standard FFL scoring.

The three-year breakdown for each player is followed with a *Per-Year Average* for each category.

The tables include the following statistics—

Year (YR)
Position (POS)
Team (TM)
Total Fantasy Points (FAN PTS)
Distance Points (DIST PTS)
Performance Points (PERF PTS)
Passing Touchdowns (0-9, 10-39, and 40+ YDS)
Rushing Touchdowns (0-9, 10-39, and 40+ YDS)
Receiving Touchdowns (0-9, 10-39, and 40+ YDS)
Field Goals (1-39, 40-49, and 50+ YDS)
Points after Touchdown (PAT)
Defense & Special Team Touchdowns (D,ST TDS)
Total Touchdowns (TOT TDS)
Games Played (GAM) ★

YR	PLAYER	POS	TM	FAN PTS	DIST PTS	PERF PTS	PASSING TD: 0-9	10-39	40+	RUSHING TD: 0-9	10-39	40+	RECEIVING TD: 0-9	10-39	40+	FIELD GOALS: 10-39	40-49	50+	PAT	D,ST TDS	TOT TDS	GAM
95	YOUNG, STEVE	QB	SF	256	198	58	8	10	2	3	0	0	0	0	0	0	0	0	0	0	23	11
94				427	358	69	20	10	5	7	0	0	0	0	0	0	0	0	0	0	42	16
93				302	273	29	11	13	5	1	1	0	0	0	0	0	0	0	0	0	31	16
				328.3	276.3	52.0	13.0	11.0	4.0	3.7	0.3	0.0	0.0	0.0	0.0	0.0	0.0	0.0	0.0	0.0	32.0	14.3
95	FAVRE, BRETT	QB	GB	429	354	75	15	18	5	2	1	0	0	0	0	0	0	0	0	0	41	16
94				346	299	47	11	21	1	1	1	0	0	0	0	0	0	0	0	0	35	16
93				162	174	-12	5	12	2	1	0	0	0	0	0	0	0	0	0	0	20	16
				312.3	275.7	36.7	10.3	17.0	2.7	1.3	0.7	0.0	0.0	0.0	0.0	0.0	0.0	0.0	0.0	0.0	32.0	16.0
95	ELWAY, JOHN	QB	DEN	296	243	53	9	9	8	1	0	0	0	0	0	0	0	0	0	0	27	16
94				219	202	17	3	10	3	3	1	0	0	0	0	0	0	0	0	0	20	14
93				230	201	29	10	13	2	0	0	0	0	0	0	0	0	0	0	0	25	16
				248.3	215.3	33.0	7.3	10.7	4.3	1.3	0.3	0.0	0.0	0.0	0.0	0.0	0.0	0.0	0.0	0.0	24.0	15.3
95	MOON, WARREN	QB	MIN	303	267	36	16	11	6	0	0	0	0	0	0	0	0	0	0	0	33	16
94				232	159	73	7	7	4	0	0	0	0	0	0	0	0	0	0	0	18	15
93				186	171	15	12	7	2	1	0	0	0	0	0	0	0	0	0	0	22	14
				240.3	199.0	41.3	11.7	8.3	4.0	0.3	0.0	0.0	0.0	0.0	0.0	0.0	0.0	0.0	0.0	0.0	24.3	15.0
95	MARINO, DAN	QB	MIA	237	186	51	13	8	3	0	0	0	0	0	0	0	0	0	0	0	24	14
94				348	267	81	11	15	4	1	0	0	0	0	0	0	0	0	0	0	31	16
93				101	90	11	1	4	3	1	0	0	0	0	0	0	0	0	0	0	9	5
				228.7	181.0	47.7	8.3	9.0	3.3	0.7	0.0	0.0	0.0	0.0	0.0	0.0	0.0	0.0	0.0	0.0	21.3	11.7
95	BLAKE, JEFF	QB	CIN	257	255	2	13	9	6	2	0	0	0	0	0	0	0	0	0	0	30	16
94				144	139	5	5	5	4	1	0	0	0	0	0	0	0	0	0	0	15	9
				200.5	197.0	3.5	9.0	7.0	5.0	1.5	0.0	0.0	0.0	0.0	0.0	0.0	0.0	0.0	0.0	0.0	22.5	12.5
95	MITCHELL, SCOTT	QB	DET	396	330	66	7	20	5	4	0	0	0	0	0	0	0	0	0	0	36	16
94				61	87	-26	5	5	0	1	0	0	0	0	0	0	0	0	0	0	11	9
93			MIA	124	105	19	4	5	3	0	0	0	0	0	0	0	0	0	0	0	12	7
				193.7	174.0	19.7	5.3	10.0	2.7	1.7	0.0	0.0	0.0	0.0	0.0	0.0	0.0	0.0	0.0	0.0	19.7	10.7
95	GEORGE, JEFF	QB	ATL	268	210	58	7	12	5	0	0	0	0	0	0	0	0	0	0	0	24	16
94				216	191	25	10	9	4	0	0	0	0	0	0	0	0	0	0	0	23	16
93			IND	80	60	20	5	2	1	0	0	0	0	0	0	0	0	0	0	0	8	11
				188.0	153.7	34.3	7.3	7.7	3.3	0.0	0.0	0.0	0.0	0.0	0.0	0.0	0.0	0.0	0.0	0.0	18.3	14.3

YR	PLAYER	POS	TM	FAN PTS	DIST PTS	PERF PTS	PASSING TD: 0-9	10-39	40+	RUSHING TD: 0-9	10-39	40+	RECEIVING TD: 0-9	10-39	40+	FIELD GOALS: 0-9	10-39	40-49	50+	PAT	D,ST TDS	TOT TDS	GAM
95	KELLY, JIM	QB	BUF	199	204	-5	3	14	5	0	0	0	0	0	0	0	0	0	0	0	0	22	15
94				201	204	-3	6	14	2	0	1	0	0	0	0	0	0	0	0	0	0	23	14
93				146	159	-13	4	11	3	0	0	0	0	0	0	0	0	0	0	0	0	18	16
				182.0	189.0	-7.0	4.3	13.0	3.3	0.0	0.3	0.0	0.0	0.0	0.0	0.0	0.0	0.0	0.0	0.0	0.0	21.0	15.0
95	EVERETT, JIM	QB	NO	244	213	31	11	11	4	0	0	0	0	0	0	0	0	0	0	0	0	26	16
94				223	187	36	7	13	2	0	0	0	0	0	0	0	0	0	0	0	0	22	16
93			RAM	68	78	-10	2	2	4	0	0	0	0	0	0	0	0	0	0	0	0	8	9
				178.3	159.3	19.0	6.7	8.7	3.3	0.0	0.0	0.0	0.0	0.0	0.0	0.0	0.0	0.0	0.0	0.0	0.0	18.7	13.7
95	BLEDSOE, DREW	QB	NE	98	99	-1	7	5	1	0	0	0	0	0	0	0	0	0	0	0	0	13	15
94				272	189	83	13	11	1	0	0	0	0	0	0	0	0	0	0	0	0	25	16
93				127	120	7	7	6	2	0	0	0	0	0	0	0	0	0	0	0	0	15	12
				165.7	136.0	29.7	9.0	7.3	1.3	0.0	0.0	0.0	0.0	0.0	0.0	0.0	0.0	0.0	0.0	0.0	0.0	17.7	14.3
95	HOSTETLER, JEFF	QB	RAI	92	99	-7	6	3	3	2	0	1	0	0	0	0	0	0	0	0	0	12	11
94				174	198	-24	6	10	4	2	0	0	0	0	0	0	0	0	0	0	0	22	16
93				208	189	19	4	7	3	4	1	0	0	0	0	0	0	0	0	0	0	19	15
				158.0	162.0	-4.0	5.3	6.7	3.3	2.0	0.3	0.0	0.0	0.0	0.0	0.0	0.0	0.0	0.0	0.0	0.0	17.7	14.0
95	BONO, STEVE	QB	KC	245	243	2	9	9	3	4	0	1	0	0	0	0	0	0	0	0	0	26	16
94				60	41	19	0	3	1	0	0	0	0	0	0	0	0	0	0	0	0	4	2
				152.5	142.0	10.5	4.5	6.0	2.0	2.0	0.0	0.5	0.0	0.0	0.0	0.0	0.0	0.0	0.0	0.0	0.0	15.0	9.0
95	TESTAVERDE, VINNY	QB	CLE	177	165	12	5	11	1	2	0	0	0	0	0	0	0	0	0	0	0	19	13
94				149	165	-16	4	9	3	2	0	0	0	0	0	0	0	0	0	0	0	18	13
93				111	117	-6	5	7	2	0	0	0	0	0	0	0	0	0	0	0	0	14	6
				145.7	149.0	-3.3	4.7	9.0	2.0	1.3	0.0	0.0	0.0	0.0	0.0	0.0	0.0	0.0	0.0	0.0	0.0	17.0	10.7
95	KRAMER, ERIK	QB	CHI	290	261	29	12	9	8	1	0	0	0	0	0	0	0	0	0	0	0	30	16
94				78	76	2	2	4	2	0	0	0	0	0	0	0	0	0	0	0	0	8	5
93			DET	63	66	-3	3	4	1	0	0	0	0	0	0	0	0	0	0	0	0	8	4
				143.7	134.3	9.3	5.7	5.7	3.7	0.3	0.0	0.0	0.0	0.0	0.0	0.0	0.0	0.0	0.0	0.0	0.0	15.3	8.3
95	HUMPHRIES, STAN	QB	SD	176	159	17	4	11	6	1	0	0	0	0	0	0	0	0	0	0	0	18	15
94				150	152	-2	7	4	6	0	0	0	0	0	0	0	0	0	0	0	0	17	15
93				101	108	-7	2	8	2	0	0	0	0	0	0	0	0	0	0	0	0	12	10
				142.3	139.7	2.7	4.3	7.7	3.3	0.3	0.0	0.0	0.0	0.0	0.0	0.0	0.0	0.0	0.0	0.0	0.0	15.7	13.3

				FAN	DIST	PERF	PASSING TD:			RUSHING TD:			RECEIVING TD:			FIELD GOALS:				D,ST	TOT	
YR	PLAYER	POS	TM	PTS	PTS	PTS	0-9	10-39	40+	0-9	10-39	40+	0-9	10-39	40+	10-39	40-49	50+	PAT	TDS	TDS	GAM
95	COLLINS, KERRY	QB	CAR	142	156	-14	6	4	4	3	0	0	0	0	0	0	0	0	0	0	17	15
95	AIKMAN, TROY	QB	DAL	164	147	17	6	7	3	1	0	0	0	0	0	0	0	0	0	0	17	16
94				112	120	-8	4	8	1	1	0	0	0	0	0	0	0	0	0	0	14	14
93				139	132	7	5	6	4	0	0	0	0	0	0	0	0	0	0	0	15	14
				138.3	133.0	5.3	5.0	7.0	2.7	0.7	0.0	0.0	0.0	0.0	0.0	0.0	0.0	0.0	0.0	0.0	15.3	14.7
95	ESIASON, BOOMER	QB	NYJ	110	126	-16	8	6	2	0	0	0	0	0	0	0	0	0	0	0	16	12
94				141	139	2	7	9	1	0	0	0	0	0	0	0	0	0	0	0	17	14
93				157	138	19	7	8	1	1	0	0	0	0	0	0	0	0	0	0	17	16
				136.0	134.3	1.7	7.3	7.7	1.3	0.3	0.0	0.0	0.0	0.0	0.0	0.0	0.0	0.0	0.0	0.0	16.7	14.0
95	ODONNELL, NEIL	QB	PIT	195	147	48	5	9	3	0	0	0	0	0	0	0	0	0	0	0	17	12
94				96	123	-27	4	7	2	1	0	0	0	0	0	0	0	0	0	0	14	14
93				87	102	-15	9	4	1	0	0	0	0	0	0	0	0	0	0	0	14	15
				126.0	124.0	2.0	6.0	6.7	2.0	0.3	0.0	0.0	0.0	0.0	0.0	0.0	0.0	0.0	0.0	0.0	15.0	13.7
95	ERICKSON, CRAIG	QB	IND	12	27	-15	0	3	0	0	0	0	0	0	0	0	0	0	0	0	3	7
94			TB	159	166	-7	3	8	5	1	0	0	0	0	0	0	0	0	0	0	17	14
93				142	171	-29	3	9	6	0	0	0	0	0	0	0	0	0	0	0	18	15
				104.3	121.3	-17.0	2.0	6.7	3.7	0.3	0.0	0.0	0.0	0.0	0.0	0.0	0.0	0.0	0.0	0.0	12.7	12.0
95	BRUNELL, MARK	QB	JAX	171	168	3	7	8	0	3	1	0	0	0	0	0	0	0	0	0	19	13
94			GB	9	12	-3	0	0	0	1	0	0	0	0	0	0	0	0	0	0	1	2
				90.0	90.0	0.0	3.5	4.0	0.0	2.0	0.5	0.0	0.0	0.0	0.0	0.0	0.0	0.0	0.0	0.0	10.0	7.5
95	CHANDLER, CHRIS	QB	HOU	174	174	0	5	8	4	2	0	0	0	0	0	0	0	0	0	0	19	13
94			RAM	68	78	-10	1	4	2	1	0	0	0	0	0	0	0	0	0	0	8	6
93			AZ	21	27	-6	0	3	0	0	0	0	0	0	0	0	0	0	0	0	3	2
				87.7	93.0	-5.3	2.0	5.0	2.0	1.0	0.0	0.0	0.0	0.0	0.0	0.0	0.0	0.0	0.0	0.0	10.0	7.0
95	HARBAUGH, JIM	QB	IND	149	168	-19	5	10	2	2	0	0	0	0	0	0	0	0	0	0	19	15
94				57	75	-18	3	5	1	0	0	0	0	0	0	0	0	0	0	0	9	9
93			CHI	57	111	-54	1	5	1	4	0	0	0	0	0	0	0	0	0	0	11	15
				87.7	118.0	-30.3	3.0	6.7	1.3	2.0	0.0	0.0	0.0	0.0	0.0	0.0	0.0	0.0	0.0	0.0	13.0	13.0
95	BROWN, DAVE	QB	NYG	106	150	-44	4	4	3	3	1	0	0	0	0	0	0	0	0	0	15	16
94				63	120	-57	6	4	2	2	0	0	0	0	0	0	0	0	0	0	14	15
				84.5	135.0	-50.5	5.0	4.0	2.5	2.5	0.5	0.0	0.0	0.0	0.0	0.0	0.0	0.0	0.0	0.0	14.5	15.5

YR	PLAYER	POS	TM	FAN PTS	DIST PTS	PERF PTS	PASSING TD: 0-9	10-39	40+	RUSHING TD: 0-9	10-39	40+	RECEIVING TD: 0-9	10-39	40+	FIELD GOALS: 10-39	40-49	50+	PAT	D,ST TDS	TOT TDS	GAM
95	SMITH, EMMITT	RB	DAL	314	174	140	0	0	0	18	6	1	0	0	0	0	0	0	0	0	25	16
94				231	141	90	0	0	0	20	1	0	1	0	0	0	0	0	0	0	22	15
93				190	78	112	0	0	0	6	2	1	1	0	0	0	0	0	0	0	10	14
				245.0	131.0	114.0	0.0	0.0	0.0	14.7	3.0	0.7	0.7	0.0	0.0	0.0	0.0	0.0	0.0	0.0	19.0	15.0
95	MARTIN, CURTIS	RB	NE	226	105	121	0	0	0	13	1	0	0	1	0	0	0	0	0	0	15	16
95	SANDERS, BARRY	RB	DET	212	108	104	0	0	0	5	2	4	1	0	0	0	0	0	0	0	12	16
94				236	72	164	0	0	0	2	4	1	1	0	0	0	0	0	0	0	8	16
93				79	24	55	0	0	0	1	2	0	0	0	0	0	0	0	0	0	3	11
				175.7	68.0	107.7	0.0	0.0	0.0	2.7	2.7	1.7	0.7	0.0	0.0	0.0	0.0	0.0	0.0	0.0	7.7	14.3
95	WARREN, CHRIS	RB	SEA	217	126	91	0	0	0	9	6	0	0	1	0	0	0	0	0	0	16	16
94				195	101	94	0	0	0	4	5	0	1	1	0	0	0	0	0	0	11	16
93				98	54	44	0	0	0	4	2	1	0	0	0	0	0	0	0	0	7	14
				170.0	93.7	76.3	0.0	0.0	0.0	5.7	4.3	0.3	0.3	0.7	0.0	0.0	0.0	0.0	0.0	0.0	11.3	15.3
95	FAULK, MARSHALL	RB	IND	155	126	29	0	0	0	7	4	0	1	2	0	0	0	0	0	0	14	16
94				166	102	64	0	0	0	8	2	1	0	0	1	0	0	0	0	0	12	16
				160.5	114.0	46.5	0.0	0.0	0.0	7.5	3.0	0.5	0.5	1.0	0.5	0.0	0.0	0.0	0.0	0.0	13.0	16.0
95	WATTERS, RICKY	RB	PHI	132	78	54	0	0	0	11	0	0	1	0	0	0	0	0	0	0	12	16
94			SF	192	123	69	0	0	0	5	1	0	2	2	1	0	0	0	0	0	11	16
93				125	90	35	0	0	0	8	2	0	0	0	1	0	0	0	0	0	11	13
				149.7	97.0	52.7	0.0	0.0	0.0	8.0	1.0	0.0	1.0	0.7	0.7	0.0	0.0	0.0	0.0	0.0	11.3	15.0
95	BENNETT, EDGAR	RB	GB	144	87	57	0	0	0	2	1	0	1	3	0	0	0	0	0	0	7	16
94				140	93	47	0	0	0	4	1	0	2	2	0	0	0	0	0	0	9	16
93				91	75	16	0	0	0	8	1	0	0	1	0	0	0	0	0	0	10	16
				125.0	85.0	40.0	0.0	0.0	0.0	4.7	1.0	0.0	1.0	2.0	0.0	0.0	0.0	0.0	0.0	0.0	8.7	16.0
95	THOMAS, THURMAN	RB	BUF	113	69	44	0	0	0	5	1	0	1	1	0	0	0	0	0	0	8	14
94				128	75	53	0	0	0	4	3	0	2	0	0	0	0	0	0	0	9	15
93				121	36	85	0	0	0	6	0	0	0	0	0	0	0	0	0	0	6	16
				120.7	60.0	60.7	0.0	0.0	0.0	5.0	1.3	0.0	1.0	0.3	0.0	0.0	0.0	0.0	0.0	0.0	7.7	15.0
95	DAVIS, TERRELL	RB	DEN	111	60	51	0	0	0	6	0	1	1	0	0	0	0	0	0	0	8	14
95	SALAAM, RASHAAN	RB	CHI	111	63	48	0	0	0	9	1	0	0	0	0	0	0	0	0	0	10	16

YR	PLAYER	POS	TM	FAN PTS	DIST PTS	PERF PTS	PASSING TD: 0-9	10-39	40+	RUSHING TD: 0-9	10-39	40+	RECEIVING TD: 0-9	10-39	40+	FIELD GOALS: 10-39	40-49	50+	PAT	D,ST TDS	TOT TDS	GAM
95	ALLEN, TERRY	RB	WAS	117	72	45	0	0	0	10	0	0	1	0	0	0	0	0	0	0	11	16
94			MIN	97	56	41	0	0	0	6	2	0	0	0	0	0	0	0	0	0	8	16
				107.0	64.0	43.0	0.0	0.0	0.0	8.0	1.0	0.0	0.5	0.0	0.0	0.0	0.0	0.0	0.0	0.0	9.5	16.0
95	PARMALEE, BERNIE	RB	MIA	115	78	37	0	0	0	7	2	1	0	1	0	0	0	0	0	0	10	16
94				95	59	36	0	0	0	4	1	1	1	0	0	0	0	0	0	0	7	13
				105.0	68.5	36.5	0.0	0.0	0.0	5.5	1.5	0.5	0.5	0.5	0.0	0.0	0.0	0.0	0.0	0.0	8.5	14.5
95	RHETT, ERRICT	RB	TB	115	72	43	0	0	0	9	2	0	0	0	0	0	0	0	0	0	11	16
94				94	44	50	0	0	0	7	0	0	0	0	0	0	0	0	0	0	7	16
				104.5	58.0	46.5	0.0	0.0	0.0	8.0	1.0	0.0	0.0	0.0	0.0	0.0	0.0	0.0	0.0	0.0	9.0	16.0
95	CENTERS, LARRY	RB	AZ	118	48	70	0	0	0	2	0	0	0	2	0	0	0	0	0	0	4	16
94				102	63	39	0	0	0	4	1	0	1	1	0	0	0	0	0	0	7	16
93				86	54	32	0	1	0	0	2	0	0	0	0	0	0	0	0	0	3	15
				102.0	55.0	47.0	0.0	0.3	0.0	2.0	1.0	0.0	0.3	1.0	0.0	0.0	0.0	0.0	0.0	0.0	4.7	15.7
95	BYARS, KEITH	RB	MIA	40	30	10	0	0	0	1	0	0	2	0	0	0	0	0	0	0	3	16
94				122	90	32	0	0	0	2	0	0	2	3	0	0	0	0	0	0	7	9
93				130	90	40	0	1	0	2	0	1	1	2	0	0	0	0	0	0	7	16
				97.3	70.0	27.3	0.0	0.3	0.0	1.7	0.0	0.3	1.7	1.7	0.0	0.0	0.0	0.0	0.0	0.0	5.7	13.7
95	KIRBY, TERRY	RB	MIA	120	93	27	0	0	0	3	1	0	1	2	0	0	0	0	0	0	8	16
94				28	14	14	0	0	0	2	0	0	0	0	0	0	0	0	0	0	2	4
93				140	78	62	0	0	0	1	2	0	1	1	1	0	0	0	0	0	6	16
				96.0	61.7	34.3	0.0	0.0	0.0	2.0	1.0	0.0	0.7	1.0	0.3	0.0	0.0	0.0	0.0	0.0	5.3	12.0
95	MEANS, NATRONE	RB	SD	65	33	32	0	0	0	4	1	0	0	0	0	0	0	0	0	0	5	10
94				141	81	60	0	0	0	9	3	0	0	0	0	0	0	0	0	0	12	16
93				78	57	21	0	0	0	6	1	1	0	0	0	0	0	0	0	0	8	16
				94.7	57.0	37.7	0.0	0.0	0.0	6.3	1.7	0.3	0.0	0.0	0.0	0.0	0.0	0.0	0.0	0.0	8.3	14.0
95	HAMPTON, RODNEY	RB	NYG	90	60	30	0	0	0	10	0	0	0	0	0	0	0	0	0	0	10	16
94				87	41	46	0	0	0	5	1	0	0	0	0	0	0	0	0	0	6	14
93				103	33	70	0	0	0	4	1	0	0	0	0	0	0	0	0	0	5	12
				93.3	44.7	48.7	0.0	0.0	0.0	6.3	0.7	0.0	0.0	0.0	0.0	0.0	0.0	0.0	0.0	0.0	7.0	14.0

YR	PLAYER	POS	TM	FAN PTS	DIST PTS	PERF PTS	PASSING TD 0-9	10-39	40+	RUSHING TD 0-9	10-39	40+	RECEIVING TD 0-9	10-39	40+	FIELD GOALS 0-39	40-49	50+	PAT	D,ST TDS	TOT TDS	GAM
95	HARMON, RONNIE	RB	SD	138	96	42	0	0	0	0	0	1	1	1	4	0	0	0	0	0	6	16
94				62	35	27	0	0	0	0	1	0	0	1	1	0	0	0	0	0	2	16
93				69	36	33	0	0	0	0	0	0	0	0	2	0	0	0	0	0	2	16
				89.7	55.7	34.0	0.0	0.0	0.0	0.0	0.3	0.3	0.3	0.3	2.3	0.0	0.0	0.0	0.0	0.0	3.3	16.0
95	THOMAS, RODNEY	RB	HOU	86	66	20	0	0	0	4	0	1	1	1	0	0	0	0	0	0	7	16
95	BETTIS, JEROME	RB	RAM	16	18	-2	0	0	0	3	0	0	0	0	0	0	0	0	0	0	3	15
94				81	34	47	0	0	0	3	1	0	0	0	0	0	0	0	0	0	4	16
93				155	51	104	0	0	0	5	1	1	0	0	0	0	0	0	0	0	7	16
				84.0	34.3	49.7	0.0	0.0	0.0	3.7	0.3	0.3	0.0	0.0	0.0	0.0	0.0	0.0	0.0	0.0	4.7	15.7
95	ALLEN, MARCUS	RB	KC	53	30	23	0	0	0	5	0	0	0	0	0	0	0	0	0	0	5	16
94				66	47	19	0	0	0	6	1	0	0	0	0	0	0	0	0	0	7	13
93				129	129	0	0	0	0	11	1	0	0	0	3	0	0	0	0	0	15	16
				82.7	68.7	14.0	0.0	0.0	0.0	7.3	0.7	0.0	0.0	0.0	1.0	0.0	0.0	0.0	0.0	0.0	9.0	15.0
95	MORRIS, BYRON	RB	PIT	76	57	19	0	0	0	8	1	0	0	0	0	0	0	0	0	0	9	13
94				72	45	27	0	0	0	6	1	0	0	0	0	0	0	0	0	0	7	13
				74.0	51.0	23.0	0.0	0.0	0.0	7.0	1.0	0.0	0.0	0.0	0.0	0.0	0.0	0.0	0.0	0.0	8.0	13.0
95	WALKER, HERSCHEL	RB	NYG	12	12	0	0	0	0	4	0	1	1	2	0	0	0	0	0	1	8	16
94				108	84	24	0	0	0	4	0	1	2	0	0	0	0	0	0	0	8	16
93				89	54	35	0	0	0	1	1	0	2	0	0	0	0	0	0	0	4	16
				69.7	50.0	19.7	0.0	0.0	0.0	1.7	0.3	0.3	1.3	0.7	0.0	0.0	0.0	0.0	0.0	0.3	4.3	16.0
95	BATES, MARIO	RB	NO	83	51	32	0	0	0	5	1	0	0	0	0	0	0	0	0	0	7	16
94				55	42	13	0	0	0	4	2	0	0	0	0	0	0	0	0	0	6	11
				69.0	46.5	22.5	0.0	0.0	0.0	4.5	1.5	0.0	0.0	0.0	0.0	0.0	0.0	0.0	0.0	0.0	6.5	13.5
95	WILLIAMS, HARVEY	RB	RAI	111	75	36	0	1	0	8	0	0	2	1	0	0	0	0	0	0	10	16
94				88	68	20	0	0	0	4	0	0	2	1	0	0	0	0	0	0	7	16
93			KC	0	0	0	0	0	0	0	0	0	0	0	0	0	0	0	0	0	0	7
				66.3	47.7	18.7	0.0	0.3	0.0	4.0	0.3	0.0	0.7	0.3	0.0	0.0	0.0	0.0	0.0	0.0	5.7	13.0
95	LOVILLE, DEREK	RB	SF	128	102	26	0	0	0	10	0	0	2	1	0	0	0	0	0	0	13	16
94				0	0	0	0	0	0	0	0	0	0	0	0	0	0	0	0	0	0	7
				64.0	51.0	13.0	0.0	0.0	0.0	5.0	0.0	0.0	1.0	0.5	0.0	0.0	0.0	0.0	0.0	0.0	6.5	11.5

YR	PLAYER	POS	TM	FAN DIST PTS	PTS	PERF PTS	PASSING TD: 0-9	10-39	40+	RUSHING TD: 0-9	10-39	40+	RECEIVING TD: 0-9	10-39	40+	FIELD GOALS: 0-9	10-39	40-49	50+	PAT	D,ST TDS	TOT TDS	GAM
95	BROWN, GARY	RB	HOU	8	0	8	0	0	0	0	0	0	0	0	0	0	0	0	0	0	0	0	9
94				36	42	-6	0	0	0	4	0	0	0	1	0	0	0	0	0	0	0	5	12
93				141	75	66	0	0	0	3	3	0	1	1	0	0	0	0	0	0	0	8	11
				61.7	39.0	22.7	0.0	0.0	0.0	2.3	1.0	0.0	0.3	0.7	0.0	0.0	0.0	0.0	0.0	0.0	0.0	4.3	10.7
95	MEGGETT, DAVID	RB	NE	24	15	9	0	0	0	1	1	0	0	0	0	0	0	0	0	0	0	2	16
94			NYG	79	69	10	0	1	0	3	1	0	1	1	1	0	0	0	0	0	0	7	16
93				66	54	12	0	1	1	0	0	0	0	0	1	0	0	0	0	0	1	3	16
				56.3	46.0	10.3	0.0	0.7	0.3	1.3	0.7	0.0	0.3	0.3	0.7	0.0	0.0	0.0	0.0	0.0	1.0	4.0	16.0
95	RUSSELL, LEONARD	RB	STL	-3	0	-3	0	0	0	0	0	0	0	0	0	0	0	0	0	0	0	0	13
94			DEN	87	63	24	0	0	0	6	3	0	0	0	0	0	0	0	0	0	0	9	14
93			NE	82	42	40	0	0	0	7	0	0	0	0	0	0	0	0	0	0	0	7	16
				55.3	35.0	20.3	0.0	0.0	0.0	4.3	1.0	0.0	0.0	0.0	0.0	0.0	0.0	0.0	0.0	0.0	0.0	5.3	14.3
95	HOARD, LEROY	RB	CLE	-3	0	-3	0	0	0	4	1	0	1	2	1	0	0	0	0	0	0	0	12
94				142	105	37	0	0	0	5	1	0	1	0	0	0	0	0	0	0	0	9	16
93				14	0	14	0	0	0	0	0	0	0	1	0	0	0	0	0	0	0	0	15
				51.0	35.0	16.0	0.0	0.0	0.0	1.3	0.3	0.0	0.3	0.7	0.3	0.0	0.0	0.0	0.0	0.0	0.0	3.0	14.3
95	MOORE, RON	RB	NYJ	-2	0	-2	0	0	0	3	1	0	0	0	0	0	0	0	0	0	0	0	15
94			AZ	51	41	10	0	0	0	3	1	0	1	0	0	0	0	0	0	0	0	5	16
93				104	63	41	0	0	0	6	3	0	0	0	0	0	0	0	0	0	0	9	15
				51.0	34.7	16.3	0.0	0.0	0.0	3.0	1.3	0.0	0.3	0.0	0.0	0.0	0.0	0.0	0.0	0.0	0.0	4.7	15.3
95	HEYWARD, CRAIG	RB	ATL	103	60	43	0	0	0	6	0	0	2	0	0	0	0	0	0	0	0	8	16
94			CHI	49	54	-5	0	0	0	7	0	0	1	0	0	0	0	0	0	0	0	8	16
93				0	0	0	0	0	0	0	0	0	0	0	0	0	0	0	0	0	0	0	16
				50.7	38.0	12.7	0.0	0.0	0.0	4.3	0.0	0.0	1.0	0.0	0.0	0.0	0.0	0.0	0.0	0.0	0.0	5.3	16.0
95	PEGRAM, ERRIC	RB	PIT	60	42	18	0	0	0	5	0	0	1	0	0	0	0	0	0	0	0	6	15
94			ATL	5	6	-1	0	0	0	1	0	0	0	0	0	0	0	0	0	0	0	1	13
93				83	21	62	0	0	0	2	1	0	0	0	0	0	0	0	0	0	0	3	15
				49.3	23.0	26.3	0.0	0.0	0.0	2.7	0.3	0.0	0.3	0.0	0.0	0.0	0.0	0.0	0.0	0.0	0.0	3.3	14.3
95	GARNER, CHARLIE	RB	PHI	56	45	11	0	0	0	4	1	1	1	0	0	0	0	0	0	0	0	6	15
94				42	21	21	0	0	0	2	1	0	0	0	0	0	0	0	0	0	0	3	10
				49.0	33.0	16.0	0.0	0.0	0.0	3.0	1.0	0.5	0.0	0.0	0.0	0.0	0.0	0.0	0.0	0.0	0.0	4.5	12.5

YR	PLAYER	POS	TM	FAN PTS	DIST PTS	PERF PTS	PASSING TD: 0-9	10-39	40+	RUSHING TD: 0-9	10-39	40+	RECEIVING TD: 0-9	10-39	40+	FIELD GOALS: 0-9	10-39	40-49	50+	PAT	D,ST TDS	TOT TDS	GAM
95	MILBURN, GLYN	RB	DEN	11	0	11	0	0	0	0	0	0	0	0	0	0	0	0	0	0	0	0	16
94				80	57	23	0	0	0	0	1	0	1	2	0	0	0	0	0	0	0	4	16
93				55	42	13	0	0	0	0	0	0	2	1	0	0	0	0	0	0	0	3	16
				48.7	33.0	15.7	0.0	0.0	0.0	0.0	0.3	0.0	1.0	1.0	0.0	0.0	0.0	0.0	0.0	0.0	0.0	2.3	16.0
95	HOLMES, DARICK	RB	BUF	48	27	21	0	0	0	3	1	0	0	0	0	0	0	0	0	0	0	4	16
95	MITCHELL, BRIAN	RB	WAS	45	39	6	0	0	0	0	1	0	0	1	0	0	0	0	0	0	0	2	16
94				57	50	7	0	0	0	0	1	0	0	0	0	0	0	0	0	0	2	3	16
93				42	21	21	0	0	0	2	0	0	0	0	1	0	0	0	0	0	0	3	16
				48.0	36.7	11.3	0.0	0.0	0.0	0.7	0.7	0.0	0.0	0.3	0.3	0.0	0.0	0.0	0.0	0.0	1.0	2.7	16.0
95	LEE, AMP	RB	MIN	59	30	29	0	0	0	1	1	1	1	0	0	0	0	0	0	0	0	3	16
94				36	24	12	0	0	0	0	0	0	2	0	0	0	0	0	0	0	0	2	13
93			SF	36	36	0	0	0	0	1	0	0	1	1	0	0	0	0	0	0	0	3	13
				43.7	30.0	13.7	0.0	0.0	0.0	0.7	0.3	0.3	1.3	0.3	0.0	0.0	0.0	0.0	0.0	0.0	0.0	2.7	14.0
95	MOORE, DERRICK	RB	CAR	50	30	20	0	0	0	3	0	1	0	0	0	0	0	0	0	0	0	4	13
94			DET	24	24	0	0	0	0	4	0	0	0	0	0	0	0	0	0	0	0	4	15
93				57	36	21	0	0	0	3	0	0	0	1	0	0	0	0	0	0	0	4	13
				43.7	30.0	13.7	0.0	0.0	0.0	3.3	0.0	0.3	0.0	0.3	0.0	0.0	0.0	0.0	0.0	0.0	0.0	4.0	13.7
95	CRAVER, AARON	RB	DEN	61	42	19	0	0	0	5	0	0	1	0	0	0	0	0	0	0	0	6	16
94			MIA	19	2	17	0	0	0	0	0	0	0	0	0	0	0	0	0	0	0	0	6
				40.0	22.0	18.0	0.0	0.0	0.0	2.5	0.0	0.0	0.5	0.0	0.0	0.0	0.0	0.0	0.0	0.0	0.0	3.0	11.0
95	BROWN, DEREK	RB	NO	21	21	0	0	0	0	1	1	0	1	0	0	0	0	0	0	0	0	2	16
95				44	36	8	0	0	0	3	0	0	0	1	0	0	0	0	0	0	0	4	16
93				52	30	22	0	0	0	2	1	0	0	1	0	0	0	0	0	0	0	4	13
				39.0	29.0	10.0	0.0	0.0	0.0	1.7	0.7	0.0	0.3	0.7	0.0	0.0	0.0	0.0	0.0	0.0	0.0	3.3	15.0
95	WILLIAMS, JOHN L.	RB	PIT	11	12	-1	0	0	0	0	0	0	1	0	0	0	0	0	0	0	0	1	12
94				54	36	18	0	0	0	1	0	0	1	1	0	0	0	0	0	0	0	3	15
93			SEA	52	42	10	0	0	0	1	2	0	0	1	0	0	0	0	0	0	0	4	16
				39.0	30.0	9.0	0.0	0.0	0.0	0.7	0.7	0.0	0.7	0.7	0.0	0.0	0.0	0.0	0.0	0.0	0.0	2.7	14.3

YR	PLAYER	POS	TM	FAN PTS	DIST PTS	PERF PTS	PASSING TD: 0-9	10-39	40+	RUSHING TD: 0-9	10-39	40+	RECEIVING TD: 0-9	10-39	40+	FIELD GOALS: 0-9	10-39	40-49	50+	PAT	D,ST TDS	TOT TDS	GAM
95	TILLMAN, LEWIS	RB	CHI	1	0	1	0	0	0	0	0	0	0	0	0	0	0	0	0	0	0	0	13
94				66	45	21	0	0	0	6	1	0	0	0	0	0	0	0	0	0	0	7	16
93			NYG	47	21	26	0	0	0	2	1	0	0	0	0	0	0	0	0	0	0	3	13
				38.0	22.0	16.0	0.0	0.0	0.0	2.7	0.7	0.0	0.0	0.0	0.0	0.0	0.0	0.0	0.0	0.0	0.0	3.3	14.0
95	FLOYD, WILLIAM	RB	SF	34	24	10	0	0	0	2	0	0	1	0	0	0	0	0	0	0	0	3	8
94				39	39	0	0	0	0	5	1	0	0	0	0	0	0	0	0	0	0	6	15
				36.5	31.5	5.0	0.0	0.0	0.0	3.5	0.5	0.0	0.5	0.0	0.0	0.0	0.0	0.0	0.0	0.0	0.0	4.5	11.5
95	LOGAN, MARC	RB	WAS	30	30	0	0	0	0	1	0	0	2	0	0	0	0	0	0	0	0	3	16
94			SF	18	18	0	0	0	0	1	0	0	1	0	0	0	0	0	0	0	0	2	9
93				56	45	11	0	0	0	6	1	0	0	0	0	0	0	0	0	0	0	7	13
				34.7	31.0	3.7	0.0	0.0	0.0	2.7	0.3	0.0	1.0	0.0	0.0	0.0	0.0	0.0	0.0	0.0	0.0	4.0	12.7
95	BUTTS, MARION	RB	HOU	24	24	0	0	0	0	4	0	0	0	0	0	0	0	0	0	0	0	4	12
94			NE	51	51	0	0	0	0	7	1	0	0	0	0	0	0	0	0	0	0	8	16
93			SD	27	27	0	0	0	0	3	1	0	0	0	0	0	0	0	0	0	0	4	16
				34.0	34.0	0.0	0.0	0.0	0.0	4.7	0.7	0.0	0.0	0.0	0.0	0.0	0.0	0.0	0.0	0.0	0.0	5.3	14.7
95	JOHNSTON, DARYL	RB	DAL	24	24	0	0	0	0	2	0	0	1	0	0	0	0	0	0	0	0	3	16
94				39	36	3	0	0	0	0	1	0	2	0	0	0	0	0	0	0	0	4	16
93				37	30	7	0	0	0	3	0	0	1	0	0	0	0	0	0	0	0	4	15
				33.3	30.0	3.3	0.0	0.0	0.0	2.3	0.0	0.0	1.3	0.0	0.0	0.0	0.0	0.0	0.0	0.0	0.0	3.7	15.7
95	ANDERS, KIMBLE	RB	KC	38	33	5	0	0	0	0	1	0	1	1	0	0	0	0	0	0	0	3	16
94				36	24	12	0	0	0	2	0	0	1	0	0	0	0	0	0	0	0	3	16
93				25	18	7	0	0	0	0	0	0	0	1	0	0	0	0	0	0	0	1	16
				33.0	25.0	8.0	0.0	0.0	0.0	0.7	0.3	0.0	0.7	0.3	0.0	0.0	0.0	0.0	0.0	0.0	0.0	2.3	16.0
95	SMITH, ROBERT	RB	MIN	62	39	23	0	0	0	3	1	1	0	0	0	0	0	0	0	0	0	5	9
94				9	9	0	0	0	0	0	1	0	0	0	0	0	0	0	0	0	0	1	13
93				26	15	11	0	0	0	1	1	0	0	0	0	0	0	0	0	0	0	2	8
				32.3	21.0	11.3	0.0	0.0	0.0	1.3	1.0	0.3	0.0	0.0	0.0	0.0	0.0	0.0	0.0	0.0	0.0	2.7	10.0
95	RICE, JERRY	WR	SF	325	186	139	0	0	0	0	1	0	4	6	5	0	0	0	0	0	1	17	16
94				211	140	71	0	0	0	2	0	0	7	4	2	0	0	0	0	0	0	15	16
93				215	144	71	0	0	1	0	0	1	7	6	2	0	0	0	0	0	0	16	16
				250.3	156.7	93.7	0.0	0.0	0.3	0.0	1.0	0.3	6.0	5.3	3.0	0.0	0.0	0.0	0.0	0.0	0.3	16.0	16.0

YR	PLAYER	POS	TM	FAN PTS	DIST PTS	PERF PTS	PASSING TD 0-9	10-39	40+	RUSHING TD 0-9	10-39	40+	RECEIVING TD 0-9	10-39	40+	FIELD GOALS 10-39	40-49	50+	PAT	D,ST TDS	TOT TDS	GAM
95	MOORE, HERMAN	WR	DET	256	132	124	0	0	0	0	0	0	1	10	3	0	0	0	0	0	14	16
94				124	84	40	0	0	0	0	0	0	6	4	1	0	0	0	0	0	11	16
93				88	54	34	0	0	0	0	0	0	1	4	1	0	0	0	0	0	6	15
				156.0	90.0	66.0	0.0	0.0	0.0	0.0	0.0	0.0	2.7	6.0	1.7	0.0	0.0	0.0	0.0	0.0	10.3	15.7
95	IRVIN, MICHAEL	WR	DAL	207	87	120	0	0	0	0	0	0	3	5	2	0	0	0	0	0	10	16
94				123	54	69	0	0	0	0	0	0	1	4	1	0	0	0	0	0	6	16
93				128	63	65	0	0	0	0	0	0	2	3	2	0	0	0	0	0	7	16
				152.7	68.0	84.7	0.0	0.0	0.0	0.0	0.0	0.0	2.0	4.0	1.7	0.0	0.0	0.0	0.0	0.0	7.7	16.0
95	GALLOWAY, JOEY	WR	SEA	148	105	43	0	0	0	0	0	0	1	3	3	0	0	0	0	1	8	16
95	BROWN, TIM	WR	RAI	175	93	82	0	0	0	0	0	0	3	3	4	0	0	0	0	0	10	16
94				127	81	46	0	0	0	0	0	0	3	5	1	0	0	0	0	0	9	16
93				136	75	61	0	0	0	0	0	0	1	5	2	0	0	0	0	0	8	16
				146.0	83.0	63.0	0.0	0.0	0.0	0.0	0.0	0.0	2.0	4.3	2.3	0.0	0.0	0.0	0.0	0.3	9.0	16.0
95	CARTER, CRIS	WR	MIN	196	132	64	0	0	0	0	0	0	8	8	1	0	0	0	0	0	17	16
94				124	61	63	0	0	0	0	0	0	4	1	2	0	0	0	0	0	7	16
93				100	66	34	0	0	0	0	0	0	5	4	0	0	0	0	0	0	9	16
				140.0	86.3	53.7	0.0	0.0	0.0	0.0	0.0	0.0	5.7	4.3	1.0	0.0	0.0	0.0	0.0	0.0	11.0	16.0
95	MILLER, ANTHONY	WR	DEN	176	138	38	0	0	0	0	0	0	2	6	6	0	0	0	0	0	14	14
94			SD	107	50	57	0	0	0	0	0	0	0	4	1	0	0	0	0	0	5	15
93			SD	137	69	68	0	0	0	0	0	0	1	3	3	0	0	0	0	0	7	16
				140.0	85.7	54.3	0.0	0.0	0.0	0.0	0.0	0.0	1.0	4.3	3.3	0.0	0.0	0.0	0.0	0.0	8.7	15.0
95	BRUCE, ISAAC	WR	RAM	244	111	133	0	0	0	0	0	0	4	7	2	0	0	0	0	0	13	16
94				27	27	0	0	0	0	0	0	0	0	3	0	0	0	0	0	0	3	11
				135.5	69.0	66.5	0.0	0.0	0.0	0.0	0.0	0.0	2.0	5.0	1.0	0.0	0.0	0.0	0.0	0.0	8.0	13.5
95	PICKENS, CARL	WR	CIN	188	135	53	0	0	0	0	0	0	9	5	3	0	0	0	0	0	17	16
94				151	87	64	0	0	0	0	0	0	6	3	2	0	0	0	0	0	11	15
93				60	48	12	0	0	0	0	0	0	2	4	0	0	0	0	0	0	6	12
				133.0	90.0	43.0	0.0	0.0	0.0	0.0	0.0	0.0	5.7	4.0	1.7	0.0	0.0	0.0	0.0	0.0	11.3	14.3

YR	PLAYER	POS	TM	FAN PTS	DIST PTS	PERF PTS	PASSING TD: 0-9	10-39	40+	RUSHING TD: 0-9	10-39	40+	RECEIVING TD: 0-9	10-39	40+	FIELD GOALS: 10-39	40-49	50+	PAT	D,ST TDS	TOT TDS	GAM
95	METCALF, ERIC	WR	ATL	129	105	24	0	0	0	0	1	0	2	3	3	0	0	0	0	1	9	16
94		RB	CLE	107	99	8	0	0	0	1	0	0	0	2	3	0	0	0	0	2	7	16
93				107	72	35	0	0	0	1	0	0	0	1	1	0	0	0	0	2	5	16
				114.3	92.0	22.3	0.0	0.0	0.0	0.7	0.7	0.0	0.7	2.0	1.7	0.0	0.0	0.0	0.0	1.7	7.0	16.0
95	SANDERS, CHRIS	WR	HOU	111	87	24	0	0	0	0	0	0	2	3	4	0	0	0	0	0	9	16
95	RISON, ANDRE	WR	CLE	50	21	29	0	0	0	0	0	0	2	1	0	0	0	0	0	0	3	16
94			ATL	110	68	42	0	0	0	0	0	0	3	4	1	0	0	0	0	0	8	14
93				169	123	46	0	0	0	0	0	0	6	7	2	0	0	0	0	0	15	16
				109.7	70.7	39.0	0.0	0.0	0.0	0.0	0.0	0.0	3.7	4.0	1.0	0.0	0.0	0.0	0.0	0.0	8.7	15.3
95	FRYAR, IRVING	WR	MIA	91	69	22	0	0	0	0	0	0	3	3	2	0	0	0	0	0	8	16
94				150	70	80	0	0	0	0	0	0	2	2	3	0	0	0	0	0	7	16
93				72	51	21	0	0	0	0	0	0	0	3	2	0	0	0	0	0	5	16
				104.3	63.3	41.0	0.0	0.0	0.0	0.0	0.0	0.0	1.7	2.7	2.3	0.0	0.0	0.0	0.0	0.0	6.7	16.0
95	BROOKS, ROBERT	WR	GB	235	123	112	0	0	0	0	0	0	3	5	5	0	0	0	0	0	13	16
94				70	60	10	0	0	0	0	0	0	2	4	0	0	0	0	0	2	6	16
93				0	0	0	0	0	0	0	0	0	0	0	0	0	0	0	0	0	0	11
				101.7	61.0	40.7	0.0	0.0	0.0	0.0	0.0	0.0	1.0	3.0	1.7	0.0	0.0	0.0	0.0	0.7	6.3	14.3
95	MATHIS, TERANCE	WR	ATL	115	81	34	0	0	0	0	0	0	1	7	1	0	0	0	0	0	9	14
94				152	88	64	0	0	0	0	0	0	7	2	2	0	0	0	0	0	11	16
93			NYJ	18	18	0	0	0	0	0	0	0	0	1	0	0	0	0	0	0	1	13
				95.0	62.3	32.7	0.0	0.0	0.0	0.0	0.0	0.0	2.7	3.3	1.0	0.0	0.0	0.0	0.0	0.0	7.0	14.3
95	ELLARD, HENRY	WR	WAS	83	51	32	0	0	0	0	0	0	2	3	2	0	0	0	0	0	5	15
94				130	57	73	0	0	0	0	0	0	2	1	3	0	0	0	0	0	6	15
93			RAM	57	21	36	0	0	0	0	0	0	0	1	1	0	0	0	0	0	2	16
				90.0	43.0	47.0	0.0	0.0	0.0	0.0	0.0	0.0	0.7	1.7	2.0	0.0	0.0	0.0	0.0	0.0	4.3	15.3
95	MARTIN, TONY	WR	SD	111	57	54	0	0	0	0	0	0	1	3	2	0	0	0	0	0	6	16
94				107	66	41	0	0	0	0	0	0	2	2	3	0	0	0	0	0	7	16
93			MIA	41	30	11	0	0	0	0	0	0	0	2	1	0	0	0	0	0	3	10
				86.3	51.0	35.3	0.0	0.0	0.0	0.0	0.0	0.0	1.0	2.3	2.0	0.0	0.0	0.0	0.0	0.0	5.3	14.0

YR	PLAYER	POS	TM	FAN PTS	DIST PTS	PERF PTS	PASSING TD: 0-9	10-39	40+	RUSHING TD: 0-9	10-39	40+	RECEIVING TD: 0-9	10-39	40+	FIELD GOALS: 0-9	10-39	40-49	50+	PAT	D,ST TDS	TOT TDS	GAM
95	REED, ANDRE	WR	BUF	28	30	-2	0	0	0	0	0	0	0	2	1	0	0	0	0	0	0	3	6
94				134	72	62	0	0	0	0	0	0	1	6	1	0	0	0	0	0	0	8	16
93				86	60	26	0	0	0	0	0	0	0	4	2	0	0	0	0	0	0	6	15
				82.7	54.0	28.7	0.0	0.0	0.0	0.0	0.0	0.0	0.3	4.0	1.3	0.0	0.0	0.0	0.0	0.0	0.0	5.7	12.3
95	PERRIMAN, BRETT	WR	DET	181	81	100	0	0	0	0	0	0	2	5	2	0	0	0	0	0	0	9	16
94				48	37	11	0	0	0	0	0	0	1	3	0	0	0	0	0	0	0	4	16
93				15	15	0	0	0	0	0	0	0	1	1	0	0	0	0	0	0	0	2	14
				81.3	44.3	37.0	0.0	0.0	0.0	0.0	0.0	0.0	1.3	3.0	0.7	0.0	0.0	0.0	0.0	0.0	0.0	5.0	15.3
95	COATES, BEN	TE	NE	45	39	6	0	0	0	0	0	0	5	1	0	0	0	0	0	0	0	6	16
94				114	54	60	0	0	0	0	0	0	4	2	1	0	0	0	0	0	0	7	16
93				73	63	10	0	0	0	0	0	0	4	3	1	0	0	0	0	0	0	8	16
				77.3	52.0	25.3	0.0	0.0	0.0	0.0	0.0	0.0	4.3	2.0	0.7	0.0	0.0	0.0	0.0	0.0	0.0	7.0	16.0
95	SCOTT, DARNAY	WR	CIN	63	51	12	0	0	0	0	0	0	1	1	3	0	0	0	0	0	0	5	16
94				89	54	35	0	0	0	0	0	0	0	2	3	0	0	0	0	0	0	5	16
				76.0	52.5	23.5	0.0	0.0	0.0	0.0	0.0	0.0	0.5	1.5	3.0	0.0	0.0	0.0	0.0	0.0	0.0	5.0	16.0
95	GRAHAM, JEFF	WR	CHI	117	39	78	0	0	0	0	0	0	1	1	2	0	0	0	0	0	0	4	16
94				78	50	28	0	0	0	0	0	0	1	2	1	0	0	0	0	0	0	5	16
93			PIT	29	0	29	0	0	0	0	0	0	0	0	0	0	0	0	0	0	0	0	12
				74.7	29.7	45.0	0.0	0.0	0.0	0.0	0.0	0.0	0.7	1.0	1.0	0.0	0.0	0.0	0.0	0.0	0.0	3.0	14.7
95	CONWAY, CURTIS	WR	CHI	151	117	34	0	0	0	0	0	0	3	3	6	0	0	0	0	0	1	12	16
94				54	41	13	0	0	0	0	0	0	0	1	1	0	0	0	0	0	0	3	12
93				18	18	0	0	1	0	0	0	0	1	2	0	0	0	0	0	0	0	3	12
				74.3	58.7	15.7	0.0	0.3	0.0	0.0	0.0	0.0	1.0	2.0	2.3	0.0	0.0	0.0	0.0	0.0	0.3	5.7	13.3
95	DAVIS, WILLIE	WR	KC	66	51	15	0	0	0	0	0	0	0	3	2	0	0	0	0	0	0	5	16
94				69	50	19	0	0	0	0	0	0	1	2	2	0	0	0	0	0	0	5	13
93				87	63	24	0	0	0	0	0	0	1	5	1	0	0	0	0	0	0	7	16
				74.0	54.7	19.3	0.0	0.0	0.0	0.0	0.0	0.0	0.7	3.3	1.7	0.0	0.0	0.0	0.0	0.0	0.0	5.7	15.0
95	HARPER, ALVIN	WR	TB	26	15	11	0	0	0	0	0	0	1	1	0	0	0	0	0	0	0	2	13
94			DAL	111	78	33	0	0	0	0	0	0	0	6	2	0	0	0	0	0	0	8	14
93				78	51	27	0	0	0	0	0	0	0	3	2	0	0	0	0	0	0	5	15
				71.7	48.0	23.7	0.0	0.0	0.0	0.0	0.0	0.0	0.3	3.3	1.3	0.0	0.0	0.0	0.0	0.0	0.0	5.0	14.0

YR	PLAYER	POS	TM	FAN PTS	DIST PTS	PERF PTS	PASSING TD: 0-9	10-39	40+	RUSHING TD: 0-9	10-39	40+	RECEIVING TD: 0-9	10-39	40+	FIELD GOALS: 10-39	40-49	50+	PAT	D,ST TDS	TOT TDS	GAM
95	JACKSON, MICHAEL	WR	CLE	107	81	26	0	0	0	0	0	0	1	7	1	0	0	0	0	0	9	13
94				15	15	0	0	0	0	0	0	0	1	1	0	0	0	0	0	0	2	7
93				86	66	20	0	0	0	0	0	0	3	4	1	0	0	0	0	0	8	15
				69.3	54.0	15.3	0.0	0.0	0.0	0.0	0.0	0.0	1.7	4.0	0.7	0.0	0.0	0.0	0.0	0.0	6.3	11.7
95	EARLY, QUINN	WR	NO	104	78	26	0	0	0	0	0	0	1	4	3	0	0	0	0	0	8	16
94				40	30	10	0	0	0	0	0	0	2	2	0	0	0	0	0	0	4	15
93				60	60	0	0	0	0	0	0	0	0	4	2	0	0	0	0	0	6	15
				68.0	56.0	12.0	0.0	0.0	0.0	0.0	0.0	0.0	1.0	3.3	1.7	0.0	0.0	0.0	0.0	0.0	6.0	15.3
95	SHARPE, SHANNON	TE	DEN	58	27	31	0	0	0	0	0	0	3	1	0	0	0	0	0	0	4	13
94				48	37	11	0	0	0	0	0	0	2	1	1	0	0	0	0	0	4	14
93				96	75	21	0	0	0	0	0	0	4	3	2	0	0	0	0	0	9	16
				67.3	46.3	21.0	0.0	0.0	0.0	0.0	0.0	0.0	3.0	1.7	1.0	0.0	0.0	0.0	0.0	0.0	5.7	14.3
95	CARRIER, MARK	WR	CAR	64	30	34	0	0	0	0	0	0	1	0	2	0	0	0	0	0	3	16
94			CLE	56	57	-1	0	0	0	0	1	0	2	3	0	0	0	0	0	0	6	13
93				80	57	23	0	0	0	0	1	0	0	3	0	0	0	0	0	1	5	15
				66.7	48.0	18.7	0.0	0.0	0.0	0.0	0.7	0.0	1.0	2.0	0.7	0.0	0.0	0.0	0.0	0.3	4.7	14.7
95	BROOKS, BILL	WR	BUF	138	108	30	0	0	0	0	0	0	3	8	3	0	0	0	0	0	11	15
94				14	15	-1	0	0	0	0	0	0	1	1	0	0	0	0	0	0	2	13
93				42	42	0	0	0	0	0	0	0	1	4	0	0	0	0	0	0	5	15
				64.7	55.0	9.7	0.0	0.0	0.0	0.0	0.0	0.0	0.7	4.3	1.0	0.0	0.0	0.0	0.0	0.0	6.0	14.3
95	EMANUEL, BERT	WR	ATL	76	36	40	0	0	0	0	0	0	3	2	0	0	0	0	0	0	5	16
94				52	39	13	0	0	0	0	0	0	3	3	1	0	0	0	0	0	4	14
				64.0	37.5	26.5	0.0	0.0	0.0	0.0	0.0	0.0	1.5	2.5	0.5	0.0	0.0	0.0	0.0	0.0	4.5	15.0
95	JEFFIRES, HAYWOOD	WR	HOU	60	60	0	0	0	0	0	0	0	4	4	0	0	0	0	0	0	8	16
94				64	54	10	0	0	0	0	0	0	2	4	0	0	0	0	0	0	6	16
93				64	51	13	0	0	0	0	0	0	2	3	1	0	0	0	0	0	6	15
				62.7	55.0	7.7	0.0	0.0	0.0	0.0	0.0	0.0	2.7	3.7	0.3	0.0	0.0	0.0	0.0	0.0	6.7	15.7
95	WILLIAMS, CALVIN	WR	PHI	28	18	10	0	0	0	0	0	0	0	2	0	0	0	0	0	0	2	16
94				48	24	24	0	0	0	0	0	0	1	2	0	0	0	0	0	0	3	16
93				112	84	28	0	0	0	0	0	0	3	6	1	0	0	0	0	0	10	16
				62.7	42.0	20.7	0.0	0.0	0.0	0.0	0.0	0.0	1.3	3.3	0.3	0.0	0.0	0.0	0.0	0.0	5.0	16.0

YR	PLAYER	POS	TM	FAN PTS	DIST PTS	PERF PTS	PASSING TD: 0-9	10-39	40+	RUSHING TD: 0-9	10-39	40+	RECEIVING TD: 0-9	10-39	40+	FIELD GOALS: 0-39	40-49	50+	PAT	D,ST TDS	TOT TDS	GAM
95	MOORE, ROB	WR	AZ	74	36	38	0	0	0	0	0	0	3	2	0	0	0	0	0	0	5	15
94			NYJ	81	55	26	0	0	0	0	0	0	2	3	1	0	0	0	0	0	6	16
93				32	6	26	0	0	0	0	0	0	1	0	0	0	0	0	0	0	1	13
				62.3	32.3	30.0	0.0	0.0	0.0	0.0	0.0	0.0	2.0	1.7	0.3	0.0	0.0	0.0	0.0	0.0	4.0	14.7
95	REED, JAKE	WR	MIN	106	72	34	0	0	0	0	0	0	5	2	2	0	0	0	0	0	9	16
94				73	36	37	0	0	0	0	0	0	0	4	0	0	0	0	0	0	4	16
93				0	0	0	0	0	0	0	0	0	0	0	0	0	0	0	0	0	0	4
				59.7	36.0	23.7	0.0	0.0	0.0	0.0	0.0	0.0	1.7	2.0	0.7	0.0	0.0	0.0	0.0	0.0	4.3	12.0
95	BLADES, BRIAN	WR	SEA	79	42	37	0	0	0	0	0	0	0	2	2	0	0	0	0	0	4	16
94				40	26	14	0	0	0	0	0	0	4	0	0	0	0	0	0	0	4	16
93				47	21	26	0	0	0	0	0	0	2	1	0	0	0	0	0	0	3	16
				55.3	29.7	25.7	0.0	0.0	0.0	0.0	0.0	0.0	2.0	1.0	0.7	0.0	0.0	0.0	0.0	0.0	3.7	16.0
95	THIGPEN, YANCEY	WR	PIT	94	45	49	0	0	0	0	0	0	1	3	1	0	0	0	0	0	5	16
94				42	42	0	0	0	0	0	0	0	0	2	2	0	0	0	0	0	4	14
93				24	24	0	0	0	0	0	0	0	1	2	0	0	0	0	0	0	3	8
				53.3	37.0	16.3	0.0	0.0	0.0	0.0	0.0	0.0	0.7	2.3	1.0	0.0	0.0	0.0	0.0	0.0	4.0	12.7
95	SHERRARD, MIKE	WR	NYG	47	36	11	0	0	0	0	0	0	1	2	1	0	0	0	0	0	4	13
94				74	54	20	0	0	0	0	0	0	2	2	2	0	0	0	0	0	6	15
93				36	24	12	0	0	0	0	0	0	0	0	2	0	0	0	0	0	2	6
				52.3	38.0	14.3	0.0	0.0	0.0	0.0	0.0	0.0	1.0	1.3	1.7	0.0	0.0	0.0	0.0	0.0	4.0	11.3
95	MITCHELL, JOHNNY	TE	NYJ	50	42	8	0	0	0	0	0	0	2	2	1	0	0	0	0	0	5	12
94				42	30	12	0	0	0	0	0	0	2	2	0	0	0	0	0	0	4	15
93				65	51	14	0	0	0	0	0	0	2	3	1	0	0	0	0	0	6	13
				52.3	41.0	11.3	0.0	0.0	0.0	0.0	0.0	0.0	2.0	2.3	0.7	0.0	0.0	0.0	0.0	0.0	5.0	13.3
95	VANOVER, TAMARICK	WR	KC	51	51	0	0	0	0	0	0	0	1	1	0	0	0	0	0	3	2	15
95	BARNETT, FRED	WR	PHI	49	36	13	0	0	0	0	0	0	3	2	0	0	0	0	0	0	5	14
94				101	57	44	0	0	0	0	0	0	0	1	4	0	0	0	0	0	5	16
93				0	0	0	0	0	0	0	0	0	0	0	0	0	0	0	0	0	0	4
				50.0	31.0	19.0	0.0	0.0	0.0	0.0	0.0	0.0	1.0	1.0	1.3	0.0	0.0	0.0	0.0	0.0	3.3	11.3

YR	PLAYER	POS	TM	FAN PTS	DIST PTS	PERF PTS	PASSING TD: 0-9	PASSING TD: 10-39	PASSING TD: 40+	RUSHING TD: 0-9	RUSHING TD: 10-39	RUSHING TD: 40+	RECEIVING TD: 0-9	RECEIVING TD: 10-39	RECEIVING TD: 40+	FIELD GOALS: 10-39	FIELD GOALS: 40-49	FIELD GOALS: 50+	PAT	D,ST TDS	TOT TDS	GAM
95	INGRAM, MARK	WR	GB	24	24	0	0	0	0	0	0	0	1	2	0	0	0	0	0	0	3	16
94			MIA	62	51	11	0	0	0	0	0	0	2	3	1	0	0	0	0	0	6	13
93				61	51	10	0	0	0	0	0	0	2	3	1	0	0	0	0	0	6	14
				49.0	42.0	7.0	0.0	0.0	0.0	0.0	0.0	0.0	1.7	2.7	0.7	0.0	0.0	0.0	0.0	0.0	5.0	14.3
95	STOKES, J.J.	WR	SF	49	39	10	0	0	0	0	0	0	0	3	1	0	0	0	0	0	4	12
95	GREEN, WILLIE	WR	CAR	110	60	50	0	0	0	0	0	0	1	2	3	0	0	0	0	0	6	16
94			DET	0	0	0	0	0	0	0	0	0	0	0	0	0	0	0	0	0	0	4
93				31	21	10	0	0	0	0	0	0	0	1	1	0	0	0	0	0	2	12
				47.0	27.0	20.0	0.0	0.0	0.0	0.0	0.0	0.0	0.3	1.0	1.3	0.0	0.0	0.0	0.0	0.0	2.7	10.7
95	MORTON, JOHNNIE	WR	DET	73	63	10	0	0	0	0	0	0	3	5	0	0	0	0	0	0	8	16
94				21	21	0	0	0	0	0	0	0	0	1	0	0	0	0	0	1	2	5
				47.0	42.0	5.0	0.0	0.0	0.0	0.0	0.0	0.0	1.5	3.0	0.0	0.0	0.0	0.0	0.0	0.5	5.0	10.5
95	SEAY, MARK	WR	SD	37	24	13	0	0	0	0	0	0	1	2	0	0	0	0	0	0	3	16
94				56	45	11	0	0	0	0	0	0	4	1	1	0	0	0	0	0	6	14
				46.5	34.5	12.0	0.0	0.0	0.0	0.0	0.0	0.0	2.5	1.5	0.5	0.0	0.0	0.0	0.0	0.0	4.5	15.0
95	BRISBY, VINCENT	WR	NE	64	27	37	0	0	0	0	0	0	1	1	1	0	0	0	0	0	3	16
94				60	39	21	0	0	0	0	0	0	2	3	0	0	0	0	0	0	5	14
93				15	15	0	0	0	0	0	0	0	1	1	0	0	0	0	0	0	2	14
				46.3	27.0	19.3	0.0	0.0	0.0	0.0	0.0	0.0	1.3	1.7	0.3	0.0	0.0	0.0	0.0	0.0	3.3	14.7
95	TAYLOR, JOHN	WR	SF	17	18	-1	0	0	0	0	0	0	0	2	0	0	0	0	0	0	2	12
94				42	33	9	0	0	0	0	0	0	4	1	0	0	0	0	0	0	5	14
93				77	51	26	0	0	0	0	0	0	0	3	2	0	0	0	0	0	5	16
				45.3	34.0	11.3	0.0	0.0	0.0	0.0	0.0	0.0	1.3	2.0	0.7	0.0	0.0	0.0	0.0	0.0	4.0	14.0
95	HAYNES, MICHAEL	WR	NO	33	33	0	0	0	0	0	0	0	1	3	0	0	0	0	0	0	4	15
94				54	45	9	0	0	0	0	0	0	1	3	1	0	0	0	0	0	5	16
93			ATL	48	30	18	0	0	0	0	0	0	3	0	1	0	0	0	0	0	4	15
				45.0	36.0	9.0	0.0	0.0	0.0	0.0	0.0	0.0	1.7	2.0	0.7	0.0	0.0	0.0	0.0	0.0	4.3	15.3
95	DILGER, KEN	TE	IND	45	33	12	0	0	0	0	0	0	1	3	0	0	0	0	0	0	4	16

			FAN	DIST	PERF	PASSING TD:			RUSHING TD:			RECEIVING TD:			FIELD GOALS:				D,ST	TOT	
YR	PLAYER	POS	TM	PTS	PTS	PTS	0-9	10-39	40+	0-9	10-39	40+	0-9	10-39	40+	10-39	40-49	50+	PAT	TDS	TDS	GAM
95	ELAM, JASON	K	DEN	177	177	0	0	0	0	0	0	0	0	0	0	21	5	5	39	0	0	16
94				140	140	0	0	0	0	0	0	0	0	0	0	22	7	1	29	0	0	16
93				155	155	0	0	0	0	0	0	0	0	0	0	18	4	4	41	0	0	16
				157.3	157.3	0.0	0.0	0.0	0.0	0.0	0.0	0.0	0.0	0.0	0.0	20.3	5.3	3.3	36.3	0.0	0.0	16.0
95	ANDERSEN, MORTEN	K	ATL	184	184	0	0	0	0	0	0	0	0	0	0	20	3	8	29	0	0	16
94			NO	134	134	0	0	0	0	0	0	0	0	0	0	19	9	0	32	0	0	16
93				146	146	0	0	0	0	0	0	0	0	0	0	16	11	1	33	0	0	16
				154.7	154.7	0.0	0.0	0.0	0.0	0.0	0.0	0.0	0.0	0.0	0.0	18.3	7.7	3.0	31.3	0.0	0.0	16.0
95	JACKE, CHRIS	K	GB	131	131	0	0	0	0	0	0	0	0	0	0	6	8	3	43	0	0	14
94				109	109	0	0	0	0	0	0	0	0	0	0	16	2	1	41	0	0	16
93				182	182	0	0	0	0	0	0	0	0	0	0	19	6	6	35	0	0	16
				140.7	140.7	0.0	0.0	0.0	0.0	0.0	0.0	0.0	0.0	0.0	0.0	13.7	5.3	3.3	39.7	0.0	0.0	15.3
95	HANSON, JASON	K	DET	149	149	0	0	0	0	0	0	0	0	0	0	22	5	1	48	0	0	16
94				103	103	0	0	0	0	0	0	0	0	0	0	13	5	0	39	0	0	16
93				165	165	0	0	0	0	0	0	0	0	0	0	24	7	3	28	0	0	16
				139.0	139.0	0.0	0.0	0.0	0.0	0.0	0.0	0.0	0.0	0.0	0.0	19.7	5.7	1.3	38.3	0.0	0.0	16.0
95	REVEIZ, FUAD	K	MIN	147	147	0	0	0	0	0	0	0	0	0	0	16	9	1	44	0	0	16
94				155	155	0	0	0	0	0	0	0	0	0	0	25	8	1	30	0	0	16
93				115	115	0	0	0	0	0	0	0	0	0	0	21	3	1	27	0	0	16
				139.0	139.0	0.0	0.0	0.0	0.0	0.0	0.0	0.0	0.0	0.0	0.0	20.7	6.7	1.0	33.7	0.0	0.0	16.0
95	JOHNSON, NORM	K	PIT	164	164	0	0	0	0	0	0	0	0	0	0	25	8	1	39	0	0	16
94			ATL	110	110	0	0	0	0	0	0	0	0	0	0	16	4	1	32	0	0	16
93				140	140	0	0	0	0	0	0	0	0	0	0	17	7	2	34	0	0	15
				138.0	138.0	0.0	0.0	0.0	0.0	0.0	0.0	0.0	0.0	0.0	0.0	19.3	6.3	1.3	35.0	0.0	0.0	15.7
95	CARNEY, JOHN	K	SD	101	101	0	0	0	0	0	0	0	0	0	0	18	3	0	32	0	0	16
94				159	159	0	0	0	0	0	0	0	0	0	0	27	5	2	33	0	0	16
93				152	152	0	0	0	0	0	0	0	0	0	0	22	7	2	31	0	0	16
				137.3	137.3	0.0	0.0	0.0	0.0	0.0	0.0	0.0	0.0	0.0	0.0	22.3	5.0	1.3	32.0	0.0	0.0	16.0

C

YR	PLAYER	POS	TM	FAN PTS	DIST PTS	PERF PTS	PASSING TD: 0-9	PASSING TD: 10-39	PASSING TD: 40+	RUSHING TD: 0-9	RUSHING TD: 10-39	RUSHING TD: 40+	RECEIVING TD: 0-9	RECEIVING TD: 10-39	RECEIVING TD: 40+	FIELD GOALS: 10-39	FIELD GOALS: 40-49	FIELD GOALS: 50+	PAT	D,ST TDS	TOT TDS	GAM
95	STOYANOVICH, PETE	K	MIA	144	144	0	0	0	0	0	0	0	0	0	0	19	6	2	37	0	0	16
94				130	130	0	0	0	0	0	0	0	0	0	0	15	8	1	35	0	0	16
93				131	131	0	0	0	0	0	0	0	0	0	0	18	4	2	37	0	0	16
				135.0	135.0	0.0	0.0	0.0	0.0	0.0	0.0	0.0	0.0	0.0	0.0	17.3	6.0	1.7	36.3	0.0	0.0	16.0
95	CHRISTIE, STEVE	K	BUF	146	146	0	0	0	0	0	0	0	0	0	0	26	3	2	33	0	0	16
94				134	134	0	0	0	0	0	0	0	0	0	0	17	5	2	38	0	0	16
93				124	124	0	0	0	0	0	0	0	0	0	0	16	6	1	36	0	0	15
				134.7	134.7	0.0	0.0	0.0	0.0	0.0	0.0	0.0	0.0	0.0	0.0	19.7	4.7	1.7	35.7	0.0	0.0	15.7
95	DEL GRECO, AL	K	HOU	155	155	0	0	0	0	0	0	0	0	0	0	14	10	3	33	0	0	16
94				87	87	0	0	0	0	0	0	0	0	0	0	8	7	1	18	0	0	15
93				162	162	0	0	0	0	0	0	0	0	0	0	21	4	4	39	0	0	16
				134.7	134.7	0.0	0.0	0.0	0.0	0.0	0.0	0.0	0.0	0.0	0.0	14.3	7.0	2.7	30.0	0.0	0.0	15.7
95	PELFREY, DOUG	K	CIN	148	148	0	0	0	0	0	0	0	0	0	0	18	10	1	34	0	0	16
94				140	140	0	0	0	0	0	0	0	0	0	0	17	9	2	24	0	0	16
93				113	113	0	0	0	0	0	0	0	0	0	0	15	7	2	13	0	0	15
				133.7	133.7	0.0	0.0	0.0	0.0	0.0	0.0	0.0	0.0	0.0	0.0	16.7	8.7	1.7	23.7	0.0	0.0	15.7
95	MURRAY, EDDIE	K	WAS	133	133	0	0	0	0	0	0	0	0	0	0	20	6	1	33	0	0	16
94			PHI	100	100	0	0	0	0	0	0	0	0	0	0	19	2	0	33	0	0	16
93			DAL	159	159	0	0	0	0	0	0	0	0	0	0	17	8	3	38	0	0	14
				130.7	130.7	0.0	0.0	0.0	0.0	0.0	0.0	0.0	0.0	0.0	0.0	18.7	5.3	1.3	34.7	0.0	0.0	15.3
95	BONIOL, CHRIS	K	DAL	133	133	0	0	0	0	0	0	0	0	0	0	24	3	0	46	0	0	16
94				126	126	0	0	0	0	0	0	0	0	0	0	16	6	0	48	0	0	16
				129.5	129.5	0.0	0.0	0.0	0.0	0.0	0.0	0.0	0.0	0.0	0.0	20.0	4.5	0.0	47.0	0.0	0.0	16.0
95	BUTLER, KEVIN	K	CHI	118	118	0	0	0	0	0	0	0	0	0	0	21	2	0	45	0	0	16
94				111	111	0	0	0	0	0	0	0	0	0	0	14	5	2	24	0	0	15
93				143	143	0	0	0	0	0	0	0	0	0	0	19	3	5	21	0	0	16
				124.0	124.0	0.0	0.0	0.0	0.0	0.0	0.0	0.0	0.0	0.0	0.0	18.0	3.3	2.3	30.0	0.0	0.0	15.7
95	JAEGER, JEFF	K	RAI	67	67	0	0	0	0	0	0	0	0	0	0	10	3	0	22	0	0	11
94				127	127	0	0	0	0	0	0	0	0	0	0	12	8	2	31	0	0	16
93				172	172	0	0	0	0	0	0	0	0	0	0	25	6	4	27	0	0	15
				122.0	122.0	0.0	0.0	0.0	0.0	0.0	0.0	0.0	0.0	0.0	0.0	15.7	5.7	2.0	26.7	0.0	0.0	14.0

YR	PLAYER	POS	TM	FAN PTS	DIST PTS	PERF PTS	PASSING TD: 0-9	10-39	40+	RUSHING TD: 0-9	10-39	40+	RECEIVING TD: 0-9	10-39	40+	FIELD GOALS: 10-39	40-49	50+	PAT	D,ST TDS	TOT TDS	GAM
95	ANDERSON, GARY	K	PHI	114	114	0	0	0	0	0	0	0	0	0	0	14	8	0	32	0	0	16
94			PIT	125	125	0	0	0	0	0	0	0	0	0	0	16	7	1	32	0	0	16
93				126	126	0	0	0	0	0	0	0	0	0	0	23	5	0	32	0	0	15
				121.7	121.7	0.0	0.0	0.0	0.0	0.0	0.0	0.0	0.0	0.0	0.0	17.7	6.7	0.3	32.0	0.0	0.0	15.7
95	KASAY, JOHN	K	CAR	130	130	0	0	0	0	0	0	0	0	0	0	16	9	1	27	0	0	16
94			SEA	104	104	0	0	0	0	0	0	0	0	0	0	13	6	1	25	0	0	16
93				127	127	0	0	0	0	0	0	0	0	0	0	16	4	3	29	0	0	16
				120.3	120.3	0.0	0.0	0.0	0.0	0.0	0.0	0.0	0.0	0.0	0.0	15.0	6.3	1.7	27.0	0.0	0.0	16.0
95	DAVIS, GREG	K	AZ	128	128	0	0	0	0	0	0	0	0	0	0	23	6	1	19	0	0	16
94				96	96	0	0	0	0	0	0	0	0	0	0	13	6	1	17	0	0	14
93				136	136	0	0	0	0	0	0	0	0	0	0	13	4	4	37	0	0	16
				120.0	120.0	0.0	0.0	0.0	0.0	0.0	0.0	0.0	0.0	0.0	0.0	16.3	5.3	2.0	24.3	0.0	0.0	15.3
95	STOVER, MATT	K	CLE	127	127	0	0	0	0	0	0	0	0	0	0	22	7	0	26	0	0	16
94				126	126	0	0	0	0	0	0	0	0	0	0	18	8	0	32	0	0	16
93				103	103	0	0	0	0	0	0	0	0	0	0	9	6	1	36	0	0	16
				118.7	118.7	0.0	0.0	0.0	0.0	0.0	0.0	0.0	0.0	0.0	0.0	16.3	7.0	0.3	31.3	0.0	0.0	16.0
95	BRIEN, DOUG	K	NO	111	111	0	0	0	0	0	0	0	0	0	0	12	6	1	35	0	0	14
94			SF	113	113	0	0	0	0	0	0	0	0	0	0	11	4	0	60	0	0	15
				112.0	112.0	0.0	0.0	0.0	0.0	0.0	0.0	0.0	0.0	0.0	0.0	11.5	5.0	0.5	47.5	0.0	0.0	14.5
95	HOLLIS, MIKE	K	JAX	109	109	0	0	0	0	0	0	0	0	0	0	14	4	2	27	0	0	16
95	LOWERY, NICK	K	NYJ	95	95	0	0	0	0	0	0	0	0	0	0	12	3	2	24	0	0	15
94				98	98	0	0	0	0	0	0	0	0	0	0	14	6	0	26	0	0	15
93			KC	127	127	0	0	0	0	0	0	0	0	0	0	15	7	1	37	0	0	16
				106.7	106.7	0.0	0.0	0.0	0.0	0.0	0.0	0.0	0.0	0.0	0.0	13.7	5.3	1.0	29.0	0.0	0.0	15.3
95	HUSTED, MICHAEL	K	TB	113	113	0	0	0	0	0	0	0	0	0	0	11	5	3	25	0	0	16
94				104	104	0	0	0	0	0	0	0	0	0	0	18	4	1	20	0	0	15
93				102	102	0	0	0	0	0	0	0	0	0	0	10	3	3	27	0	0	14
				106.3	106.3	0.0	0.0	0.0	0.0	0.0	0.0	0.0	0.0	0.0	0.0	13.0	4.0	2.3	24.0	0.0	0.0	15.0

C

YR	PLAYER	POS	TM	FAN PTS	DIST PTS	PERF PTS	PASSING TD: 0-9	10-39	40+	RUSHING TD: 0-9	10-39	40+	RECEIVING TD: 0-9	10-39	40+	FIELD GOALS: 10-39	40-49	50+	PAT	D,ST TDS	TOT TDS	GAM
95	BAHR, MATT	K	NE	120	120	0	0	0	0	0	0	0	0	0	0	16	5	2	27	0	0	16
94				125	125	0	0	0	0	0	0	0	0	0	0	23	4	0	36	0	0	16
93			PHI	71	71	0	0	0	0	0	0	0	0	0	0	11	2	0	28	0	0	14
				105.3	105.3	0.0	0.0	0.0	0.0	0.0	0.0	0.0	0.0	0.0	0.0	16.7	3.7	0.7	30.3	0.0	0.0	15.3
95	BLANCHARD, CARY	K	IND	103	103	0	0	0	0	0	0	0	0	0	0	11	7	1	25	0	0	12
93			NYJ	92	92	0	0	0	0	0	0	0	0	0	0	12	5	0	31	0	0	16
				97.5	97.5	0.0	0.0	0.0	0.0	0.0	0.0	0.0	0.0	0.0	0.0	11.5	6.0	0.5	28.0	0.0	0.0	14.0
95	SAN FRANCISCO	DT	SF	158	84	74	0	0	0	0	0	0	0	0	0	0	0	0	0	8	8	16
94				145	72	73	0	0	0	0	0	0	0	0	0	0	0	0	0	6	6	16
93				120	57	63	0	0	0	0	0	0	0	0	0	0	0	0	0	5	5	16
				141.0	71.0	70.0	0.0	0.0	0.0	0.0	0.0	0.0	0.0	0.0	0.0	0.0	0.0	0.0	0.0	6.3	6.3	16.0
95	MINNESOTA	DT	MIN	135	51	84	0	0	0	0	0	0	0	0	0	0	0	0	0	5	5	16
94				144	75	69	0	0	0	0	0	0	0	0	0	0	0	0	0	7	7	16
93				98	21	77	0	0	0	0	0	0	0	0	0	0	0	0	0	2	2	16
				125.7	49.0	76.7	0.0	0.0	0.0	0.0	0.0	0.0	0.0	0.0	0.0	0.0	0.0	0.0	0.0	4.7	4.7	16.0
95	PHILADELPHIA	DT	PHI	147	60	87	0	0	0	0	0	0	0	0	0	0	0	0	0	6	6	16
94				114	37	77	0	0	0	0	0	0	0	0	0	0	0	0	0	3	3	16
93				116	52	64	0	0	0	0	0	0	0	0	0	0	0	0	0	5	5	16
				125.7	49.7	76.0	0.0	0.0	0.0	0.0	0.0	0.0	0.0	0.0	0.0	0.0	0.0	0.0	0.0	4.7	4.7	16.0
95	SAN DIEGO	DT	SD	130	63	67	0	0	0	0	0	0	0	0	0	0	0	0	0	6	6	16
94				160	84	76	0	0	0	0	0	0	0	0	0	0	0	0	0	7	7	16
93				66	12	54	0	0	0	0	0	0	0	0	0	0	0	0	0	1	1	16
				118.7	53.0	65.7	0.0	0.0	0.0	0.0	0.0	0.0	0.0	0.0	0.0	0.0	0.0	0.0	0.0	4.7	4.7	16.0
95	KANSAS CITY	DT	KC	158	78	80	0	0	0	0	0	0	0	0	0	0	0	0	0	7	7	16
94				109	32	77	0	0	0	0	0	0	0	0	0	0	0	0	0	2	2	16
93				83	27	56	0	0	0	0	0	0	0	0	0	0	0	0	0	3	3	16
				116.7	45.7	71.0	0.0	0.0	0.0	0.0	0.0	0.0	0.0	0.0	0.0	0.0	0.0	0.0	0.0	4.0	4.0	16.0
95	PITTSBURGH	DT	PIT	140	63	77	0	0	0	0	0	0	0	0	0	0	0	0	0	6	6	16
94				109	24	85	0	0	0	0	0	0	0	0	0	0	0	0	0	3	3	16
93				96	30	66	0	0	0	0	0	0	0	0	0	0	0	0	0	3	3	16
				115.0	39.0	76.0	0.0	0.0	0.0	0.0	0.0	0.0	0.0	0.0	0.0	0.0	0.0	0.0	0.0	4.0	4.0	16.0

YR	PLAYER	POS	TM	FAN PTS	DIST PTS	PERF PTS	PASSING TD: 0-9	10-39	40+	RUSHING TD: 0-9	10-39	40+	RECEIVING TD: 0-9	10-39	40+	FIELD GOALS: 0-9	10-39	40-49	50+	PAT	D,ST TDS	TOT TDS	GAM
95	HOUSTON	DT	HOU	116	45	71	0	0	0	0	0	0	0	0	0	0	0	0	0	0	4	4	16
94				82	25	57	0	0	0	0	0	0	0	0	0	0	0	0	0	0	2	2	16
93				142	60	82	0	0	0	0	0	0	0	0	0	0	0	0	0	0	6	6	16
				113.3	43.3	70.0	0.0	0.0	0.0	0.0	0.0	0.0	0.0	0.0	0.0	0.0	0.0	0.0	0.0	0.0	4.0	4.0	16.0
95	CAROLINA	DT	CAR	112	39	73	0	0	0	0	0	0	0	0	0	0	0	0	0	0	4	4	16
95	CLEVELAND	DT	CLE	83	30	53	0	0	0	0	0	0	0	0	0	0	0	0	0	0	3	3	16
94				124	54	70	0	0	0	0	0	0	0	0	0	0	0	0	0	0	5	5	16
93				126	57	69	0	0	0	0	0	0	0	0	0	0	0	0	0	0	5	5	16
				111.0	47.0	64.0	0.0	0.0	0.0	0.0	0.0	0.0	0.0	0.0	0.0	0.0	0.0	0.0	0.0	0.0	4.3	4.3	16.0
95	WASHINGTON	DT	WAS	103	36	67	0	0	0	0	0	0	0	0	0	0	0	0	0	0	4	4	16
94				131	79	52	0	0	0	0	0	0	0	0	0	0	0	0	0	0	7	7	16
93				97	45	52	0	0	0	0	0	0	0	0	0	0	0	0	0	0	4	4	16
				110.3	53.3	57.0	0.0	0.0	0.0	0.0	0.0	0.0	0.0	0.0	0.0	0.0	0.0	0.0	0.0	0.0	5.0	5.0	16.0
95	NEW ORLEANS	DT	NO	84	12	72	0	0	0	0	0	0	0	0	0	0	0	0	0	0	1	1	16
94				124	57	67	0	0	0	0	0	0	0	0	0	0	0	0	0	0	5	5	16
93				122	57	65	0	0	0	0	0	0	0	0	0	0	0	0	0	0	5	5	16
				110.0	42.0	68.0	0.0	0.0	0.0	0.0	0.0	0.0	0.0	0.0	0.0	0.0	0.0	0.0	0.0	0.0	3.7	3.7	16.0
95	DETROIT	DT	DET	94	12	82	0	0	0	0	0	0	0	0	0	0	0	0	0	0	1	1	16
94				132	82	50	0	0	0	0	0	0	0	0	0	0	0	0	0	0	7	7	16
93				101	39	62	0	0	0	0	0	0	0	0	0	0	0	0	0	0	4	4	16
				109.0	44.3	64.7	0.0	0.0	0.0	0.0	0.0	0.0	0.0	0.0	0.0	0.0	0.0	0.0	0.0	0.0	4.0	4.0	16.0
95	LA RAIDERS	DT	RAI	133	54	79	0	0	0	0	0	0	0	0	0	0	0	0	0	0	6	6	16
94				111	48	63	0	0	0	0	0	0	0	0	0	0	0	0	0	0	5	5	16
93				80	21	59	0	0	0	0	0	0	0	0	0	0	0	0	0	0	2	2	16
				108.0	41.0	67.0	0.0	0.0	0.0	0.0	0.0	0.0	0.0	0.0	0.0	0.0	0.0	0.0	0.0	0.0	4.3	4.3	16.0
95	ARIZONA	DT	AZ	132	60	72	0	0	0	0	0	0	0	0	0	0	0	0	0	0	6	6	16
94				87	16	71	0	0	0	0	0	0	0	0	0	0	0	0	0	0	1	1	16
93				96	45	51	0	0	0	0	0	0	0	0	0	0	0	0	0	0	4	4	16
				105.0	40.3	64.7	0.0	0.0	0.0	0.0	0.0	0.0	0.0	0.0	0.0	0.0	0.0	0.0	0.0	0.0	3.7	3.7	16.0

			FAN	DIST	PERF	PASSING TD:			RUSHING TD:			RECEIVING TD:			FIELD GOALS:				D,ST	TOT	
YR	PLAYER	POS	TM	PTS	PTS	PTS	0-9	10-39	40+	0-9	10-39	40+	0-9	10-39	40+	10-39	40-49	50+	PAT	TDS	TDS	GAM
95	DALLAS	DT	DAL	99	39	60	0	0	0	0	0	0	0	0	0	0	0	0	0	4	4	16
94				134	57	77	0	0	0	0	0	0	0	0	0	0	0	0	0	5	5	16
93				81	33	48	0	0	0	0	0	0	0	0	0	0	0	0	0	3	3	16
				104.7	43.0	61.7	0.0	0.0	0.0	0.0	0.0	0.0	0.0	0.0	0.0	0.0	0.0	0.0	0.0	4.0	4.0	16.0
95	NY GIANTS	DT	NYG	118	54	64	0	0	0	0	0	0	0	0	0	0	0	0	0	5	5	16
94				90	32	58	0	0	0	0	0	0	0	0	0	0	0	0	0	2	2	16
93				87	24	63	0	0	0	0	0	0	0	0	0	0	0	0	0	2	2	16
				98.3	36.7	61.7	0.0	0.0	0.0	0.0	0.0	0.0	0.0	0.0	0.0	0.0	0.0	0.0	0.0	3.0	3.0	16.0
95	SEATTLE	DT	SEA	93	36	57	0	0	0	0	0	0	0	0	0	0	0	0	0	3	3	16
94				99	37	62	0	0	0	0	0	0	0	0	0	0	0	0	0	3	3	16
93				101	25	76	0	0	0	0	0	0	0	0	0	0	0	0	0	3	3	16
				97.7	32.7	65.0	0.0	0.0	0.0	0.0	0.0	0.0	0.0	0.0	0.0	0.0	0.0	0.0	0.0	3.0	3.0	16.0
95	NY JETS	DT	NYJ	120	39	81	0	0	0	0	0	0	0	0	0	0	0	0	0	4	4	16
94				100	33	67	0	0	0	0	0	0	0	0	0	0	0	0	0	3	3	16
93				67	12	55	0	0	0	0	0	0	0	0	0	0	0	0	0	1	1	16
				95.7	28.0	67.7	0.0	0.0	0.0	0.0	0.0	0.0	0.0	0.0	0.0	0.0	0.0	0.0	0.0	2.7	2.7	16.0
95	BUFFALO	DT	BUF	104	27	77	0	0	0	0	0	0	0	0	0	0	0	0	0	3	3	16
94				62	10	52	0	0	0	0	0	0	0	0	0	0	0	0	0	1	1	16
93				118	54	64	0	0	0	0	0	0	0	0	0	0	0	0	0	5	5	16
				94.7	30.3	64.3	0.0	0.0	0.0	0.0	0.0	0.0	0.0	0.0	0.0	0.0	0.0	0.0	0.0	3.0	3.0	16.0
95	INDIANAPOLIS	DT	IND	91	33	58	0	0	0	0	0	0	0	0	0	0	0	0	0	3	3	16
94				138	78	60	0	0	0	0	0	0	0	0	0	0	0	0	0	7	7	16
93				49	18	31	0	0	0	0	0	0	0	0	0	0	0	0	0	2	2	16
				92.7	43.0	49.7	0.0	0.0	0.0	0.0	0.0	0.0	0.0	0.0	0.0	0.0	0.0	0.0	0.0	4.0	4.0	16.0
95	ST. LOUIS	DT	RAM	124	48	76	0	0	0	0	0	0	0	0	0	0	0	0	0	5	5	16
94				95	49	46	0	0	0	0	0	0	0	0	0	0	0	0	0	4	4	16
93				52	6	46	0	0	0	0	0	0	0	0	0	0	0	0	0	1	1	16
				90.3	34.3	56.0	0.0	0.0	0.0	0.0	0.0	0.0	0.0	0.0	0.0	0.0	0.0	0.0	0.0	3.3	3.3	16.0

YR	PLAYER	POS	TM	FAN PTS	DIST PTS	PERF PTS	PASSING TD: 0-9	10-39	40+	RUSHING TD: 0-9	10-39	40+	RECEIVING TD: 0-9	10-39	40+	FIELD GOALS: 10-39	40-49	50+	PAT	D,ST TDS	TOT TDS	GAM
95	ATLANTA	DT	ATL	105	45	60	0	0	0	0	0	0	0	0	0	0	0	0	0	4	4	16
94				95	30	65	0	0	0	0	0	0	0	0	0	0	0	0	0	3	3	16
93				64	24	40	0	0	0	0	0	0	0	0	0	0	0	0	0	2	2	16
				88.0	33.0	55.0	0.0	0.0	0.0	0.0	0.0	0.0	0.0	0.0	0.0	0.0	0.0	0.0	0.0	3.0	3.0	16.0
95	CHICAGO	DT	CHI	83	15	68	0	0	0	0	0	0	0	0	0	0	0	0	0	2	2	15
94				63	12	51	0	0	0	0	0	0	0	0	0	0	0	0	0	1	1	15
93				106	42	64	0	0	0	0	0	0	0	0	0	0	0	0	0	5	5	16
				84.0	23.0	61.0	0.0	0.0	0.0	0.0	0.0	0.0	0.0	0.0	0.0	0.0	0.0	0.0	0.0	2.7	2.7	16.0
95	GREEN BAY	DT	GB	61	6	55	0	0	0	0	0	0	0	0	0	0	0	0	0	1	1	16
94				101	33	68	0	0	0	0	0	0	0	0	0	0	0	0	0	3	3	16
93				89	21	68	0	0	0	0	0	0	0	0	0	0	0	0	0	2	2	16
				83.7	20.0	63.7	0.0	0.0	0.0	0.0	0.0	0.0	0.0	0.0	0.0	0.0	0.0	0.0	0.0	2.0	2.0	16.0
95	MIAMI	DT	MIA	80	21	59	0	0	0	0	0	0	0	0	0	0	0	0	0	2	2	16
94				73	12	61	0	0	0	0	0	0	0	0	0	0	0	0	0	1	1	16
93				78	36	42	0	0	0	0	0	0	0	0	0	0	0	0	0	3	3	16
				77.0	23.0	54.0	0.0	0.0	0.0	0.0	0.0	0.0	0.0	0.0	0.0	0.0	0.0	0.0	0.0	2.0	2.0	16.0
95	BENNETT, TONY	LB	IND	25	9	16	0	0	0	0	0	0	0	0	0	0	0	0	0	2	2	16
94				22	12	10	0	0	0	0	0	0	0	0	0	0	0	0	0	1	1	14
93			GB	6	0	6	0	0	0	0	0	0	0	0	0	0	0	0	0	0	0	9
				17.7	7.0	10.7	0.0	0.0	0.0	0.0	0.0	0.0	0.0	0.0	0.0	0.0	0.0	0.0	0.0	1.0	1.0	13.0
95	LEWIS, MO	LB	NYJ	16	9	7	0	0	0	0	0	0	0	0	0	0	0	0	0	1	1	16
94				30	21	9	0	0	0	0	0	0	0	0	0	0	0	0	0	2	2	15
93				6	0	6	0	0	0	0	0	0	0	0	0	0	0	0	0	0	0	16
				17.3	10.0	7.3	0.0	0.0	0.0	0.0	0.0	0.0	0.0	0.0	0.0	0.0	0.0	0.0	0.0	1.0	1.0	15.7
95	PAUP, BRYCE	LB	BUF	20	0	20	0	0	0	0	0	0	0	0	0	0	0	0	0	0	0	15
94			GB	20	9	11	0	0	0	0	0	0	0	0	0	0	0	0	0	1	1	16
93				12	0	16	0	0	0	0	0	0	0	0	0	0	0	0	0	0	0	15
				17.3	3.0	15.7	0.0	0.0	0.0	0.0	0.0	0.0	0.0	0.0	0.0	0.0	0.0	0.0	0.0	0.3	0.3	15.3

YR	PLAYER	POS	TM	FAN PTS	DIST PTS	PERF PTS	PASSING TD: 0-9	10-39	40+	RUSHING TD: 0-9	10-39	40+	RECEIVING TD: 0-9	10-39	40+	FIELD GOALS: 0-9	10-39	40-49	50+	PAT	D,ST TDS	TOT TDS	GAM
95	THOMAS, DERRICK	LB	KC	10	0	10	0	0	0	0	0	0	0	0	0	0	0	0	0	0	0	0	15
94				10	0	10	0	0	0	0	0	0	0	0	0	0	0	0	0	0	0	0	16
93				20	12	8	0	0	0	0	0	0	0	0	0	0	0	0	0	0	1	1	13
				13.3	4.0	9.3	0.0	0.0	0.0	0.0	0.0	0.0	0.0	0.0	0.0	0.0	0.0	0.0	0.0	0.0	0.3	0.3	14.7
95	SMITH, ANTHONY	LB	RAI	11	0	11	0	0	0	0	0	0	0	0	0	0	0	0	0	0	0	0	16
94				15	9	6	0	0	0	0	0	0	0	0	0	0	0	0	0	0	1	1	16
93				12	0	12	0	0	0	0	0	0	0	0	0	0	0	0	0	0	0	0	16
				12.7	3.0	9.7	0.0	0.0	0.0	0.0	0.0	0.0	0.0	0.0	0.0	0.0	0.0	0.0	0.0	0.0	0.3	0.3	16.0
95	GREENE, KEVIN	LB	PIT	12	0	12	0	0	0	0	0	0	0	0	0	0	0	0	0	0	0	0	16
94				13	0	13	0	0	0	0	0	0	0	0	0	0	0	0	0	0	0	0	16
93				12	0	12	0	0	0	0	0	0	0	0	0	0	0	0	0	0	0	0	15
				12.3	0.0	12.3	0.0	0.0	0.0	0.0	0.0	0.0	0.0	0.0	0.0	0.0	0.0	0.0	0.0	0.0	0.0	0.0	15.7
95	MILLS, SAM	LB	CAR	23	9	14	0	0	0	0	0	0	0	0	0	0	0	0	0	0	1	1	16
94			NO	2	0	2	0	0	0	0	0	0	0	0	0	0	0	0	0	0	0	0	16
93				11	9	2	0	0	0	0	0	0	0	0	0	0	0	0	0	0	1	1	9
				12.0	6.0	6.0	0.0	0.0	0.0	0.0	0.0	0.0	0.0	0.0	0.0	0.0	0.0	0.0	0.0	0.0	0.7	0.7	13.7
95	SCROGGINS, TRACY	LB	DET	23	12	11	0	0	0	0	0	0	0	0	0	0	0	0	0	0	1	1	16
94				2	0	2	0	0	0	0	0	0	0	0	0	0	0	0	0	0	0	0	13
93				9	0	9	0	0	0	0	0	0	0	0	0	0	0	0	0	0	1	1	12
				11.3	4.0	7.3	0.0	0.0	0.0	0.0	0.0	0.0	0.0	0.0	0.0	0.0	0.0	0.0	0.0	0.0	0.7	0.7	13.7
95	THOMAS, WILLIAM	LB	PHI	19	9	10	0	0	0	0	0	0	0	0	0	0	0	0	0	0	1	1	16
94				7	0	7	0	0	0	0	0	0	0	0	0	0	0	0	0	0	0	0	16
93				8	0	8	0	0	0	0	0	0	0	0	0	0	0	0	0	0	0	0	16
				11.3	3.0	8.3	0.0	0.0	0.0	0.0	0.0	0.0	0.0	0.0	0.0	0.0	0.0	0.0	0.0	0.0	0.3	0.3	16.0
95	COLLINS, ANDRE	LB	CIN	6	0	6	0	0	0	0	0	0	0	0	0	0	0	0	0	0	0	0	16
94			WAS	27	21	6	0	0	0	0	0	0	0	0	0	0	0	0	0	0	2	2	16
93				0	0	7	0	0	0	0	0	0	0	0	0	0	0	0	0	0	0	0	12
				11.0	7.0	6.3	0.0	0.0	0.0	0.0	0.0	0.0	0.0	0.0	0.0	0.0	0.0	0.0	0.0	0.0	0.7	0.7	14.7

YR	PLAYER	POS	TM	FAN PTS	DIST PTS	PERF PTS	PASSING TD: 0-9	10-39	40+	RUSHING TD: 0-9	10-39	40+	RECEIVING TD: 0-9	10-39	40+	FIELD GOALS: 0-39	40-49	50+	PAT	D,ST TDS	TOT TDS	GAM
95	SLADE, CHRIS	LB	NE	15	9	6	0	0	0	0	0	0	0	0	0	0	0	0	0	1	1	16
94				8	0	8	0	0	0	0	0	0	0	0	0	0	0	0	0	0	0	16
93				9	0	9	0	0	0	0	0	0	0	0	0	0	0	0	0	0	0	10
				10.7	3.0	7.7	0.0	0.0	0.0	0.0	0.0	0.0	0.0	0.0	0.0	0.0	0.0	0.0	0.0	0.3	0.3	14.0
95	HARVEY, KEN	LB	WAS	10	0	10	0	0	0	0	0	0	0	0	0	0	0	0	0	0	0	16
94	½			12	0	12	0	0	0	0	0	0	0	0	0	0	0	0	0	0	0	16
93	½		AZ	9	0	9	0	0	0	0	0	0	0	0	0	0	0	0	0	0	0	15
				10.3	0.0	10.3	0.0	0.0	0.0	0.0	0.0	0.0	0.0	0.0	0.0	0.0	0.0	0.0	0.0	0.0	0.0	-5.7
95	WOODALL, LEE	LB	SF	19	12	7	0	0	0	0	0	0	0	0	0	0	0	0	0	1	1	16
94				1	0	1	0	0	0	0	0	0	0	0	0	0	0	0	0	0	0	15
				10.0	6.0	4.0	0.0	0.0	0.0	0.0	0.0	0.0	0.0	0.0	0.0	0.0	0.0	0.0	0.0	0.5	0.5	15.5
95	LLOYD, GREG	LB	PIT	11	0	11	0	0	0	0	0	0	0	0	0	0	0	0	0	0	0	16
94				11	0	11	0	0	0	0	0	0	0	0	0	0	0	0	0	0	0	15
93				6	0	6	0	0	0	0	0	0	0	0	0	0	0	0	0	0	0	15
				9.3	0.0	9.3	0.0	0.0	0.0	0.0	0.0	0.0	0.0	0.0	0.0	0.0	0.0	0.0	0.0	0.0	0.0	15.3
95	BENNETT, CORNELIUS	LB	BUF	17	12	5	0	0	0	0	0	0	0	0	0	0	0	0	0	1	1	14
94				5	0	5	0	0	0	0	0	0	0	0	0	0	0	0	0	0	0	16
93				5	0	5	0	0	0	0	0	0	0	0	0	0	0	0	0	0	0	15
				9.0	4.0	5.0	0.0	0.0	0.0	0.0	0.0	0.0	0.0	0.0	0.0	0.0	0.0	0.0	0.0	0.3	0.3	15.0
95	HALEY, CHARLES	LB	DAL	10	0	10	0	0	0	0	0	0	0	0	0	0	0	0	0	0	0	13
94	½			13	0	13	0	0	0	0	0	0	0	0	0	0	0	0	0	0	0	15
93	½			4	0	4	0	0	0	0	0	0	0	0	0	0	0	0	0	0	0	12
				9.0	0.0	9.0	0.0	0.0	0.0	0.0	0.0	0.0	0.0	0.0	0.0	0.0	0.0	0.0	0.0	0.0	0.0	13.3
95	JOHNSON, MIKE	LB	DET	8	0	8	0	0	0	0	0	0	0	0	0	0	0	0	0	1	1	16
94	⅛			14	12	2	0	0	0	0	0	0	0	0	0	0	0	0	0	0	0	16
93			CLE	5	0	5	0	0	0	0	0	0	0	0	0	0	0	0	0	0	0	16
				9.0	4.0	5.0	0.0	0.0	0.0	0.0	0.0	0.0	0.0	0.0	0.0	0.0	0.0	0.0	0.0	0.3	0.3	16.0
95	LATHON, LAMAR	LB	CAR	9	0	9	0	0	0	0	0	0	0	0	0	0	0	0	0	0	0	15
94			HOU	11	4	7	0	0	0	0	0	0	0	0	0	0	0	0	0	0	0	14
93				6	4	2	0	0	0	0	0	0	0	0	0	0	0	0	0	0	0	11
				8.7	2.7	6.0	0.0	0.0	0.0	0.0	0.0	0.0	0.0	0.0	0.0	0.0	0.0	0.0	0.0	0.0	0.0	13.3

YR	PLAYER	POS	TM	FAN PTS	DIST PTS	PERF PTS	PASSING TD: 0-9	10-39	40+	RUSHING TD: 0-9	10-39	40+	RECEIVING TD: 0-9	10-39	40+	FIELD GOALS: 0-39	40-49	50+	PAT	D,ST TDS	TOT TDS	GAM
95	NORTON, KEN	LB	SF	22	18	4	0	0	0	0	0	0	0	0	0	0	0	0	0	2	2	16
94				1	0	1	0	0	0	0	0	0	0	0	0	0	0	0	0	0	0	16
93			DAL	3	0	3	0	0	0	0	0	0	0	0	0	0	0	0	0	0	0	16
				8.7	6.0	2.7	0.0	0.0	0.0	0.0	0.0	0.0	0.0	0.0	0.0	0.0	0.0	0.0	0.0	0.7	0.7	16.0
95	JACKSON, RICKEY	LB	SF	11	0	11	0	0	0	0	0	0	0	0	0	0	0	0	0	0	0	16
⅛				3	0	3	0	0	0	0	0	0	0	0	0	0	0	0	0	0	0	15
⅛			NO	11	0	11	0	0	0	0	0	0	0	0	0	0	0	0	0	0	0	16
				8.3	0.0	8.3	0.0	0.0	0.0	0.0	0.0	0.0	0.0	0.0	0.0	0.0	0.0	0.0	0.0	0.0	0.0	15.7
95	SEAU, JUNIOR	LB	SD	16	9	7	0	0	0	0	0	0	0	0	0	0	0	0	0	1	1	15
94				6	0	6	0	0	0	0	0	0	0	0	0	0	0	0	0	0	0	16
93				2	0	2	0	0	0	0	0	0	0	0	0	0	0	0	0	0	0	16
				8.0	3.0	5.0	0.0	0.0	0.0	0.0	0.0	0.0	0.0	0.0	0.0	0.0	0.0	0.0	0.0	0.3	0.3	15.7
95	MCCANTS, KEITH	LB	AZ	9	6	3	0	0	0	0	0	0	0	0	0	0	0	0	0	1	1	16
94				14	12	2	0	0	0	0	0	0	0	0	0	0	0	0	0	1	1	9
93			HOU	0	0	0	0	0	0	0	0	0	0	0	0	0	0	0	0	0	0	5
				7.7	6.0	1.7	0.0	0.0	0.0	0.0	0.0	0.0	0.0	0.0	0.0	0.0	0.0	0.0	0.0	0.7	0.7	10.0
95	ARMSTEAD, JESSIE	LB	NYG	15	12	3	0	0	0	0	0	0	0	0	0	0	0	0	0	1	1	16
94				4	0	4	0	0	0	0	0	0	0	0	0	0	0	0	0	0	0	14
93				1	0	1	0	0	0	0	0	0	0	0	0	0	0	0	0	0	0	15
				6.7	4.0	2.7	0.0	0.0	0.0	0.0	0.0	0.0	0.0	0.0	0.0	0.0	0.0	0.0	0.0	0.3	0.3	15.0
95	CORYATT, QUENTIN	LB	IND	6	0	6	0	0	0	0	0	0	0	0	0	0	0	0	0	1	1	16
94				13	12	1	0	0	0	0	0	0	0	0	0	0	0	0	0	1	1	15
93				1	0	1	0	0	0	0	0	0	0	0	0	0	0	0	0	0	0	16
				6.7	4.0	2.7	0.0	0.0	0.0	0.0	0.0	0.0	0.0	0.0	0.0	0.0	0.0	0.0	0.0	0.3	0.3	15.7
95	CONNOR, DARION	LB	CAR	7	0	7	0	0	0	0	0	0	0	0	0	0	0	0	0	0	0	16
94			ATL	11	0	11	0	0	0	0	0	0	0	0	0	0	0	0	0	0	0	15
93				1	0	1	0	0	0	0	0	0	0	0	0	0	0	0	0	0	0	13
				6.3	0.0	6.3	0.0	0.0	0.0	0.0	0.0	0.0	0.0	0.0	0.0	0.0	0.0	0.0	0.0	0.0	0.0	14.7
95	THOMAS, ORLANDO	DB	MIN	33	21	12	0	0	0	0	0	0	0	0	0	0	0	0	0	2	2	16

YR	PLAYER	POS	TM	FAN PTS	DIST PTS	PERF PTS	PASSING TD: 0-9	10-39	40+	RUSHING TD: 0-9	10-39	40+	RECEIVING TD: 0-9	10-39	40+	FIELD GOALS: 0-9	10-39	40-49	50+	PAT	D,ST TDS	TOT TDS	GAM
95	HUGHES, TYRONE	DB	NO	0	0	0	0	0	0	0	0	0	0	0	0	0	0	0	0	0	0	0	16
94				50	48	2	0	0	0	0	0	0	0	0	0	0	0	0	0	0	4	4	15
93				36	36	0	0	0	0	0	0	0	0	0	0	0	0	0	0	0	3	3	16
				28.7	28.0	0.7	0.0	0.0	0.0	0.0	0.0	0.0	0.0	0.0	0.0	0.0	0.0	0.0	0.0	0.0	2.3	2.3	15.7
95	WILLIAMS, AENEAS	DB	AZ	41	33	8	0	0	0	0	0	0	0	0	0	0	0	0	0	0	3	3	16
94				9	0	9	0	0	0	0	0	0	0	0	0	0	0	0	0	0	0	0	15
93				23	21	2	0	0	0	0	0	0	0	0	0	0	0	0	0	0	2	2	15
				24.3	18.0	6.3	0.0	0.0	0.0	0.0	0.0	0.0	0.0	0.0	0.0	0.0	0.0	0.0	0.0	0.0	1.7	1.7	15.3
95	MCDANIEL, TERRY	DB	RAI	18	12	6	0	0	0	0	0	0	0	0	0	0	0	0	0	0	1	1	16
94				37	30	7	0	0	0	0	0	0	0	0	0	0	0	0	0	0	3	3	15
93				14	9	5	0	0	0	0	0	0	0	0	0	0	0	0	0	0	1	1	16
				23.0	17.0	6.0	0.0	0.0	0.0	0.0	0.0	0.0	0.0	0.0	0.0	0.0	0.0	0.0	0.0	0.0	1.7	1.7	15.7
95	WILLIAMS, WILLIE	DB	PIT	20	12	8	0	0	0	0	0	0	0	0	0	0	0	0	0	0	1	1	16
95	MCDONALD, TIM	DB	SF	25	21	4	0	0	0	0	0	0	0	0	0	0	0	0	0	0	2	2	16
94				26	24	2	0	0	0	0	0	0	0	0	0	0	0	0	0	0	2	2	16
93				3	0	3	0	0	0	0	0	0	0	0	0	0	0	0	0	0	0	0	16
				18.0	15.0	3.0	0.0	0.0	0.0	0.0	0.0	0.0	0.0	0.0	0.0	0.0	0.0	0.0	0.0	0.0	1.3	1.3	16.0
95	PARKER, ANTHONY	DB	MIN	15	9	6	0	0	0	0	0	0	0	0	0	0	0	0	0	0	1	1	16
94				37	33	4	0	0	0	0	0	0	0	0	0	0	0	0	0	0	3	3	15
93				1	0	1	0	0	0	0	0	0	0	0	0	0	0	0	0	0	0	0	10
				17.7	14.0	3.7	0.0	0.0	0.0	0.0	0.0	0.0	0.0	0.0	0.0	0.0	0.0	0.0	0.0	0.0	1.3	1.3	13.7
95	SANDERS, DEION	DB	DAL	2	0	2	0	0	0	0	0	0	0	0	0	0	0	0	0	0	0	0	9
94			SF	42	36	6	0	0	0	0	0	0	0	0	0	0	0	0	0	0	3	3	11
93			ATL	7	0	7	0	0	0	0	0	0	0	0	0	0	0	0	0	0	0	0	11
				17.0	12.0	5.0	0.0	0.0	0.0	0.0	0.0	0.0	0.0	0.0	0.0	0.0	0.0	0.0	0.0	0.0	1.0	1.0	10.3
95	WRIGHT, TOBY	DB	RAM	20	12	8	0	0	0	0	0	0	0	0	0	0	0	0	0	0	1	1	16
94				12	12	0	0	0	0	0	0	0	0	0	0	0	0	0	0	0	1	1	1
				16.0	12.0	4.0	0.0	0.0	0.0	0.0	0.0	0.0	0.0	0.0	0.0	0.0	0.0	0.0	0.0	0.0	1.0	1.0	8.5

YR	PLAYER	POS	TM	FAN PTS	DIST PTS	PERF PTS	PASSING TD: 0-9	10-39	40+	RUSHING TD: 0-9	10-39	40+	RECEIVING TD: 0-9	10-39	40+	FIELD GOALS: 0-9	10-39	40-49	50+	PAT	D,ST TDS	TOT TDS	GAM
95	DAVIS, ERIC	DB	SF	16	12	4	0	0	0	0	0	0	0	0	0	0	0	0	0	0	1	1	15
94				1	0	1	0	0	0	0	0	0	0	0	0	0	0	0	0	0	0	0	16
93				28	24	4	0	0	0	0	0	0	0	0	0	0	0	0	0	0	2	2	16
				15.0	12.0	3.0	0.0	0.0	0.0	0.0	0.0	0.0	0.0	0.0	0.0	0.0	0.0	0.0	0.0	0.0	1.0	1.0	15.7
95	COLLINS, MARK	DB	KC	10	9	1	0	0	0	0	0	0	0	0	0	0	0	0	0	0	1	1	16
94				16	12	4	0	0	0	0	0	0	0	0	0	0	0	0	0	0	1	1	14
93			NYG	17	12	5	0	0	0	0	0	0	0	0	0	0	0	0	0	0	1	1	16
				14.3	11.0	3.3	0.0	0.0	0.0	0.0	0.0	0.0	0.0	0.0	0.0	0.0	0.0	0.0	0.0	0.0	1.0	1.0	15.3
95	CLAY, WILLIE	DB	DET	8	0	8	0	0	0	0	0	0	0	0	0	0	0	0	0	0	0	0	16
94				12	9	3	0	0	0	0	0	0	0	0	0	0	0	0	0	0	1	1	16
93				19	18	1	0	0	0	0	0	0	0	0	0	0	0	0	0	0	2	2	13
				13.0	9.0	4.0	0.0	0.0	0.0	0.0	0.0	0.0	0.0	0.0	0.0	0.0	0.0	0.0	0.0	0.0	1.0	1.0	15.0
95	V8JACKSON, GREG	DB	PHI	16	12	4	0	0	0	0	0	0	0	0	0	0	0	0	0	0	1	1	16
94				18	12	6	0	0	0	0	0	0	0	0	0	0	0	0	0	0	1	1	16
93			NYG	4	0	4	0	0	0	0	0	0	0	0	0	0	0	0	0	0	0	0	16
				12.7	8.0	4.7	0.0	0.0	0.0	0.0	0.0	0.0	0.0	0.0	0.0	0.0	0.0	0.0	0.0	0.0	0.7	0.7	16.0
95	GREEN, DARRELL	DB	WAS	9	6	3	0	0	0	0	0	0	0	0	0	0	0	0	0	0	1	1	16
94				12	9	3	0	0	0	0	0	0	0	0	0	0	0	0	0	0	1	1	15
93				16	12	4	0	0	0	0	0	0	0	0	0	0	0	0	0	0	1	1	16
				12.3	9.0	3.3	0.0	0.0	0.0	0.0	0.0	0.0	0.0	0.0	0.0	0.0	0.0	0.0	0.0	0.0	1.0	1.0	15.7
95	HANKS, MERTON	DB	SF	15	9	6	0	0	0	0	0	0	0	0	0	0	0	0	0	0	1	1	16
94				7	0	7	0	0	0	0	0	0	0	0	0	0	0	0	0	0	0	0	16
93				15	12	3	0	0	0	0	0	0	0	0	0	0	0	0	0	0	1	1	15
				12.3	7.0	5.3	0.0	0.0	0.0	0.0	0.0	0.0	0.0	0.0	0.0	0.0	0.0	0.0	0.0	0.0	0.7	0.7	15.7
95	LEWIS, DARYLL	DB	HOU	19	12	7	0	0	0	0	0	0	0	0	0	0	0	0	0	0	1	1	16
94				5	0	5	0	0	0	0	0	0	0	0	0	0	0	0	0	0	0	0	16
93				13	12	1	0	0	0	0	0	0	0	0	0	0	0	0	0	0	1	1	4
				12.3	8.0	4.3	0.0	0.0	0.0	0.0	0.0	0.0	0.0	0.0	0.0	0.0	0.0	0.0	0.0	0.0	0.7	0.7	12.0

YR	PLAYER	POS	TM	FAN PTS	DIST PTS	PERF PTS	PASSING TD: 0-9	10-39	40+	RUSHING TD: 0-9	10-39	40+	RECEIVING TD: 0-9	10-39	40+	FIELD GOALS: 0-9	10-39	40+	50+	PAT	D,ST TDS	TDS	TOT TDS	GAM
95	VINCENT, TROY	DB	MIA	17	12	5	0	0	0	0	0	0	0	0	0	0	0	0	0	0	1	1	16
94				17	12	5	0	0	0	0	0	0	0	0	0	0	0	0	0	0	1	1	13
93				2	0	2	0	0	0	0	0	0	0	0	0	0	0	0	0	0	0	0	13
				12.0	8.0	4.0	0.0	0.0	0.0	0.0	0.0	0.0	0.0	0.0	0.0	0.0	0.0	0.0	0.0	0.0	0.7	0.7	14.0
95	WASHINGTON, BRIAN	DB	NYJ	16	12	4	0	0	0	0	0	0	0	0	0	0	0	0	0	0	1	1	16
94				2	0	2	0	0	0	0	0	0	0	0	0	0	0	0	0	0	0	0	14
93				18	12	6	0	0	0	0	0	0	0	0	0	0	0	0	0	0	1	1	16
				12.0	8.0	4.0	0.0	0.0	0.0	0.0	0.0	0.0	0.0	0.0	0.0	0.0	0.0	0.0	0.0	0.0	0.7	0.7	15.3
95	LYNCH, LORENZO	DB	AZ	15	12	3	0	0	0	0	0	0	0	0	0	0	0	0	0	0	1	1	13
94				2	0	2	0	0	0	0	0	0	0	0	0	0	0	0	0	0	0	0	15
93				16	12	4	0	0	0	0	0	0	0	0	0	0	0	0	0	0	1	1	15
				11.0	8.0	3.0	0.0	0.0	0.0	0.0	0.0	0.0	0.0	0.0	0.0	0.0	0.0	0.0	0.0	0.0	0.7	0.7	14.3
95	HARMON, ANDY	DB	PHI	11	0	11	0	0	0	0	0	0	0	0	0	0	0	0	0	0	0	0	15
94				10	0	10	0	0	0	0	0	0	0	0	0	0	0	0	0	0	0	0	15
93				11	0	11	0	0	0	0	0	0	0	0	0	0	0	0	0	0	0	0	15
				10.7	0.0	10.7	0.0	0.0	0.0	0.0	0.0	0.0	0.0	0.0	0.0	0.0	0.0	0.0	0.0	0.0	0.0	0.0	15.0
95	BROWN, LARRY	DB	DAL	27	21	6	0	0	0	0	0	0	0	0	0	0	0	0	0	0	2	2	16
94				4	0	4	0	0	0	0	0	0	0	0	0	0	0	0	0	0	0	0	13
93				0	0	0	0	0	0	0	0	0	0	0	0	0	0	0	0	0	0	0	15
				10.3	7.0	3.3	0.0	0.0	0.0	0.0	0.0	0.0	0.0	0.0	0.0	0.0	0.0	0.0	0.0	0.0	0.7	0.7	14.7
95	ZORDICH, MIKE	DB	PHI	16	12	4	0	0	0	0	0	0	0	0	0	0	0	0	0	0	1	1	15
94			AZ	14	9	5	0	0	0	0	0	0	0	0	0	0	0	0	0	0	1	1	15
93				1	0	1	0	0	0	0	0	0	0	0	0	0	0	0	0	0	0	0	10
				10.3	7.0	3.3	0.0	0.0	0.0	0.0	0.0	0.0	0.0	0.0	0.0	0.0	0.0	0.0	0.0	0.0	0.7	0.7	13.3
95	REYNOLDS, RICKY	DB	NE	7	0	7	0	0	0	0	0	0	0	0	0	0	0	0	0	0	0	0	16
94			TB	21	18	3	0	0	0	0	0	0	0	0	0	0	0	0	0	0	2	2	14
93				2	0	2	0	0	0	0	0	0	0	0	0	0	0	0	0	0	0	0	14
				10.0	6.0	4.0	0.0	0.0	0.0	0.0	0.0	0.0	0.0	0.0	0.0	0.0	0.0	0.0	0.0	0.0	0.7	0.7	14.7

YR	PLAYER	POS	TM	FAN PTS	DIST PTS	PERF PTS	PASSING TD: 0-9	10-39	40+	RUSHING TD: 0-9	10-39	40+	RECEIVING TD: 0-9	10-39	40+	FIELD GOALS: 0-9	10-39	40-49	50+	PAT	D,ST TDS	TOT TDS	GAM
95	GLENN, VENCIE	DB	NYG	19	12	7	0	0	0	0	0	0	0	0	0	0	0	0	0	0	1	1	15
94			MIN	5	0	5	0	0	0	0	0	0	0	0	0	0	0	0	0	0	0	0	16
93				5	0	5	0	0	0	0	0	0	0	0	0	0	0	0	0	0	0	0	15
				9.7	4.0	5.7	0.0	0.0	0.0	0.0	0.0	0.0	0.0	0.0	0.0	0.0	0.0	0.0	0.0	0.0	0.3	0.3	15.3
95	SMITH, OTIS	DB	PHI	18	12	6	0	0	0	0	0	0	0	0	0	0	0	0	0	0	1	1	11
94				1	0	1	0	0	0	0	0	0	0	0	0	0	0	0	0	0	0	0	13
				9.5	6.0	3.5	0.0	0.0	0.0	0.0	0.0	0.0	0.0	0.0	0.0	0.0	0.0	0.0	0.0	0.0	0.5	0.5	12.0
95	SMITH, NEIL	DL	KC	14	0	14	0	0	0	0	0	0	0	0	0	0	0	0	0	0	0	0	16
94				13	0	13	0	0	0	0	0	0	0	0	0	0	0	0	0	0	0	0	14
93				16	0	16	0	0	0	0	0	0	0	0	0	0	0	0	0	0	0	0	15
				14.3	0.0	14.3	0.0	0.0	0.0	0.0	0.0	0.0	0.0	0.0	0.0	0.0	0.0	0.0	0.0	0.0	0.0	0.0	15.0
95	JONES, SEAN	DL	GB	17	6	11	0	0	0	0	0	0	0	0	0	0	0	0	0	0	1	1	16
94				9	0	9	0	0	0	0	0	0	0	0	0	0	0	0	0	0	0	0	16
93			HOU	13	0	13	0	0	0	0	0	0	0	0	0	0	0	0	0	0	0	0	16
				13.0	2.0	11.0	0.0	0.0	0.0	0.0	0.0	0.0	0.0	0.0	0.0	0.0	0.0	0.0	0.0	0.0	0.3	0.3	16.0
95	ONEAL, LESLIE	DL	SD	14	0	14	0	0	0	0	0	0	0	0	0	0	0	0	0	0	0	0	16
94				12	0	12	0	0	0	0	0	0	0	0	0	0	0	0	0	0	0	0	16
93				12	0	12	0	0	0	0	0	0	0	0	0	0	0	0	0	0	0	0	16
				12.7	0.0	12.7	0.0	0.0	0.0	0.0	0.0	0.0	0.0	0.0	0.0	0.0	0.0	0.0	0.0	0.0	0.0	0.0	16.0
95	DOUGLAS, HUGH	DL	NYJ	12	0	12	0	0	0	0	0	0	0	0	0	0	0	0	0	0	0	0	15
95	FLANIGAN, JIM	DL	CHI	12	0	12	0	0	0	0	0	0	2	0	0	0	0	0	0	0	0	2	16
95	WHITE, REGGIE	DL	GB	14	0	14	0	0	0	0	0	0	0	0	0	0	0	0	0	0	0	0	15
94				9	0	9	0	0	0	0	0	0	0	0	0	0	0	0	0	0	0	0	15
93				13	0	13	0	0	0	0	0	0	0	0	0	0	0	0	0	0	0	0	16
				12.0	0.0	12.0	0.0	0.0	0.0	0.0	0.0	0.0	0.0	0.0	0.0	0.0	0.0	0.0	0.0	0.0	0.0	0.0	15.3
95	RANDLE, JOHN	DL	MIN	10	0	10	0	0	0	0	0	0	0	0	0	0	0	0	0	0	0	0	16
94				13	0	13	0	0	0	0	0	0	0	0	0	0	0	0	0	0	0	0	16
93				12	0	12	0	0	0	0	0	0	0	0	0	0	0	0	0	0	0	0	15
				11.7	0.0	11.7	0.0	0.0	0.0	0.0	0.0	0.0	0.0	0.0	0.0	0.0	0.0	0.0	0.0	0.0	0.0	0.0	15.7

YR	PLAYER	POS	TM	FAN PTS	DIST PTS	PERF PTS	PASSING TD: 0-9	10-39	40+	RUSHING TD: 0-9	10-39	40+	RECEIVING TD: 0-9	10-39	40+	FIELD GOALS: 10-39	40-49	50+	PAT	D,ST TDS	TOT TDS	GAM
95	SMITH, BRUCE	DL	BUF	12	0	12	0	0	0	0	0	0	0	0	0	0	0	0	0	0	0	15
94				9	0	9	0	0	0	0	0	0	0	0	0	0	0	0	0	0	0	15
93				14	0	14	0	0	0	0	0	0	0	0	0	0	0	0	0	0	0	16
				11.7	0.0	11.7	0.0	0.0	0.0	0.0	0.0	0.0	0.0	0.0	0.0	0.0	0.0	0.0	0.0	0.0	0.0	15.3
95	CARTER, KEVIN	DL	RAM	11	0	11	0	0	0	0	0	0	0	0	0	0	0	0	0	1	1	16
95	DOLEMAN, CHRIS	DL	ATL	12	0	12	0	0	0	0	0	0	0	0	0	0	0	0	0	0	0	16
94				8	0	8	0	0	0	0	0	0	0	0	0	0	0	0	0	0	0	14
93				13	0	13	0	0	0	0	0	0	0	0	0	0	0	0	0	0	0	16
				11.0	0.0	11.0	0.0	0.0	0.0	0.0	0.0	0.0	0.0	0.0	0.0	0.0	0.0	0.0	0.0	0.0	0.0	15.3
95	FULLER, WILLIAM	DL	PHI	13	0	13	0	0	0	0	0	0	0	0	0	0	0	0	0	0	0	14
94				10	0	10	0	0	0	0	0	0	0	0	0	0	0	0	0	0	0	16
93				10	0	10	0	0	0	0	0	0	0	0	0	0	0	0	0	0	0	13
				11.0	0.0	11.0	0.0	0.0	0.0	0.0	0.0	0.0	0.0	0.0	0.0	0.0	0.0	0.0	0.0	0.0	0.0	14.3
95	SIMMONS, CLYDE	DL	AZ	21	9	12	0	0	0	0	0	0	0	0	0	0	0	0	0	1	1	16
94				6	0	6	0	0	0	0	0	0	0	0	0	0	0	0	0	0	0	16
93				6	0	6	0	0	0	0	0	0	0	0	0	0	0	0	0	0	0	16
				11.0	3.0	8.0	0.0	0.0	0.0	0.0	0.0	0.0	0.0	0.0	0.0	0.0	0.0	0.0	0.0	0.3	0.3	16.0
95	SEALS, RAY	DL	PIT	10	0	10	0	0	0	0	0	0	0	0	0	0	0	0	0	0	0	16
94				7	0	7	0	0	0	0	0	0	0	0	0	0	0	0	0	0	0	13
93			TB	15	6	9	0	0	0	0	0	0	0	0	0	0	0	0	0	1	1	14
				10.7	2.0	8.7	0.0	0.0	0.0	0.0	0.0	0.0	0.0	0.0	0.0	0.0	0.0	0.0	0.0	0.3	0.3	14.3
95	SMITH, CHUCK	DL	ATL	8	0	8	0	0	0	0	0	0	0	0	0	0	0	0	0	0	0	14
94				21	9	12	0	0	0	0	0	0	0	0	0	0	0	0	0	1	1	12
93				3	0	3	0	0	0	0	0	0	0	0	0	0	0	0	0	0	0	12
				10.7	3.0	7.7	0.0	0.0	0.0	0.0	0.0	0.0	0.0	0.0	0.0	0.0	0.0	0.0	0.0	0.3	0.3	12.7
95	TOLBERT, TONY	DL	DAL	7	0	7	0	0	0	0	0	0	0	0	0	0	0	0	0	0	0	16
94				18	12	6	0	0	0	0	0	0	0	0	0	0	0	0	0	1	1	16
93				7	0	7	0	0	0	0	0	0	0	0	0	0	0	0	0	0	0	16
				10.7	4.0	6.7	0.0	0.0	0.0	0.0	0.0	0.0	0.0	0.0	0.0	0.0	0.0	0.0	0.0	0.3	0.3	16.0

YR	PLAYER	POS	TM	FAN PTS	DIST PTS	PERF PTS	PASSING TD: 0-9	10-39	40+	RUSHING TD: 0-9	10-39	40+	RECEIVING TD: 0-9	10-39	40+	FIELD GOALS: 10-39	40-49	50+	PAT	D,ST TDS	TOT TDS	GAM
95	BUCKNER, BRENSTON	DL	PIT	18	12	6	0	0	0	0	0	0	0	0	0	0	0	0	0	1	1	16
94				2	0	2	0	0	0	0	0	0	0	0	0	0	0	0	0	0	0	7
				10.0	6.0	4.0	0.0	0.0	0.0	0.0	0.0	0.0	0.0	0.0	0.0	0.0	0.0	0.0	0.0	0.5	0.5	11.5
95	MARTIN, WAYNE	DL	NO	15	0	15	0	0	0	0	0	0	0	0	0	0	0	0	0	0	0	16
94				10	0	10	0	0	0	0	0	0	0	0	0	0	0	0	0	0	0	16
93				5	0	5	0	0	0	0	0	0	0	0	0	0	0	0	0	0	0	15
				10.0	0.0	10.0	0.0	0.0	0.0	0.0	0.0	0.0	0.0	0.0	0.0	0.0	0.0	0.0	0.0	0.0	0.0	15.7
95	SAPP, WARREN	DL	TB	10	6	4	0	0	0	0	0	0	0	0	0	0	0	0	0	1	1	16
95	THOMAS, HENRY	DL	DET	14	0	14	0	0	0	0	0	0	0	0	0	0	0	0	0	0	0	16
94			MIN	6	0	6	0	0	0	0	0	0	0	0	0	0	0	0	0	0	0	15
93				9	0	9	0	0	0	0	0	0	0	0	0	0	0	0	0	0	0	13
				9.7	0.0	9.7	0.0	0.0	0.0	0.0	0.0	0.0	0.0	0.0	0.0	0.0	0.0	0.0	0.0	0.0	0.0	14.7
95	CROSS, JEFF	DL	MIA	8	0	8	0	0	0	0	0	0	0	0	0	0	0	0	0	0	0	16
94				10	0	10	0	0	0	0	0	0	0	0	0	0	0	0	0	0	0	10
93				10	0	10	0	0	0	0	0	0	0	0	0	0	0	0	0	0	0	16
				9.3	0.0	9.3	0.0	0.0	0.0	0.0	0.0	0.0	0.0	0.0	0.0	0.0	0.0	0.0	0.0	0.0	0.0	14.0
95	BUTNETT, ROB	DL	CLE	10	0	10	0	0	0	0	0	0	0	0	0	0	0	0	0	0	0	16
94				8	0	8	0	0	0	0	0	0	0	0	0	0	0	0	0	0	0	16
93				9	0	9	0	0	0	0	0	0	0	0	0	0	0	0	0	0	0	15
				9.0	0.0	9.0	0.0	0.0	0.0	0.0	0.0	0.0	0.0	0.0	0.0	0.0	0.0	0.0	0.0	0.0	0.0	15.7
95	COOK, ANTHONY	DL	GB	9	0	9	0	0	0	0	0	0	0	0	0	0	0	0	0	1	1	11
95	MCGLOCKTON, CHESTER	DL	RAI	10	0	10	0	0	0	0	0	0	0	0	0	0	0	0	0	0	0	16
94				9	0	9	0	0	0	0	0	0	0	0	0	0	0	0	0	0	0	15
93				8	0	8	0	0	0	0	0	0	0	0	0	0	0	0	0	0	0	15
				9.0	0.0	9.0	0.0	0.0	0.0	0.0	0.0	0.0	0.0	0.0	0.0	0.0	0.0	0.0	0.0	0.0	0.0	15.3
95	EDWARDS, ANTONIO	DL	SEA	20	12	8	0	0	0	0	0	0	0	0	0	0	0	0	0	1	1	13
94				2	0	2	0	0	0	0	0	0	0	0	0	0	0	0	0	0	0	14
93				3	0	3	0	0	0	0	0	0	0	0	0	0	0	0	0	0	0	5
				8.3	4.0	4.3	0.0	0.0	0.0	0.0	0.0	0.0	0.0	0.0	0.0	0.0	0.0	0.0	0.0	0.3	0.3	10.7

YR	PLAYER	POS	TM	FAN PTS	DIST PTS	PERF PTS	PASSING TD: 0-9	10-39	40+	RUSHING TD: 0-9	10-39	40+	RECEIVING TD: 0-9	10-39	40+	FIELD GOALS: 0-9	10-39	40-49	50+	PAT	D,ST TDS	TOT TDS	GAM
	SWANN, ERIC	DL	AZ																				
95				11	0	11	0	0	0	0	0	0	0	0	0	0	0	0	0	0	0	0	12
94				11	4	7	0	0	0	0	0	0	0	0	0	0	0	0	0	0	0	0	15
93				3	0	3	0	0	0	0	0	0	0	0	0	0	0	0	0	0	0	0	9
				8.3	1.3	7.0	0.0	0.0	0.0	0.0	0.0	0.0	0.0	0.0	0.0	0.0	0.0	0.0	0.0	0.0	0.0	0.0	12.0

C.34

Appendix D—Final '95 Fantasy Rankings

Presented in this section are tables presenting the *Top 310* NFL players of the 1995 season based upon standard FFL scoring.

The tables include the following statistics—

Ranking (R)
Position (POS)
Team (TM)
Total Fantasy Points (FAN PTS)
Distance Points (DIST PTS)
Performance Points (PERF PTS)
Passing Touchdowns (0-9, 10-39, and 40+ YDS)
Rushing Touchdowns (0-9, 10-39, and 40+ YDS)
Receiving Touchdowns (0-9, 10-39, and 40+ YDS)
Field Goals (1-39, 40-49, and 50+ YDS)
Points after Touchdown (PAT)
Defense & Special Team Touchdowns (D,ST TDS)
Total Touchdowns (TOT TDS) ★

R	PLAYER	POS	TM	FAN PTS	DIST PTS	PERF PTS	PASSING TD: 0-9	10-39	40+	RUSHING TD: 0-9	10-39	40+	RECEIVING TD: 0-9	10-39	40+	FIELD GOALS: 0-39	40-49	50+	PAT	D,ST TDS	TOT TDS
1	FAVRE, BRETT	QB	GB	429	354	75	15	18	5	2	1	0	0	0	0	0	0	0	0	0	41
2	MITCHELL, SCOTT	QB	DET	396	330	66	7	20	5	4	0	0	0	0	0	0	0	0	0	0	36
3	RICE, JERRY	WR	SF	325	186	139	0	0	1	0	1	0	4	6	5	0	0	0	0	1	17
4	SMITH, EMMITT	RB	DAL	314	174	140	0	0	0	18	6	1	0	0	0	0	0	0	0	0	25
5	MOON, WARREN	QB	MIN	303	267	36	16	11	6	0	0	0	0	0	0	0	0	0	0	0	33
6	ELWAY, JOHN	QB	DEN	296	243	53	9	9	8	0	0	1	0	0	0	0	0	0	0	0	27
7	KRAMER, ERIK	QB	CHI	290	261	29	12	9	8	0	0	0	0	0	0	0	0	0	0	0	30
8	GEORGE, JEFF	QB	ATL	268	210	58	7	12	5	0	0	0	0	0	0	0	0	0	0	0	24
9	BLAKE, JEFF	QB	CIN	257	255	2	13	9	6	2	0	0	0	0	0	0	0	0	0	0	30
10	MOORE, HERMAN	WR	DET	256	132	124	0	0	0	0	0	0	1	10	3	0	0	0	0	0	14
11	YOUNG, STEVE	QB	SF	256	198	58	8	10	2	3	0	0	0	0	0	0	0	0	0	0	23
12	BONO, STEVE	QB	KC	245	243	2	9	9	3	4	0	1	0	0	0	0	0	0	0	0	26
13	BRUCE, ISAAC	WR	RAM	244	111	133	0	0	0	0	0	0	4	7	2	0	0	0	0	0	13
14	EVERETT, JIM	QB	NO	244	213	31	11	11	4	0	0	0	0	0	0	0	0	0	0	0	26
15	MARINO, DAN	QB	MIA	237	186	51	13	8	3	0	0	0	0	0	0	0	0	0	0	0	24
16	BROOKS, ROBERT	WR	GB	235	123	112	0	0	0	0	0	0	3	5	5	0	0	0	0	0	13
17	MARTIN, CURTIS	RB	NE	226	105	121	0	0	0	13	1	0	0	1	0	0	0	0	0	0	15
18	WARREN, CHRIS	RB	SEA	217	126	91	0	0	0	9	6	0	0	1	0	0	0	0	0	0	16
19	SANDERS, BARRY	RB	DET	212	108	104	0	0	0	5	2	4	1	0	0	0	0	0	0	0	12
20	IRVIN, MICHAEL	WR	DAL	207	87	120	0	0	0	0	0	0	3	5	2	0	0	0	0	0	10
21	KELLY, JIM	QB	BUF	199	204	-5	3	14	5	0	0	0	0	0	0	0	0	0	0	0	22
22	CARTER, CRIS	WR	MIN	196	132	64	0	0	0	0	0	0	8	8	1	0	0	0	0	0	17
23	ODONNELL, NEIL	QB	PIT	195	147	48	5	9	3	0	0	0	0	0	0	0	0	0	0	0	17
24	PICKENS, CARL	WR	CIN	188	135	53	0	0	0	0	0	0	9	5	3	0	0	0	0	0	17
25	ANDERSEN, MORTEN	K	ATL	184	184	0	0	0	0	0	0	0	0	0	0	20	3	8	29	0	0
26	PERRIMAN, BRETT	WR	DET	181	81	100	0	0	0	0	0	0	2	5	2	0	0	0	0	0	9
27	ELAM, JASON	K	DEN	177	177	0	0	0	0	0	0	0	0	0	0	21	5	5	39	0	0
28	TESTAVERDE, VINNY	QB	CLE	177	165	12	5	11	1	2	0	0	0	0	0	0	0	0	0	0	19
29	HUMPHRIES, STAN	QB	SD	176	159	17	4	11	2	1	0	0	0	0	0	0	0	0	0	0	18
30	MILLER, ANTHONY	WR	DEN	176	138	38	0	0	0	0	0	0	2	6	6	0	0	0	0	0	14
31	BROWN, TIM	WR	RAI	175	93	82	0	0	0	0	0	0	3	3	4	0	0	0	0	0	10

				FAN	DIST	PERF	PASSING TD:			RUSHING TD:			RECEIVING TD:			FIELD GOALS:					D,ST	TOT
R	PLAYER	POS	TM	PTS	PTS	PTS	0-9	10-39	40+	0-9	10-39	40+	0-9	10-39	40+	0-9	10-39	40-49	50+	PAT	TDS	TDS
32	CHANDLER, CHRIS	QB	HOU	174	174	0	5	8	4	2	0	0	0	0	0	0	0	0	0	0	0	19
33	BRUNELL, MARK	QB	JAX	171	168	3	7	8	0	3	1	0	0	0	0	0	0	0	0	0	0	19
34	AIKMAN, TROY	QB	DAL	164	147	17	6	7	3	1	0	0	0	0	0	0	0	0	0	0	0	17
35	JOHNSON, NORM	K	PIT	164	164	0	0	0	0	0	0	0	0	0	0	25	8	1	0	39	0	0
36	KANSAS CITY	DT	KC	158	78	80	0	0	0	0	0	0	0	0	0	0	0	0	0	0	7	7
37	SAN FRANCISCO	DT	SF	158	84	74	0	0	0	0	0	0	0	0	0	0	0	0	0	0	8	8
38	DEL GRECO, AL	K	HOU	155	155	0	0	0	0	0	0	0	0	0	0	14	10	3	0	33	0	0
39	FAULK, MARSHALL	RB	IND	155	126	29	0	0	0	7	4	0	1	2	0	0	0	0	0	0	0	14
40	CONWAY, CURTIS	WR	CHI	151	117	34	0	0	0	0	0	0	3	3	6	0	0	0	0	0	0	12
41	HANSON, JASON	K	DET	149	149	0	0	0	0	0	0	0	0	0	0	22	5	1	0	48	0	0
42	HARBAUGH, JIM	QB	IND	149	168	-19	5	10	2	2	0	0	0	0	0	0	0	0	0	0	0	19
43	GALLOWAY, JOEY	WR	SEA	148	105	43	0	0	0	0	0	0	1	3	3	0	0	0	0	0	1	8
44	PELFREY, DOUG	K	CIN	148	148	0	0	0	0	0	0	0	0	0	0	18	10	1	0	34	0	0
45	PHILADELPHIA	DT	PHI	147	60	87	0	0	0	0	0	0	0	0	0	0	0	0	0	0	6	6
46	REVEIZ, FUAD	K	MIN	147	147	0	0	0	0	0	0	0	0	0	0	16	9	1	0	44	0	0
47	CHRISTIE, STEVE	K	BUF	146	146	0	0	0	0	0	0	0	0	0	0	26	3	2	0	33	0	0
48	BENNETT, EDGAR	RB	GB	144	87	57	0	0	0	2	1	0	1	3	0	0	0	0	0	0	0	7
49	STOYANOVICH, PETE	K	MIA	144	144	0	0	0	0	0	0	0	0	0	0	19	6	2	0	37	0	0
50	COLLINS, KERRY	QB	CAR	142	156	-14	6	4	4	3	0	0	0	0	0	0	0	0	0	0	0	17
51	PITTSBURGH	DT	PIT	140	63	77	0	0	0	0	0	0	0	8	3	0	0	0	0	0	6	6
52	BROOKS, BILL	WR	BUF	138	108	30	0	0	0	0	0	0	0	4	0	0	0	0	0	0	0	11
53	HARMON, RONNIE	RB	SD	138	96	42	0	0	0	0	0	1	1	4	0	0	0	0	0	0	0	6
54	MINNESOTA	DT	MIN	135	51	84	0	0	0	0	0	0	0	0	0	0	0	0	0	0	5	5
55	BONIOL, CHRIS	K	DAL	133	133	0	0	0	0	0	0	0	0	0	0	24	3	0	0	46	0	0
56	MURRAY, EDDIE	K	WAS	133	133	0	0	0	0	0	0	0	0	0	0	20	6	1	0	33	0	0
57	LA RAIDERS	DT	RAI	133	54	79	0	0	0	0	0	0	0	0	0	0	0	0	0	0	6	6
58	ARIZONA	DT	AZ	132	60	72	0	0	0	0	0	0	0	0	0	0	0	0	0	0	6	6
59	WATTERS, RICKY	RB	PHI	132	78	54	0	0	0	11	0	0	1	0	0	0	0	0	0	0	0	12
60	JACKE, CHRIS	K	GB	131	131	0	0	0	0	0	0	0	0	0	0	6	8	3	0	43	0	0
61	MILLER, CHRIS	QB	RAM	131	147	-16	7	9	2	0	0	0	0	0	0	0	0	0	0	0	0	18
62	GRBAC, ELVIS	QB	SF	130	99	31	2	3	3	2	0	0	0	0	0	0	0	0	0	0	0	10

R	PLAYER	POS	TM	FAN PTS	DIST PTS	PERF PTS	PASSING TD: 0-9	10-39	40+	RUSHING TD: 0-9	10-39	40+	RECEIVING TD: 0-9	10-39	40+	FIELD GOALS: 10-39	40-49	50+	PAT	D,ST TDS	TOT TDS
63	KASAY, JOHN	K	CAR	130	130	0	0	0	0	0	0	0	0	0	0	16	9	1	27	0	0
64	SAN DIEGO	DT	SD	130	63	67	0	0	0	0	0	0	0	0	0	0	0	0	0	6	6
65	METCALF, ERIC	WR	ATL	129	105	24	0	0	0	0	1	0	2	3	3	0	0	0	0	1	9
66	DAVIS, GREG	K	AZ	128	128	0	0	0	0	0	0	0	0	0	0	23	6	1	19	0	0
67	LOVILLE, DEREK	RB	SF	128	102	26	0	0	0	10	0	0	2	1	0	0	0	0	0	0	13
68	STOVER, MATT	K	CLE	127	127	0	0	0	0	0	0	0	0	0	0	22	7	0	26	0	0
69	PETERSON, TODD	K	SEA	125	125	0	0	0	0	0	0	0	0	0	0	15	8	0	40	0	0
70	ST. LOUIS	DT	RAM	124	0	124	0	0	0	0	0	0	0	0	0	0	0	0	0	5	5
71	BAHR, MATT	K	NE	120	120	0	0	0	0	0	0	0	0	0	0	16	5	2	27	0	0
72	ELLIOTT, LIN	K	KC	120	120	0	0	0	0	0	0	0	0	0	0	17	7	0	34	0	0
73	KIRBY, TERRY	RB	MIA	120	93	27	0	0	0	3	1	0	1	2	0	0	0	0	0	0	8
74	NY JETS	DT	NYJ	120	39	81	0	0	0	0	0	0	0	0	0	0	0	0	0	4	4
75	KRIEG, DAVE	QB	AZ	119	123	-4	7	9	0	0	0	0	0	0	0	0	0	0	0	0	16
76	BUTLER, KEVIN	K	CHI	118	118	0	0	0	0	0	0	0	0	0	0	21	2	0	45	0	0
77	CENTERS, LARRY	RB	AZ	118	48	70	0	0	0	2	0	0	0	2	0	0	0	0	0	0	4
78	NY GIANTS	DT	NYG	118	54	64	0	0	0	0	0	0	0	0	0	0	0	0	0	5	5
79	ALLEN, TERRY	RB	WAS	117	72	45	0	0	0	10	0	0	1	0	0	0	0	0	0	0	11
80	GRAHAM, JEFF	WR	CHI	117	39	78	0	0	0	0	0	0	1	1	2	0	0	0	0	0	4
81	HOUSTON	DT	HOU	116	45	71	0	0	0	0	0	0	0	0	0	0	0	0	0	4	4
82	MATHIS, TERANCE	WR	ATL	115	81	34	0	0	0	0	0	0	1	7	1	0	0	0	0	0	9
83	PARMALEE, BERNIE	RB	MIA	115	78	37	0	0	0	7	2	0	0	1	0	0	0	0	0	0	10
84	RHETT, ERRICT	RB	TB	115	72	43	0	0	0	9	2	0	0	0	0	0	0	0	0	0	11
85	ANDERSON, GARY	K	PHI	114	114	0	0	0	0	0	0	0	0	0	0	14	8	0	32	0	0
86	HUSTED, MICHAEL	K	TB	113	113	0	0	0	0	0	0	0	0	0	0	11	5	3	25	0	0
87	THOMAS, THURMAN	RB	BUF	113	69	44	0	0	0	5	1	0	1	1	0	0	0	0	0	0	8
88	CAROLINA	DT	CAR	112	39	73	0	0	0	0	0	0	0	0	0	0	0	0	0	4	4
89	BRIEN, DOUG	K	NO	111	111	0	0	0	0	0	0	0	0	0	0	12	6	1	35	0	0
90	DAVIS, TERRELL	RB	DEN	111	60	51	0	0	0	6	0	1	1	0	0	0	0	0	0	0	8
91	MARTIN, TONY	WR	SD	111	57	54	0	0	0	0	0	0	1	3	2	0	0	0	0	0	6
92	SALAAM, RASHAAN	RB	CHI	111	63	48	0	0	0	9	1	0	0	0	0	0	0	0	0	0	10
93	SANDERS, CHRIS	WR	HOU	111	87	24	0	0	0	0	0	0	2	3	4	0	0	0	0	0	9

R	PLAYER	POS	TM	FAN PTS	DIST PTS	PERF PTS	PASSING TD 0-9	PASSING TD 10-39	PASSING TD 40+	RUSHING TD 0-9	RUSHING TD 10-39	RUSHING TD 40+	RECEIVING TD 0-9	RECEIVING TD 10-39	RECEIVING TD 40+	FG 10-39	FG 40-49	FG 50+	PAT	D,ST TDS	TOT TDS
94	WILLIAMS, HARVEY	RB	RAI	111	75	36	0	1	0	8	1	0	0	0	0	0	0	0	0	0	10
95	ESIASON, BOOMER	QB	NYJ	110	126	-16	8	6	2	0	0	0	0	0	0	0	0	0	0	0	16
96	GREEN, WILLIE	WR	CAR	110	60	50	0	0	0	0	0	0	3	0	3	0	0	0	0	0	6
97	HOLLIS, MIKE	K	JAX	109	109	0	0	0	0	0	0	0	0	0	0	14	4	2	27	0	0
98	FREROTTE, GUS	QB	WAS	108	120	-12	6	4	3	1	0	0	0	0	0	0	0	0	0	0	14
99	JACKSON, MICHAEL	WR	CLE	107	81	26	0	4	0	0	0	0	1	2	0	0	0	0	0	0	9
100	BROWN, DAVE	QB	NYG	106	150	-44	4	4	3	3	1	0	0	0	0	0	0	0	0	0	15
101	DALUISO, BRAD	K	NYG	106	106	0	0	0	0	0	0	0	0	0	0	16	2	2	28	0	0
102	REED, JAKE	WR	MIN	106	72	34	0	0	0	0	0	0	5	2	0	0	0	0	0	0	9
103	ATLANTA	DT	ATL	105	45	60	0	0	0	0	0	0	0	0	0	0	0	0	0	4	4
104	BUFFALO	DT	BUF	104	27	77	0	0	0	0	0	0	0	0	0	0	0	0	0	3	3
105	EARLY, QUINN	WR	NO	104	78	26	0	0	0	0	0	0	1	4	3	0	0	0	0	0	8
106	BLANCHARD, CARY	K	IND	103	103	0	0	0	0	0	0	0	0	0	0	11	7	1	25	0	0
107	HEYWARD, CRAIG	RB	ATL	103	60	43	0	0	0	6	0	0	2	0	0	0	0	0	0	0	8
108	WASHINGTON	DT	WAS	103	36	67	0	0	0	0	0	0	0	0	0	0	0	0	0	4	4
109	CARNEY, JOHN	K	SD	101	101	0	0	0	0	0	0	0	0	0	0	18	3	0	32	0	0
110	DALLAS	DT	DAL	99	39	60	0	0	0	0	0	0	0	0	0	0	0	0	0	4	4
111	BLEDSOE, DREW	QB	NE	98	99	-1	7	5	1	0	0	0	0	0	0	0	0	0	0	0	13
112	LOWERY, NICK	K	NYJ	95	95	0	0	0	0	0	0	0	0	0	0	12	3	2	24	0	0
113	DETROIT	DT	DET	94	12	82	0	0	0	0	0	0	0	0	0	0	0	0	0	1	1
114	THIGPEN, YANCEY	WR	PIT	94	45	49	0	0	0	0	0	0	1	3	1	0	0	0	0	0	5
115	MIRER, RICK	QB	SEA	93	144	-51	2	6	5	1	0	0	0	0	0	0	0	0	0	0	14
116	SEATTLE	DT	SEA	93	0	93	0	0	0	0	0	0	0	0	0	0	0	0	0	3	3
117	HOSTETLER, JEFF	QB	RAI	92	99	-7	6	3	3	0	0	0	0	0	0	0	0	0	0	0	12
118	FRYAR, IRVING	WR	MIA	91	69	22	0	0	0	0	0	0	3	3	2	0	0	0	0	0	8
119	INDIANAPOLIS	DT	IND	91	33	58	0	0	0	0	0	0	0	0	0	0	0	0	0	3	3
120	RYPIEN, MARK	QB	RAM	91	66	25	5	4	0	0	0	0	0	0	0	0	0	0	0	0	9
121	HAMPTON, RODNEY	RB	NYG	90	60	30	0	0	0	10	0	0	0	0	0	0	0	0	0	0	10
122	THOMAS, RODNEY	RB	HOU	86	66	20	0	0	0	4	0	0	1	1	1	0	0	0	0	0	7
123	NEW ENGLAND	DT	NE	84	21	63	0	0	0	0	0	0	0	0	0	0	0	0	0	2	2
124	NEW ORLEANS	DT	NO	84	12	72	0	0	0	0	0	0	0	0	0	0	0	0	0	1	1

R	PLAYER	POS	TM	FAN PTS	DIST PTS	PERF PTS	PASSING TD 0-9	10-39	40+	RUSHING TD 0-9	10-39	40+	RECEIVING TD 0-9	10-39	40+	FIELD GOALS 0-9	10-39	40-49	50+	PAT	D,ST TDS	TOT TDS
125	BATES, MARIO	RB	NO	83	51	32	0	0	0	5	1	1	0	0	0	0	0	0	0	0	0	7
126	CHICAGO	DT	CHI	83	15	68	0	0	0	0	0	0	0	0	0	0	0	0	0	0	2	2
127	CINCINNATI	DT	CIN	83	9	74	0	0	0	0	0	0	0	0	0	0	0	0	0	0	1	1
128	CLEVELAND	DT	CLE	83	30	53	0	0	0	0	0	0	0	0	0	0	0	0	0	0	3	3
129	ELLARD, HENRY	WR	WAS	83	51	32	0	0	0	0	0	0	3	2	0	0	0	0	0	0	0	5
130	MIA	DT	MIA	80	21	59	0	0	0	0	0	0	0	0	0	0	0	0	0	0	2	2
131	BLADES, BRIAN	WR	SEA	79	42	37	0	0	0	0	0	0	4	0	0	0	0	0	0	0	0	4
132	LEVENS, DORSEY	RB	GB	77	66	11	0	0	0	3	0	0	3	1	0	0	0	0	0	0	0	7
133	EMANUEL, BERT	WR	ATL	76	36	40	0	0	0	0	0	0	3	2	0	0	0	0	0	0	0	5
134	MORRIS, BYRON	RB	PIT	76	57	19	0	0	0	8	1	0	0	0	0	0	0	0	0	0	0	9
135	MOORE, ROB	WR	AZ	74	36	38	0	0	0	0	0	0	3	2	0	0	0	0	0	0	0	5
136	MORTON, JOHNNIE	WR	DET	73	63	10	0	0	0	0	0	0	3	5	0	0	0	0	0	0	0	8
137	TAMPA BAY	DT	TB	73	0	73	0	0	0	0	0	0	0	0	0	0	0	0	0	0	2	2
138	MILLS, ERNIE	WR	PIT	71	72	-1	0	0	0	0	0	0	2	4	2	0	0	0	0	0	0	8
139	CHMURA, MARK	TE	GB	70	48	22	0	0	0	0	0	0	5	2	0	0	0	0	0	0	0	7
140	JAEGER, JEFF	K	RAI	67	67	0	0	0	0	0	0	0	0	0	0	10	3	0	0	22	0	0
141	MURRELL, ADRIAN	RB	NYJ	67	42	25	0	0	0	1	0	0	1	1	0	0	0	0	0	0	0	3
142	DAVIS, WILLIE	WR	KC	66	51	15	0	0	0	0	0	0	0	3	2	0	0	0	0	0	0	5
143	JACKSONVILLE	DT	JAX	66	24	42	0	0	0	0	0	0	0	0	0	0	0	0	0	0	2	2
144	MEANS, NATRONE	RB	SD	65	33	32	0	0	0	4	1	0	0	0	0	0	0	0	0	0	0	5
145	WILKINS, JEFF	K	SF	65	65	0	0	0	0	0	0	0	0	0	0	11	1	0	0	27	0	0
146	BRISBY, VINCENT	WR	NE	64	27	37	0	0	0	0	0	0	1	1	1	0	0	0	0	0	0	3
147	CARRIER, MARK	WR	CAR	64	30	34	0	0	0	0	0	0	1	0	2	0	0	0	0	0	0	3
148	SCOTT, DARNAY	WR	CIN	63	51	12	0	0	0	0	0	0	1	1	3	0	0	0	0	0	0	5
149	DENVER	DT	DEN	62	12	50	0	0	0	0	0	0	0	0	0	0	0	0	0	0	1	1
150	SMITH, ROBERT	RB	MIN	62	39	23	0	0	0	3	1	0	0	0	0	0	0	0	0	0	1	5
151	CRAVER, AARON	RB	DEN	61	42	19	0	0	0	5	0	0	1	0	0	0	0	0	0	0	0	6
152	GREEN BAY	DT	GB	61	6	55	0	0	0	0	0	0	0	0	0	0	0	0	0	0	1	1
153	JEFFIRES, HAYWOOD	WR	HOU	60	60	0	0	0	0	0	0	0	4	4	0	0	0	0	0	0	0	8
154	MCDUFFIE, O.J.	WR	MIA	60	60	0	0	0	0	0	0	0	4	4	0	0	0	0	0	0	0	8
155	PEGRAM, ERRIC	RB	PIT	60	42	18	0	0	0	5	0	0	1	0	0	0	0	0	0	0	0	6

R	PLAYER	POS	TM	FAN PTS	DIST PTS	PERF PTS	PASSING TD 0-9	10-39	40+	RUSHING TD 0-9	10-39	40+	RECEIVING TD 0-9	10-39	40+	FIELD GOALS 0-39	40-49	50+	PAT	D,ST TDS	TOT TDS
156	BYNER, EARNEST	RB	CLE	59	42	17	0	0	0	2	0	0	1	1	0	0	0	0	0	0	4
157	LEE, AMP	RB	MIN	59	30	29	0	0	0	1	0	1	1	0	0	0	0	0	0	0	3
158	SHARPE, SHANNON	TE	DEN	58	27	31	0	0	0	0	0	0	3	1	0	0	0	0	0	0	4
159	SMALL, TORRANCE	WR	NO	58	57	1	0	0	0	0	0	0	4	1	0	0	0	0	0	0	6
160	GARNER, CHARLIE	RB	PHI	56	45	11	0	0	0	4	1	1	1	0	0	0	0	0	0	0	6
161	STEWART, KORDELL	QB	PIT	55	48	7	1	0	0	0	1	0	0	0	0	0	0	0	0	0	3
162	ALLEN, MARCUS	RB	KC	53	30	23	0	0	0	5	0	0	0	1	0	0	0	0	0	0	5
163	EVANS, VINCE	QB	RAI	51	60	-9	1	2	3	0	0	0	0	0	0	0	0	0	0	0	6
164	VANOVER, TAMARICK	WR	KC	51	51	0	0	0	0	0	0	0	0	0	0	0	0	0	0	3	2
165	MITCHELL, JOHNNY	TE	NYJ	50	42	8	0	0	0	0	0	0	2	2	1	0	0	0	0	0	5
166	MOORE, DERRICK	RB	CAR	50	30	20	0	0	0	3	0	0	1	0	0	0	0	0	0	0	4
167	RISON, ANDRE	WR	CLE	50	21	29	0	0	0	0	0	0	2	1	0	0	0	0	0	0	3
168	BARNETT, FRED	WR	PHI	49	36	13	0	0	0	0	0	0	3	2	0	0	0	0	0	0	5
169	BIASUCCI, DEAN	K	RAM	49	49	0	0	0	0	0	0	0	0	0	0	7	1	1	13	0	0
170	HEARST, GARRISON	RB	AZ	49	18	31	0	0	0	1	0	0	3	0	0	0	0	0	0	0	4
171	MCGEE, TONY	TE	CIN	49	30	19	0	0	0	0	0	0	1	2	0	0	0	0	0	0	3
172	STOKES, J.J.	WR	SF	49	39	10	0	0	0	0	0	0	2	2	0	0	0	0	0	0	4
173	COPELAND, HORACE	WR	TB	48	21	27	0	0	0	0	0	0	3	3	1	0	0	0	0	0	4
174	HOLMES, DARICK	RB	BUF	48	27	21	0	0	0	3	1	0	0	1	1	0	0	0	0	0	2
175	ISMAIL, QADRY	WR	MIN	48	36	12	0	0	0	0	0	0	0	1	1	0	0	0	0	0	4
176	JACKSON, WILLIE	WR	JAX	48	36	12	0	0	0	0	0	0	3	0	3	0	0	0	0	0	3
177	STRONG, MACK	RB	SEA	48	48	0	0	0	0	1	0	0	2	0	0	0	0	0	0	0	5
178	HOBERT, BILLY JOE	QB	RAI	47	54	-7	2	2	0	0	0	0	0	0	0	0	0	0	0	0	4
179	MCNAIR, TODD	RB	HOU	47	18	29	0	0	0	0	0	0	5	1	0	0	0	0	0	0	6
180	SHERRARD, MIKE	WR	NYG	47	36	11	0	0	0	0	0	0	0	0	1	0	0	0	0	0	1
181	DAWKINS, SEAN	WR	IND	46	24	22	0	0	0	0	0	0	1	2	1	0	0	0	0	0	4
182	ISMAIL, RAGHIB	WR	RAI	46	36	10	0	0	0	0	0	0	1	2	0	0	0	0	0	0	3
183	COATES, BEN	TE	NE	45	39	6	0	0	0	0	0	0	5	1	0	0	0	0	0	0	6
184	DAWSON, LAKE	WR	KC	45	45	0	0	0	0	0	0	0	1	3	1	0	0	0	0	0	5
185	DILGER, KEN	TE	IND	45	33	12	0	0	0	0	0	0	1	3	0	0	0	0	0	0	4
186	MITCHELL, BRIAN	RB	WAS	45	39	6	0	0	0	0	1	0	0	1	0	0	0	0	0	1	2

R	PLAYER	POS	TM	FAN PTS	DIST PTS	PERF PTS	PASSING TD 0-9	PASSING TD 10-39	PASSING TD 40+	RUSHING TD 0-9	RUSHING TD 10-39	RUSHING TD 40+	RECEIVING TD 0-9	RECEIVING TD 10-39	RECEIVING TD 40+	FG 0-39	FG 40-49	FG 50+	PAT	D,ST TDS	TOT TDS
187	FRIESZ, JOHN	QB	SEA	44	51	-7	2	3	1	0	0	0	0	0	0	0	0	0	0	0	6
188	KOSAR, BERNIE	QB	MIA	43	39	4	0	3	0	0	1	0	0	0	0	0	0	0	0	0	4
189	MCCARDELL, KEENAN	WR	CLE	43	33	10	0	0	0	0	0	0	1	3	0	0	0	0	0	0	4
190	MCLAUGHLIN, STEVE	K	RAM	43	43	0	0	0	0	0	0	0	0	0	0	7	1	0	17	0	0
191	SHEPERD, LESLIE	WR	WAS	43	30	13	0	0	0	1	0	0	0	0	1	0	0	0	0	0	3
192	JENNINGS, KEITH	TE	CHI	42	42	0	0	0	0	0	0	0	4	2	0	0	0	0	0	0	6
193	LOHMILLER, CHIP	K	NO	42	42	0	0	0	0	0	0	0	0	0	0	7	0	0	11	0	0
194	FENNER, DERRICK	RB	RAI	41	36	5	0	0	0	0	0	0	3	0	0	0	0	0	0	0	3
195	WILLIAMS, AENEAS	DB	AZ	41	33	8	0	0	0	0	0	0	0	0	0	0	0	0	0	3	0
196	BIENIEMY, ERIC	RB	CIN	40	18	22	0	0	0	3	0	0	0	0	0	0	0	0	0	0	3
197	BYARS, KEITH	RB	MIA	40	30	10	0	0	0	1	0	0	2	0	0	0	0	0	0	0	3
198	CALLOWAY, CHRIS	WR	NYG	40	30	10	0	0	0	0	0	0	1	2	0	0	0	0	0	0	3
199	HOBBS, DARYL	WR	RAI	40	27	13	0	0	0	0	0	0	0	1	1	0	0	0	0	0	3
200	PEETE, RODNEY	QB	PHI	40	75	-35	3	5	0	1	0	0	0	0	0	0	0	0	0	0	9
201	TURNER, FLOYD	WR	IND	40	36	4	0	0	0	0	0	0	1	2	1	0	0	0	0	0	4
202	WILLIAMS, KEVIN	WR	DAL	40	21	19	0	0	0	0	0	0	0	1	1	0	0	0	0	0	2
203	BAILEY, AARON	WR	IND	39	39	0	0	0	0	0	0	0	0	3	0	0	0	0	0	0	3
204	DRAYTON, TROY	TE	STL	39	30	9	0	0	0	0	0	0	2	2	0	0	0	0	0	0	4
205	SANDERS, FRANK	WR	AZ	39	15	24	0	0	0	0	0	0	1	1	0	0	0	0	0	0	2
206	ANDERS, KIMBLE	RB	KC	38	33	5	0	0	0	0	1	0	3	0	0	0	0	0	0	0	3
207	NOVACEK, JAY	TE	DAL	37	36	1	0	0	0	0	0	0	3	2	0	0	0	0	0	0	5
208	SEAY, MARK	WR	SD	37	24	13	0	0	0	0	0	0	1	1	0	0	0	0	0	0	3
209	FORD, COLE	K	RAI	36	36	0	0	0	0	0	0	0	0	0	0	7	0	0	15	0	0
210	MORGAN, ANTHONY	WR	GB	36	36	0	0	0	0	0	0	0	0	4	0	0	0	0	0	0	4
211	LEWIS, THOMAS	WR	NYG	35	24	11	0	0	0	0	0	0	1	0	0	0	0	0	0	1	1
212	WESTBROOK, MICHAEL	WR	WAS	35	30	5	0	0	0	0	0	0	1	0	1	0	0	0	0	0	2
213	FLOYD, WILLIAM	RB	SF	34	24	10	0	0	0	2	0	0	1	0	0	0	0	0	0	0	3
214	MITCHELL, PETE	TE	JAX	34	18	16	0	0	0	0	0	0	1	0	1	0	0	0	0	0	2
215	BAILEY, JOHNNY	RB	RAM	33	15	18	0	0	0	1	1	0	0	0	0	0	0	0	0	0	2
216	ELLISON, JERRY	RB	TB	33	33	0	0	0	0	4	1	0	0	0	0	0	0	0	0	0	5
217	HAYNES, MICHAEL	WR	NO	33	33	0	0	0	0	0	0	0	1	3	0	0	0	0	0	0	4

R	PLAYER	POS	TM	FAN PTS	DIST PTS	PERF PTS	PASSING TD 0-9	PASSING TD 10-39	PASSING TD 40+	RUSHING TD 0-9	RUSHING TD 10-39	RUSHING TD 40+	RECEIVING TD 0-9	RECEIVING TD 10-39	RECEIVING TD 40+	FG 0-39	FG 40-49	FG 50+	PAT	D,ST TDS	TOT TDS
218	THOMAS, ORLANDO	DB	MIN	33	21	12	0	0	0	0	0	0	0	0	0	0	0	0	0	2	0
219	CHREBET, WAYNE	WR	NYJ	32	33	-1	0	0	0	0	0	0	1	3	0	0	0	0	0	0	4
220	COLEMAN, ANDRE	WR	SD	32	36	-4	0	0	0	0	0	0	0	0	0	0	0	0	0	3	0
221	JORDAN, RANDY	RB	JAX	32	24	8	0	0	0	0	0	0	0	0	1	0	0	0	0	0	1
222	POTTS, ROOSEVELT	RB	IND	31	24	7	0	0	0	0	0	0	0	0	1	0	0	0	0	0	1
223	WALLS, WESLEY	TE	NO	31	30	1	0	0	0	0	0	0	0	1	0	0	0	0	0	0	1
224	WRIGHT, ALEXANDER	WR	RAM	31	18	13	0	0	0	0	0	0	2	2	0	0	0	0	0	0	4
225	COFER, MIKE	K	IND	30	30	0	0	0	0	0	0	0	0	0	0	2	1	0	9	0	2
226	HAYDEN, AARON	RB	SD	30	18	12	0	0	0	3	0	0	0	0	0	0	0	0	0	0	3
227	JEFFERSON, SHAWN	WR	SD	30	18	12	0	0	0	0	0	0	0	2	0	0	0	0	0	0	2
228	LOGAN, MARC	RB	WAS	30	30	0	0	0	0	1	0	0	2	0	0	0	0	0	0	0	3
229	NEAL, LORENZO	RB	NO	30	24	6	0	0	0	0	0	0	0	2	0	0	0	0	0	0	2
230	WILSON, CHARLES	WR	NYJ	30	30	0	0	0	0	0	0	0	2	2	0	0	0	0	0	0	4
231	GREEN, HAROLD	RB	CIN	29	30	-1	0	0	0	2	0	0	1	0	0	0	0	0	0	0	3
232	HARRIS, JACKIE	TE	TB	29	9	20	0	0	0	0	0	0	0	1	0	0	0	0	0	0	1
233	TASKER, STEVE	WR	BUF	29	24	5	0	0	0	0	0	0	1	2	0	0	0	0	0	0	3
234	ZEIER, ERIC	QB	CLE	29	30	-1	2	2	0	0	0	0	0	0	0	0	0	0	0	0	4
235	REED, ANDRE	WR	BUF	28	30	-2	0	0	0	0	0	0	1	2	0	0	0	0	0	0	3
236	WILLIAMS, CALVIN	WR	PHI	28	18	10	0	0	0	0	0	0	0	2	1	0	0	0	0	0	2
237	ARMOUR, JUSTIN	WR	BUF	27	27	0	0	0	0	0	0	0	0	3	0	0	0	0	0	0	3
238	BROWN, LARRY	DB	DAL	27	21	6	0	0	0	0	0	0	0	0	0	0	0	0	0	2	0
239	TIMPSON, MICHAEL	WR	CHI	27	27	0	0	0	0	0	0	0	1	0	0	0	0	0	0	0	3
240	GRAHAM, SCOTTIE	RB	MIN	26	15	11	0	0	0	1	1	0	0	0	0	0	0	0	0	0	2
241	GREEN, ERIC	TE	MIA	26	24	2	0	0	0	0	0	0	1	2	0	0	0	0	0	0	3
242	HARPER, ALVIN	WR	TB	26	15	11	0	0	0	0	0	0	1	1	0	0	0	0	0	0	2
243	HILL, GREG	RB	KC	26	6	20	0	0	0	1	0	0	0	0	0	0	0	0	0	0	1
244	PRITCHARD, MIKE	WR	DEN	26	27	-1	0	0	0	0	0	0	0	1	1	0	0	0	0	0	3
245	BENNETT, TONY	LB	IND	25	9	16	0	0	0	0	0	0	0	0	0	0	0	0	0	0	0
246	GREEN, ROBERT	RB	CHI	25	21	4	0	0	0	2	1	0	0	0	0	0	0	0	0	0	3
247	MCDONALD, TIM	DB	SF	25	21	4	0	0	0	0	0	0	0	0	0	0	0	0	0	2	0
248	YARBOROUGH, RYAN	WR	NYJ	25	15	10	0	0	0	0	0	0	1	1	0	0	0	0	0	0	2

R	PLAYER	POS	TM	FAN PTS	DIST PTS	PERF PTS	PASSING TD 0-9	10-39	40+	RUSHING TD 0-9	10-39	40+	RECEIVING TD 0-9	10-39	40+	FIELD GOALS 0-39	40-49	50+	PAT	D,ST TDS	TOT TDS
249	BRUENER, MARK	TE	PIT	24	24	0	0	0	0	0	0	0	1	2	0	0	0	0	0	0	3
250	BUTTS, MARION	RB	HOU	24	24	0	0	0	0	4	0	0	0	0	0	0	0	0	0	0	4
251	HESTER, JESSIE	WR	RAM	24	24	0	0	0	0	0	0	0	0	2	1	0	0	0	0	0	3
252	INGRAM, MARK	WR	GB	24	24	0	0	0	0	0	0	0	1	2	0	0	0	0	0	0	3
253	JOHNSTON, DARYL	RB	DAL	24	24	0	0	0	0	2	0	0	1	0	0	0	0	0	0	0	3
254	MEGGETT, DAVID	RB	NE	24	15	9	0	0	0	1	1	0	1	0	0	0	0	0	0	0	3
255	SLAUGHTER, WEBSTER	WR	KC	24	24	0	0	0	0	0	0	0	4	0	0	0	0	0	0	0	4
256	SMITH, JIMMY	WR	JAX	24	24	0	0	0	0	0	0	0	1	2	0	0	0	0	0	0	3
257	COPELAND, RUSSELL	WR	BUF	23	12	11	0	0	0	0	0	0	0	1	1	0	0	0	0	0	2
258	GIVINS, ERNEST	WR	JAX	23	24	−1	0	0	0	0	0	0	0	1	0	0	0	0	0	0	1
259	MILLS, SAM	LB	CAR	23	9	14	0	0	0	0	0	0	0	0	0	0	0	0	0	3	3
260	SCROGGINS, TRACY	LB	DET	23	12	11	0	0	0	0	0	0	0	0	0	0	0	0	0	3	3
261	TILLMAN, CEDRIC	WR	JAX	23	24	−1	0	0	0	0	0	0	1	2	0	0	0	0	0	0	3
262	NORTON, KEN	LB	SF	22	18	4	0	0	0	0	0	0	0	0	0	0	0	0	0	2	2
263	SMITH, IRV	TE	NO	22	21	1	0	0	0	0	0	0	2	1	0	0	0	0	0	0	3
264	STEWART, JAMES	RB	JAX	22	24	−2	0	0	0	2	0	0	1	0	0	0	0	0	0	0	3
265	BROWN, DEREK	RB	NO	21	21	0	0	0	0	0	1	0	1	0	0	0	0	0	0	0	2
266	GAYLE, SHAUN	DB	SD	21	18	3	0	0	0	0	0	0	0	0	0	0	0	0	0	2	2
267	GLOVER, ANDREW	TE	RAI	21	21	0	0	0	0	0	0	0	2	1	0	0	0	0	0	0	3
268	GULIFORD, ERIC	WR	MIN	21	21	0	0	0	0	0	0	0	0	0	1	0	0	0	0	0	1
269	HOWARD, DESMOND	WR	JAX	21	21	0	0	0	0	0	0	0	0	1	0	0	0	0	0	1	1
270	KAUFMAN, NAPOLEON	RB	RAI	21	21	0	0	0	0	1	0	0	0	0	0	0	0	0	0	0	1
271	SIMMONS, CLYDE	DL	AZ	21	9	12	0	0	0	0	0	0	0	0	0	0	0	0	0	1	1
272	SPIKES, IRVING	RB	MIA	21	21	0	0	0	0	1	0	0	0	0	0	0	0	0	0	0	1
273	WYCHECK, FRANK	TE	HOU	21	21	0	0	0	0	1	0	0	1	0	0	0	0	0	0	0	2
274	CASH, KEITH	TE	KC	20	9	11	0	0	0	0	0	0	0	0	0	0	0	0	0	2	2
275	CHRISTIAN, BOB	RB	CAR	20	12	8	0	0	0	0	0	0	1	0	0	0	0	0	0	0	1
276	DORN, TORIN	DB	RAI	20	18	2	0	0	0	0	0	0	0	0	0	0	0	0	0	1	1
277	EDWARDS, ANTONIO	DL	SEA	20	12	8	0	0	0	0	0	0	0	0	0	0	0	0	0	2	2
278	HASTINGS, ANDRE	WR	CAR	20	21	−1	0	0	0	0	0	0	1	0	0	0	0	0	0	1	1
279	JONES, BRENT	TE	SF	20	21	−1	0	0	0	0	0	0	2	1	0	0	0	0	0	0	3

R	PLAYER	POS	TM	FAN PTS	DIST PTS	PERF PTS	PASSING TD 0-9	PASSING TD 10-39	PASSING TD 40+	RUSHING TD 0-9	RUSHING TD 10-39	RUSHING TD 40+	RECEIVING TD 0-9	RECEIVING TD 10-39	RECEIVING TD 40+	FG 0-39	FG 40-49	FG 50+	PAT	D,ST TDS	TOT TDS
280	KINCHEN, TODD	WR	RAM	20	24	-4	0	0	0	0	0	0	4	0	0	0	0	0	0	0	4
281	MCNAIR, STEVE	QB	HOU	20	27	-7	0	3	0	0	0	0	0	0	0	0	0	0	0	0	3
282	PAUP, BRYCE	LB	BUF	20	0	20	0	0	0	0	0	0	0	0	0	0	0	0	0	0	0
283	WHEATLEY, TYRONE	RB	NYG	20	21	-1	0	0	0	2	1	0	0	0	0	0	0	0	0	0	3
284	WILLIAMS, WILLIE	DB	PIT	20	12	8	0	0	0	0	0	0	0	0	0	0	0	0	0	1	0
285	WRIGHT, TOBY	DB	RAM	20	12	8	0	0	0	0	0	0	0	0	0	0	0	0	0	1	0
286	EDWARDS, ANTHONY	WR	AZ	19	18	1	0	0	0	0	0	0	0	2	0	0	0	0	0	0	2
287	GLENN, VENCIE	DB	NYG	19	12	7	0	0	0	0	0	0	0	0	0	0	0	0	0	1	0
288	LEWIS, DARRYLL	DB	HOU	19	12	7	0	0	0	0	0	0	0	0	0	0	0	0	0	1	0
289	SMITH, RICO	WR	CLE	19	9	10	0	0	0	0	0	0	1	0	0	0	0	0	0	0	1
290	THOMAS, WILLIAM	LB	PHI	19	9	10	0	0	0	0	0	0	0	0	0	0	0	0	0	1	0
291	WOODALL, LEE	LB	SF	19	12	7	0	0	0	0	0	0	0	0	0	0	0	0	0	1	0
292	AVERY, STEVE	RB	PIT	18	18	0	0	0	0	0	0	0	1	0	0	0	0	0	0	0	1
293	BISHOP, BLAINE	DB	HOU	18	12	6	0	0	0	0	0	0	0	0	0	0	0	0	0	1	0
294	BUCKNER, BRENSTON	DL	PIT	18	12	6	0	0	0	0	0	0	0	0	0	0	0	0	0	1	0
295	CLARK, GARY	WR	MIA	18	18	0	0	0	0	0	0	0	0	1	0	0	0	0	0	0	2
296	CULVER, RODNEY	RB	IND	18	18	0	0	0	0	3	0	0	0	0	0	0	0	0	0	0	3
297	EVANS, CHARLES	RB	MIN	18	18	0	0	0	0	1	0	0	1	0	0	0	0	0	0	0	2
298	GANNON, RICH	QB	KC	18	18	0	0	0	0	0	1	0	0	0	0	0	0	0	0	0	1
299	GRAHAM, HASON	WR	NE	18	18	0	0	0	0	0	0	0	0	2	0	0	0	0	0	0	2
300	GRIFFITH, HOWARD	RB	CAR	18	18	0	0	0	0	1	0	0	1	0	0	0	0	0	0	0	2
301	MAYHEW, MARTIN	DB	TB	18	12	6	0	0	0	0	0	0	0	0	0	0	0	0	0	1	0
302	MCDANIEL, TERRY	DB	RAI	18	12	6	0	0	0	0	0	0	0	0	0	0	0	0	0	1	0
303	METZELAARS, PETE	TE	CAR	18	18	0	0	0	0	0	0	0	3	0	0	0	0	0	0	0	3
304	ROBINSON, EDDIE	LB	PIT	18	12	6	0	0	0	0	0	0	0	0	0	0	0	0	0	1	0
305	SMITH, OTIS	DB	PHI	18	12	6	0	0	0	0	0	0	0	0	0	0	0	0	0	1	0
306	VAN PELT, ALEX	QB	BUF	18	18	0	0	2	0	0	0	0	0	0	0	0	0	0	0	0	2
307	ZENDEJAS, TONY	K	RAM	18	18	0	0	0	0	0	0	0	0	0	0	1	2	0	5	0	0
308	BENNETT, CORNELIUS	LB	BUF	17	12	5	0	0	0	0	0	0	0	0	0	0	0	0	0	1	0
309	CARTER, ANTONIO	RB	CHI	17	18	-1	0	0	0	0	0	0	0	1	0	0	0	0	0	0	1
310	JONES, SEAN	DL	GB	17	6	11	0	0	0	0	0	0	0	0	0	0	0	0	0	1	0

Appendix E— FFL Merchandise

It's easy to get into the *"winning spirit"* with Official FFL Sportswear and other products.

To order, call toll-free at 1-800-872-0335. *American Express, Discover, MasterCard,* and *Visa* credit cards accepted.

Baseball Cap—
Cotton twill; one size fits all.
Red & White with Blue FFL logotype.
$9.95

The Official Tee-Shirt—
Premium heavyweight cotton.
White with Red & Blue FFL logotype.
Sizes M-XL: $14.95
Size XXL: $16.95

Crewneck Sweatshirt—
Premium wieght 7-ounce, 50/50 fleece.
White with Red & Blue FFL logotype.
Sizes M-XL: $24.95
Size XXL: $26.95

Golf Shirt—
Premium quality 100% cotton interlock.
White with Red & Blue embroidered
FFL logotype.
Sizes M-XL: $29.95
Size XXL: $31.95

Commissioner's Portfolio—
11" x 16" zippered portfolio.
A *must* for keeping and carrying your league records!
Red with White FFL logotype.
$11.95

3-Sided, 3-Color Ballpoint Pen—
Comfortable grip—won't roll!
The official pen for your league records!
$0.99 Each

Ceramic Coffee Cup—
Handsome, extra large, 15-ounce capacity hot beverage mug!
Navy Blue with White FFL logotype.
$9.95 Each

Thermal Sports Mug—
Large covered mug that won't spill and won't sweat!
$4.95 Each ★

Appendix F—
Quick Start, '96
TBFF for DOS

The following is a quick reference guide to the *Terry Bradshaw Fantasy Football* software. Every aspect of the program is addressed here. If, however, you need further instructions for using the software they are available in the complete manual which has been included on the CD. You can view or print the manual using Microsoft Word 6 (or later), or through DOS using the **TYPE** or **PRINT** command.

The two versions of the manual are :
- DOSMAN96.DOC for Microsoft Word
- DOSMAN96.TXT for DOS

To view or print the manual using Word, simply insert the CD into your CD-ROM drive and start Word as you normally would, then select the appropriate file (DOSMAN.DOC) to open from your word processor's *File Menu*. (*Note:* You may be able to use other word processors to view or print the manual provided they support Word 6 file formats) Consult your word processor manual for further information.

To view or print the DOS text version of the manual, you need to be at a DOS prompt, and type the following (commands you need to type are in **bold**):
D:[ENTER] (to change to your CD-ROM drive)
CD\[ENTER]
CD\FFL96[ENTER]
TYPE DOSMAN.TXT|MORE[ENTER] to view the manual on screen
or
PRINT DOSMAN.TXT[ENTER] to print to your printer

Getting Started—
Installing & Running the Terry Bradshaw Fantasy Football Software

In order to run the *Terry Bradshaw Fantasy Football* software, the following is the minimum required configuration for your PC:

- 386DX/25MHZ or compatible computer and DOS 3.3 or higher.
- CD ROM drive (for CD-ROM version)
- Hard Disk Drive with 35-45MB available for program and a complete season of statistics
- Printer (*optional*)
- Modem (*optional*)

Note: The 1996 Terry Bradshaw FFL software *cannot* be run on a system using disk compression, nor should it be run on a network. Although some people have managed an entire season under these circumstances, we do not recommend it, and cannot offer technical support for users trying to run the software under these conditions.

Installing and Running the Program—

Windows users: You will need to first exit Windows before installing (or running once installed) the *Terry Bradshaw Fantasy Football* software. Once you have exited Windows, follow the instructions below for installing the software:

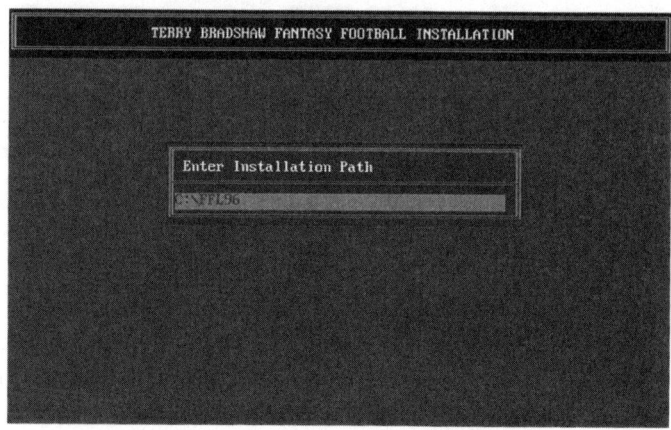

For the purpose of this manual it is assumed your hard drive is "c". Commands you need to type are in BOLD.

Place the FFL program DISKETTE #1 or CD ROM into its drive.

Access the appropriate drive—
A: [ENTER] if your floppy drive is A:
B: [ENTER] if your floppy drive is B:
D: [ENTER] if your CD-ROM is D:
Once you access the appropriate drive, your prompt will change to the letter of that drive.

Begin the installation program by typing:
INSTALL [ENTER]

An installation window will be displayed. The program will prompt you for the directory in which to install the program. The system will default to the C:\FFL96 directory. If that is the directory you wish to use, simply press [ENTER]. If you wish to install the program in a directory other than the default, simply type the directory name and press [ENTER]. If the directory does not exist on your system, the installation program will create it for you. If installing from floppy disks, when the program prompts you, place the Fantasy Football program DISKETTE #2 into the floppy drive and press [ENTER]. When the installation is complete, a message will display indicating a successful installation and prompt you to press any key to exit the installation program. You can now begin using the software.

Each time you want to use the *Terry Bradshaw Fantasy Football* software you will have to first exit Windows and start the program by typing STARTFFL [ENTER] at the FFL96 DOS prompt. If you are at a different directory (i.e., C:\WINDOWS), first change to your root directory by typing CD\ [ENTER], then at the C:\ prompt type CD\FFL96 [ENTER]. Windows95 users see below for instructions on running the software under Windows95.

Important!
If you get the following message "*The Fantasy Football was unable to all of your files. You must have the settings FILES=50 and BUFFERS=30 in your CONFIG.SYS file*" please follow these instructions for *Editing Your System's* CONFIG.SYS *File*.

Editing Your System's CONFIG.SYS File—

To edit the CONFIG.SYS file:

1. Access your system's root directory (C:\>).
   If you are not at the root directory type C: [ENTER], then type CD\ [ENTER]. You should now be at the root directory of your "C" drive.

2. Type EDIT [SPACEBAR] CONFIG.SYS [ENTER].
   The MSDOS editor screen will now be displayed with the contents of your current CONFIG.SYS file.

3. If you have the lines for FILES, and BUFFERS but they are not FILES=50, and BUFFERS=30, simply use the arrow keys to move the cursor to the numbers and delete them using the [DEL] key, replacing them with the required settings, 50 for files, 30 for buffers.

   If you are missing one or both of these settings entirely simply move the cursor to the end of the file and enter FILES=50[ENTER] and BUFFERS=30 [ENTER].

4. Hold down the [ALT] and [F] keys together to bring up the *File Menu*. Select *Exit* and hit [ENTER], (you will be prompted that the loaded file is not saved, so you need to save it now by selecting YES).

5. *That's it!* Now just reboot (reset or turn off and back on) your computer and you're ready to run the Fantasy Football software.

Running the Program Under Windows 95—

After installing the software, following the installation instructions in this manual, return to your Windows 95 Desktop. The *1996 Terry Bradshaw Fantasy Football* program will run without problems under Windows 95 provided you follow these simple instructions:

1. From the Windows 95 Desktop double-click the "*My Computer*" icon.

2. Double-click on the icon for your "c" drive.

3. From the folder listings for your "c" drive select the FFL96 folder by double-clicking its icon.

4. Locate the file "START FFL.BAT". Click and hold the right mouse button on this icon and "*drag*" it to a spot over your desktop and release the mouse button (*if the desktop isn't visible click on the middle button in the upper right-hand of your screen to resize the folder listing's window*). A menu will appear, select "*Create Shortcut*" and a new icon will be created on your desktop.

5. Close the windows for your "c" drive and "*My Computer.*"

6. You should now have the MSDOS icon on your Desktop for "*Shortcut to STARTFFL.BAT*". Right-click on this icon and select "*Properties*".

7. Click on the "*Program*" tab at the top of the form and make sure the box reading "*Close on Exit*" is checked.

8. Click on the "*Advanced*" button, then click the first two checkboxes: "*Prevent MSDOS based programs from detecting Windows*" and "*Suggest MSDOS mode as necessary*" and click the "OK" button.

9. Next, click on the "*Screen*" tab at the top of the form and, under "*Usage*" make sure "*Full-Screen*" is selected, then click on the "OK" button.

You're done!
That's all there is to it. You can now run the *Terry Bradshaw Fantasy Football* software directly from your Windows 95 Desktop simply by double-clicking its icon.

Setting Up Your League—

Option 'A' from the *Main Menu*, *League Setup*, takes you to the *League Setup Menu* where all of the necessary steps for setting up your league and configuring your system can be accomplished. The following is a guide to the options available through the *League Setup Menu*.

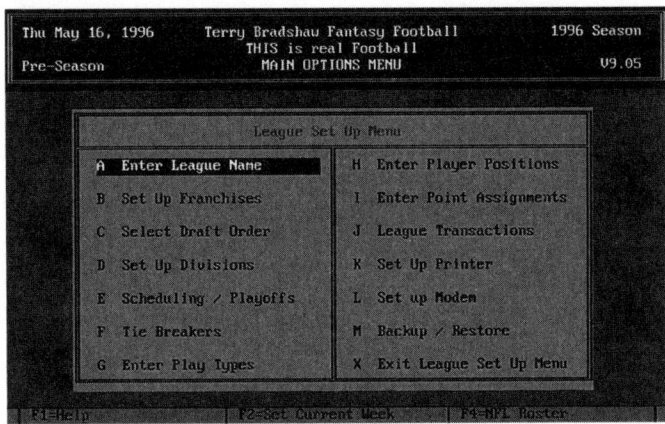

'A' Enter League Name—

Selecting 'A' from the *League Setup Menu* allows you to enter your league's name. The name can be anything that you choose up to 25 characters in length.

'B' Set Up Franchises—

Selecting 'B' from the *League Setup Menu* takes you to another menu. From this second menu you can **Add Franchises, Display/Edit Franchises, Print Franchises**, and **Print Mailing Labels**.

Add Franchise:
When you select this option you will be presented with the *Franchise Entry* screen. Here you enter the franchise name, whether or not the franchise's dues have been paid, *Salary Cap, Draft Order,* and *Scoring Method*. If your league does not use a salary cap leave the *Salary Cap* field blank. You can assign the draft order from this screen by entering the appropriate number in the *Draft Order* field, if you do not enter anything the order will default to the order franchises are entered. Finally, you have the option for *Scoring Method*. This will be '1' *Drafted Player Performance* for *all* franchises. The other options, *League Average*, and *Fixed Points* are only used for assigning a value to be beaten by teams having a bye week. You should only need to use this if you have a league with an odd number of franchises and want teams to have to beat the league average or a fixed number of points on their bye week.

Display/Edit Franchises:
After you have entered franchise information using the **Add Franchise** option you can *Display* and/or *Edit* them with this menu selection. The same screen is used and you can edit any information you need to for your franchises.

Print Franchises:
Select this option to print out all franchise information. You can print the information, display it to your screen, or save it to a file.

Print Mailing Labels:
Select this option to print mailing labels to use for envelopes if you mail information out to franchise owners. There are two options available, both using Avery labels. You will need to buy Avery #4145 if you are using a dot-matrix printer, Avery #5161 for lasers, ink-jet, or other single sheet fed printers.

'c' Select Draft Order—

Selecting 'c' from the *League Setup Menu* allows you to choose the method you want to use for your draft. The options are **Normal Draft, Reverse Order Draft, Reset Draft Order Each Round,** and **Reset Current Drafting Order.**

Normal Draft:
Selecting this option will give franchises the same draft pick each round. The team picking first in the first round will do so in every round through the draft.

Reverse Order Draft:
This is the most common, and most fair, method of running a fantasy draft. The order of the draft remains the same for all odd numbered rounds, and reverses for even numbered rounds. Thus the team that picks last in round one gets the first pick in round two, picking two picks in a row.

Reset Draft Order Each Round:
Use this option if your league will choose a new drafting order for each round of the draft. After each round you will select a new drafting order.

Reset Current Drafting Order:
Use this option to change your league's drafting order in the middle of the draft. You can use this option in combination with the above selections to change the drafting order after running through a pre-determined number of rounds.

'D' Set Up Divisions—

Selecting option 'D' from the *League Setup Menu* allows you to *Set Up Divisions, Assign Franchises to Divisions,* and *Print Division Setup.* If you do not set up divisions the Terry Bradshaw Fantasy Football program will assign all franchises to one division by default.

Set Up Divisions:
Select this option to enter the name or names of your divisions. You can select up to eight divisions maximum.

Assign Franchises to Divisions:
After you have selected and named your divisions you use this option to assign your franchises to one of them. You will first select the division you want to assign franchises to, and will be given two windows displaying unassigned franchises in the left and the division with any assigned franchises on the right. Highlighting a franchise and hitting [ENTER] will move that franchise into the opposite window.

Print Division Setup:
For a printout of your current division alignments, choose this option. The divisions will be printed out showing the franchises currently assigned to it.

'E' Scheduling/Playoffs—

Selecting option 'E' from the *League Setup Menu* takes you to the *Scheduling and Playoff Setup* module. Here you can *Edit Current Schedule, Print Current Schedule, Re-Load Default Schedule,* and input your *Playoff Schedule.*

Edit Current Schedule:
If you want to change the schedule that was loaded for your league by default, you can do it here. Simply select a week to change, and then edit the week's matchups. Simply use the commands listed at the bottom of your screen make deletions, then enter the new matchups you want by hitting F10 and selecting the teams. Playoff matchups can also be edited here, once your regular season has ended.

Print Current Schedule:
Before making any changes to your schedule, it is a good idea to print it out. Make changes then, based upon the default that was loaded, and re-print the schedule to be sure it as you want it to be for all the weeks in the season.

Re-Load Default Schedule:
If your league structure changes (i.e., you add an additional team after first setting up your schedule) or you have made changes and want to go back to the original schedule, select this option. The default schedule will be re-loaded based upon your current league configuration.

Playoff Setup:
You will need to enter this information in order for your league's playoffs to run properly. When you select this option you will see a form for entering the number of weeks in your league's regular season, the playoff starting and ending weeks, and the number of teams that you allow in the playoffs for the first round.

'F' Tie Breakers—

Selecting option 'F' from the *League Setup Menu* takes you to the *Tie Breakers* setup. This section is where you will define how your league will settle ties. There are two types of ties to be considered, **Head-to-Head** and **Franchise Standings**. With **Head-to-Head** ties, teams end up with the same points in a weekly matchup. These ties can be settled or left to stand, and be reflected in the *Weekly League Summary Report* as a tie for each team. If you don't want ties, select one of the methods for breaking **Head-to-Head** ties.

'G' Enter Play Types—

Selecting option 'G' from the *League Setup Menu* takes you to the *Play Types Menu*. If your league uses any play types not already set up, you enter them here using **Add a Play Type** (remember, these user defined play types will not be supported through the download files, and have to be tracked manually). You can also *Display/Edit Play Types* to change properties such as whether the play is tracked as a *Statistical* or *Scoring Play* type, and whether or not the play type is active in your league. You should set the play types you won't be using to inactive. This will save hard disk space and allow for faster processing of the weekly stats. There is also an option to *Print Play Types*.

'H' Enter Player Positions—

Selecting option 'H' from the *League Setup Menu* takes you to the *Player Position Menu*. The options here are the same as for Play Types. You can **Add a Position, Display/Edit Positions,** or **Print Positions**. When you select *Display/Edit Positions,* you have the option to set your draft and start limits for each position, as well as setting whether or not the position is active. As with *Play Types*, setting unused positions to not active will save hard disk space and allow for faster processing of weekly updates.

'I' Enter Point Assignments—

Selecting option 'I' from the *League Setup Menu* takes you to the **Point Assignments Options Menu**. This is where you will enter all the information for the way your league scores plays and stats. There is an official FFL recommended scoring system already in place, but you can edit this or replace it completely with your own scoring system. Making sure you have all point assignments correct before starting the season will eliminate the headaches and frustration of trying to get it all right while the other members of your league are complaining about why they haven't received their reports yet. To make testing your point assignments easy, we have provided you with an instant testing feature. By hitting the F4 key you can enter the value you want to test for the currently highlighted point assignment.

After you have gone through and tested all of your point assignments, you can, and should, further test them by running an update with the included sample stats. Make sure all the scoring plays are being awarded the proper points in accordance with your league's scoring system, and make sure all stats are being awarded the proper points too. If not, simply edit the point assignment in question, and then recalculate the points for the week and check your reports again.

For 1996, the *Terry Bradshaw Fantasy Football* software point assignment section is easier to use than ever before. The point assignment entry screen is now structured in a sentence format to help you better understand how the points will be awarded. To edit an existing point assignment simply highlight it and hit [ENTER]. To add an additional point assignment hit the *Insert* key and then select the position, followed by the play type you want to create a point assignment for. Type in the values you want to use and then test the assignment using the F4 key to see if you are getting the results you want.

'j' League Transactions—

Selecting option *'j'* from the League Setup Menu takes you to the *Transactions Option Menu*. Here is where you will enter in the fees your league uses, if any, for various roster transactions throughout the season. You can also delete transactions here, as well as print transactions and transaction fees. Your options are **Setup League Transaction Fees**, **Delete League Transactions**, and **Print League Transaction Fees**.

Setup League Transaction Fees:
Enter the amount your league charges for drafting players (after the season starts), cutting players, trading players, and placing players on or taking players off the *Injured Reserve* list.

Delete League Transactions:
If you have incorrectly entered a trade or other player transaction, and do not want it reflected on the transaction reports you can delete it here. First undo the incorrectly entered transaction using the appropriate menu option. Then select *League Transactions* and then *Delete League Transactions* to remove the incorrect transaction, as well as the reversal of the transaction. The franchises involved will not be charged, and neither of these transactions will appear on the transaction reports.

Print League Transactions:
Select this option to print out all league transactions. You can select *Print by Franchise*, or *Print by Week*. This is a good report to view on screen if you have just deleted some unwanted transactions and want to check that the transaction report is now correct.

Print League Transaction Fees:
After you have setup all your league's transaction fees you can print out a copy for each franchise using the *Print League Transaction Fees* menu selection.

'K' Set Up Printer—

Selecting option 'K' from the *League Setup Menu* takes you to your *Print Setup*. When you first enter this module, you will see *"Printer Not Selected"* as option 'A,' *Print to Screen, Print to Disk File, Set Print File Path, Selection List of Printers*, and *Set Lines per Page*.

Printer Not Selected:
Select this option to setup your printer.
There is a list of printer drivers for most major printer manufacturers printers included. If you cannot find your exact printer listed you will need to consult your printer's manual for a list of compatible drivers. After you have selected a printer, the name will replace Printer Not Selected. To make a change to the printer then, select option 'E' *Selection List of Printers*.

Print to Screen:
This sets the default path for printing to print to your screen. You can then print to the printer from the screen. You can also select to print to your printer from the *Print Options Menu* that appears each time you enter the *Reports* module of the program.
Selecting *Print to Screen* here simply sets the highlight to that option in the *Print Options Menu*.

Print to Disk File:
This sets the default path for printing to a file. You can then print to the printer from the screen. You can also select to print to your printer from the *Print Options Menu* that appears each time you enter the *Reports* module of the program. Selecting *Print to Disk File* here simply sets the highlight to that option in the *Print Options Menu*. (if you select this option, make sure you also select option 'D' to select the destination for the file)

Set Print File Path:
Select this option and enter the path (example: C:\FFLREPTS\ ) where you wish print files to be stored. This can be any valid DOS path, including floppy drives.

Set Lines per Page:
If your printed reports are not filling the entire page, or are ending with a few lines on the next page then change the *Lines per Page* setting. The default of 55 should work fine with most printers, though some will work better with a slightly higher setting.

'L' Set Up Modem—

Selecting option 'L' from the *League Setup Menu* takes you into *Modem Setup*. You only need to set up a modem if you will be downloading stats through the download module built into the program. When you first enter this you will see a list of modems from which to select. After you have selected your modem, you will need to set the com port you are using (normally COM1). You can now make any changes to this that you need by exiting *Modem Setup* and then selecting it again. You will be able to change the modem, port, add a dial prefix or suffix, change your connect wait time, and edit the modem initialization string. If you do not see your modem listed, try using the Hayes compatible that most closely matches the modem you are using. You can also enter your own initialization string if you know it, or edit an existing string. If you encounter difficulties, try just putting 'AT' for the initialization string.

'M' Backup / Restore—

Selecting option 'M' from the *League Setup Menu*, takes you to the *Backup/Restore* setup. You will want to make sure you backup your league each week, and here is where you will set the default location for the backup data to be stored. You have the option to change this when you actually run the backup; this is simply the default path that will be displayed and used if you do not make changes when running a backup. For more information on the *Backup/Restore* process, see the *System Utilities* section later in this manual. There you will have an explanation of the actual process, which you should become familiar with. Backing up your league's data each week allows you to completely restore your league should your data files become corrupted.

'X' Exit League Setup:
Selecting option 'X' from the *League Setup Menu* (or from any menu in the Terry Bradshaw Fantasy Football program) will return you to the previous menu.

Player Management—

Player management is the function of *Main Menu* options '*B*', '*C*', '*D*', and '*E*', they are all covered here, and are very simple to understand and easy to use.

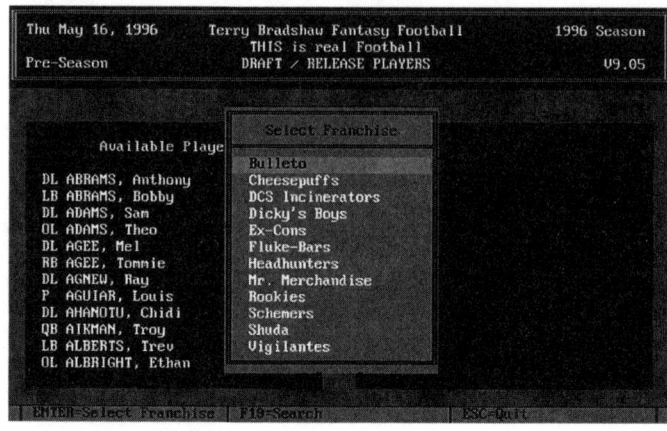

Draft/Release Players, Select Starting Players,
Trade Players, and Injured Reserve—

Draft/Release Players:
Initially you will use this option, '*B*' from the *Main Menu*, to run through your league's draft. Drafting can be done "*by Round*" or "*by Franchise*". If you will be using the *Terry Bradshaw Fantasy Football* software to run your draft, you will probably want to choose *Draft by Round*. Otherwise, if you are simply entering in the rosters after the draft has been completed it is much easier to use *Draft by Franchise*. To select a player for drafting, find him on the list of available players (the right window), and then hit [ENTER]. You will have to select the franchise to draft the player first, of course. For drafting by round, the franchise that has the current pick will be selected for you, and after that franchise drafts you advance to the next pick by hitting F1, F2 to reverse the pick if you have entered it by mistake. There is a quick way to find the player you want to draft: with the highlight in the available players window, begin typing the last name of the player you want to draft. Enter the name just as the names appear in the list, all caps for the last name (which you type first), followed by the first name if necessary. For example, to locate Emmitt Smith you type: SMITH, **Emmitt**.

For player acquisitions during the season, you will be presented first with the franchise list then, after selecting the franchise, the two player windows. This is the same as *Draft by Franchise* in the preseason. You can set up fees for drafting and releasing players under *League Transactions*, (these fees will not apply during the preseason).

Select Starting Players:
Each week you will need to enter the starting lineups for your league's franchises. You do so through option 'c' from the *Main Menu*, *Select Starting Players*. The display in this module is very similar to that of *Draft/Release Players*. You will have a franchise list initially, and once a franchise selected you will have two player windows. The non-starting players on the left, starters on the right. Just highlight the player to be started and press [ENTER] to move them to the started window, or vice versa. Each week, the starting rosters will be carried forward, so all you need to do is make the changes from week to week.

Trade Players:
In the event of a trade, you enter option 'd' from the *Main Menu*, *Trade Players*. Again the interface is very similar to the *Draft/Release* one. The only difference is that you must select two franchise to trade between. Then, highlight the players to be trade for one team, press [ENTER], and then repeat the process for the other team. You can set up fees for trades under *League Transactions*.

Injured Reserve:
If your league uses IR status, then this is where you place players on, and remove them from, the *Injured Reserve* list. Select the franchise, followed by the player(s) to be placed on IR. Later, when the player is ready to be taken off IR, simply reverse these steps to place them back on the active roster. You can set up fees for both of these actions under *League Transactions*.

Updating Your League's Standings—

Weekly Stats—

From the *Main Menu*, option '*F*' takes you to the *Update* module where you will either manually enter stats, download them using the built in communications package, or copy them if they have been downloaded through one of the other FSPI download services. Stats downloads are available by 6:00 AM Mondays, and again Tuesdays to include the Monday night game. They are available through the FSPI BBS, our web site at HTTP://WWW.FSPI.COM, Compuserve, MSN, and Prodigy. (*Note:* FSPI *has no control over when the stats are posted on Prodigy. They are available, however, by 6:00 AM through all other sources. If you have signed up through one of the commercial online services you will only be able to download stats via that service.*)

```
Thu May 16, 1996       Terry Bradshaw Fantasy Football         1996 Season
U                      Franchise Rosters

       Player Name          PN Team         Franchise          Points
       AIKMAN, Troy         QB Dallas       Bulleto                 6
       BETTIS, Jerome       RB St.Louis     Vigilantes
       BLAKE, Jeff          QB Cincinnati   Schemers                6
       BLEDSOE, Drew        QB New Englan   Dicky's Boys           10
       BONIOL, Chris        K  Dallas       Vigilantes              5
       BRISBY, Vincent      WR New Englan   Vigilantes
       BROOKS, Robert       WR Green Bay    Vigilantes
       BRUCE, Isaac         WR St.Louis     Vigilantes              9
       CUNNINGHAM, Randall  QB Philadelph   Shuda                  -6
       ELWAY, John          QB Denver       Cheesepuffs             8
       FAVRE, Brett         QB Green Bay    Ex-Cons                17
       GEORGE, Jeff         QB Atlanta      Fluke-Bars             20
       INDIANAPOLIS         DT Indianapol   Vigilantes              1
       IRVIN, Michael       WR Dallas       Ex-Cons                16
       KRAMER, Erik         QB Chicago      Mr. Merchandise        28
       MARINO, Dan          QB Miami        Vigilantes             26
       MARTIN, Curtis       RB New Englan   DCS Incinerators       16
```

Updating Manually—

For 1996, the Terry Bradshaw Fantasy Football software features an all new, easier to use, manual stats entry procedure. Each week when you are ready to enter the stats and scoring plays from the weeks NFL games, you simply select option '*F*', *Weekly Stats* from the *Main Menu*, followed by the week you wish to update. From there select *Manually Add/Edit Stats*, then *Add/Edit Player Stats* from the *Update Options Menu* and you will be presented with a list of players. By hitting F4 you can toggle this list between *Starters*, *Drafted*, or *All* players. If you only track stats for the starters or drafted players, then that is all you will see on your screen when you select that option for display. You also have the option, by hitting F9, to sort this list of players by *Player Name*, *Player Team* (NFL team), or *Franchise* (Fantasy Football team)

To actually enter stats and scoring plays, simply highlight the player you want to enter them for, and by hitting F2 you can enter scoring plays (i.e., touchdowns, field goals, etc.), F3 for stats. When you enter the F3 stats window you can select to view all stats, or just those you have point assignments set up for. Again, highlight the play type you wish to enter stats for and then enter the stats (not the points) for the stat (i.e., yards gained). Repeat this process for all play types necessary, and for all players you want to enter stats for. Once you are done with this, you will want to finish your update by selecting *Finish Update* from the *Update Options Menu*. Once this process has been completed, advance your lineups when prompted (do not advance the lineups if you are doing an update on Monday, you will advance the lineups after Tuesday's final update) and you are done. You can now run your weekly reports.

Updating through a Download Service—

Once you have subscribed to one of the update services and are downloading stats each week, you begin your update by selecting *Weekly Stats* from the *Main Menu*. You will now be given the option of downloading the stats using the built in communications, option 'A' from the *Select Import Option Menu*, or *Copy Week Download File* if you have already downloaded through your own communications software, the FSPI www site (HTTP://WWW.FSPI.COM), or one of the commercial on-line services.

Using the built-in communications:

There is a simple and easy way to use the communications module included with the *Terry Bradshaw Fantasy Football* software. This requires a toll call to our BBS located in Reston, Virginia but should take less than 3 minutes on average to download the weekly stat file.

To use the *Download Manager*, select option 'A' *Download File From* FSPI BBS from the *Import Options Menu*. The first time you use the built in communications, you will be prompted for your *User ID and Password* the first time you use the *Download Manager*, and will need to enter some information for on-line registration. You should also have set up your modem and port settings in *League Setup*. After you have your *User ID and Password* info entered, have filled out the on-line registration form, and setup your modem, you are ready to download.

FSPI www Site—Using a Web Browser:

If you already have access to the World Wide Web via an Internet provider or other commercial on-line service, you may wish to download your stats through FSPI's web site at URL HTTP://WWW.FSPI.COM. Launch your web browser and go to the FSPI site by typing in our URL in place of the one listed for your browser's default home page (the one that loads automatically when you launch the browser). There you will see an icon (or other graphic) indicating Fantasy Football stats, click on that and then follow the instructions to download the stat file. After you have downloaded the file you will need to know the path it was downloaded to. This is normally the directory of your browser, (C:\NETSCAPE\PROGRAM if you are using

Netscape) or on-line service (C:\PRODIGY if you are using Prodigy). Go to your Windows File Manager (or Explorer in Win95) and click on the directory where the Fantasy Football download file is located (this will be on the left side of your File Manger window). Double-click on the file name (*example*: FFL01.EXE) to decompress the .EXE file you downloaded and create the FFLSTAT.1 the Terry Bradshaw Fantasy Football program needs (*the file will be on the right side of the File Manager window*). You are now ready to run your weekly update.

Compuserve—

You can sign up for and download the stats via Compuserve. To do so, GO to SIFFL and follow the instructions on screen. Please note that if you have signed up for the download service from FSPI, you will not be able to download the stats through Compuserve. Compuserve will bill you for the stats when you sign up on-line.
If you have signed up through FSPI, you can access the stats using Compuserve's web browser (*see above—Using a Web Browser*).

The Microsoft Network—

You can sign up for and download the stats via The Microsoft Network (MSN). To do so, GO to *Fantasy Football* and follow the instructions on screen. Please note that if you have signed up for the download service from FSPI, you will not be able to download the stats through MSN. MSN will bill you for the stats when you sign up on-line.
If you have signed up through FSPI, you can access the stats using MSN's Internet Explorer (*see above—Using a Web Browser*).

Prodigy—

You can sign up for and download the stats via Prodigy. To do so, *Jump* to *Fantasy Football* and follow the instructions on screen. Please note that if you have signed up for the download service from FSPI, you will not be able to download the stats through Prodigy. Prodigy will bill you for the stats when you sign up on-line.
If you have signed up through FSPI, you can access the stats using Prodigy's web browser (*see above—Using a Web Browser*).

Finishing the Update—

Once you have downloaded the stat file, and copied it into your Fantasy Football directory, you will need to finish the update. Select *Finish Update*, and then advance your lineups when prompted (do not advance the lineups until you have run the *final* update for the week, i.e., do not advance them if you are running an update on Monday). Now you are ready to print your weekly reports.

Reports, Reports, and More Reports—

For those of you that just can't get enough reports and stat information, the 1996 *Terry Bradshaw Fantasy Football* software has got you covered. There are more than 30 different reports that you can use to keep you and your franchise owners up to speed. The following is a brief description of the reports so that you can decide which ones will be the most useful for your league.

Weekly Reports—

User Defined Weekly Reports:
This is not a report, but rather a selection of reports that you can customize. When you select this option you will be given a list of reports. Select *Customize Weekly Reports* (see below) and then select the reports you want to print. Then, each week by selecting *User Defined Weekly Reports* you will get a print out of each of these reports you have selected.

Weekly Winning Report:
The *Weekly Winning Report* lists total franchise points scored for the current week, as well as the cumulative season totals for all franchises, and lists them in order. There is also a *Top Twenty Individual Performances* section which will list the top twenty players scores for the current week, along with the player's franchise and starting status. Your newsletter can be printed on this report in place of the *Individual Top 20* list, although it will appear at the top of the report.

Weekly League Summary Report:
The *Weekly League Summary Report* is your league's standings report. It will list the standings (separated by division where applicable), the weekly head-to-head results, along with the next week's matchups and NFL schedule, including NFL teams on a bye week if there are any. Your newsletter can be printed on this report in place of the NFL schedule, although it will appear at the *top* of the report.

Weekly Winners Ranking Report:
The *Weekly Winners Ranking Report* is a week by week listing of the franchise points for each week. It is the same information that is displayed in the *Weekly Winning Report* under current week franchise points.

Player Scoring Report:
The *Player Scoring Report* lists the starting and non-starting points for each franchise for the current week along with the player's YTD totals.

Scoring Plays Report:
The *Scoring Plays Report* is a detailed listing of all scoring plays and stats for each player broken down by player and franchise. You can list all stats and plays, or only those that resulted in fantasy points. This report is a good tool for the commissioner should a question arise regarding a certain franchise's points. It is an invaluable tool for solving point assignment problems.

Starting Lineup Worksheets:
The *Starting Lineup Worksheets* can be passed out to the franchise owners each week to allow them to select their starting lineups for the next week. The worksheets list all franchise players along with their starting status and points for the current week, and their points for the year-to-date.

Pre-Game Starting Players Report:
This report is similar to the *Starting Lineup Worksheets* only that it lists all franchises together rather than printing each on a separate page. It is also a week *beginning* report as opposed to a week ending report and should be printed out *after* the starting lineups have been put in for the week.

Starting Roster Report:
Similar to the *Player Scores Report*, the *Starting Roster Report* lists only starting players with their points for the week.

Customize Weekly Reports:
This is where you will select which reports print out when you select *User Defined Weekly Reports*. Select or de-select reports using the F2 key, and then hit [END] to save your selections.

League Setup Reports—

Player Point Assignments Report:
This report gives you a printout of your *Point Assignments*. You can use this to review if everything is entered correctly, and to give to the franchise owners so they will know their scoring system.

Player Positions Report:
This is a printout of all the *Player Positions* along with their status (*Active/Non-Active*).

Play Types Report:
This is a printout of all the *Play Types* and their status.

Division Setup Report:
A printout of your league's division setup, showing the divisions and the franchise assigned to them.

Mailing Labels:
If you mail reports to your league's owners, then you can print out mailing labels. The labels will contain the franchise owner name and address. You have two options for labels, Avery #5161 for laser printing, and Avery #4145 for tractor feed dot matrix printing. Avery labels should be available at your local office supplies store.

League Rules Report:
A summary of your league's rules that is created from the information you enter for transaction fees, etc. This report may not be as detailed as one you create yourself in a word processor, but is an outline of how you have used the *Terry Bradshaw Fantasy Football* software to set up your league.

Player Information—

NFL Roster Report:
A complete listing of all NFL players contained in the roster file, which can be sorted by *Player Position* or *NFL Team*.

Franchise Rosters Report:
A printout, franchise by franchise, of all the players currently drafted on to one of your franchises.

Draft Night Player List Report:
A handy report to aid in your draft. All active positions are printed along with a line for entering the name of the owner or franchise that the player was drafted by.

Weekly Player Scores Report:
This is a printout of players (you can select *Drafted, Non-Drafted,* or *All*) with their weekly points totals. You will be able to tell how a player has gotten his total points at any time during the season, by seeing the points listed for each week. A good way to analyze non-drafted player performance before making any moves to pick up new players.

Top 40 Point Leaders Report:
This report gives you the *Top 40 Point Leaders* for any or all positions. You can select which positions to print out, or just print them all.

Released Players Report:
A report of all players that have been released from a franchise. This is a good report to give to your franchise owners so they will now what players have become available.

Injured Reserve Report:
This report will show you all players currently on the IR list.

Roster Transactions Report:
The *Roster Transactions Report* will show you all player transactions for the season. You can sort the report by franchise or by week. If you use transaction fees, you can use this report to track what your franchise owners owe.

Roster Transaction Fees Report:
A printout of your *Roster Transaction Fee* structure.

Post Draft Report:
This is only applicable to leagues that use the *Draft-by-Round* method. After the draft, or at any time during the draft, you can print out a round by round summary of which players have been drafted, and by whom.

Player Salary Report:
If your league uses a salary structure, you can get a printout of the players and their salaries here. There is an option to print *Drafted* or *Non-Drafted* players.

NFL and FFL Schedules—

Schedule by Week Report:
This is a printout of your FFL schedule, broken down by week.

Schedule by Franchise Report:
This is a printout of your FFL schedule, broken down by franchise.

Schedule with Playoff Report:
This is the same as *Schedule by Week Report* with the addition of the playoffs. During the season this will display only the first playoff round, and the teams that would be in the first round based upon the current standings, and your playoff setup criteria.

1996 NFL Schedule Report:
A week by week NFL schedule for 1996 including game times and national television games.

Stat Reports—

Drafted Stat Detail Report:
A printout of all drafted players with their year to date stats.

Non-Drafted Stat Detail Report:
A printout of all non-drafted players with their year to date stats.

Franchise Stat History Report:
Similar to the *Drafted Stat History Report*, with a breakdown by franchise.

Top 40 Stat Leaders Report:
The *Top 40 Stat Leaders.* You can print out *any* or *all* positions.

Season Player Scoring Summary Report:
Using the official Terry Bradshaw Fantasy Football scoring system, this report gives you a detailed breakdown of players points for the year, and where they fell within the Fantasy Football scoring system.

Box Score Report:
A quarter-by-quarter box score style report of your league's weekly matchups. Stat and scoring information is also included.

```
PLAYER PERFORMANCE SCREEN              SMITH, Emmitt  RB  Dallas

Total Points..: 46      Total Yardage  163      Through Week: 1

Rushing Att..:    21    Rushing Yards:   163    Rushing Avg...:    7.8
Rushing TDs..:     4    2 Point Run..:     0    Rushing Points:     46

Passing Att..:     0    Passing Comp:      0    Sacks:       0    Passing TDs:      0
Passing Yards:     0    Pass Comp%..:    0.0    INT..:       0    2 Pt Pass..:      0
Passing Avg..:   0.0    Fumbles Lost:      0                      Pass Points:      0

No. Receptions:    1    Receiving Yrds:    0    Receiving Avg..:        0.0
Receiving TDs:     0    2 Point Recpt:     0    Receiving Points:         0

PAT Attempts..:    0    PATs Made..:       0    PAT%:      0.00  PAT Points:        0
Field Goal Att:    0    FGs Made..:        0    FG%:       0.00  FG Points.:        0

Kick Return Yards:      0    Punt Return Yards:    0    Def / ST Points:      0
Kick Return TD..:       0    Punt Return TD..:     0    Blocked Kick TD:      0
Interception TD.:       0    Fumble Return TD.:    0    Safety........:       0
Tackles.........:       0    Sacks..........:    0.0    Assists.......:       0
Interceptions..:        0    Fumbles Recovered:    0

                             Strike any Key
```

Stat Analysis—

Option '**H**' from the *Main Menu* is *Stat Analysis*. Think of *Stat Analysis* as your on-screen information center, a quick and easy way to check stats and points for any player you want without the need for running reports. Select option '**H**' from the *Main Menu* to go to the *Stat Analysis* screen. Then, just select whether you wish to view information on drafted or non-drafted players, and then hit enter on the franchise, or player name to bring up the stat screen. This is a great reference tool to use if one of your league owners has a question about a particular player. There is no need to thumb through page after page of reports, or print out a new report, just go to the *Stat Analysis* module and you can get what you want there.

System Utilities and Troubleshooting—

System Utilities—

There are several valuable tools for you to use under option '*i*' from the *Main Menu, System Utilities*. Each of these is covered below. You will want to be familiar with these as they can help you avoid problems during the season.

File Indexing:
The *Terry Bradshaw Fantasy Football* software is a database application, and as such uses extensive indexing to keep track of your league. From time to time you should re-index each of the files from the *File Indexing* option under *System Utilities*: **Player File, Franchise File, Roster Transaction File, Point Assignment File, Play Type File, Position File, Franchise Roster File, Play File,** and **Play Transaction File.** This is the first thing you should do whenever you encounter a strange problem with rosters. points or franchises. If you are sure you have the *Point Assignment* right for a particular play, but the points are still wrong, re-indexing can often take care of the problem. Please be sure to re-index *all* of your files before calling for technical assistance. This will be the first step the technician will have you perform if you have not done so before you call.

Reset Season:
If you want to run a few sample weeks (which you should) to test your point assignments and become familiar with the updating process, you can do so and then reset your season. You have the option of saving roster and franchise information, so you can do your sample weeks with your actual franchises, or you can simply draft some dummy franchises.

Backup/Restore:
Backing up your league each and every week can save you a lot of headaches should your database files ever become corrupted. If that happens, and you have backed up your league's data, you simply select this option to restore the data, and all will be fine. If your database files become corrupted and you have not been backing up, then you will have no choice but to *Start Your Season Over*, there is nothing that can be done to repair a corrupted database, and our technical support department will not be able to help you. Make it a regular part of your updating to first run a backup! You have the option of backing up to any valid drive and path you choose. By default, the files will be backed up in a sub directory of your Fantasy Football directory. You can also use a floppy to backup and then restore your league to a different computer. Just run the backup utility to a floppy disk, then run the restore utility on the other computer (*Terry Bradshaw Fantasy Football must be installed on that computer as well*) and you will have all the information input for you to the second computer.

Frequently Asked Questions/Troubleshooting—

Move Line-ups Ahead:

If you are not starting your Fantasy Football season in week one of the NFL season, you will need to first delete the schedules for the week(s) you are not playing (see option 'E' *Scheduling/Playoffs* under *League Setup Menu* earlier in this guide for instructions on deleting schedules. The instructions are listed in *Edit Current Schedule*), and then move your lineups ahead to the week you are starting in. This will prevent you from having to run an update in the weeks you are not playing, and having ties for all your franchises.

Can I run more than one league with the Terry Bradshaw Fantasy Football software?

Yes. To install a second league, you need to install the *Terry Bradshaw Fantasy Football* software again, selecting a new directory (like Fantasy Football96B). You can then run the second league through that directory.

My points aren't coming out right, what could be wrong?

The first step to identifying a problem with points is to print out a *Scoring Plays Report*. This report will give you a breakdown of how all the points were awarded to each franchise. Compare this to the points you think a player should be getting. Make a note of any stats or scoring plays that are being awarded the wrong points. Go back to the *Point Assignment* section of the program and check the point assignments for the stat and/or scoring plays that are wrong. Make any changes needed and return to the *Update Manager* and *Recalculate* your points. Print out another *Scoring Plays Report* and re-check the points in question. You may find you need to repeat this process until you have everything working the way you want it. You will only have to do this once, after it's correct you shouldn't need to make any further changes to your point assignments. *You should be sure to do this in the preseason using the sample (or manually enter) stats to avoid problems during the regular season.*

My standings are wrong, why is this?

You probably don't have your *Franchise Standings Tiebreakers* set up properly. Go back into the *Franchise Manager*, and then into *Tiebreakers*. Be sure that you have the tiebreakers you want to use selected and in the proper order. Make any necessary changes and print out another *Weekly League Summary*. You should now have the standings in the correct order.

Can I draft the same player for different franchises?

Yes—but only if your league is set up for *multiple player positions*. For example, Team A could draft Eric Metcalf as a *wide receiver* and Team B could draft Eric Metcalf as a *kick returner*.

I ran the update, but had a starting lineup wrong. What can I do?

This is an easy problem to fix. With the *Terry Bradshaw Fantasy Football* software, you can go into any previous week and make a starting lineup or roster change. Simply go to the *Main Menu*, and select the week you need to make changes for by hitting F2. Then make the lineup changes, and re-run your reports, there is no need to run through the update process again. Make sure you then reset the current week though.

My modem isn't listed in the modems list, what should I do?

If you don't see your modem listed in the modem setup, or don't know what type of modem you are using, try using one of the Hayes compatible modems. Most modems are Hayes compatible and one of these should work. If it does not work, try editing one of the Hayes initialization strings to just read AT.

Can I fax reports right from the Terry Bradshaw Fantasy Football software?

Not directly from the software, no. If you have fax software, however, here is what you can do. Run your word processor software and go to the file menu to open a file. Select your Fantasy Football directory, and look for files with a .PRN extension. These are your reports files, and you can tell which report by the name. Open the file you want, and format it using 1/2-inch margins and 7-point Courier, or Courier new font. Now you can fax the report through your fax software, but you will need to refer to its manual if you need help with that.

Can the software be run on an Apple Macintosh?

Unless you are running SoftPC or similar Mac software which enables you to run IBM-compatible PC software, you will be unable to use the *Terry Bradshaw Fantasy Football* software. There is no support, however, for those Mac users that do have the ability to run PC software.

I have some players missing, or players that are showing up more than once.

A simple problem, this is probably because of file indexing. Go to *System Utilities* from the *Main Menu*, and select *File Indexing*. Re-index all of your files and this should solve the problem. Try to be sure to re-index on a regular basis—every three or four weeks.

My printer isn't listed, what should I do?

You need to consult your Printer Manual to find out what driver listed is compatible with your printer. Please do not call our technical support department if you cannot find your printer on the list. You need to resolve that by finding a compatible driver that is on the list.

My reports are printing too many lines and going past the page's end.

You probably just need to adjust your lines per page setting. This is done in the *League Setup Menu* under *Printer Setup*. Try reducing the lines per page and printing the report again.

Technical Support— Please be aware that the first two weeks of the NFL season are *extremely* busy ones for our Technical Support Department. We make every effort to answer all calls, but you may find long hold times and busy signals frequently during these first two weeks of the season.

To avoid having to call during that time, we ask that you make every effort possible to first resolve your problem by referring to both this printed version of the *Quick Start* guide, as well as the full manual that is included on your CD/diskette. We also strongly advise that you set your league up and test your scoring system and downloading of the stat files before the season starts.

Many of the problems you experience are the result of improperly set up point assignments, or misplaced stat files after download. Becoming familiar with the program and the updating process will mean you probably won't have any need to call the FSPI Technical Support Department during the season.

If, after you have exhausted all possibilities for solving a problem yourself, you still need further assistance with the Terry Bradshaw Fantasy Football software, you can get it by contacting FSPI's Technical Support Department. This can be done by phone, or via E-MAIL. Please be at your computer with the Terry Bradshaw Fantasy Football software running when you call. Please also be sure that you have made every attempt possible to resolve your problem using the on-line help and printed documentation before calling. The technicians may need certain information regarding your PC system, so please be sure to have the following information available:

- Type of CPU (i.e., 486/DX2-66, Pentium 133, etc.)
- Version of Windows you are running
- Amount of memory installed
- Amount of available disk space
- Make and model of your modem
  (*necessary only for downloading problems*)
- Make and model of your printer
  (*necessary only for printing problems*)
- What procedure you were attempting when the problem occurred
- What steps you have taken to solve the problem

Please refer first to the section on *System Utilities*, and the *Frequently Asked Questions and Troubleshooting* section of this guide before calling for technical assistance. Please also be sure to go through the steps outlined under *System Utilities* first, these steps can resolve most of the problems you could encounter running the *1996 Terry Bradshaw Fantasy Football* software.

To reach the Fantasy Sports Properties, Inc. Technical Support Department, call or write using the following:

FSPI Technical Support Hotline:
(703) 391-0395
Hours: Monday-Friday 9:00 AM-9:00PM EST

FSPI Technical Support E-MAIL:
AOL: TECHSUPPORT@FSPI.COM
Compuserve: 76702,3573
Internet: TECHSUPPORT@FSPI.COM
MSN: TECHSUPPORT@FSPI.COM
Prodigy: GDXS68F

Please be aware that the first two weeks of the NFL season are *extremely* busy ones for our Technical Support Department. We make every effort to answer all calls, but you may find long hold times and busy signals frequently during these first two weeks of the season. To avoid having to call during that time, we ask that you make every effort possible to first resolve your problem by referring to both this printed version of the *Quick Start* guide, as well as the full manual that is included on your CD/diskette. We also strongly advise that you set your league up and test your scoring system, and downloading of the stat files before the season starts. Many of the problems you experience are the result of improperly set up point assignments, or misplaced stat files after download. Becoming familiar with the program and the updating process will mean you probably won't have any need to call the FSPI Technical Support Department during the season. ★

Appendix G—Quick Start, '96 TBFF for Windows

The following is a quick reference guide to the *Terry Bradshaw Fantasy Football for Windows* software. Every aspect of the program is addressed here. If, however, you need further instructions for using the software they are available in the complete manual which has been included on the CD. You can view or print the manual using Microsoft Word 6 (or later), or through DOS using the TYPE or PRINT command.

The two versions of the manual are :
- WINMAN96.DOC for Microsoft Word
- WINMAN96.TXT for DOS

To view or print the manual using Word, simply insert the CD into your CD-ROM drive and start Word as you normally would, then select the appropriate file (WINMAN.DOC) to open from your word processor's *File Menu*. (*Note:* You may be able to use other word processors to view or print the manual provided they support Word 6 file formats) Consult your word processor manual for further information.

To view or print the DOS text version of the manual, you need to be at a DOS prompt, and type the following (commands you need to type are in **bold**):
D:[ENTER] (to change to your CD-ROM drive)
CD\[ENTER]
CD\FFL96[ENTER]
TYPE WINMAN.TXT|MORE[ENTER] to view the manual on screen
or
PRINT WINMAN.TXT[ENTER] to print to your printer

Getting Started—Installing & Running Terry Bradshaw Fantasy Football for Windows

In order to run the *Terry Bradshaw Fantasy Football* software, the following is the minimum required configuration for your PC:

- 486DX/33MHZ or compatible computer with a minimum of 4MB of RAM (8MB recommended), and WINDOWS 3.X or WINDOWS 95 installed.
- CD ROM drive (for CD-ROM version)
- Hard Disk Drive with 35MB available for program and a complete season of statistics
- Printer (*optional*)
- Modem (*optional*)

Note: You cannot run the *Terry Bradshaw Fantasy Football for Windows* software on a system using disk compression.

Installing the Program—	*Windows 3.x users:* Insert the CD or program DISKETTE #1 into the appropriate drive. Click on *File* in your *Program Manger's* menu, then select **Run**. In the *Run* dialog box type D:\SETUP.EXE, (where 'D' is the letter of your floppy or CD-ROM drive) then click **OK**. Follow the instructions on your screen to complete the installation. *Windows 95 users:* Insert the CD or program DISKETTE #1 into the appropriate drive. Click on **Start** from the *Taskbar* and select **Run**. In the *Run* dialog box type D:\SETUP.EXE, (where 'D' is the letter of your floppy or CD-ROM drive) then click **OK**. Follow the instructions on your screen to complete the installation.
Starting the Program—	*Windows 3.x users:* Find the new Program Group "*Fantasy Sports*" and double-click on its icon. You will now see the *Terry Bradshaw Fantasy Football Icon*. Double-clicking this icon will launch the program. *Windows 95 users:* Click on **Start** from the Taskbar and select **Programs**. Locate the "*Fantasy Sports*" folder, and then click on *Terry Bradshaw Fantasy Football* to launch the program.

Setting Up Your League.

The League Manager.

Setting up your league is easy using the *Terry Bradshaw Fantasy Football* software. When you first run the program you will automatically be placed in the **League Manager Module.** All the necessary steps to completing your league's setup are presented here. The following gives a brief overview of each of these steps. If you find that, after reading these, you need more help on setting up your league, please refer to the complete manual contained on the CD. The instructions for viewing and/or printing the manual are in the previous section.

Enter League Name—

Enter the name that's been decided upon by your league. This name can be up to 40 characters long. You don't have to enter anything if you don't want to, or you can enter a name at a later time. The *League Name* will appear in report headings for personalization purposes.

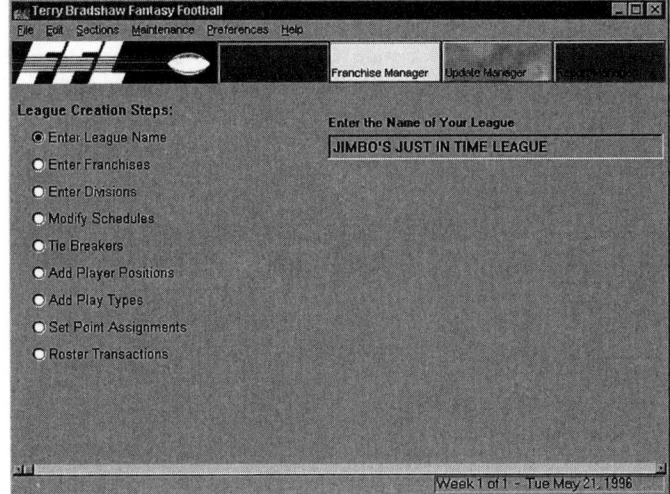

Enter Franchises—

Selecting this option will present you with the *Franchise Entry Screen.* This is where you enter all information about your league's franchise owners. Each franchise can have up to four different owners, and all information regarding those owners can be entered here. This information can also be edited at any time during the season by the league commissioner.

Click on *Add Franchise* to enter new franchises, and then enter the owner information. You can also reflect whether or not the dues (*League Entry Fee*) have been paid, as well as enter the amount of that fee. This information can be changed, or updated, at any time by highlighting the franchise and clicking *Edit Franchise.* You might want to do this for owners who haven't yet paid there dues, updating *Dues Paid* once they have.

Enter Divisions—

Selecting this option allows you to set up your division structure and assign franchises to those divisions. You may have up to six divisions, and can use the default "*Division 1*" for a name, or give each division its own unique name. As with the franchise entry, this information can be changed or updated at any time. You should not, however, make any changes to the division structure, or franchises assigned to divisions, once the regular season has started. Doing so will create problems with your schedule, and could give you results you aren't expecting.

Modify Schedules—

When you first select this option the *Terry Bradshaw Fantasy Football* program will create a schedule based on your franchise and division setup. You may then make any changes you wish to the schedule by editing the weekly matchups. You can edit the schedule at any time during the season, including the playoff weeks, to reflect the matchups you want. (*Note:* You should not make changes to the schedule for any weeks that have a completed update. Doing so could give you results you aren't expecting.)

Tie Breakers—

Selecting this option allows you to decide how your league will handle ties, both in head-to-head games, and in the weekly standings. The program will always use the overall league records to first determine the standings, but you can choose any or all of the options for breaking ties from the list presented. Ties will then be settled using the tie breaker criteria in the order you have selected.

For *Head-to-Head* ties you have the option of *Allowing Ties*, using *Total Non-Starting Points*, or *Number of Scoring Plays* (i.e., one team has 5 scoring plays and 25 points, the other has 4 scoring plays and 25 points. The team with the 5 scoring plays would be awarded the win). Just click on the *Head-to-Head Tie Breakers* button and select the method (you can use only one) that your league will use for *Head-to-Head Ties*.

For weekly standings, ties can be settled by using the following options in any order (and in any number, you don't have to use them all): *League Points, Head-to-Head Record, Head-to-Head Points, Division Record, Division Points*, and *Non-Division Record*. Simply click on the *Set Tie Breaker Criteria* button and then set the criteria for how your league will settle ties within the standings.

Add Player Positions—

Selecting this option will display a list of the *System Defined Player Positions*. Note that *System Defined Positions* are the only positions which will be supported through the weekly stats download service. You may add additional positions here if you would like, but stats for positions you enter must be tracked manually. By clicking on *Edit Position* while a system defined position highlighted, you can select your league's draft and start limits for each position you use. This will help keep your draft organized by warning you when a franchise owner is attempting to draft a position that he already has drafted the maximum allowed number of players for. The same will happen if you are entering starting lineups and try to start too many players in any position.

Add Play Types—

Selecting this option displays a list of the system defined *Play Types*. As with positions, you may add any play type your league wishes to use, but will have to track stats for those additional play types manually. To add a new play type, click the *Add Play Types* button, and then enter the name for your new play type. You can also edit or delete *User Defined Play Types*. You cannot, however, edit or delete system defined play types.

Set Point Assignments—

Selecting this option takes you into point assignments. Here you will set up your league's scoring system. The official FFL recommended scoring system is already set up for you, but it can be edited, or replaced completely. You enter point assignments by first selecting the *Position* you want to enter the point assignment for. You then select the *Play Type* to edit and input the values you want to use to determine points. There are two different ways to set up point assignments, and you need to be aware of the differences.

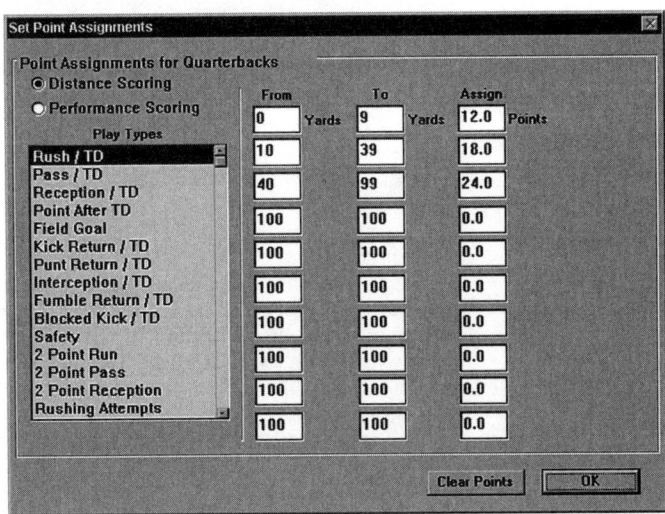

Performance Scoring vs. Distance Scoring—

Here is an example of how the same play can be awarded points differently. Let's look at a 9-yard touchdown run by a RB. *Distance* scoring would be used to award 6 points for any rushing touchdown from 1 to 9 yards. *Performance* scoring adds an extra dimension to this and allows you to award points *per yard* in a scoring play. So a 9-yard touchdown run could be worth 9 points if a *Performance Scoring* method was used and set up to award 1 point per yard. In this scenario a 1-yard run would only be worth 1 point. This applies to statistic categories also, but not necessarily on a *per yard* basis—it may be sacks, tackles, completion percentage, etc. It depends on the play type the point assignment is set up for.

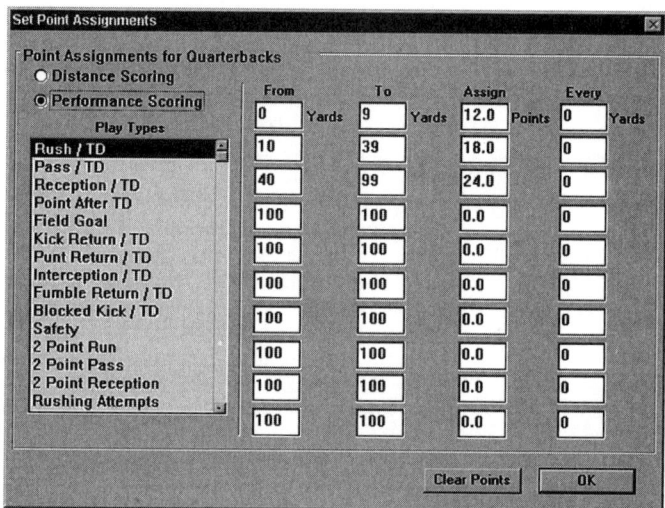

If you are still confused, read on, and this should help clarify the difference between these two scoring types. We will use two examples, a *Pass/TD* for a QB of 25 yards, and *5 Sacks for a Defense* in a game.

First, the *25-yard Pass/TD* by a QB. If you set this up as a *Distance* scoring play you select QB under *Set Point Assignments*, then select *Pass/TD*, and make sure *Distance Scoring* is selected. You will have three fields in the point assignment screen: *From*, *To*, and *Assign*. You enter in yardage in the "*From*" and "*To*" fields, and the amount of points you want awarded for any *Pass/TD* that falls within this range in the "*Assign*" field. So, if you have a range that is "*From*" 1 "*To*" 29 "*Assign*" 6 then the *25-yard Pass/TD* by the QB is worth 6 points, as is any *Pass/TD* by a QB from 1 to 29 yards. Your next point assignment will automatically start from 30, and you would enter the end range in the "*To*" field, followed by the points in the "*Assign*" field. You do this until you have the range of possibilities covered (1 to 99 yards in this case). If you select *Performance* for the *Pass/TD* play type under QB, you will see the additional field "*Every*" now. What the "*Every*" field does is add an additional factor to the point assignment. If you took the *Pass/TD* point assignment from above, and added a 1 in the "*Every*" field then that same 25-yard *Pass/TD* would now be given the 6 points for every 1 yard, making the 25-yard *Pass/TD* now worth 150 points (that is 6 points *per yard*).

Still confused? Okay, let's look at the difference using a statistic—*sacks*—rather than a scoring play. We will take the example of *5 Sacks for a Defense* in a game.

While there is really no distance involved in the scoring of sacks, the same format applies to setting up your point assignment. For *Distance* scoring you will award points for sacks based on a *range* that the sacks fall in, whereas with *Performance*, you will award points for sacks based on an *increment* that you set up. So, for awarding one point (and only one point) for 1, 2, 3, 4, or 5 sacks you use the *Distance* scoring method. Your point assignment would be "*From*" 1 "*To*" 5 "*Assign*" 1. This way the defense (or defensive player if your league uses individual defensive positions) with 5 sacks would be awarded 1 point. Any sack *total* falling in this range is worth 1 point.

Normally, you will want to award points *per sack* and that is done through the *Performance* scoring setup. To award 1 point per sack, your point assignment would be "*From*" 1 "*To*" 99 "*Assign*" 1 "*Every*" 1. We use 99 in this example, but the "*To*" number only needs to be higher than what might be possible in a game. You could put 15 here if you wanted, but for the sake of consistency, FSPI's scoring system will always use 99 or 999 for the "*To*" field of the last point assignment for a play type.

There is one more thing that is important to remember. Using the *Distance Scoring* method will only award points for a scoring play or stat that falls *within* a particular range set up in your point assignments. So if you want to award a point for sacks from 1 to 5, and 2 points for sacks from 6 to 10, you will need to put 2 in the *Assign* field for the second range. If a defense ends up with 6 sacks, the first point assignment is ignored, only sacks between 1 and 5 will be awarded points based on that assignment. The 6 sacks falls into the second range, and points will be awarded based on that (and only that) assignment. Conversely, for *Performance* scoring point assignments, each point assignment up to the total is used. For the defense with 6 sacks, they would be awarded 1 point for the first 5 sacks, and 2 points for the 6th sack. (assuming that your point assignment after 1 to 5 is something like "*From*" 6 "*To*" 10 "*Assign*" 2 "*Every*" 1)

So the difference between *Distance* and *Performance* scoring is really that *Distance* looks only at the one *range* (what you put in the "*From*" and "*To*" fields) a play, or stat, falls in and *Performance* looks at all the ranges, and then the *increment* (what you put in the "*Every*" field) to determine how to award points for a scoring play or stat.

Hopefully you now have a good understanding of how to enter point assignments for your league's scoring system. Try to input a few different point assignments, draft a few "*dummy*" franchises and run an update for the first week. You can check your points after you do so, and then make any necessary changes or adjustments to your point assignments to get things right before the season starts. Making sure your point assignments are right *before* the season starts can help you avoid the headaches trying to get it right *during* the season.

Roster Transactions—

Selecting this option takes you to *Roster Transactions*. This is where you set up the fees your league charges, if any, for transactions during the season. You can also edit transactions or delete them completely here. Note that deletions here have *no* effect on rosters, only on the *Roster Transaction Report*.

Drafting, Transactions, and Lineups.

Draft Night/ Franchise Manager.

Before you have drafted you will see a button for *Draft Night* as one of the selections in the main program window. Enter the *Draft Night* when you are ready to begin your league's draft. You will be prompted for the method you wish to use: *Draft by Round*, or *Draft by Franchise*. If you select *Draft by Round*, you will be prompted for the order you wish to use for your draft. After you have selected the method you wish to use you can begin drafting players on to your franchises. After the draft has been completed you are ready to end *Draft Night* and begin the regular season. At this time the *Draft Night* button will become the *Franchise Manager*.

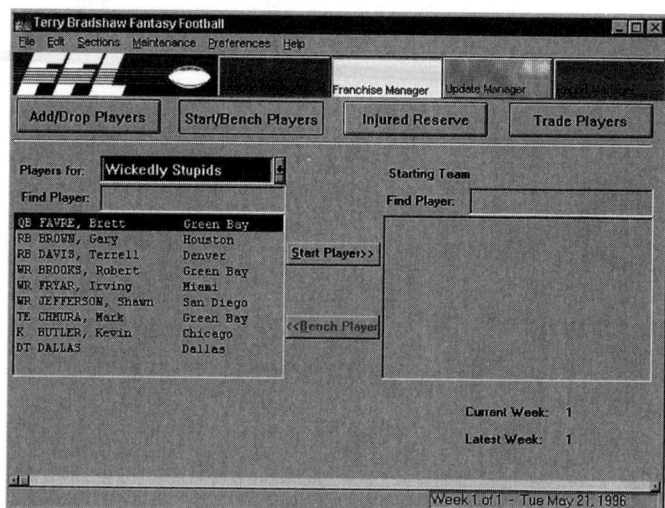

The *Franchise Manager* is where you will manage all of your league's player transactions. You *Add/Drop* players here, place injured players on *Injured Reserve* and *Trade Players*. This is also where you will insert each franchise's starting lineups each week using the *Start/Bench* option. To accomplish any of these tasks is easy. In the case of a trade, simply select the franchise or franchises you want to make moves for, then select the player to be moved and click on the arrow button between the two windows. This will *Add, Drop, Place on IR, Trade,* or *Start/Bench* the player you have highlighted.

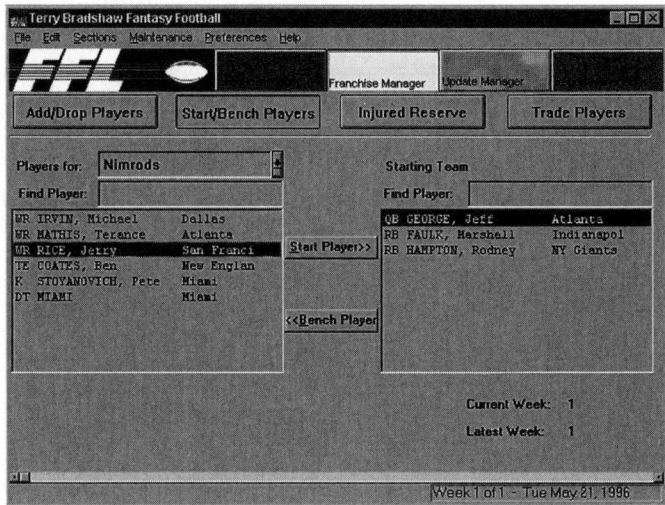

Updating Your League's Standings.

The Update Manager.

After all of the NFL games have been played each weekend, you will want to update your league's franchise points. You do this through the *Update Manager*. When updating, you have the choice to update manually, or through one of the FSPI stats download services. Stats are available by 6:00 AM Mondays and again on Tuesdays to include the Monday night game. Stats can be downloaded from the FSPI BBS using the built in *Download Manager* via the *World Wide Web* at HTTP://WWW.FSPI.COM, or through the FSPI BBS using your own communications software. Stats are also available through Compuserve, MSN, and Prodigy. However, they must be purchased on-line with, and downloaded from, the individual service.

Updating Manually—

For commissioners who do not subscribe to any of the download services, you will update your league's stats each week by entering them manually through the *Edit Scoring Plays*, and *Edit Player Stats* buttons. Find the player you want to enter stats or scoring plays for and highlight him. Once a player is highlighted, clicking on either of the buttons will take you into the *Edit* screen. For scoring plays you click the *Edit Scoring Plays* button, then click the *Add* button.

Select the type of play (i.e., *Pass/TD*) and enter the distance of the score. (*Note:* for certain plays there is no distance entered—you must use "0" for the quantity. These play types are *Safety*, *Two-Point Conversion*, and *Point After TD*). Click the *Okay* button and the points will be calculated for you based on your point assignments. Repeat this process until you have entered all scoring plays for the highlighted player. If you have stats to enter you do so by clicking the *Edit Player Stats* button and enter the stats for each category you wish to track. Click on *Okay*, and again the points will be calculated for you. Repeat this process for all players and team units that have scoring plays and/or stats for the week. Once you have all of these entered, and are through updating, click the *Finish Update* button to assign all the points to the franchises. You are now ready to run your reports for the week.

Updating through a download service—

If you have subscribed to one of the update services and are downloading stats each week, you begin your update by clicking the *Import Stat File* button. You will now be given the option of downloading the stats using the FSPI *Download Manager* or *Copy Week xx Download File* (where *xx* is the week number you wish to update) if you have already downloaded through your own communications software, the FSPI WWW site (HTTP://WWW.FSPI.COM), or one of the commercial on-line services.

FSPI *Download Manager:*

There is a simple and easy way to use the *Download Manager* included with the *Terry Bradshaw Fantasy Football for Windows* software. This requires a toll call to our BBS located in Reston, Virginia but should take less than two minutes on average to download the weekly stat file.

To use the *Download Manager*, click on *Download Stats* after selecting *Import Stat File* from the *Update Manager*. You will be prompted for your *User ID and Password* the first time you use the *Download Manager*, and will need to enter some information for on-line registration. You will also have to set up your modem and port settings. These can be changed at any time during the season, by clicking the *Modem Setup* button in the *Download Manager*. After you have your *User ID and Password* info entered, have filled out the on-line registration form, and setup your modem, you are ready to download. Do so by clicking the *Download* button in the *Download Manager*. If you have everything entered correctly, you will not have to do anything more than click the *Download* button for the rest of the season. After a successful download you will be returned to the *Terry Bradshaw Fantasy Football* program to finish updating.

FSPI WWW Site:

If you already have access to the *World Wide Web* via an *Internet* provider or other commercial on-line service, you may wish to download your stats through FSPI's web site at URL HTTP://WWW.FSPI.COM. Launch your web browser and go to the FSPI site by typing in our URL in place of the one listed for your browser's default home page (the one that loads automatically when you launch the browser). There you will see an icon (or other graphic) indicating FFL stats, click on that and then follow the instructions to download the stat file. After you have downloaded the file you will need to know the path it was downloaded to. This is normally the directory of your browser, (C:\NETSCAPE\PROGRAM if you are using Netscape) or on-line service (C:\PRODIGY if you are using Prodigy). Go to your *Windows File Manager* (or *Explorer* in Win95) and click on the directory where the FFL download file is located (this will be on the left side of your *File Manager* window). Double-click on the file name (*example:* FFL01.EXE) to decompress the .EXE file you downloaded and create the FFLSTAT.1 the *Terry Bradshaw Fantasy Football* program needs. (the file will be on the right side of the *File Manager* window). You are now ready to run your weekly update.

Start *Terry Bradshaw Fantasy Football for Windows*, and in the **Update Manager**, click on **Import Stat File**, and then select **Copy Week Download File**. You should now have a Windows dialog box on the screen. Locate the directory where the FFLSTAT file is located again, then highlight the FFLSTAT file for the current week and click **Okay**. The program will now begin the update process by reading in the stat file and assigning players points based on your league's point assignments. After this is done, check to make sure your points look right, and then click **Finish Update**. You are now ready to run your reports for the week.

Compuserve:

You can sign up for and download the stats via Compuserve. To do so, GO to SIFFL and follow the instructions on screen. Please note that if you have signed up for the download service from FSPI, you will not be able to download the stats through Compuserve. Compuserve will bill you for the stats when you sign up on-line. If you have signed up through FSPI, you can access the stats using Compuserve's web browser (see above).

The Microsoft Network:

You can sign up for and download the stats via The Microsoft Network (MSN). To do so, GO to FFL and follow the instructions on screen. Please note that if you have signed up for the download service from FSPI, you will not be able to download the stats through MSN. MSN will bill you for the stats when you sign up on-line. If you have signed up through FSPI, you can access the stats using MSN's Internet Explorer (see above).

Prodigy:

You can sign up for and download the stats via Prodigy. To do so, JUMP to FFL and follow the instructions on screen. Please note that if you have signed up for the download service from FSPI, you will not be able to download the stats through Prodigy. Prodigy will bill you for the stats when you sign up on-line. If you have signed up through FSPI, you can access the stats using Prodigy's web browser (see above).

Sorting It All Out.

The Reports Manager.

When you want to find out what's going on in your league, this is the place to do it. Each week after you have finished running your updates, you will probably want to print out reports to show everyone in your league how they, and their fellow competitors, have fared. With the *Reports Manager* you can print out or view on screen, a *Weekly League Summary*, *Weekly Winning Reports*, *Transaction Reports*, *Scoring Plays Reports*, and more. There are reports to analyze non-drafted players, trades, and who is on IR. Use any of the reports you want, and you will keep your league members informed of what is going on from week to week. A well informed league member is more likely to be an active and involved participant, so consider this when you select the reports to hand out each week. Everyone benefits from being in a well informed league, competition is better, and trading and player transactions are more frequent.

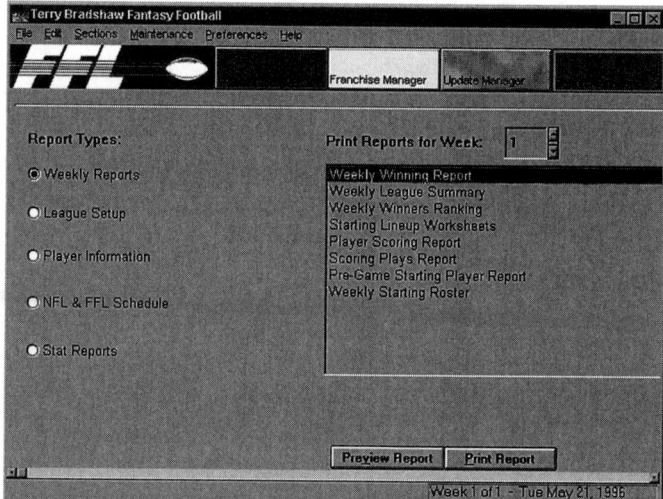

The following is a list of the reports available in the *Terry Bradshaw Fantasy Football for Windows* program along with a brief description for each:

Weekly Reports—

Weekly Winning Report:
The *Weekly Winning Report* lists total franchise points scored for the current week, as well as the cumulative season totals for all franchises, and lists them in order. There is also a *Top Twenty Individual Performances* section which will list the top twenty players scores for the current week, along with the player's franchise and starting status.

Weekly League Summary Report:
The *Weekly League Summary Report* is your league's standings report. It will list the standings (separated by division where applicable), the weekly head to head results, along with the next week's matchups and NFL schedule, including NFL teams on a bye week if there are any.

Weekly Winners Ranking:
The *Weekly Winners Ranking Report* is a week by week listing of the franchise points for each week. It is the same information that is displayed in the *Weekly Winning Report* under current week franchise points.

Starting Lineup Worksheets:
The *Starting Lineup Worksheets* can be passed out to the franchise owners each week to allow them to select their starting lineups for the next week. The worksheets list all franchise players along with their starting status and points for the current week, and their points for the year to date.

Player Scoring Report:
The *Player Scoring Report* lists the starting and non-starting points for each franchise for the current week along with the player's YTD totals.

Scoring Plays Report:
The *Scoring Plays Report* is a detailed listing of all scoring plays and stats for each player broken down by franchise. You can list all stats and plays, or only those that resulted in fantasy points. This report is a good tool for the commissioner should a question arise regarding a certain franchise's points.

Pre-Game Starting Player Report:
This report is similar to the *Starting Lineup Worksheets* only that it lists all franchises together rather than printing each on a separate page. It is also a week *beginning* report as opposed to a week ending report and should be printed out *after* the starting lineups have been put in for the week.

Weekly Starting Roster:
This report is similar to the *Player Scoring Report*, with the exception of non-starting players. Non-starting players are *not* listed in the *Weekly Starting Roster Report*.

League Setup—

Player Point Assignments Report:
The *Player Point Assignments Report* is used to get a printout of your league's point assignment setup. You can use this report to pass out to all the league owners so that they can see how points will be awarded and also to verify you have the point assignments set the way you want them for your scoring system.

Player Positions Report:
The *Player Positions Report* will give you a printout of all the *System Defined* and *User Defined* positions.

Play Types Report:
The *Play Types Report* will give you a printout of all the *System Defined* and *User Defined Play Types*.

Mailing Labels:
You can use this report if you will be mailing reports to the franchise owners in your league. You have the option of two types of Avery labels you can use. There is a report using two column labels, and one using single column labels.

Player Information—

NFL Roster:
A complete printout of all NFL players contained in the software's database. This report can come in handy on draft night. The NFL roster will be printed alphabetized by position.

Franchise Roster Report:
The *Franchise Roster Report* will give you a printout of all franchises rosters. This report is a handy tool for keeping franchise owners up to date on the players on other franchises rosters, as well as those that are not drafted.

Weekly Player Scores Report:
The *Weekly Player Scores Report* is a week by week breakdown of how players have scored their season YTD points. This report can be printed for drafted players only, non-drafted players only, or for all players. The report will list the player's name along with the total fantasy points he scored for each week in the season. An indispensable tool for analyzing the available players in the "*free agent*" market for your league.

Roster Transactions Report:
The *Roster Transactions Report* will give you a printout of all the transactions made by your league's owners throughout the season. You can choose to print this information by week or by franchise.

NFL & FFL Schedules—

NFL Schedule:
A complete week by week printout of the official 1996 NFL schedule.

Schedule by Week:
The Schedule by Week report is a printout of your league's franchise schedules week by week. Here is a good place to start before editing your schedule. Load the default schedule and then print the *Schedule by Week* report to see what changes, if any, you wish to make.

Stat Reports—

Non-Drafted Stat Detail Report:
The *Non-Drafted Stat Detail Report* is another valuable tool in analyzing the "*free agent*" market for your league. Here you can get a printout of the YTD stats for all the non-drafted players in your fantasy league.

Franchise Stat History Report:
The *Franchise Stat History Report* is similar to the *Non-Drafted Stat Detail Report*, only it is for the drafted players and is listed by franchise. Thinking about a trade? Here is a good report to take a look at before making the deal.

Frequently Asked Questions—

Can I run more than one league with the Terry Bradshaw Fantasy Football software?

Yes. To install a second league select the *File*, then select *New League*. You can then enter information for this second league, and choose which league loads by default under the *Preferences Menu*.

My points aren't coming out right, what could be wrong?

The first step to identifying a problem with points is to print out a *Scoring Plays Report*. This report will give you a breakdown of how all the points were awarded to each franchise. Compare this to the points you think a player should be getting. Make a note of any stats or scoring plays that are being awarded the wrong points. Go back to the *Point Assignment* section of the program and check the point assignments for the stat and/or scoring plays that are wrong. Make any changes needed and return to the *Update Manager* and *Recalculate* your points. Print out another *Scoring Plays* report and re-check the points in question. You may find you need to repeat this process until you have everything working the way you want it. You will only have to do this once, after it's correct you shouldn't need to make any further changes to your point assignments. *You should be sure to do this in the preseason using the sample (or manually enter) stats to avoid problems during the regular season.*

My standings are wrong, why is this?

You probably don't have your *Franchise Standings* tiebreakers set up properly. Go back into the *Franchise Manager*, and then into *Tiebreakers*. Be sure that you have the tiebreakers you want to use selected and in the proper order. Make any necessary changes and print out another *Weekly League Summary*. You should now have the standings in the correct order.

Can I draft the same player for different franchises?

Yes—but only if your league is set up for *multiple player positions*. For example, Team A could draft Eric Metcalf as a *wide receiver* and Team B could draft Eric Metcalf as a *kick returner*.

I ran the update, but had a starting lineup wrong. What can I do?

This is an easy problem to fix. With the *Terry Bradshaw Fantasy Football* software, you can go into any previous week and make a starting lineup or roster change. Simply go into the *Franchise Manager*, and select the week you need to make changes for. Then make the lineup changes, and re-run your reports, there is no need to run through the update process again.

My modem isn't listed in the modems list, what should I do?

If you don't see your modem listed in the modem setup, or don't know what type of modem you are using, try using one of the Hayes-compatible modems. Most modems are Hayes-compatible and one of these should work. If it does not work, try editing one of the Hayes initialization strings to just read AT.

Can I fax reports right from the Terry Bradshaw Fantasy Football software?

Yes, if you have software such as Delrina's WinFax. Normally, these software packages install a driver that you select to print to instead of your printer. Consult your fax software's manual for further information.

Can the software be run on an Apple Macintosh?

Unless you are running SoftPC or similar Mac software which enables you to run IBM-compatible PC software, you will be unable to use the *Terry Bradshaw Fantasy Football for Windows* software. There is no support, however, for those Mac users that do have the ability to run PC software.